HANDBOOKS

PUERTO RICO

SUZANNE VAN ATTEN

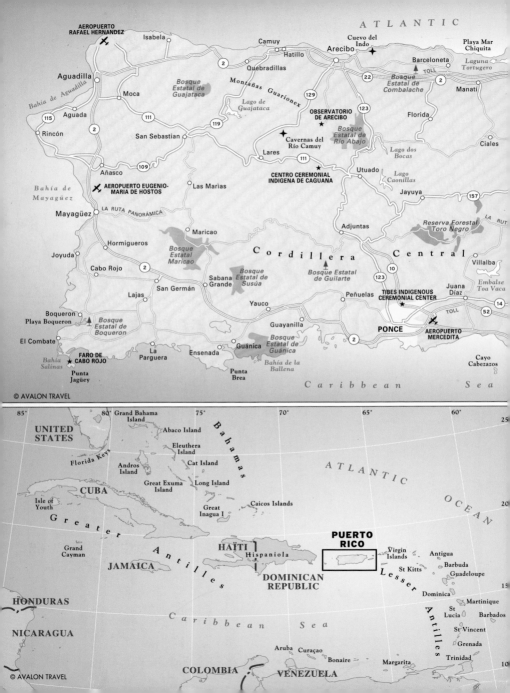

Contents

Discover Puerto Rico

 Puerto Rico's nickname, Island of Enchantment, is a fitting sobriquet. Sandy beaches, palm trees, and tropical breezes make it a favorite getaway for the sun and surf crowd. Rugged mountains and a verdant rain forest attract adventure travelers, and lavish hotels with ocean-side golf courses embrace vacationers who crave luxury.

But Puerto Rico is much more than a picture postcard. Four hundred years of Spanish heritage has left its mark on the island, giving it an Old World elegance. Its vibrant cultural life reflects not only the island's European history, but also its indigenous origins and African influences.

An added bonus is the hip, bustling metropolis of San Juan, which boasts world-class restaurants, nightclubs, and casinos that keep the party-hearty set up until dawn. Yet, a simple stroll through the cobble-stone streets of Old San Juan steeps visitors in a concentrated dose of the island's history and cultural life.

Just 111 miles long and 36 miles wide, Puerto Rico has a population of 3.9 million people, making it one of the most densely populated places in the world. Despite the traffic jams and overdevelopment in some areas, natural beauty abounds in the many protected coves, mangrove lagoons, caves, and mountain streams. They provide the perfect backdrop for an immersion into the sensual pleasures of the tropics.

Less than an hour's drive from San Juan is one of the island's most popular sights, El Yunque Caribbean National Forest, which contains a semitropical rainforest. In the northwest karst country, there are limestone caves, easily explored at Las Cavernas del Río Camuy park, and several bioluminescent bays where kayakers can commune with the tiny luminescent organisms that turn the water a glittery green- or blue-specked sea on moonless nights.

Puerto Rico's central mountain region is one of the dramatic, beautiful areas of the island, where high mountain peaks, canyons, ferns, orchids, streams, and cooler temperatures prevail. The indigenous Taíno culture was once a stronghold here, and their ancient ruins and petroglyphs can be found throughout the area.

All that is to say, there is a lot more to Puerto Rico than beaches. But if it is spectacular beaches one wants, there are plenty to be found, as is a bounty of water sports from surfing and diving to fishing and sailing.

Life is vivid in Puerto Rico, so prepare to have your slumbering senses awakened in this enchanted land where the sun shines brightly, rainbow-hued buildings pop with color, and tropical music fills the air.

Planning Your Trip

▶ WHERE TO GO

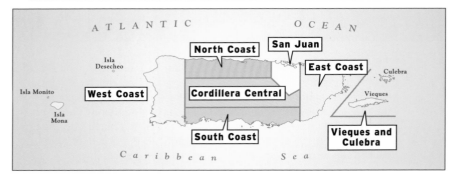

San Juan

Situated on the northeast coast, sophisticated, fast-paced San Juan is Puerto Rico's capital and largest city. Its heart is Old San Juan, the original walled city founded by Spanish settlers in 1521, home to two enormous fortresses: Castillo de San Felipe del Morro and Castillo de San Cristóbal. Other

Castillo de San Felipe del Morro protected Old San Juan from attack by sea.

significant neighborhoods include Isla Verde, with the city's best beaches and most exclusive hotels, and Condado, considered the tourist district and where you'll find many high-rise hotels, high-end shops, and casinos. In nearby Santurce is the lovely new showplace of local artwork, Museo de Arte de Puerto Rico.

East Coast

The east coast contains Puerto Rico's most popular tourist sight, El Yunque Caribbean National Forest, a 28,000-acre nature preserve in the Sierra de Luquillo. The second-most popular sight on the island is Balneario La Monserrate, a beautiful beach in Luquillo. Fajardo is the boating center of Puerto Rico, where you can go diving, snorkeling, fishing, sailing, and kayaking. It is also home to the small but ecologically diverse Reserva Natural Las Cabezas de San Juan, which contains a terrific bioluminescent bay. The southern part of the east coast is the least touristy part of the island and features several nice beaches and good seafood restaurants.

IF YOU HAVE . . .

- **Three days:** Old San Juan, Luquillo, El Yunque
- **Five days:** Add Condado, Santurce, and Ponce
- **One week:** Add Vieques or Culebra
- **Two weeks:** Add Rincón and Cordillera Central

South Coast

In the center of the south coast is Ponce, the third-largest city in Puerto Rico, once a wealthy international port town and a major player in the sugar and coffee industries. The city boasts gorgeous neoclassical and Spanish Revival architecture, a thriving plaza, and a strong cultural heritage. Just north of town is one of the island's two major Taíno Indian centers. Centro Ceremonial Indígena de Tibes was once home to two indigenous tribes, the Igneri and the Pre-Taínos. The south coast is the site of a unique 10,000-acre subtropical dry forest, Bosque Estatal de Guánica, featuring hiking trails, beaches, and the ruins of a Spanish fort.

West Coast

Within the west coast region are the fun-loving surf towns of Isabela, Rincón, and Aguadilla; the colonial cities of Mayagüez and San Germán; the fishing village of Boquerón; the biolumi-nescent bay in La Parguera; and the salt flats of Cabo Rojo. In addition to being a major destination for surfing and diving, the west coast is home to Bosque Estatal de Guajataca, a 2,357-acre forest reserve, and Balneario de Boquerón, one of the island's loveliest public beaches. The airport in Aguadilla makes it possible to bypass San Juan altogether for those who just want to explore the west coast.

North Coast

Much of the north coast is karst country, distinguished by limestone hills and caves, which makes for lots of rocky beaches and seaside cliffs. But there are two terrific sandy beaches—Balneario Cerro Gordo in Vega Alta and Playa Mar Chiquita in Manatí. Perhaps the biggest draw on this coast is Las Cavernas del Río Camuy, a gorgeous cave park featuring hikes through enormous

You know you're in karst country when you spot the naturally forming haystack-shaped hills called *mogotes*.

caverns by a subterranean river. Another popular site is Observatorio de Arecibo, the world's largest radio telescope. And a bit off the beaten path is Cueva del Indio, huge petrified sand dunes where you can see natural arches, blow holes, and ancient Taíno petroglyphs.

Cordillera Central

The central mountain region is a wonderland of natural beauty and Taíno Indian culture. La Ruta Panorámica is a well-marked route that takes visitors on a scenic tour through the region. Toro Negro Forest, in the center of the region, contains the island's highest peak. Jayuya is the site of Museo del Cemi, an amulet-shaped museum containing indigenous artifacts, and La Piedra Escrita, a boulder covered with Taíno petroglyphs. But probably the most significant site is Centro Ceremonial Indígena de Caguana, a Taíno archaeological site dating to A.D. 1100 in Utuado. Also in Utuado is Bosque Estatal de Río Abajo, a 5,000-acre subtropical humid forest.

Vieques and Culebra

Vieques and Culebra are two small islands off the main island's east coast. Both offer some

Balneario Sun Bay is Vieques's most popular beach.

of the best wilderness beaches to be found in Puerto Rico—if not the entire Caribbean. Balneario Sun Bay in Vieques is a mile-long sandy crescent on crystal-blue waters. Playa Flamenco on Culebra is considered one of the best beaches in the United States. Both islands are renowned for their spectacular diving and snorkeling. Vieques is also the site of Mosquito Bay, Puerto Rico's most outstanding bioluminescent bay, where the water glows an electric blue at night. If you need a history fix, Vieques is home to El Fortín Conde del Mirasol and Museum, the last fort built by colonial Spain.

Museo del Cemi in Jayuya, in the Cordillera Central, is shaped like a Taíno amulet.

▶ WHEN TO GO

The climate in Puerto Rico is classified as tropical marine, which means it is sunny, hot, and humid year-round. The only seasonal change in Puerto Rico is in the amount of precipitation that falls.

Rainy season is May–October, which is also hurricane season. A daily shower can be expected, although they don't typically last very long. Airline ticket prices and hotel room rates are usually discounted during this time.

Dry season is January–May, which coincides with the tourist industry's high season in most parts of the island, including San Juan. Note that rain does occur during dry season, but at a much lower rate than in summer and fall.

Some parts of the island have a high season that differs from the norm. Because surfing is its main attraction, Rincón's high season is December–April, when the swells are highest. In Boquerón and other places that cater to Puerto Rican tourists, the high season is during the summer when children are out of school.

Explore Puerto Rico

▶ BEST OF PUERTO RICO

It would take at least a month to fully explore Puerto Rico, but this two-week tour gives visitors a little taste of everything Puerto Rico has to offer: beaches, nature preserves, colonial cities, surf and dive spots, indigenous culture, and golf.

Day 1

Catch an early flight into San Juan and spend the day wandering Old San Juan's cobblestone streets and checking out some shops, such as Puerto Rican Arts and Crafts on Calle

Fortaleza. Enjoy a hearty traditional Puerto Rican lunch of *mofongo* or *arroz con pollo* at Restaurante Raices on Calle Recinto Sur. That afternoon, tour El Morro, a huge Spanish fort overlooking San Juan Bay. At night, do like the locals do and dine late on seviche and oysters at Aguaviva on Calle Fortaleza. End the day at Nuyorican Café for some live salsa music.

Day 2

In the morning, tour Museo de Las Americas, a museum in Old San Juan containing an extensive collection of folk art from countries throughout Latin America. It's located in Cuartel de Ballajá, a former Spanish military barracks. For lunch, head to Kasalta Bakery on Calle McLeary in Ocean Park for the best Cuban sandwich, and you're just a few blocks from the Museo de Arte de Puerto Rico in Santurce, which has an extensive collection of local artwork on exhibition that spans five centuries. That evening, dine in elegance inside the clamshell-shaped Perla at La Concha

Renaissance Resort in Condado. Enjoy an after-dinner drink at Wet, a glamorous rooftop lounge at the Water Club, or go to the casino for some gambling action at the InterContinental San Juan hotel, both in Isla Verde.

Day 3

In San Juan, rent a car and drive 25 miles east to Luquillo to spend the day at Balneario La Monserrate, one of the island's most beautiful government-maintained beaches. Stop along the way at Luquillo Kioskos and lunch on fritters and meat pies and wash it down with a cold beer. No need to stock up before hitting the sand and surf: There are more vendors selling snacks and beverages at the beach. Use the public showers to freshen up before heading back to your hotel in San Juan, but stop in Rio Grande on your way for a traditional Puerto Rican meal at Antojitos Puertorriqueños.

Day 4

Eat a hearty breakfast at La Bombonera on Calle San Francisco in Old San Juan, then put on your hiking shoes and drive 30 miles east to El Yunque Caribbean National Forest.

El Portal Tropical Forest Center marks the entrance to El Yunque Caribbean National Forest.

Some of the best traditional Puerto Rican cuisine can be found at the Luquillo Kioskos.

Spend the day hiking the trails, bird-watching, and swimming in the rivers and pools that dot the area. Return to San Juan and enjoy a meal of creative Caribbean cuisine in the courtyard of The Parrot Club on Calle Fortaleza in Old San Juan. That night, join the perennial pub crawl along Calle San Sebastian.

Day 5

Drive 33 miles east to Ceiba (allow an hour) and catch a plane to Vieques (be sure to reserve a car ahead of time). Spend the morning soaking in the sun at Balneario Sun Bay. That afternoon, visit the Vieques Museum of Art and History, located in El Fortín Conde de Mirasol, Spain's last fort in the New World. In the evening, dine at one of several restaurants that line the main strip in Esperanza. If it's a moonless night, be sure to take a tour of bioluminescent Mosquito Bay. Spend the night on Vieques.

Day 6

Catch an early flight back to Ceiba and drive 89 miles southwest to Ponce. The halfway point is Cayey, a great place to stop and have a roast-pork lunch at one of this mountain town's many *lechoneras*. Spend the afternoon on a walking tour of central Ponce to see its lovely European architecture. That evening, have dinner overlooking the water at Paseo Tablado La Guancha

Paseo Tablado La Guancha, a new waterfront development in Ponce, features a panoramic seaside boardwalk as well as lots of restaurants and bars.

and stroll off the calories along the boardwalk. Stay the night in Ponce, preferably in one of the hotels overlooking Plaza de Las Delicias.

Day 7

In the morning, tour Museo de Arte de Ponce, featuring an impressive collection of European and Puerto Rican art from the 18th through 21st centuries. Pick up picnic supplies at Classic Delights Bakery & Café on Calle Marina in Ponce and drive 24 miles west to Guánica. Put your hiking shoes on and explore the subtropical dry forest at Bosque Estatal de Guánica. That evening, drive 10 miles west to La Parguera for a seafood dinner and spend the night.

Day 8

Take a boat tour of the Los Canales Manglares mangrove channels in La Parguera. That night, take a tour of the Bahía Fosforescente bioluminescent bay. Spend another night in La Parguera.

Day 9

Drive 15 miles west into the Cabo Rojo Peninsula and check into Bahía Salinas Beach Hotel, a lovely, sprawling hotel tucked far away from everything on the farthest southwestern point of the island. Relax on its many porches or verandas on hammocks or chaise lounges surrounded by tangles of tropical plants. Or perhaps you'd rather soak in an outdoor mineral bath. Nearby are the Cabo Rojo salt flats, a 1,200-acre reserve where salt is mined and excellent bird-watching is to be found.

Day 10

Get an early start and drive 30 miles north to Rincón. From Black Eagle Marina take a dive or snorkeling tour to Desecheo Island, a 45-minute boat ride off the coast where divers and snorkelers can skirt around the fringes of this uninhabited island and see a variety of marine life. Spend the evening checking out some of the funky bars in Rincón and meet some expatriates who've made this happening town their home.

Day 11

From Rincón, drive 35 miles inland to Las Cavernas del Río Camuy and spend the morning exploring the island's magical sub-terranean world. In the afternoon, drive 8 miles east to Observatorio de Arecibo and see the world's largest radio telescope. Drive 17 miles north to Hatillo and spend the night.

Day 12

Drive 10 miles east to Cueva del Indio and scramble (carefully!) over the petrified sand dunes where the coastline is drop-dead gorgeous and you can see natural arches, blow holes, and Taíno petroglyphs. Head 30 miles east to Dorado for an afternoon of sunbathing and spend the night in the lap of luxury at the Dorado Beach Club.

Day 13

Get in a round of golf at one of two courses designed by Robert Trent Jones Sr. at the Dorado Beach Club followed by a massage in the afternoon. For dinner, go into Dorado and dine on local cuisine at El Ladrillo. Spend the night in Dorado.

See the world's largest radio telescope at Observatorio de Arecibo.

Day 14

Drive 17 miles east to San Juan. If there's time before your flight, check out Castillo de San Cristóbal, the large fortress at the entrance to Old San Juan by Plaza de Colón.

Construction of Castillo de San Cristóbal in Old San Juan began in 1634 to protect the walled city from ground attack.

► EXPLORING THE CORDILLERA CENTRAL

As enticing as Puerto Rico's beaches are, there are plenty of good reasons to spend time in the Cordillera Central, the island's interior mountain range. Gorgeous tropical jungle, hiking trails, natural pools, and indigenous culture are just some of the attractions to be explored.

One of the great things about the Cordillera Central is that it's possible to get a taste of its charms on a day trip from just about anywhere on the island. Travelers seeking a mountain getaway may want to escape to the Cordillera Central for two or three days, while more ambitious travelers will want to reserve four or five days to fully explore the mountainous terrain.

Day 1

Fly into San Juan and drive to Cayey. Eat your fill at one of the *lechoneras* serving pit-roasted pork and other local delicacies, and walk it off on the 0.5-mile hike in Reserva Forestal de Carite, a subtropical humid forest. Go for a swim in the natural pool at Charco Azul. Camp there for the night or stay in a nearby hotel.

Day 2

Drive to Barranquitas and tour the quaint town, stopping by Museo Luis Muñoz Rivera, a museum home honoring the poet, journalist, and politician who lived here. If you want something a little more adventurous, take a hiking and rappelling tour of San Cristóbal Cañon, between Barranquitas and Aibonito. Head to Coamo for the night and relax in the natural hot springs.

Day 3

Head to Jayuya and tour Museo del Cemí, a museum shaped like a Taíno amulet and featuring excavated artifacts from the island's indigenous culture. In the afternoon, visit La Piedra Escrita, a boulder covered with Taíno petroglyphs located in a river by a large natural pool where you can take a cool dip.

Day 4

Go to Utuado and explore Centro Ceremonial Indígena de Caguana, an archaeological site dating back to A.D. 1100 featuring *bateys* (ball courts), monoliths, and petroglyphs left behind by the Taíno.

Day 5

Spend the day underground at Las Cavernas del Río Camuy, a massive cave park. In the afternoon go to Lares and have some refreshing pineapple ice cream at Heladería de Lares.

Although visitors to Las Cavernas del Río Camuy enter through a man-made entrance, this is the natural mouth of the cave.

▶ SUNBATHING, SWIMMING, AND SURFING

No two beaches are alike in Puerto Rico. *Balnearios* are large, government-maintained beaches with bathroom and shower facilities, picnic tables, and snack bars. Some have lounge-chair rentals, lifeguards, and campsites. Expect to pay $3–5 per vehicle to get in, and be aware that they get crowded on weekends and holidays. There are also many wilderness beaches, which are typically remote and devoid of development and facilities. Some beaches have big waves best suited to surfing, and others are as calm as bathwater and ideal for swimming. One thing all the beaches have in common is their accessibility to the public. There is no such thing as a private beach in Puerto Rico.

Best *Balnearios*

BALNEARIO LA MONSERRATE

Balneario La Monserrate, commonly called Luquillo Beach, is considered one of the island's most beautiful beaches. It features a wide flat crescent of sand, a shady palm grove, and calm shallow waters. A couple of food vendors sell fritters and piña coladas, among other refreshments. There are several picnic shelters, as well as toilets and shower facilities. Camping is allowed with a permit.

BALNEARIO SUN BAY

Balneario Sun Bay is Vieques's crowning jewel of beaches. Pull your car to the edge of a sand dune and mark your spot on the smooth sand. Shade is spotty here, so bring a beach umbrella if you plan to stay for the day. Modest picnic shelters, bathrooms, and shower facilities are available. Camping is allowed with a permit.

PLAYA FLAMENCO

Culebra is the lucky site of Playa Flamenco, one of "America's Best Beaches," according to the Travel Channel. The wide, mile-long, horseshoe-shaped beach boasts fine white sand and calm, aquamarine water. Unlike Puerto Rico's other publicly maintained beaches, Playa Flamenco is home to two hotels—Villa Flamenco Beach and Culebra Beach Villas (the latter operates Coconuts Beach Grill, serving sandwiches and beverages to beachgoers). An abandoned graffiti-covered tank on the sand is a reminder of the U.S. Navy's presence. Camping is allowed with a permit.

A reminder of the U.S. Navy's former presence on Culebra, this abandoned tank on the northwestern edge of Playa Flamenco provides a makeshift canvas for graffiti artists.

ROMANTIC ESCAPES

It's no wonder Puerto Rico is such a popular destination for honeymooners. The beautiful beaches, balmy breezes, and lush tropical foliage provide a perfect backdrop to a romantic getaway. But there's more to it than that. There is a palpable sensuality to life in Puerto Rico. The Spanish architecture, the salsa music, the Caribbean cuisine, the heat — all those elements and more come together to enliven the senses and set the stage for amorous pursuits. Whether it's soaking in the natural hot springs in Coamo or taking a nighttime boat ride through a bioluminescent bay, learning the art of flamenco dancing or dining under the stars, couples can't help but fall under the sway of Puerto Rico's many aphrodisiacal charms.

OLD SAN JUAN

Book your stay at **Hotel El Convento,** a former Carmelite convent in Old San Juan that dates back to 1651. Start the day with a couples massage. That night, dine beneath great swaths of silk organza on the sensuous culinary creations at **Marmalade,** then take an evening stroll through the historic town's cobblestone streets. Take a taxi to nearby Hato Rey and catch the flamenco show at **Divino Bocadito,** a Spanish restaurant and lounge.

LA PARGUERA

Old San Juan may be the most romantic place in Puerto Rico, but La Parguera on the southwestern coast is an easy second. Stay the night at **Parador Villa Parguera,** a lovely old-fashioned inn with charming grounds right on the water. The next day go sailing on *Fondo de Cristal III,* a 72-seat glass-bottom catamaran, to one of the nearby cays, where you can swim, sun, and snorkel on your own private beach. Dine at any number of excellent seafood restaurants in town, and take a nighttime boat tour of glittery **Bahía Fosforescente.**

COAMO

From San Juan, take a scenic drive through the Cordillera Central to Coamo. Although rustic Hotel Baños Coamo caters more to families than couples seeking romance, it's the perfect place to spend the night because it's located right beside **Baños de Coamo,** a natural hot spring that has brought tourists to this tiny pueblo since colonial times. The springs are contained in a tile and cement pool on the hotel grounds, but for a more authentic experience, hike a short distance behind the hotel to the public pool located in a wooded area. That evening, drive 13 miles southeast to **Salinas,** where you can dine at one of the many seafood restaurants that line the coast in this tiny fishing village. **Ladi's** is a good choice, especially if you can get a seat right on the water.

BALNEARIO DE BOQUERÓN

In addition to its long white beach and calm waters, this publicly maintained beach is exceptional because of its excellent facilities, which are bigger, nicer, and more modern than those found at most *balnearios*. The property is quite shady, and in addition to the usual showers, toilets, and picnic tables, there is a huge events pavilion, a baseball field, and a cafeteria.

BALNEARIO CERRO GORDO

Balneario Cerro Gordo in Vega Alta on the north coast is a large protected cove with calm waters and a pristine sandy beach surrounded by hills covered in lush vegetation. It boasts the best campgrounds of any of the *balnearios* because of its spacious location atop a hilly peninsula overlooking the ocean. There's also great surfing to be had here.

Best Wilderness Beaches

BOSQUE ESTATAL DE PIÑONES

Bosque Estatal de Piñones offers several miles of gorgeous wilderness beach just minutes east of San Juan. Drive along Carretera 187 and look for sandy unmarked roads along the coast where you can pull your car right up to the beach and climb down the sand dunes into the water. For lunch, grab an *empanadilla* and *coco frio* from one of the food kiosks on the way. Plan on leaving by late afternoon because the sand fleas tend to attack when the sun starts to go down.

PLAYA MAR CHIQUITA

Playa Mar Chiquita in Manatí is a tiny little protected cove located at the base of limestone cliffs on the north coast. A coral reef nearly encloses the calm, shallow basin of water ideal for taking small children swimming. When you need some respite from the sun, explore the cliff-side caves.

CULEBRITA

It requires a boat ride to get there, but Culebrita, a *cayo* off the coast of Culebra, is the place to go if you really want to get away from it all. In addition to multiple beaches perfect for swimming or shore snorkeling, there are several tidal pools and a lovely, abandoned lighthouse. To get there, either rent a boat or catch a water taxi at the docks in Dewey.

Culebrita, off the coast of Culebra, is the place to go to really get away from it all.

PUERTO RICO FOR THRILLSEEKERS

One of Puerto Rico's best-kept secrets is its wealth of adventure travel options. Novices and experts alike can find plenty of rewarding activities that will challenge their skills and immerse them in the island's unparalleled natural beauty.

BACKCOUNTRY HIKING

Discover the most remote part of **El Yunque Caribbean National Forest** by bypassing the paved trails in El Yunque Recreation Center and hiking **El Toro Trail,** a primitive trail starting at Carretera 186, kilometer 10.6, that passes through Tabonuco, Sierra Palm, and cloud forests, offering spectacular views of the south coast. The arduous 2.2-mile trail connects with **Trade Winds Trail,** a 3.9-mile primitive trail that ends at the southern tip of El Yunque Recreation Center.

El Yunque Caribbean National Forest

RAPPELLING

Hike, rappel, and body-surf your way through **San Cristóbal Cañon,** one of the biggest canyons in the Caribbean, located between Aibonito and Barranquitas in the Cordillera Central. Several adventure tour operators offer guided expeditions into the canyon and provide all the equipment and expertise you'll need. Thick with vegetation, the canyon is 4.5 miles long and 500–800 feet deep, providing a great place to test your mountaineering skills.

SPELUNKING

Puerto Rico has the third largest underground river cave system in the world. The tamest way to witness this fascinating subterranean world is to visit **Las Cavernas del Río Camuy** on the north coast. Explore Cueva Clara, featuring a 170-foot-high room thick with stalagmites and stalactites and an underwater waterfall. For a more adventurous exploration of the cave system, contact one of several adventure tour operators and test your rappelling skills.

WILDERNESS CAMPING

Travel by boat at night over the choppy waters of Mona Passage and pitch a tent on uninhabited **Mona Island,** a semiarid subtropical island with 20 miles of coastline, most of which is vertical cliffs more than 200 feet high. Hike the island's trails, where you can spot feral pigs and goats as well as the prehistoric-looking Mona Iguana, which grows up to four feet long. Snorkel or dive the crystal-clear waters that surround the island's perimeter. Several local outfitters provide transportation and equipment.

DIVING

Thanks to a modest fishing trade, Puerto Rico has some of the healthiest, most intact underwater reefs to be found in the Caribbean, which makes it ideal for diving and snorkeling. There are several world-class dive sites around the island, but one of the most spectacular is **La Pared** in La Parguera. The reef wall runs parallel to the coast from Guánica to Cabo Rojo, dropping from 55 feet to more than 1,500 feet in depth, with visibility ranging from 60 to 150 feet.

KITE-BOARDING

Is old-school surfing too tame for you? Step up the action by attaching a sail to your board and harnessing the wind for more go-power in **Isla Verde,** San Juan. Velauno (787/982-0543, www.velauno.com) offers classes and equipment rental for first-timers, or tips and equipment sales for experienced kite-boarders.

Playa Carlos Rosario offers easy access to a site rich in marine life.

Best Beaches for Surfing

Although surf spots can be found all around Puerto Rico's coastline, the most popular area is the northwest coast in the municipalities of Isabela, Aguadilla, and Rincón.

PLAYA DE JOBOS

Playa de Jobos in Isabela is an island favorite. The breakpoint off Puntas Jacinto is renowned for its right-breaking tube, and a shady parking lot right on the beach provides easy access. Within walking distance are a number of casual restaurants and bars. Happy Belly offers beachside service.

DOMES

Rincón is the surfing capital of Puerto Rico, thanks to literally dozens of popular surf sites. By far the favorite is Domes, located in front of the green domes of an abandoned nuclear power plant known by the acronym BONUS. This easy-access spot features long hollow waves that reach a height of eight feet. Domes is often crowded, especially on weekends.

TRES PALMAS

This is another world-class site in Rincón. The waves here are very long and fast, and require a 10-minute hike to access.

WILDERNESS

Aguadilla also boasts several outstanding surf spots. One popular spot is Wilderness, located on the former Ramey Air Force Base. Just drive right through the golf course to get there. Waves break right and left, and swells reach up to 16 feet in height. Nearby El Rincón Surf Shop is a great source of information on current conditions and hot spots.

Best Beach for Snorkeling and Diving

Puerto Rico's best dive sites require a boat ride to access, but excellent snorkeling and diving can be found along the shore in some spots.

PLAYA CARLOS ROSARIO

For easy access to a site rich in marine life, visit Playa Carlos Rosario, a narrow beach flanked by boulders and a protruding coral reef in Culebra. The underwater visibility is usually quite good here, and the coral reef, where you can see all kinds of colorful fish and coral formations, is teeming with marine life.

SAN JUAN

San Juan, Puerto Rico, is arguably the most cosmopolitan city in the Caribbean. The second-oldest European settlement in the Americas, it is a place where world-class restaurants and luxury hotels compete for space alongside glitzy nightclubs and casinos; where Spanish colonial and neoclassical buildings line cobblestone streets; where designer stores and import shops beckon spend-happy tourists; where art, music, and dance thrive in its theaters, museums, and festivals; and where you're never very far from wide strips of sand and surf, ideal for sailing, sunbathing, and swimming.

Situated on the northeastern coast of Puerto Rico, San Juan stretches along 25 miles of coastline and 10 miles inland. It spans 30,000 acres of coastal plain, encompassing rivers, bays, and lagoons, and is home to 1.1 million residents in the greater San Juan area. Established by Spain as the island's capital in 1521, the city's early role as a military stronghold is evident in its 16th- and 17th-century fortresses and a nearly 400-year-old city wall erected around the oldest part of the city to protect it from foreign attacks.

The heart of the city is historic Old San Juan, a 45-block grid of blue cobblestone streets lined with pastel 16th–18th-century buildings trimmed with ornamental ironwork and hanging balconies. By day its streets crawl with tourists shopping for souvenirs and designer duds. At night it throbs with locals and tourists alike, both partaking of some of the city's finest restaurants and nightclubs.

But Old San Juan is only the tip of the city. Travel eastward along the coast to Condado,

© OMAR VEGA

considered the city's tourist district. High-rise hotels, condos, and apartment buildings overlook the Atlantic Ocean. High-end shops line the main thoroughfare, Avenida Ashford, and many fine restaurants and casinos serve night crawlers.

Continue eastward to Ocean Park, a gated residential community on a fine beach with a handful of guesthouses and restaurants. Beside it is Isla Verde, where the city's best beaches and most exclusive hotels are, along with fast-food restaurants and a cockfight arena.

Though it may seem so, San Juan isn't all beachfront property. Travel inland for a lo-cals-only experience in Hato Rey, San Juan's commercial district; Río Piedras, home of the University of Puerto Rico; and Bayamón, a bedroom community.

As in any large city, all is not paradise. San Juan is a densely populated metropolis thick with automobile traffic. A heavy cruise-ship trade dumps thousands of tourists in the city several days a week, and the number of trin-ket shops catering to day-trippers has prolifer-ated. Burger Kings and Pizza Huts are not an uncommon sight. Neither are pockets of poor neighborhoods, some of whose residents con-tribute to a petty street-crime problem.

But despite its big-city ways, San Juan's nat-ural beauty is apparent in its miles of sandy beaches, its shady plazas, and its beloved *coquí,* a tiny tree frog whose "co-QUI" song fills the air. As it's a commonwealth of the United States, American influence is clearly present, but San Juan proudly maintains its Spanish heritage in its language, its culture, and its customs. And although its future is firmly planted in the 21st century, San Juan's rich history endures in its carefully preserved ar-chitecture, its stately fortresses, and the hearts of its inhabitants.

PLANNING YOUR TIME

It's possible to hit San Juan's highlights in a single long weekend, but it's equally possible to spend a whole month here and not see all the city has to offer.

Six municipalities make up greater San Juan.

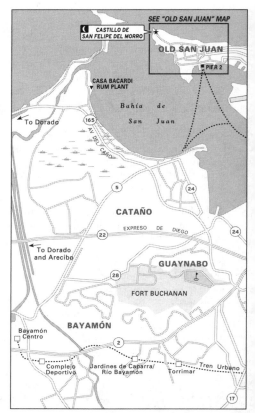

They include San Juan, Cataño, Bayamón, Guaynabo, Trujillo Alto, and Carolina. The four sectors that visitors gravitate to are Old San Juan, Condado, Ocean Park, and Isla Verde in the municipalities of San Juan and Carolina. Not surprisingly, all four areas are along the coast, and luckily they are within about 20 minutes of one another by car or taxi. Most are also accessible by bus.

Old San Juan

Old San Juan is the cultural center of Puerto Rico. The 500-year-old city is filled with many historic buildings, Spanish forts, museums, res-taurants, bars, shops, and ship docks. Beach access is very limited in Old San Juan, and a

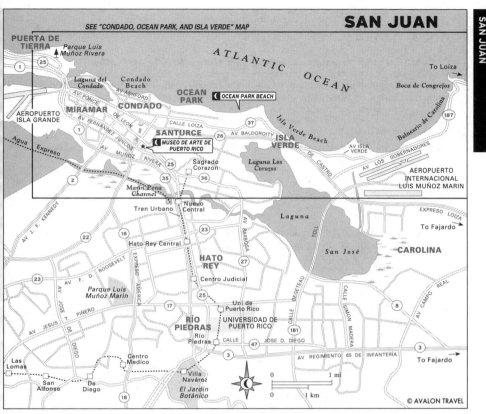

SEE "CONDADO, OCEAN PARK, AND ISLA VERDE" MAP   **SAN JUAN**

thick concentration of tourists can be found here, especially on days the cruise ships dock. But its charm is undeniable.

Among Old San Juan's many must-see sites are the city's two Spanish fortresses, **Castillo de San Felipe del Morro** and **Castillo de San Cristóbal;** the significant religious sites of **Catedral de San Juan Bautista** and **Capilla del Cristo;** and two terrific museums, Museo de Las Americas and La Casa de Libro.

The best way to see Old San Juan is by foot. The roads are drivable, but they're narrow and one-way, and only residents' automobiles are permitted in at night. If walking gets to be too much, there is a free trolley service that runs through the southern half of the city where most of the shops

are. Navigation in and out of Old San Juan is easy. The main public bus terminal is near the cruise-ship piers on Calle de Marina, just below Plaza de Colón in Old San Juan, and there are taxi stands in front of most plazas and hotels.

Condado and Miramar

Condado is considered San Juan's tourist district, although Old San Juan and Isla Verde could qualify for the same designation. The community, which runs along a stretch of beach between Old San Juan and Isla Verde, is undergoing a dramatic transformation. Once the height of glamour, this strip of flashy resorts and hotels fell onto hard times during the recession of the early 1980s, and many hotels closed.

HIGHLIGHTS

((Ocean Park Beach: Easy access and pristine sand make Ocean Park Beach an excellent place to spend the day in the sun. Due to its central location, it's a short cab ride from anywhere in the city. On weekends, lounge chairs are available for rent and street vendors patrol the area selling snacks and beverages (page 28).

((Castillo de San Felipe del Morro: Established in 1539, this imposing Spanish colonial fortress was designed so sentries could spot enemies entering San Juan Bay. That's what makes it such an exceptional place to admire the views. The vast lawn is a great spot to fly a kite too (page 28).

((Castillo de San Cristóbal: Built to protect San Juan from attack by land, San Cristóbal was begun in 1634 and eventually encompassed 27 acres, making it the largest fort on the island. It provides an excellent vantage point for checking out stunning views of the city (page 28).

((Museo de Arte de Puerto Rico: This impressive new 130,000-square-foot museum showcases Puerto Rican art from the 17th century to the present, from classical portraiture to politically charged conceptual art. As an added bonus, the wall text is in Spanish and English (page 33).

((Catedral de San Juan Bautista: Established in 1521, the cathedral lays claim to being the oldest existing church in the Western Hemisphere. The current structure dates from the 1800s or early 1900s and contains the tomb of Juan Ponce de León (page 34).

((Nuyorican Café: The casual Old San Juan nightclub is the hot spot for live salsa music every night but Monday. This is where locals go to dance the night away on the tiny dance floor. Get there early if you want a seat (page 41).

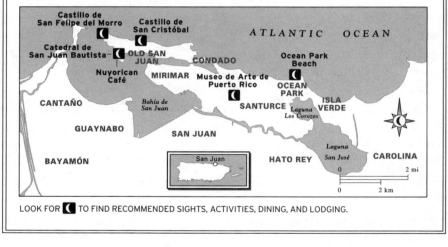

LOOK FOR ((TO FIND RECOMMENDED SIGHTS, ACTIVITIES, DINING, AND LODGING.

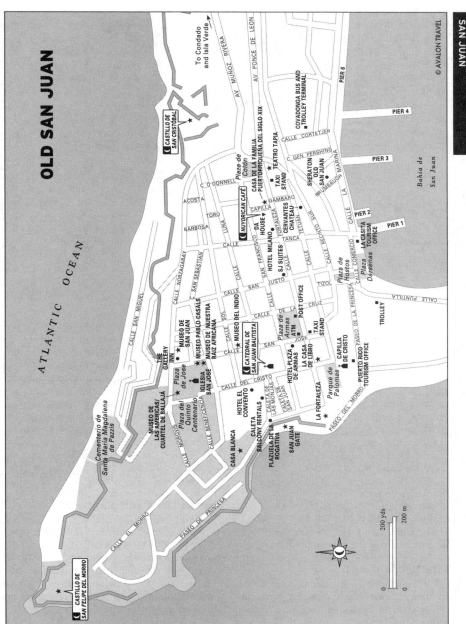

OLD SAN JUAN

ATLANTIC OCEAN

© AVALON TRAVEL

Bahia de San Juan

To Condado and Isla Verde

CASTILLO DE SAN CRISTÓBAL

CASTILLO DE SAN FELIPE DEL MORRO

Cementerio de Santa Maria Magdalena de Pazzis

AV MUÑOZ RIVERA
AV PONCE DE LEON

PIER 6
PIER 4
PIER 3
PIER 2
PIER 1

COVADONGA BUS AND TROLLEY TERMINAL
CALLE CORTETJER
C GEN PERSHING
SHERATON OLD SAN JUAN
BRUMBAUGH MARINA

CALLE MORROS
PASEO DEL MORRO
CALLE EL MORRO
PASEO DE PRINCESA
PASEO DEL MORRO

CALLE SAN MIGUEL
CALLE NORZAGARAY
CALLE SAN SEBASTIAN
CALLE SOL
CALLE LUNA
CALLE SAN FRANCISCO
CALLE FORTALEZA
CALLE TETUAN
CALLE SAN JUSTO

O'DONNELL
ACOSTA
TORO
BARBOSA

Plaza de Colón
CAPILLA
DA HOUSE
CASA DE LA FAMILIA PUERTORRIQUEÑA DEL SIGLO XIX
TEATRO TAPIA
TAXI STAND
GAMBARO
CERVANTES CHATEAU
HOTEL MILANO
SJ SUITES
TANCA
NUYORICAN CAFÉ

CALLE RECINTO SUR
CALLE COMERCIO
CALLE CRUZ
CALLE TIZOL
CALLE BENITO SUR

Plaza de Hostos
Plaza Dársenas
LA CASITA TOURISM OFFICE
POST OFFICE
TAXI STAND
TROLLEY
CALLE PUNTILLA

Plaza de la Catedral
CATEDRAL DE SAN JUAN BAUTISTA
HOTEL PLAZA DE ARMAS
Plaza de Armas
ATM
LA CASA DE LIBRO
CAPILLA DE CRISTO
PUERTO RICO TOURISM OFFICE

THE GALLERY
Plaza del San José
MUSEO DE SAN JUAN
MUSEO PABLO CASALS
MUSEO DE NUESTRA RAIZ AFRICANA
MUSEO DEL INDIO
IGLESIA SAN JOSÉ

MUSEO DE LAS AMÉRICAS/ CUARTEL DE BALLAJÁ
Plaza del Quinto Centenario
CALLE BENEFICENCIA
CALLE DE LAS MONJAS
CALLETA DE SAN JUAN
HOTEL EL CONVENTO
CALLE DEL CRISTO

CASA BLANCA
CALETA
BALCONY RENTALS
PLAZUELA DE LA ROGATIVA
SAN JUAN GATE
LA FORTALEZA
Parque de Palomas

200 yds
200 m
0

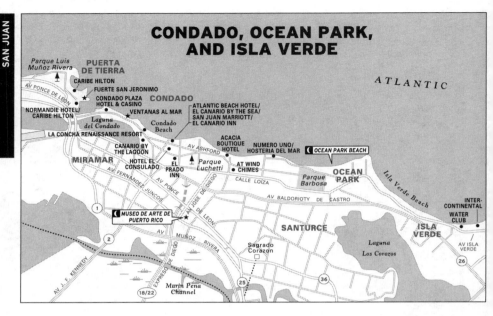

CONDADO, OCEAN PARK, AND ISLA VERDE

But things are on the upswing. Several cranes hang over Avenida Ashford as old buildings are undergoing renovation and new construction is under way. New parks have blossomed, giving passersby access to the Atlantic Ocean and a great place to relax and people-watch.

Aside from its beaches and hotels, Condado is home to some excellent restaurants and casinos, and it is the best place to go for upscale shopping at places such as Louis Vuitton and Cartier. Taxis and public buses traverse the area frequently, and its wide sidewalks and browse-friendly businesses make it an excellent place for pedestrians.

Miramar, an upscale residential area overlooking Laguna del Condado, has recently been designated a historic district and is scheduled for millions of dollars in improvements.

Isla Verde
Isla Verde is renowned for its long, wide beaches, its luxury resorts, and some pretty spectacular nightclubs and casinos. When you're catching some rays on the beach or partying the night away

in a glitzy hot spot, it can feel as glamorous as a mini–South Beach. Unfortunately, the only way to actually see Isla Verde's gorgeous coast is from one of the high-rise hotels and condominiums that line every inch of the way. And the traffic-choked main thoroughfare, Avenida Isla Verde, is a jumble of fast-food restaurants, pizzerias, souvenir shops, tattoo parlors, condom shops, and so on. The community is also home to the Aeropuerto Internacional Luis Muñoz Marín.

The best way to enjoy Isla Verde is to ensconce oneself in one of the community's cushy seaside resorts and stay there.

Ocean Park and Santurce
Wedged between Condado and Isla Verde is a tiny oasis of quiet gentility called Ocean Park. Primarily a gated residential neighborhood, the ocean-side community has only a handful of restaurants, and shopping is nonexistent. But there are several very nice guesthouses right on the beach, and they're excellent places to stay if you want a refuge from busy urban settings and crowded tourist attractions. There's also

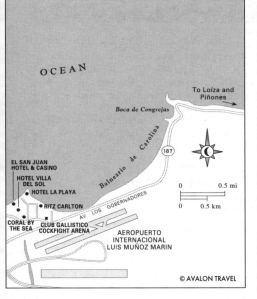

OCEAN

To Loíza and Piñones

Boca de Congrejas

Balneario de Carolina

187

EL SAN JUAN HOTEL & CASINO

HOTEL VILLA DEL SOL

HOTEL LA PLAYA

RITZ CARLTON

AV LOS GOBERNADORES

CORAL BY THE SEA

CLUB GALLISTICO COCKFIGHT ARENA

AEROPUERTO INTERNACIONAL LUIS MUÑOZ MARIN

0   0.5 mi

0   0.5 km

© AVALON TRAVEL

women. It's connected by the new 10-mile Tren Urbano metro system to Río Piedras, home of the University of Puerto Rico and El Jardín Botánico, and the residential area of Bayamón, home of Parque de las Ciencias Luis A. Ferre science park.

Several spectacular day trips are less than an hour's drive east of San Juan, the most popular being **El Yunque Caribbean National Forest,** the rain forest, and **Balneario La Monserrate,** considered one of Puerto Rico's most beautiful beaches.

HISTORY

Christopher Columbus was on his second voyage in his quest to "discover" the New World when he arrived in Puerto Rico in 1493. He christened the island San Juan Bautista after John the Baptist, claimed it as a property of Spain, and went on his merry way. But among his crew was a lieutenant named Juan Ponce de León, who shared Columbus's passion for exploration and colonization. In 1508 Ponce de León returned to the island to establish a settlement in a nearly landlocked bit of marshland just west of San Juan, which he called Caparra. He couldn't have made a poorer choice for a new settlement. Virtually uninhabitable and strategically ineffective, the settlement was relocated around 1521 to what is now Old San Juan. Originally the new settlement was called Puerto Rico for its "rich port." It's not clear why—possibly a cartographer's mistake—but soon after it was founded, the name of the settlement was switched with the name of the island.

The history of San Juan is inextricable from that of the island itself; for more information on San Juan's and Puerto Rico's history, see the *History* section in the *Background* chapter.

an excellent stretch of well-maintained public beach with parking.

Just a few blocks inland from Condado is Santurce, a congested conglomeration of small shops and businesses that cater to residents of the island. Tourists are advised to take precautions when visiting the area at night as it has a high rate of street crime. Nevertheless, it is home to the superb **Museo de Arte de Puerto Rico** and several popular nightclubs.

Hato Rey, Río Piedras, and Bayamón

Outside San Juan's popular tourist areas are communities central to the lives of San Juan residents. Hato Rey is the city's business and financial district, chock-full of banks and restaurants that cater to businessmen and

Sights

BEACHES

Isla Verde Beach (along Ave. Isla Verde) is one of San Juan's most stellar beaches. Roughly two miles long, its wide stretches of sand and rolling surf make for great swimming, surfing, and windsurfing. Like all beaches in Puerto Rico, Isla Verde Beach is open to the public, but because it's lined cheek by jowl with high-rise hotels and apartment buildings, access is limited to narrow walkways between buildings and the occasional dead-end street. Compounding the access problem is the dearth of parking, except for a multilevel lot on the far eastern end.

Condado Beach (along Ave. Ashford) is a less picture-perfect beach than Isla Verde Beach. The terrain is hillier, the sand coarser, and the water less crystalline. But it's got sand, surf, and sun, so it's still got a lot to offer. Like Isla Verde Beach, it's lined with high-rises, but it's much more easily accessible to the general public.

Balneario de Carolina (Carr. 187, Ave. Boca de Congrejas, 787/778-8811, $2) is a public beach maintained by the municipality of Carolina. There are picnic shelters, bathroom facilities, and plenty of parking.

Balneario Escambrón (Carr. 25 in Puerta de Tierra) is the closest beach to Old San Juan. It is a small strip of sand but there's plenty of parking, food vendors, a children's playground, and lifeguards on duty until 5 P.M. Shady characters are known to loiter here after dark.

◖ Ocean Park Beach

Ocean Park Beach is a terrific little residential beach that benefits from ample free parking at Parque Barbosa at the end of Calle McLeary. Due to its central location, it's a short cab ride from anywhere in the city. The section of the beach across from the park is cleaned and raked daily, and a swimming area is marked off with nets to keep out sea creatures. The only drawback is that this part of the beach gets very crowded on weekends and holidays. On weekends, lounge chairs are available for rent, and street vendors patrol the area selling snacks and beverages. Farther east the wind and surf are a little rougher, which makes it popular with sailboarders and kite-surfers. The area in front of the guesthouses inside the gated community of Ocean Park is a popular gay beach.

HISTORIC SIGHTS

◖ Castillo de San Felipe del Morro

It doesn't matter from which direction you approach El Morro (501 Calle Norzagaray, Old San Juan, 787/729-6777, daily 9 A.M.–6 P.M. Dec.–May, daily 9 A.M.–5 P.M. June–Nov., $3 adults, $5 for both forts, $2 seniors over 62, free for children under 16, English tours at 11 A.M. and 3 P.M.), it's an impressive sight to behold. From San Juan Bay, which it was constructed to protect from attack, it's an awesome feat of engineering and a daunting display of military defense featuring four levels of cannon-bearing batteries that rise 140 feet from the sea. From Old San Juan, the approach is more welcoming, thanks to an enormous expanse of grassy lawn and breathtaking views of the shore. It's easy to see why this is such a popular spot for kite-flyers.

Inside El Morro is a maze of rooms, including gun rooms, soldiers' quarters, a chapel, turreted sentry posts, and a prison connected by tunnels, ramps, and a spiral stairway. The foundations for El Morro were laid in 1539, but it wasn't completed until 1787. It successfully endured many foreign attacks by the English in 1595, 1598, and 1797, and by the Dutch in 1625. During the Spanish-American War, the United States fired on El Morro and destroyed the lighthouse, which was later rebuilt.

◖ Castillo de San Cristóbal

San Cristóbal (Calle Norzagaray at the

© SUZANNE VAN ATTEN

Castillo de San Cristóbal

entrance to Old San Juan, 787/729-6777, daily 9 A.M.–6 P.M. Dec.–May, daily 9 A.M.–5 P.M. June–Nov., $3 adults, $5 for both forts, $2 seniors over 62, free for children under 16, English tours at 10 A.M. and 2 P.M.) is the large fortress at the entrance to Old San Juan by Plaza de Colón. Before it was built, two significant attacks from land—first by the Earl of Cumberland in 1598, later by the Dutch in 1625—convinced the Spanish that protecting the walled city from attack by sea alone was not adequate.

The fort's construction began in 1634 and was completed in 1783. The fort eventually encompassed 27 acres of land, although some of it was destroyed to accommodate the expanding city. The fort's defense was tested in 1797 by another unsuccessful attack by the British. After the United States won the Spanish-American War, it took control of the fort and used it as a World War II observation post. Today, a section of the fort is open to the public, who can wander freely among its intriguing array of tunnels, ramps, stairways, batteries, magazines, soldiers' quarters, and turreted sentry posts.

Old San Juan

The recently renovated **Casa Blanca** (1 Calle San Sebastían, Old San Juan, 787/725-1454, Tues.–Sat. 9 A.M.–noon and 1–4 P.M., $2) was originally built as a home for the island's first governor, Juan Ponce de León, although he died on his quest for the Fountain of Youth before he could ever take up residence. Construction was begun in 1523, and for more than 200 years it served as the residence of Ponce de León's descendants. Today it's a museum of 17th- and 18th-century domestic life featuring lots of impressive Spanish antiques. Don't miss the cool, lush gardens that surround the house and the views of both San Juan Bay and the Atlantic Ocean.

La Fortaleza (Calle Fortaleza, Old San Juan, 787/721-7000, ext. 2211, 2323, and 2358, Mon.–Fri. 9 A.M.–3:30 P.M., free) was the first fort built in Puerto Rico, completed in 1540 to provide refuge for the island's original Spanish settlers. Partially burned by the Dutch in 1625, it was rebuilt in the 1640s and received a new facade in 1846. It has been the official residence of the governor of Puerto Rico since the 16th century, which gives it the distinction of the longest continuous use of an executive mansion in the western hemisphere. Tours are limited mostly to the lovely gardens and first floor, with audio narration in Spanish and English.

Aside from El Morro and San Cristóbal's iconic turreted sentry boxes, the most distinguishing characteristic of Old San Juan is **La Muralla,** the grand, dramatic, and impenetrable wall that once surrounded the city and still stands strong along the coast and bay. Nearly 400 years old, the wall took 200 years to complete and stands 48 feet high in some places and 20 feet thick at its base. The wall once had five gates that permitted access into the city, but only one remains today. The commanding red **La Puerta de San Juan** was built in the late 1700s and is on the eastern end of Old San Juan beside La Fortaleza. Sixteen feet tall and 20 feet thick, the door is best seen from the wide bayside promenade,

LA MURALLA

The most enduring symbol of Puerto Rico is La Muralla. Nearly 400 years old, the city wall is composed of rock, rubble, and mortar that wraps around Old San Juan from the cruise-ship piers on San Juan Harbor to the capitol on the Atlantic Ocean. Its iconic sentry boxes serve as a symbol of the island's Spanish heritage and resilience in an ever-changing world.

Begun by Spanish colonists in the 1600s, the wall took 200 years to complete and has withstood multiple attacks by the English, the Dutch, and the Americans. But what proved nearly impenetrable to foreign attack has been rendered defenseless by modern life. Automobile traffic, pollution, and misguided attempts to preserve it have endangered the wall.

Forty-five feet wide and 40 feet high in some spots, La Muralla is crumbling in places. In 2004 a 70-foot section below the heavily traveled Calle Norzagaray fell, underscoring the urgency of stepping up preservation efforts. It wasn't the first time the wall's fragility was made apparent. A larger section fell into San Juan Bay in 1938, and in 1999, a Soviet oil tanker ran aground, damaging the wall's northwest corner.

When the U.S. Army seized Puerto Rico in 1898, it took over maintenance of the wall and attempted its first preservation efforts. Concrete was used to patch La Muralla, but that only served to add weight to the wall and trap moisture inside it, which weakened the structure through time.

Now a National Historic Site, La Muralla is maintained by the National Park Service, which has been overseeing efforts to repair the wall. Experts have spent years studying the 16th-century methods used to build the structure in an attempt to recreate the magic mixture of sand, water, and limestone used to stucco the wall. Not only is the repair method they've developed more effective than concrete, it serves to preserve the wall's historic integrity. The process is now being used to repair the wall's beloved sentry boxes. But it's a painstaking and costly process, requiring the services of specially trained masons, which the Park Service is hard-pressed to fund for large-scale repairs.

But La Muralla endures. Along with the fortresses El Morro and San Cristóbal that adjoin it, the wall attracts 1.2 million visitors a year. Chances are, with the help of preservation efforts, it will continue to assert its soaring beauty and cultural significance as the proud protector of Old San Juan for years to come.

©OMAR VEGA

Construction of La Muralla, the city wall, began nearly 400 years ago.

© SUZANNE VAN ATTEN

Paseo de Princesa, a bayside promenade where festivals and events are frequently held

Paseo de Princesa. Named after La Princesa, a 19th-century prison that now houses the Puerto Rico Tourism Company, the promenade begins across from Plaza de Hostos at Calle Tizol near the cruise-ship piers in Old San Juan. Glorious royal palms, a view of the bay, the soaring city wall, the city gate, and an outlandish fountain comprising naked sea nymphs and goats are some of the sights along the way. The promenade continues along El Morro, ending dramatically at the point containing the oldest part of the fort. Paseo de Princesa is the site of frequent festivals and events, and you can usually find a variety of vendors here selling *piraguas* (snow cones), popcorn, and *dulces* (sweets).

Cuartel de Ballajá (Calle Norzagaray beside Plaza del Quinto Centenario near the entrance to El Morro, Old San Juan) is a massive structure that once housed 1,000 Spanish soldiers. Built in 1854, the former barracks are three levels high with interior balconies and a dizzying series of arches that overlook an enormous courtyard. It was the last major building constructed by the Spanish in the New World. Today it houses the Museo de Las Americas, featuring a fantastic folk art collection.

Cementerio de Santa María Magdalena de Pazzis is the city's historic cemetery, outside the city wall just east of El Morro and accessible from Calle Norzagaray in Old San Juan. In addition to a neoclassical chapel, there are many significant burial sites of some of the city's early colonists, as well as the tomb of Pedro Albizu Campos, the revered revolutionary who sought independence for the island of Puerto Rico. Avoid going alone or at night. Next door is **La Perla,** an impoverished community notorious for its drug trade; its illicit activities are known to spill over into the cemetery. If you don't want to venture in, you can get a great view of it from Plaza del Quinto Centenario on Calle Norzagaray.

Condado

Information about the small lagoon-based **Fuerte San Jerónimo** (behind Caribe Hilton in Puerta de Tierra) is difficult to come by, perhaps because it's the only fort in San Juan that isn't part of the San Juan National Historic

Site. Instead, it's overseen by the Institute of Puerto Rican Culture and managed by the Caribe Hilton, on whose property it now sits. Various sources date its origins to the 17th and 18th centuries. Unfortunately, it's rarely open to the public.

Greater San Juan

El Cañuelo (end of Carr. 870 on Isla de Cabras, Toa Alta, daily 8:30 A.M.–5:30 P.M., $2) is the ruins of a tiny fortress across the bay from El Morro. Originally constructed of wood in the 1500s, it was destroyed in an attack by the Dutch in 1625. The current stone structure was built in the 1670s. Its purpose was to work in concert with El Morro to create cannon cross-fire at the mouth of the bay. Unfortunately, the public is not allowed to enter the fort, but it provides a terrific view of El Morro. There's a small recreation area with picnic tables.

A few crumbling walls and foundations are all that's left of **Ruinas de Caparra** (Carr. 2, km 6.4, Guaynabo, 787/781-4795, Mon.–Fri. 9 A.M.–4 P.M.), the site of Juan Ponce de León's first settlement on the island, established in 1508. Attempts to develop the settlement didn't last long. The property is in a swamp that proved nearly uninhabitable, so settlers quickly relocated to Old San Juan. The small museum contains historical documents and Taíno artifacts pertaining to the site.

Rum plays a long, colorful role in the history and economic development of Puerto Rico. Established in 1862 by Don Facundo Bacardi Masó, Bacardi is the top-selling rum in the United States and is still owned and operated by its founder's descendants. For an interactive lesson on its production, **Casa Bacardi Visitor Center** (Carr. 165, km 6.2, Cataño, 787/788-8400, www.casabacardi .org, Mon.–Sat. 8:30 A.M.–5:30 P.M., last tour at 4:15 P.M.; Sun. 10 A.M.–5 P.M., last tour at 3:45 P.M., free) offers audiotaped tours of its largest distillery, bottling operation, and museum of historic artifacts. Admission includes two drinks and a trolley tour of the surrounding gardens. The factory is a 20-minute drive from San Juan. Alternatively, visitors can catch the AquaExpreso ferry (6 A.M.–10 P.M., $0.50) at Pier 2 in Old San Juan to Cataño, where a *publico* van will provide transportation to the factory for $2–6, depending on the number of riders.

HISTORY MUSEUMS

Museo de Arte e Historia de San Juan (150 Calle Norzagaray, Old San Juan, 787/724-1875, Wed.–Fri. 9 A.M.–noon and 1–4 P.M., Sat.–Sun. 10 A.M.–4 P.M., free) is in the city's former marketplace, built in 1857. In 1979 it was converted into a city museum. It contains two exhibition spaces, one housing temporary exhibits illuminating various aspects of the city's history, the other a permanent exhibition that gives a comprehensive look at the city's history from its geographical roots to the 21st century. Superbly produced wall graphics and text include reproductions of old photographs, maps, prints, and paintings that tell the city's story. All the exhibits are in Spanish, but a photocopied handout in English encapsulates the exhibition highlights.

Two museums in one, **Casa de la Familia Puertorriqueña del Siglo XIX** and **Museo de la Farmacia** (319 Calle Fortaleza, Old San Juan, 787/977-2700 or 787/977-2701, Tues.–Sat. 8:30 A.M.–4:20 P.M., free) is a re-creation of a typical (albeit wealthy) family's residence from the late 1800s filled with antiques, both locally made and imported from Germany, Belgium, and Italy. Downstairs are vessels, cabinets, scales, and various other accoutrements from a 19th-century pharmacy in Cayey.

Museo de Nuestra Raíz Africana (Calle San Sebastían beside Plaza de San José, Old San Juan, 787/724-4294 or 787/724-4184, Tues.–Sat. 8:30 A.M.–4:20 P.M.) explores the African influence on Puerto Rican culture. Slavery and abolition figure prominently, including a display of handcuffs and collars and a simulated re-creation of what it was like to cross the ocean in a slave ship.

Museo del Indio (119 San José, Old San Juan, 787/721-2864, Tues.–Sat. 9:30 A.M.–3:30 P.M., free) is San Juan's newest museum. Devoted to the history of the island's Taíno Indian population, it contains many artifacts unearthed in excavations around the island including pottery, stone tools, and *cemíes,* small carved stone talismans representative of various gods.

ART MUSEUMS AND GALLERIES
Santurce
◖ MUSEO DE ARTE DE PUERTO RICO
Without a doubt, the crowning jewel of San Juan's cultural institutions is Museo de Arte de Puerto Rico (299 Ave. José de Diego, Santurce, 787/977-6277, fax 787/977-4446, www.mapr .org, Tues. and Thurs.–Sat. 10 A.M.–5 P.M., Wed. 10 A.M.–8 P.M., Sun. 11 A.M.–6 P.M., $6 adults, $3 children 5–12, seniors, students with ID, and visitors with disabilities; valet parking). Visitors with even a passing interest in art will be bowled over by the volume and quality of work produced by the many gifted artists who hail from this small island.

The modern, new 130,000-square-foot, neoclassical structure opened in 2000 and is devoted to Puerto Rican art from the 17th century to the present. And joy! The wall text is in Spanish and English. Exhibition highlights include works by the celebrated Francisco Manuel Oller, a European-trained 17th-century realist-impressionist, and a striking selection of *cartels,* a mid-century poster-art form distinguished by bold graphics and socially conscious themes.

Contemporary art is on the second floor, and it is not to be missed. One room is devoted to Rafael Trelles's 1957 installation *Visits to the Wake,* inspired by Oller's famous 19th-century painting of a family attending a child's wake, called *El Veloria.* The piece combines video, sculpture, found objects, and life-size cutouts of the painting's characters to astounding effect. Another remarkable work is Pepón Osorio's installation titled *No Crying Allowed in the Barbershop.* The simulated barbershop explores issues of male vanity, rites of passage, and early lessons in masculinity.

There are also temporary exhibition spaces for rotating shows, a children's gallery, a five-acre modern sculpture garden, and the Raul

Julia Theater, featuring an intriguing curtain made of mundillo, a traditional handmade lace. A museum shop is also on-site, as is Pikayo, a pricey fine-dining restaurant.

OTHER ART MUSEUMS AND GALLERIES
Before Museo de Arte de Puerto Rico opened, **Museo de Arte Contemporáneo de Puerto Rico** (Escuela Rafael M. de Labra, corner of Roberto H. Todd and Ponce de León, Santurce, 787/977-4030, 787/977-4031, or 787/977-4032, www.museocontemporaneo pr.org, Tues.–Sat. 10 A.M.–4 P.M., Sun. noon–4 P.M., free) was the place to go for modern art. Unfortunately, it's a bit of a disappointment in comparison. But it's worth a visit just to see the building, an atypical red-brick Georgian structure completed in 1918. Two small exhibition spaces feature rotating exhibits from the permanent collection. Wall text is in Spanish only.

Espacio 1414 (1414 Ave. Fernández Juncos, 787/725-3899, www.espacio1414.com, Sat. 2 P.M.–6 P.M.) is a contemporary art space established in a former warehouse. In addition to its permanent collection of contemporary Latin American art, it features three levels of temporary exhibition space.

Old San Juan
MUSEO DE LAS AMERICAS
The other side of the art pendulum from Museo de Arte de Puerto Rico is Museo de Las Americas (Cuartel de Ballajá, second floor, on Calle Norzagaray beside Plaza del Quinto Centenario, Old San Juan, 787/724-5052, fax 787/722-2848, musame@prtc.net, www .prtc.net/~musame, Tues.–Fri. 10 A.M.–4 P.M., Sat.–Sun. 11 A.M.–5 P.M., free). Inside an enormous structure that once housed 1,000 Spanish soldiers, the museum contains a fantastic collection of Latin American folk art, including masks, musical instruments, clothing, pottery, baskets, and tools. Highlights include altars representing Santeria, voodoo, and Mexico's Day of the Dead celebration. Don't miss the collection of vintage Santos, Puerto Rican wood carvings of saints.

Wall text is in Spanish and English except in the second smaller exhibit dedicated to Puerto Rico's African heritage. The **Tienda de Artesanías** on the first floor (Tues.–Fri. 10 A.M.–4 P.M., Sat.–Sun. 11 A.M.–5 P.M., 787/722-6057) has a small but quality selection of locally made crafts for sale.

OTHER ART MUSEUMS AND GALLERIES
La Casa de Libro (255 Calle Cristo, Old San Juan, 787/723-0354, lcdl@prw.net, www.lacasa dellibro.org, Tues.–Sat. 11:30 A.M.–4:30 P.M., free) is a little gem of a museum in a former residence. It has an impressive collection of historic books displayed in exhibits that rotate about every three months. In 2005 it featured an exhibit honoring the 400-year anniversary of Cervantes's *Don Quixote* that included a first edition from 1605.

Museo Pablo Casals (101 Calle San Sebastían, Old San Juan, 787/723-9185, Tues.–Sat. 9:30 A.M.–5:30 P.M., $1) commemorates the career and accomplishments of Pablo Casals, the renowned cellist who performed for Queen Victoria and President Theodore Roosevelt, among other world movers and shakers. Born in Catalonia, Casals moved to Puerto Rico in 1956. A year later, the island established the annual Casals Festival of classical music, which continues today. Inside an 18th-century building, the museum contains Casals's music manuscripts, cello, and piano. You can hear recordings of Casals performing in the music room upstairs.

One of the oldest theaters in the Western Hemisphere is **Teatro Tapia** (Calle Fortaleza at Plaza de Colón, Old San Juan, 787/721-0180 or 787/721-0169), a lovely Romantic-style building constructed in 1824 and renovated in 1987. Named after Puerto Rican playwright Alejandro Tapia y Rivera, the 642-seat theater still hosts a variety of performance art events.

Several interesting galleries are in Old San Juan. Among the best is **Galería Botello** (208 Calle Cristo, Old San Juan, 787/723-9987 or 787/723-2879, fax 787/724-6776, botello sj@msn.com, www.botello.com, Mon.–Sat. 10 A.M.–6 P.M.). Although he was born in Spain, renowned artist Angel Botello spent most of his life in the Caribbean, eventually settling in Puerto Rico, where he opened this gallery. Although he died in 1986, the artist lives on through his paintings and sculptures on view at the gallery, which also exhibits solo shows by contemporary artists. **Galería Exodo** (200-B Calle Cristo, Old San Juan, 787/725-4252 or 787/671-4159, galeriaexodo@gmail.com, www .galeriaexodo.com, Mon.–Fri. 11 A.M.–7 P.M., Sat. 10 A.M.–6 P.M., Sun. 11 A.M.–5 P.M.)—formerly Fósil Arte—has a wide diversity of mostly high-quality works by contemporary artists, both Puerto Rican and international. **The Butterfly People** (257 Calle de la Cruz, Old San Juan, 787/723-2432 or 787/723-2201, info@butterflypeople.com, www.butterfly people.com, 10 A.M.–6 P.M. daily) is a unique gallery that sells fantastic colorful pieces composed of real butterflies mounted in Lucite.

RELIGIOUS SITES
◖ Catedral de San Juan Bautista
Catedral de San Juan Bautista (151–153 Calle del Cristo, Old San Juan, 787/722-0861, www.catedralsanjuan.com, Mon.–Thurs. 9 A.M.–noon and 1:30–4 P.M., Fri. 9 A.M.–noon; Mass Sat. 9 A.M., 11 A.M., and 7 P.M., Sun.–Fri. 12:15 P.M.) holds the distinction of being the second-oldest church in the western hemisphere, the first being Catedral Basilica Menor de Santa in the Dominican Republic. The church was first built of wood and straw in 1521 but was destroyed by hurricanes and rebuilt multiple times. In 1917 the cathedral underwent major restoration and expansion. The large sanctuary features a marble altar and rows of arches with several side chapels appointed with elaborate statuary primarily depicting Mary and Jesus. In stark contrast is a chapel featuring an enormous contemporary oil painting of a man in a business suit. It was erected in honor of Carlos "Charlie" Rodríguez, a Puerto Rican layman who was beatified in 2001 by Pope John Paul II. Catedral de San Juan Bautista is the final resting place of Juan de Ponce de León, whose remains are encased in a marble tomb, and a relic of San Pio, a Roman martyr.

© OMAR VEGA

Capilla del Cristo is a tiny chapel at the end of Calle de la Cristo overlooking San Juan Bay.

Capilla del Cristo

Built in 1753, the tiny picturesque Capilla del Cristo (south end of Calle de la Cristo, Old San Juan, 787/722-0861) is one of the most photographed sights in San Juan. Legend has it that horse races were held on Calle del Cristo, and one ill-fated rider was speeding down the hill so fast he couldn't stop in time and tumbled over the city wall to his death, and the chapel was built to prevent a similar occurrence. An alternative end to the legend is that the rider survived and the church was built to show thanks to God. Either way, the result was the construction of a beloved landmark.

Unfortunately, Capilla del Cristo is rarely open, but it's possible to peer through the windows and see the ornate gilded altarpiece. Beside it is **Parque de Palomas,** a gated park overlooking San Juan Harbor that is home to more pigeons than you might think imaginable. Bird seed is available for purchase if you want to get up close and personal with your fine feathered friends.

Iglesia San José

Although Catedral de San Juan Bautista gets all the glory, Iglesia San José (Calle San Sebastián at Plaza de San José, Old San Juan, 787/725-7501) is one of the oldest structures in Old San Juan. Built in the 1530s, it was originally a chapel for the Dominican monastery, but it was taken over in 1865 by the Jesuits. The main chapel is an excellent example of 16th-century Spanish Gothic architecture. Originally Iglesia San José was Juan Ponce de León's final resting place, but his body was later moved to Catedral de San Juan Bautista. Ponce de León himself is said to have donated the wooden 16th-century crucifix. Unfortunately, the church has been closed for many years while it undergoes a seemingly endless renovation project.

FAMILY ATTRACTIONS

El Jardín Botánico (Hwy. 1 at Carr. 847 in Río Piedras, 787/250-0000, ext. 6578, or 787/767-1701, daily 6 A.M.–6 P.M., free, guides available by special arrangement 10 A.M.–1 P.M.) is a 289-acre urban garden filled with tropical and subtropical vegetation, including orchids, heliconias, bromeliads, palms, and bamboo. There's also a native Taíno garden display of native plants. It is maintained by the University of Puerto Rico.

For hands-on educational activities geared toward children, head to **Museo del Niño** (150 Calle Cristo near El Convento Hotel, Old San Juan, 787/722-3791, info@museodelninopr .org, www.museodelninopr.org, Tues.–Thurs. 9 A.M.–3:30 P.M., Fri. 9 A.M.–5 P.M., Sat.–Sun. 12:30–5 P.M., $5 adults, $7 children). This three-story museum contains exhibits in geography, nutrition, weather, astronomy, biology, and more.

An even more elaborate interactive educational opportunity can be found at **Parque de las Ciencias Luis A. Ferré** (Carr. 167, off Hwy. 22 in Bayamón, 787/740-6878, 787/740-6868, 787/740-6869, or 787/740-6871, Wed.–Fri. 9 A.M.–4 P.M., Sat.–Sun. and holidays 10 A.M.–6 P.M., ticket booth closes two hours before park closing, $5 adults, $3 children, $2.50 seniors 65 and older and those with disabilities; parking $1; planetarium $3 adults, $2 children). Basically an amusement park devoted to science, it encompasses 37 acres and features an aerospace museum with NASA rockets, a natural-science museum, an art museum, a small zoo, a planetarium, an archaeology museum, a transportation museum, a lake with paddleboats, and food vendors selling hot dogs and pizza.

PLAZAS AND PARKS

Colonial Spanish towns are traditionally anchored by a plaza that serves as an important gathering place for the community, and Old San Juan is lucky enough to have several. There's no better way to spend the morning than strolling the perimeter of a plaza or spending time on a bench sipping coffee, fending off pigeons, and watching the parade of people pass by. The plazas are also popular sites for arts festivals and evening concerts.

Metropolitan San Juan also has several modern parks with all the jogging trails and children's playgrounds modern man (or woman) could want.

© SUZANNE VAN ATTEN

Artisans rolling handmade cigars can be found in the plazas of Old San Juan.

Old San Juan

Not surprisingly, the largest concentration of historic plazas and parks is in Old San Juan. **Plaza de Armas** (Calle San Francisco, at Calle de la Cruz and Calle San José) is the main square in Old San Juan and a great place to people-watch. Once the site of military drills, it contains a large gazebo and a fountain surrounded by four 100-year-old statues that represent the four seasons. A couple of vendors sell coffee and snacks, and there's a bank of pay phones popular with cruise-ship visitors eager to check in with those back home. Across the street on Calle de la Cruz is a small grocery store. Across Calle Cordero is an ATM, and a taxi stand is just around the corner on Calle San José at Calle Fortaleza.

Plaza de Colón (between Calle Fortaleza, Calle San Francisco, and Calle O'Donnell) is a large square at the entrance to Old San Juan by San Cristóbal fortress. In the center is a huge pedestal topped with a statue of Christopher Columbus, whom the plaza is named after.

There's a small newsstand on one corner, and several restaurants and shops surround it on two sides. Unfortunately, there's little shade, so it's not that pleasant for lingering when the sun is high.

Old San Juan's newest square is **Plaza del Quinto Centenario** (between Calle Norzagaray and Calle Beneficencia near the entrance to El Morro, Old San Juan). Built to commemorate the 500th anniversary of Christopher Columbus's "discovery" of the New World, the plaza features a striking 40-foot totem made from black granite and ceramic pieces created by local artist Jaime Suárez. The plaza provides a great view of the historic cemetery, El Morro, and all the kite flyers who gather on the fort's long green lawn.

One of Puerto Rico's most beautiful pieces of public art is in **Plazuela de la Rogativa,** a tiny sliver of a park tucked between the city wall and Calle Clara Lair just west of El Convento in Old San Juan. At its center is a spectacular bronze sculpture called *La Rogativa,* designed by New Zealand artist Lindsay Daen in the 1950s. The piece depicts a procession of three women and a priest bearing crosses and torches. It commemorates one of San Juan's most beloved historic tales. In 1797 a British fleet led by Sir Ralph Abercrombie entered San Juan Bay and prepared to launch an attack in hopes of capturing the city. Because the city's men were away protecting the city's inland fronts, the only people remaining behind were women and clergy. In hopes of staving off an attack, the governor ordered a *rogativa,* a divine entreaty to ask the saints for help. As the story goes, the town's brave women formed a procession, carrying torches and ringing bells throughout the streets, which duped the British into thinking reinforcements had arrived, prompting them to sail away, leaving the city safe once again.

Plaza de José (Calle San Sebastían and Calle Cristo, Old San Juan) is in front of the Iglesia de San José and features a statue of its most celebrated parishioner, Juan Ponce de León. After successfully thwarting another attack by the British in 1797, citizens of San Juan melted the enemy's cannons to make the statue. This is a popular gathering place for young locals, especially at night when the string of nearby bars gets crowded.

Plaza de Hostos (between Calle San Justo and Calle Tizol, Old San Juan) is a bustling shady spot near the cruise-ship piers. On weekends it turns into a craft fair, and there are often food vendors selling fritters and snow cones. Just across the street, at **Plaza Dársenas,** concerts are often held on the weekends on a covered stage overlooking the harbor.

Beside Capilla de Cristo on the south end of Calle de la Cristo in Old San Juan is **Parque de Palomas,** a small gated park packed with a zillion pigeons. A vendor sells small bags of feed for those who take pleasure in being swarmed with the feathered urban dwellers. Kids love it!

Condado

Aside from its long stretch of beach, Condado is mostly concrete and asphalt, but there are several very nice, compact parks there. **Ventanas al Mar, Plaza Ancla,** and **Parque del Indio** are all on the ocean side of Avenida Ashford, and although they're primarily concrete, they feature excellent pieces of contemporary public art, benches for resting, and access to the water. Plaza Ancla has the added bonus of a terrific open-air restaurant, Barlovento, which has a full bar and serves Mediterranean cuisine. Another waterside park between Condado and Miramar is **Parque Laguna del Condado** (by Dos Hermanos bridge). Having recently undergone a $500,000 renovation, the park features hiking, biking, and jogging trails that run along Condado Lagoon and has kayak rentals available.

Condado's best park, though, is **Parque Luchetti** (between Calle Magdalena and Calle Luchetti at Calle Cervantes), a lovely oasis of quiet and lush green flora just two blocks away from the hubbub of Avenida Ashford. Shaded benches, flowering shrubs, palm trees, and public art make this the perfect spot to relax or picnic. One of the highlights is a whimsical bronze sculpture called *Juan Bobo and the Basket*. Created in 1991 by New Zealand artist Lindsay Daen, who made the more famous *La Rogativa* statue in Old San Juan, it's inspired by a local fable.

Puerta de Tierra

Puerta de Tierra is a spot of land between Condado and Old San Juan that is home to **Parque Luis Muñoz Rivera** (between Ave. Ponce de León and Ave. Muñoz Rivera), another lovely green space that provides a welcome reprieve from the city's urban atmosphere. Shady gardens, fountains, walking trails, a children's play area, and the Peace Pavilion can be found in this 27-acre park.

Ocean Park

Ocean Park's **Parque Barbosa** (end of Calle McLeary) isn't the prettiest or best-maintained park in San Juan, but it does have hiking, jogging, and bike paths. Its proximity to a large public-housing project may deter some visitors, but it's the perfect place to park when visiting Ocean Park beach, which is right across the street.

Hato Rey

Parque Luis Muñoz Marín (off Hwy. 18 between Ave. Jesús Piñero and Ave. F. D. Roosevelt, Wed.–Sun. and holidays) in Hato Rey is a modern 140-acre park with walking and bike trails, a children's play area, golf practice grounds, an amphitheater, pavilions, and more.

Sports and Recreation

When it comes to water sports, San Juan pales in comparison to the rest of Puerto Rico, but there are many tour operators in the area that will provide transportation to nearby sweet spots for snorkeling, diving, fishing, and more.

DIVING AND SNORKELING

Ocean Sports (77 Ave. Isla Verde, 787/268-2329, www.osdivers.com, Mon.–Sat. 10 A.M.–7 P.M.) rents and sells snorkel and scuba equipment from its two stores and operates scuba and snorkel tours from Fajardo. Road transportation to and from San Juan is available. **Caribbean School of Aquatics** (1 Calle Taft, 787/728-6606 or 787/383-5700, greg@saildiveparty.com, www.saildiveparty.com) offers full- and half-day sail, scuba, snorkel, and fishing trips from San Juan and Fajardo on a luxury catamaran with Captain Greg Korwek. Snorkel trips start at $79 per person; scuba trips start at $139 per person. **Scuba Dogs** (D-13 Buen Samaritano Gardenville, Guaynabo, 787/783-6377, www.scubadogs.net) provides scuba and snorkeling trips all around the island for everyone from first-timers to those seeking PADI dive training. It also sells and rents equipment. **Caribe Aquatic Adventures** (Hotel Normandie, 499 W. Ave. Muñoz Rivera, 787/281-8858 or 787/724-1882, www.diveguide.com/p2046.htm) offers snorkel and reef dives four times daily, as well as light-tackle and deep-sea fishing trips.

SURFING

Costazul (264 Calle San Francisco, Old San Juan, 787/722-0991 or 787/724-8085, fax 787/725-1097, sferco@caribe.net, Mon.–Sat. 9 A.M.–7 P.M.) sells surfboards and related equipment. But if you need instruction, **Caribbean Surf School** (787/637-8363, www.caribbeansurfpr.com) offers daily and weekly lessons with avid surfers and certified lifeguards at various locations. The school has a 3:1 student-to-instructor ratio, as well as individual instruction.

Velauno (2430 Calle Loíza, San Juan, 787/982-0543 or 866/PR-VELA-1— 866/778-3521, www.velauno.com) is the go-to place for all things surfing, including kite-surfing and windsurfing. They sell and rent equipment and offer lessons for adults

© OMAR VEGA

windsurfing in Condado

and children, including weeklong summer camps for windsurfers.

BOATING

There are three marinas in San Juan, the largest being **San Juan Bay Marina** (787/721-8062), with a capacity of 191 boats, including 125 wet slips, 60 dry-stack spaces, and six spaces for yachts more than 100 feet long. There's also a restaurant on-site. **Club Náutico de San Juan** (787/722-0177) has 117 wet slips and **Congrejas Yacht Club** in Piñones (787/791-1015) has 180 wet slips, a boat ramp, and a restaurant. All three have fuel and water.

FISHING

Mike Benitez Marina Services (Club Náutico de San Juan, 787/723-2292 or 787/724-6265, fax 787/725-4344, Fishpr2001@yahoo.com, www.mikebenitezfishingpr.com) offers deep-sea fishing trips daily. Half-day trips last 8 A.M.–noon and 1–5 P.M. Full-day excursions depart at 8 A.M. and return at 4 P.M. Reservations are required, and there's a six-passenger maximum.

Caribbean Outfitters (Congrejas Yacht Club, 787/396-8346, www.fishinginpuertorico.com/captbig.htm) offers fishing and fly-fishing charters throughout Puerto Rico, Vieques, Culebra, the Dominican Republic, and St. Thomas with Captain Omar.

ADVENTURE SPORTS

The go-to outfitters for rappelling in the rain forest, cave tubing, zipline rides, and hiking is **EcoQuest** (New San Juan Building 6471, Suite 5A, Isla Verde, 787/616-7543 or 787/529-2496, info@ecoquest.com, www.ecoquestpr.com).

TENNIS

There is no shortage of tennis courts in San Juan. Many of the large hotels have courts. In addition, there are several public courts, including: **Caribbean Mountain Villas Tennis Court** (Carr. 857, km 857, Canovanillas Sector, Carolina, 787/769-0860); **Central Park** (Calle Cerra off Carr. 2, Santurce, 787/722-1646); **Isla Verde Tennis Club** (Villamar, Isla Verde, 787/727-6490).

SPAS

Eden Spa (331 Recinto Sur, bldg. Acosta, Old San Juan, 787/721-6400, www.secretsofeden spa.net, Mon.–Sat. 10 A.M.–7 P.M., VIP services 7–9 P.M.) offers pure luxury pampering, including caviar facials, four-hands massage, honeybutter body wrap, chakra-balancing treatments, Reiki—you name it, Eden Spa has got it.

Zen Spa (1054 Ave. Ashford, Condado, 787/722-8433, www.zen-spa.com, Mon.–Fri. 7 A.M.–9 P.M., Sat. 8 A.M.–6 P.M., Sun. 9 A.M.–6 P.M.) offers massage, body wraps, facials, manicures, and hair care. Day-spa packages run $125–400. There's also a health club on the premises.

Entertainment and Events

FESTIVALS

San Juan loves a festival. It seems as though there's one going on every weekend. Some have traditional origins, and others are products of the local tourism department, but they all promise insight into the island's culture and are loads of fun.

Noches de Galerías (787/723-7080) is held the first Tuesday of the month February–May and September–December. Roughly 20 museums and galleries throughout Old San Juan open 6–9 P.M. for this festive gallery crawl. Though its intentions may be high-minded, as the night progresses the event becomes more of a raucous pub crawl as young adults and teenagers fill the streets in revelry. Arts and crafts booths also line Plaza de San José.

Held in June, **Noche de San Juan Bautista** is the celebration of the island's patron saint. Festivities last several days and include religious processions, concerts, and dance performances. But the highlight of the event is on June 24, when celebrants from all over the island flock to the beach for the day for picnics and recreation. Then at midnight, everyone walks backward into the ocean three times to ward off evil spirits.

Founded in honor of the renowned cellist and composer Pablo Casals, the **Festival Casals** (787/725-7334) is held in June and July and features a slate of classical music concerts at the Fine Arts Center (Ave. de Diego at Ave. Ponce de León). Concerts are also held in Ponce and Mayagüez.

Street festivals don't get any more lively

than **Festival de la Calle de San Sebastían** (787/724-0910), held in January on Calle San Sebastían in Old San Juan. For three days the street is filled with parades, folkloric dances, music, food, and crafts.

Each year the **Heineken Jazz Festival** (Anfiteatro Tito Puente in Hato Rey, 866/994-0001) selects a single jazz master to celebrate with three nights of concerts, 8 P.M.–midnight.

The Puerto Rico Tourism Company presents an annual three-day arts festival in early June called **Feria de Artesanías** (787/723-0692, www.gotopuertorico.com). More than 200 artisans fill the walkways along Paseo La Princesa and Plaza Dársena, and the days are filled with music and dance performances as well as a folk-singer competition.

Less an actual festival and more a cultural series, **La Casita Festival** takes place every Saturday 5:30–7:30 P.M. year-round in Plaza de la Dársena by Pier 1 in Old San Juan. Musicians and dance groups perform, and artisans sell their wares.

Similarly, **LeLoLai Festival** (787/723-3135, 787/791-1014, or 800/223-6530) presents traditional concerts and dance performances year-round at various sites throughout the island, including InterContinental Hotel San Juan in Isla Verde and Castillo de San Cristóbal in Old San Juan.

NIGHTLIFE

If club- and bar-hopping is your thing, you've come to the right place. San Juan definitely knows how to party. The most popular nightclubs and bars tend to be in Old San Juan, Condado, Santurce, and Isla Verde. Electronic music is prevalent, as is reggaetón, Puerto Rico's homegrown brand of hip-hop, combined with Jamaican dancehall and Caribbean musical styles. The legal drinking age is 18, and there's no official bar-closing time, so many establishments stay open until 6 A.M. Things don't really get started until after midnight, so take a disco nap and put on your dancing shoes. It's sure to be a long fun-filled night.

Old San Juan
◖ NUYORICAN CAFÉ
By far the best nightclub for live contemporary Latin music—from rock and jazz to salsa and merengue—is Nuyorican Café (312 Calle San Francisco, 787/977-1276, Tues.–Wed. 7 P.M.–3 A.M., Thurs.–Sun. 7 P.M.–5 A.M., free every night except $5 Fri., full bar). Don't bother looking for a sign; there isn't one. Just look for a gaggle of club-goers clustered around a side door down Capilla alley, which connects Calle San Francisco and Calle Fortaleza. Primarily a locals' place, although tourists are welcome, this casual music-lovers' club packs in a young bohemian crowd, especially on weekends when the tiny dance floor gets jammed. The kitchen serves a limited menu of Puerto Rican cuisine until midnight. The music usually starts around 11 P.M. There's no direct link between this café and New York City's Nuyorican Poets Café, which was and still is the epicenter of the Nuyorican movement, although the name is a nod to the club in New York City.

OTHER BARS AND CLUBS
San Juan's hippest nightclub scene revolves around electronic music and reggaetón, and there are any number of clubs devoted to the forms. Old San Juan's veteran nightclub is **Club Lazer** (251 Calle de la Cruz, 787/725-7581, www.clublazer.com, Wed.–Sun. 10 P.M.–3 or 4 A.M.). The three-level 1980s-era disco complete with a light show is popular with both

gays and straights. The hottest DJs spin here, and Sunday is reggaetón night.

The hottest new dance club for the young techno crowd is **Milk** (314 Calle Fortaleza, 787/721-3548, www.myspace.com/clubmilkpr, Thurs.–Sat. 10 P.M.–5 A.M.). The narrow, two-level spot sports a chic minimalist look, and patrons are expected to dress to impress—no baggy jeans, baseball caps, flip-flops, sneakers, or tank tops allowed. DJs spin all night long, and there's great people-watching from the balcony. Reservations required for table service.

Raven Room (305 Recinto Sur, 787/667-9651, www.ravenroompr.com, Wed.–Sat. 10 P.M.–3 or 4 A.M., $7), formerly Oleo Lounge, is a popular new club for the 21 and up set featuring minimalist decor and DJs spinning everything from the latest dance tunes to hits from the '70s and '80s.

The Noise (203 Calle Tanca, 787/724-3739) is a white-hot club in a former house in Old San Juan, where reggaetón keeps the beat going until the wee hours. Popular with the 18–21 crowd.

Blend (309 Calle Fortaleza, 787/977-7777, Tues.–Sat. 5 P.M.–3:30 A.M.) is a chic restaurant and lounge centered around an indoor patio and dramatic wall fountain. Local and touring DJs spin all forms of techno.

Club Le Cirque (357 Calle San Francisco, 787/725-3246, Wed.–Sat. 6 P.M.–4 A.M.) is a gay bar and lounge serving lunch and dinner. Smoking is allowed on the patio.

Another popular late-night bar for the casual bohemian crowd is **Galería Candela** (110 Calle San Sebastian, 787/594-5698 or 787/977-4305). The space is a hipster art gallery by day, but at night DJs spin into the wee hours.

If you need a place to rest your feet and just chill with a cool beverage, there is a wide variety of bars, both casual and upscale, where you can actually have a conversation, at least in the early part of the evening. The later it gets, though, the more crowded and louder it gets.

Although primarily an Indo-Latino fusion restaurant, **Tantra** (356 Calle Fortaleza, 787/977-8141, fax 787/977-4289, www.tantra pr.com, Sun.–Thurs. noon–11 P.M., Fri.–Sat.

noon–midnight) turns into a late-night party spot for the hip and trendy after-dinner crowd who flock here for the sophisticated ambiance, the creative martinis, and a toke or two on one of the many hookahs that line the bar. The kitchen serves a limited late-night menu.

For something completely different, frozen tropical drinks and old kitschy decor create the perfect place for a shopping break at **María's** (204 Calle de la Cristo, no telephone, daily 10:30 A.M.–3 A.M.). The tiny, pleasantly seedy bar primarily serves a variety of frozen drinks—piña colada, papaya frost, coconut blossom, and so on (with or without rum). Avoid the pedestrian tacos and nachos ($3.75–7) and check out the cheesy celebrity photos behind the bar. If the dark, narrow bar is full, there are a couple of tables in the back.

Looking for all the world like an old jail cell, **El Batey** (101 Calle Cristo, 787/725-1787, daily noon–4 A.M., cash only) is a barren dive bar covered top to bottom with drunken-scrawled graffiti and illuminated by bare bulbs suspended from the ceiling. There's one pool table and an interesting jukebox with lots of jazz mixed in with classic discs by the likes of Tom Waits, Jimi Hendrix, and Sly Stone. If you order a martini, they'll laugh at you. This is a beer and shots kind of place.

The barred windows and garish orange exterior don't offer much of a welcome at **Krugger** (52 Calle San José, 787/723-2474, Thurs.–Sat.), but the word is that this loud dive bar is the place to go for karaoke.

Isla Verde

One of San Juan's most glamorous bars is **Ⓒ Wet,** atop the Water Club hotel (2 Calle Tartak, 787/728-3666 or 888/265-6699, fax 787/728-3610, www.waterclubsanjuan.com). This posh rooftop bar looks like the set for *The Real World,* and the clientele are just as young and trendy as that show's cast members. Huge white leather sofas and beds arranged around tiny tables under a white awning set the tone for its chill vibe. The minimal lighting is limited to elaborate Indonesian lanterns and candles, which complement the panoramic view of the city lights. Sushi and supersweet martinis, with porn-star names such as Mango Do Me and Mojito Lips, are typical fare. If you need further proof that this is the place to see and be seen, Donatella Versace was reportedly spotted in the ladies' room.

On the first floor of The Water Club is **Liquid,** a more intimate bar that shares space with the hotel's restaurant, Tangerine. The attraction here is the interesting wall behind the bar—it's made from corrugated tin over which water pours all night long.

Another popular hotel hotspot is **Brava** (El San Juan Hotel, 6063 Ave. Isla Verde, 787/791-2761 or 787/791-2781, www.bravapr.com). Formerly Club Babylon, this popular dance club still packs in the upscale trendy set, who dance to an eclectic mix of dance-club tunes, salsa, and '80s rock. Reservations required for table service.

For something more casual, **Drums** (Isla Verde Mall, 787/253-1443, www.drums puertorico.com, Mon.–Tues. 11 A.M.–11 P.M., Wed. 11 A.M.–1 A.M., Thurs. 11 A.M.–2 A.M., Fri.–Sat. 11 A.M.–4 A.M., Sun. 11:30 A.M.–2:30 A.M.) is a huge, crowded spot that packs 'em in for live rock music, DJs, and karaoke. It serves an extensive menu of pub grub, as well entrées including steak, fish, and ribs.

Condado

The large open-air pavilion bar **La Terraza Condado** (intersection of Ave. Ashford and Calle McLeary, 787/723-2770, Sun.–Thurs. 5 P.M.–midnight, Fri.–Sat. 5 P.M.–2 A.M.) is popular with a young crowd that flocks here on the weekends for the cheap drinks, and it's an ideal perch for people-watching. There's a full bar, and it serves Puerto Rican cuisine ($9–18).

There are two types of strip clubs in Puerto Rico—those that don't serve alcohol and feature nude dancers, and those that serve alcohol and feature dancers who keep their G-strings on. **Divas** (1104 Ave. Ashford, 787/721-8270, www.myspace.com/divasinternational, $10) is the latter. Fairly upscale and well controlled by several large no-nonsense men in suits, it's a safe, saucy environment that attracts both men and women. It features a full bar and a private VIP room upstairs.

Santurce

Santurce's club scene primarily serves the gay community, but beware that it can be a rough part of town, especially at night. Panhandlers and petty thieves are known to prowl the area, so take precautions.

Santurce is home to several gay clubs. **Krash** (1257 Ave. Ponce de León, 787/722-1131, www.krashpr.com, Wed.–Sat. 10 P.M.–3 A.M., $6 after midnight), formerly Eros, is a major two-level party scene. Wednesday is urban pop night with three DJs spinning R&B, hip-hop, and reggaetón. Thursday and Friday nights feature DJs spinning house, tribal, and retro.

For a casual low-key gay bar, check out **Junior's Bar** (613 Calle Condado, 787/723-9477, daily, two-drink minimum). This is the place to have a beer, play some tunes on the jukebox, and check out the occasional drag queen or male stripper show.

Yet another popular gay bar and lounge in Santurce is **Starz** (365 Ave. de Diego, 787/721-8645).

The local lesbian crowd gathers in the laid-back ambiance of **Cups** (1708 Calle San Mateo, 787/268-3570, Wed.–Fri. 7 P.M.–3 A.M., Sat. 8 P.M.–3 A.M.). DJs spin dance music on Wednesday nights, karaoke is Thursday nights, and live music is Friday nights. There are pool tables too.

Hato Rey

For a little taste of España, check out the Saturday night flamenco show at ◖ **Divino Bocadito** (574 Ave. Ponce de Leon, Hato Rey, 787/765-8282, www.divinobocadito .com, Wed.–Thurs. 11 A.M.–midnight, Fri. 11 A.M.–2 A.M., Sat. 7 P.M.–2 A.M., Sun. 7 P.M.–midnight). Formerly located in Old San Juan, this lively Spanish bar and restaurant serves tapas and paella, but the real reason to come is to dance. Flamenco shows are Saturdays at 9 P.M., Andalusian dance performances are Thursdays and Fridays at 8 P.M., and dance classes are Wednesdays 7:30–8:30 P.M.

PARTY DISTRICTS

There's no doubt about it: Puerto Ricans love a good party, and it seems as if there's always one going on somewhere. San Juan has a couple of unofficial party districts where the concentration of bars and restaurants creates a street-party atmosphere that attracts young locals and tourists alike to barhop and people-watch. Although generally safe and contained, these areas can experience a certain level of rowdiness and petty crime, particularly when heavy drinking is involved. Visitors are encouraged to have a good time, but they should take care to keep their wits about them.

One popular party spot just a short taxi ride from Condado is **Plaza del Mercado** (Calle Roberts in Santurce), a small grid of narrow streets that surround Santurce's historic marketplace. The area contains a high concentration of tiny bars and restaurants serving cheap drinks and local cuisine. The streets get especially crowded Thursday, Friday, and Saturday nights with locals celebrating the weekend. If the walk-up bars and street scene get to be

© SUZANNE VAN ATTEN

Plaza del Mercado in Santurce

too much, duck into **Buyé Bistro Criolla** (202 Calle Canals, by Plaza del Mercado, Santurce, 787/725-4826, Mon.–Wed. 1–3 P.M., Thurs.–Fri. 1–3 P.M. and 5 P.M.–1 A.M., Sat. 5 P.M.–1 A.M.), especially on a Friday night. DJs spin here until the wee hours of the morning at this casual bar and restaurant. Check the chalkboard for daily specials ($7.95–16.95).

Another popular party district is **Boca de Cangrejas** (end of Ave. Isla Verde, just past the airport), a sandy patch of beachfront bars, restaurants, clubs, and food kiosks. Since this is also a popular weekend beach spot, the party tends to start early here, but the fun still lasts late into the night. The best way to get to Boca de Cangrejas is to drive or take a taxi, although you'll have to call one to pick you up when you're ready to leave. If you drive, be sure not to leave anything of value visible in the car; break-ins are not uncommon.

Although most establishments are open-air concrete structures, there are a few more-upscale places, such as **Soleil Beach Club** (Carr. 187, km 4.6, 787/253-1033, www.soleilbeachclub.com, Sun.–Thurs. 11 A.M.–11 P.M., Fri.–Sat. 11 A.M.–2 A.M.), near Boca de Cangrejas in Piñones. The beachside establishment with the palm-frond entrance serves Puerto Rican cuisine and offers live Latin music.

In Old San Juan, party central is along **Calle San Sebastián.** Bars, clubs, and pool halls of every stripe line the street, making it a great place to barhop door-to-door. Standard stops include **Nono's** (109 Calle San Sebastián, 787/725-7819, daily noon–2 A.M.) and **Cafe San Sebastián** (153 Calle San Sebastián, 787/725-3998, Wed.–Sun. 8 P.M.–3 A.M.).

CASINOS

Puerto Rico's greatest concentration of casinos can be found in San Juan. It has a total of 10 gambling palaces, all in hotels. Although jacket and tie are not required, attire tends to be dressy. All the casinos have banks of slot machines, blackjack tables, and roulette wheels. Most have craps tables, Caribbean stud poker, and three-card poker. Some have mini-baccarat, let it ride, progressive blackjack, and Texas hold 'em.

The largest casino is at the **Ritz-Carlton San Juan Hotel** (Isla Verde, 787/253-1700, 10 A.M.–6 A.M.). Within its 17,000 square feet are 335 slots, 11 blackjack tables, four mini-baccarat games, and Texas hold 'em. **El San Juan Hotel** (787/791-1000, 10 A.M.–4 A.M.) has the largest number of blackjack tables—14—and the added bonus of proximity to one of the most glamorous old-school hotel lobbies on the island, filled with gorgeous ornate woodwork and a massive antique chandelier. The only 24-hour casino in Isla Verde is **Courtyard by Marriott** (787/791-0404). Other casinos in the area include **InterContinental San Juan** (787/791-6100, 10 A.M.–4 A.M.) and **Embassy Suites Hotel** (787/791-0505, 10 A.M.–4 A.M.).

For a concentration of casino action, Condado is the place to go. **Condado Plaza Hotel** (787/721-1000) boasts 402 slots, as well as 13 blackjack tables, six mini-baccarat games, and Texas hold 'em. Other 24-7 casinos in the area include **San Juan Marriott Resort** (787/722-7000) and the small **Diamond Palace Hotel and Casino** (787/721-0810). Condado is also home to **Radisson Ambassador Plaza Hotel** (787/721-7300, 10 A.M.–4 A.M.), with a whopping 489 slots.

Old San Juan has only one casino, **Sheraton Old San Juan Hotel** (787/721-5100, 8 A.M.–2 A.M.).

HORSE RACING

Just 20 minutes east of San Juan, **Hipodromo Camarero** (Carr. 3, km 15.3, Canóvanas, 787/641-6060, www.comandantepr.com, free) is a modern upscale racetrack with a restaurant, sports bar, and clubhouse with a panoramic view of the track. Races are Friday–Sunday and Wednesday, 2:30–6:30 P.M.

COCKFIGHTS

Granted, cockfighting isn't for everyone, but it is a part of Puerto Rican culture. Most cockfight arenas are in rural areas of the island, but San Juan has a large, modern, tourist-friendly facility in **Club Gallistico de Puerto Rico** (Ave. Isla Verde at Ave. Los Gobernadores,

787/791-1557, Sat. 2–10 P.M., $5 tourists, $10 general admission). Most of the betting action takes place in the seats closest to the ring. Odds are haggled over and then bets are placed on the honor system by shouting wagers until a taker is secured. Bets are made not only on which bird will win, but on how long the fight will last. Regulars tend to be high rollers who take their bets seriously, so novices may have difficulty placing bets. Food and beer are available for purchase. This is a highly charged, testosterone-rich environment. Women are welcome, but they are advised not to dress provocatively or go alone.

Shopping

In the current era of globalization, shopping is fast becoming similarly homogenized the world over, and Puerto Rico is no different. The island is rife with large shopping malls and outlet stores selling the same designer names you could buy at Anywhere, USA. But there is also a strong culture of artisanship in Puerto Rico, and many stores sell locally made traditional crafts and contemporary artwork in varying degrees of quality. Haitian, Indonesian, and Indian import shops are plentiful too, as are high-end fine-jewelry stores. And thanks to Condado, San Juan is the place to go for high-end fashion, including Louis Vuitton and Cartier.

OLD SAN JUAN

People love to shop in Old San Juan because it offers the widest variety of unique shopping options in one pedestrian-friendly place. This is the place to go for fine jewelry, imported clothing and furnishings, cigars, folk art, tourist trinkets, and American chain stores, such as Marshalls, Walgreens, and Radio Shack.

Arts and Crafts

For visitors seeking high-quality crafts by local artisans, **Puerto Rican Arts and Crafts** (204 Calle Fortaleza, 787/725-5596, daily 9:30 A.M.–6 P.M.) is your one-stop shopping spot. This large two-level store has everything from original paintings and prints to ceramics, sculpture, jewelry, and more.

For a small selection of authentic Caribbean crafts, stop by **Tienda de Artesanías** (Museo de Las Americas in Ballajá Barracks, on Calle Norzagaray beside Quincentennial Plaza, 787/722-6057, Tues.–Fri. 10 A.M.–4 P.M., Sat.–Sun. 11 A.M.–5 P.M.). It has a nice but small mix of quality baskets, shawls, pottery, jewelry, Santos, art posters, and CDs.

Máscaras de Puerto Rico (La Calle, 105 Calle Fortaleza, 787/725-1306, Chilean@coqui.net, http://home.coqui.net/chilean, Mon.–Sat. 10 A.M.–6:30 P.M., Sun. 10:30 A.M.–5:30 P.M.) is a funky, narrow shop in a covered alleyway selling quality contemporary crafts, including masks and small reproductions of vintage *cartel* posters.

There are two nearly identical shops on the same street called **Haitian Gallery** (367 Calle Fortaleza, 787/721-4362; and 206 Calle Fortaleza, 787/725-0986, haitiangallery@aol.com, www.haitiangallerypr.com, daily 10 A.M.–6 P.M.). They both sell a great selection of Haitian folk art, including brightly colored primitive-style paintings and tons of woodwork, from sublime bowls to ornately sculpted furniture. There's a small selection of Indonesian imports, such as leaf-covered picture frames and photo albums, and tourist trinkets.

Puerto Rico Homemade Crafts Gallery (403 Calle San Francisco, 787/724-3840, http://tallercocuyopr.com, Mon.–Sat. 10:30 A.M.–8 P.M., Sun. 10:30 A.M.–6 P.M.) is an excellent source for authentic local crafts and folk art—both traditional and contemporary. The shop carries a large selection of *vejigante* masks, plus native Taíno reproductions, *cartel* posters, coconut-shell tea sets, jewelry, and Santos.

The Poets Passage (203 Calle Cruz, 787/567-9275, daily 10 A.M.–6 P.M.) offers a funky collection of local arts, crafts, and books. The store is owned by local poet and publisher Lady Lee Andrews. Poetry nights are held every Tuesday at 7 P.M.

Tourist tchotchkes, shell jewelry, *vejigante* masks, gourds, beaded necklaces, and seed jewelry can be found at **Ezense** (353 Calle Fortaleza, 787/725-1782, ezense@yahoo.com, daily 10 A.M.–7 P.M.).

Cigars

Like Cuba, Puerto Rico has a long history of hand-rolled cigar-making, and you can often find a street vendor rolling and selling his own in Plaza de Hostos's Mercado de Artesanías, a plaza near the cruise-ship piers at Calle Recinto Sur. There are also several good cigar shops selling anything you could want—except Cubans, of course. The biggest selection has to be at **The Cigar House** (255 Calle Fortaleza, 787/723-5223; 258 Calle Fortaleza, 787/725-9604; and 253 Calle San Justo, 787/725-0652; www.thecigarhousepr .com, daily 10 A.M.–6 P.M.). Trinidad, Monte Cristo, Padron 1926 and 1964, Cohiba, Perdomo, Macanudo, Partagas, Romeo and Julieta, and Puerto Rican cigars aged in rum are among those sold. They also sell tons of tourist trinkets.

For a more intimate setting, visit **El Galpón** (154 Calle del Cristo, 787/725-3945 or 888/842-5766, daily 10 A.M.–6 P.M.). This small selective shop sells a variety of quality cigars, Panama hats, masks, art prints, and superb vintage and contemporary Santos.

Imports

San Juan has several Indonesian import shops. **Eclectica** (204 Calle O'Donnell, Plaza de Colón, and 205 Calle de la Cruz, 787/721-7236 or 787/725-3163, www.eclectikasanjuan .com, daily 10 A.M.–7 P.M.) has Indonesian imports specializing in home decor, purses, and jewelry.

Hecho a Mano (260 Calle San Francisco, 787/722-0203, and 250 Calle San José, 787/725-3992, fax 787/723-0880, hechom@ coqui.net) sells Indonesian decorative imports, locally designed women's wear, funky purses, and jewelry. There's another location at 1126 Avenida Ashford in Condado.

Kamel International Bazaar and Art Gallery (154–156 Calle de la Cristo, 787/722-1455 or 787/977-7659, kamelimports@yahoo .com, daily 10:30 A.M.–6 P.M.) sells inexpensive Indian clothing, jewelry, rugs, beaded handbags, and reproduction paintings on canvas.

Surf Shop

Costazul (264 Calle San Francisco, 787/722-0991 or 787/724-8085, fax 787/725-1097, sferco@caribe.net, Mon.–Sat. 9 A.M.–7 P.M.) sells a great selection of surf and skate wear for men and women, including Oakley sunglasses and clothes by Billabong and Quiksilver. During surf season, it also stocks boards and related gear.

Fine Jewelry

There are dozens of high-end fine-jewelry stores in Old San Juan, especially along Calle Fortaleza, including **N. Barquet Joyers** (201 Calle Fortaleza, 787/721-3366 or 787/721-4051, fax 787/721-4051, nbarquet@spiderlink .net, daily 10 A.M.–5 P.M.); **Casa Diamante** (252 Calle Fortaleza, 787/977-5555, daily 10 A.M.–6 P.M.); and **Emerald Isles** (105 Calle Fortaleza, 787/977-3769, Mon.–Sat. 11 A.M.–6 P.M.).

Vogue Bazaar (364 Calle San Francisco, 787/722-1100, Mon.–Wed. and Fri.–Sat. 10 A.M.–6:30 P.M. specializes in pre-Columbian reproductions, gemstones from South America, and purses from Thailand.

Used Records and Collectibles

Thrift-store shoppers and collectors of vinyl will love **Frank's Thrift Store** (363 Calle San Francisco, 787/722-0691, daily 10 A.M.–6 P.M.). Come here to peruse the enormous used-record collection, from '80s kitsch to fresh electronica. There's even a turntable available, so you can listen to the stock before you buy. But this cluttered labyrinth of rooms is also packed with the widest assortment of junk and collectibles you could ever imagine. Decorative items, old photographs, dishes, toys, clothes—you name it.

Kitchen Goods
Spicy Caribbee (154 Calle de la Cristo, 888/725-7529, www.spicycaribbee.com, Mon.– Sat. 10 A.M.–7 P.M., Sun. 11 A.M.–5 P.M.) sells Caribbean sauces, spice mixes, coffees, soaps, fragrances, candles, cookbooks, and more.

CONDADO
Except for a few trinket sellers, most of the shopping in Condado is high-end clothing, accessories, and furnishings in the center of the neighborhood along Avenida Ashford.

Designer Clothes and Furnishings
For a fantastic variety of modern pop furniture and housewares, as well as museum-quality collectibles, go to **Articulos** (1300 Ave. Ashford, 787/723-3950, fax 787/722-5667, Mon.–Sat. 10 A.M.–6 P.M., Sun. 11 A.M.–5 P.M.). This is the place to go for monochromatic molded plastic furnishings and home decor by Alessi and Kartell. There are also great light fixtures, kitchenware, and a large selection of international bath and skin-care products. Check out the corner glass cabinet containing the highly collectible designs of Yoshitomo Nara and Marcel Dzama.

For one-of-a-kind designs, visit the eponymous store of one of the island's most renowned designers of casual wear and haute couture for both men and women, **Nono Maldonado** (1051 Ave. Ashford, 787/721-0456, 10 A.M.–6 P.M., 11 A.M.–5 P.M.). He was the former fashion editor of *Esquire* magazine.

Monsieur (1126 Ave. Ashford, 787/722-0918, Mon.–Sat. 10 A.M.–6 P.M.) sells casual designer menswear for the young and clubby.

Trendy Clothes
For something completely different, **HipHop** (1124 Ave. Ashford, 787/722-6081, Mon.– Sat. 10 A.M.–7 P.M., Sun. noon–5 P.M.) sells trendy teen wear for girls, plus Vans shoes and Kiplinger luggage.

Indonesian imports and locally designed women's wear are available at **Hecho a Mano** (1126 Ave. Ashford, 787/722-5322, fax 787/723-0880, hechom@coqui.net, Mon.–Wed. 10 A.M.–7 P.M., Thurs.–Sat. 10:30 A.M.–8 P.M., Sun. 11 A.M.–6 P.M.). It also has two locations in Old San Juan at 260 Calle San Francisco and 250 Calle San José.

Vintage Clothes
Fans of quality vintage clothing must beat a path to owner Jose Quinones' eclectic boutique, **Rockabilly** (53 Calle Barranquitas, 787/725-4665, Tues.–Sat. 10 A.M.–5 P.M.). We're talking about classic pieces by Chanel and Halston here, not to mention vintage prom dresses, stilettos, platforms, and purses. There are new vintage-inspired clothing styles too. In the back is a hair salon.

Accommodations

In addition to an enormous array of hotels, inns, and guesthouses offering every kind of accommodation imaginable, San Juan has a variety of daily, weekly, and monthly apartment rentals available to those seeking a homier or long-term place to stay. **El Viejo Adoquin** (6 Calle de la Cruz, Old San Juan, 787/977-3287, reservations@stayinpr.com, www.stayinpr.com) offers several superbly located and decorated apartments in Old San Juan, as well as one in Rincón. **The Caleta Realty** (151 Calle Clara Lair, 787/725-5347, fax 787/977-5642, reservations@thecaleta.com, www.thecaleta.com) also has many properties in Old San Juan and Condado.

OLD SAN JUAN
Aside from a large, fairly new Sheraton and a recently renovated Howard Johnson, there are

GAY PUERTO RICO

Long before Columbus arrived in Puerto Rico, native Taíno men used to beseech the moon to send them wives with a ceremonial dance in which they wore female garb. Legend has it that when the colonists witnessed the ritual, they assumed the men were homosexuals and sicced their dogs on them.

Boy, would the colonists be shocked today. Today Puerto Rico has an active, out, and proud gay community, and it is a popular destination for gay travelers. Although homosexual acts are illegal in Puerto Rico, the law is rarely if ever enforced, and there are plenty of accommodations, nightclubs, and beaches that cater to the LGBT traveler.

The island's largest gay community is in San Juan, and that's where you'll find the biggest concentration of businesses that specialize in serving gay clientele.

Accommodations popular with gay and lesbian travelers include the laid-back Ocean Park properties and **Numero Uno Guest House** (1 Santa Ana, 787/726-5010 or 866/726-5010, fax 787/727-5482, info@numero1guesthouse .com, www.numero1guesthouse.com, $143-287 s, $277-287 suite, plus $25 per additional guest, plus 9 percent tax and 15 percent service charge, children under 12 stay with parents for free), as well as the more party-central **Atlantic Beach Hotel** (1 Calle Vendig, 787/721-6900, fax 787/721-6917, www.atlantic beachhotel.com, $115-149 s/d) in Condado. The beaches in front of these properties are the most popular gay beaches, although everyone is welcome.

There's no shortage of gay and lesbian nightclubs in San Juan. Most of the gay bars can be found in Santurce. **Atlantic Beach Bar** (1 Calle Vendig, Condado, 787/721-6900) is a casual bar at the Atlantic Beach House hotel right on the ocean, offering happy hour 5-7 P.M. **Krash** (1257 Ave. Ponce de León, 787/722-1131, www .krashpr.com, Wed.-Sat. 10 P.M.-3 A.M., $6 after midnight), formerly Eros, is a popular party spot. Wednesday is urban pop night with three DJs spinning R&B, hip-hop, and reggaetón. Thursday and Friday nights feature DJs spinning house, tribal, and retro.

In Condado, fans of salsa, reggae, and pop music flock to **Junior's** (615 Calle Condado, 787/723-9477, daily 8 P.M.-late, no cover). And in Old San Juan, **Club Le Cirque** (357 Calle San Francisco, 787/725-3246, Wed.-Sat. 6 P.M.-4 A.M.) is a gay bar and lounge with a patio that also serves lunch and dinner.

Catering to the lesbian crowd is **Cups** (1708 Calle San Mateo, Santurce, 787/268-3570, Wed.-Fri. 7 P.M.-3 A.M., Sat. 8 P.M.-3 A.M.), a laid-back spot for karaoke, live music, dance music, and a game of pool.

---

a handful of small independent hotels and inns in Old San Juan that tend to book up quickly. No matter where you stay in Old San Juan, you're within easy walking distance to some of the city's finest restaurants, shops, and cultural sights. It's worth booking ahead to stay in Old San Juan.

$100-150

By far the hippest new place to stay in San Juan, **☾ Da House** (312 Calle San Francisco, 787/366-5074 or 787/977-1180, fax 787/725-3436, www.dahousehotelpr.com, $80–120 s/d) is owned and operated by the folks behind one of the city's hottest music clubs, Café Nuyorican. It's also located directly

above the nightclub, making it a great spot for the late-night party crowd. Those inclined to go to bed early will no doubt be kept awake by the club downstairs, which doesn't close until 3 or 4 in the morning. But night owls looking to stay in elegant but casual surroundings on a student's budget would be hard-pressed to find a better hotel. The 27 units are small and sparsely furnished with just the basics—bed, lamp, mini-fridge, ceiling fan, and remote-control air-conditioning. There is no TV or phone, and fresh linens, irons, and hair dryers are available only upon request. And there's no elevator, so be prepared to walk up as many as four flights to your room—carrying your own luggage. Service is minimal—the pierced and tattooed set that runs the reception desk often do double duty in the bar downstairs. So what makes Da House so great? Besides the inexpensive rates and location in the heart of Old San Juan, it is a gorgeous building filled with fantastic contemporary art exhibitions that change every month.

When it comes to bang for the buck, you can't do much better than **《 Hotel Milano** (307 Calle Fortaleza, 787/729-9050 or 877/729-9050, fax 787/722-3379, hmilano@ coqui.net, www.hotelmilanopr.com, $95–185 s/d plus 9 percent tax). Here you get all the modern amenities you could want but in a historic setting ideally situated among many of Old San Juan's most popular restaurants and shops. Thirty clean corporate-style rooms come with new furnishings, air-conditioning, satellite TV, hair dryers, and mini-refrigerators. An added bonus is the serviceable rooftop restaurant and bar, which provide fantastic views of the city and harbor.

Ideally located in the heart of Old San Juan on Plaza de Armas, **Hotel Plaza de Armas** (202 Calle San Jose, 787/722-9191, fax 787/725-3091, plazadearmas@hotmail .com, www.hojopr.com, $109 s, $169–179 d, $185 suites) is a simple modern hotel in a historic building renovated in 2005. The Howard Johnson property has 50 units, which comes with air-conditioning, satellite TV, and Wi-Fi. Suites come with balconies and small refrigerators; king suites sleep up to five people and have DVD players. Free continental breakfast.

$150-250

On the edge of Old San Juan overlooking the Atlantic Ocean is **The Gallery Inn** (204–206 Calle Norzagaray, 787/722-1808, fax 787/724-7360, reservations@thegalleryinn.com, www.the galleryinn.com, $175–350 s/d, plus 18 percent tax and tariff, includes breakfast buffet), one of the unique hotels in San Juan. This 18th-century home is packed with 22 small rooms tucked into a multilevel labyrinth of patios, courtyards, balconies, archways, fountains, and interior gardens. As if that weren't enough, the hotel is chock-full of portrait

sculptures and plaster reliefs by artist-owner Jan D'Esopo, as well as potted plants, hanging baskets, and an assortment of tropical birds, which have the run of the place. If the chockablock decor begins to feel a bit claustrophobic, there's an elegant, airy music room with a grand piano and a rooftop deck for a change of scenery. Small rooms are well appointed with quality antiques and reproductions. Each comes with air-conditioning and a telephone.

Nearby is the equally modern, corporate-style **SJ Suites** (253 Calle Fortaleza, 787/977-4873, 787/977-4873, or 787/725-1351, fax 787/977-7682, sjsuites@hotmail.com, www .sjsuites.com, $130–300 s/d, plus 9 percent tax, includes continental breakfast). Fifteen spanking-new, self-serve suites come with air-conditioning, satellite TV, and mini-refrigerators. There's no reception desk or on-site management. Check-in is inside Kury Jewelry Store next door.

Over $250

《 Cervantes Chateau (329 Recinto Sur, 787/724-7722, fax 787/289-8909, reservations@ cervantespr.com, www.cervantespr.com, $225 s/d, $285 junior suite, $425 suite, $975 split-level penthouse suite, plus taxes and resort fees) is a new luxury boutique hotel near the piers in Old San Juan. Tastefully but playfully decorated by clothing designer and former fashion editor at *Esquire* magazine Nono Maldonado, the hotel combines mid-century modern elements with Spanish colonial style. The emphasis is on luxury, apparent in the Egyptian linens, HDTV flat-screen TVs, and free wireless Internet. The fine dining restaurant, Panza, is on-site.

To get a true sense of history, spend the night in a Carmelite convent completed in 1651 by order of King Phillip IV of Spain. **Hotel El Convento** (100 Calle Cristo, 787/723-9020, 787/721-2877, or 800/468-2779, elconvento@ aol.com, www.elconvento.com, $325–445 s/d, $710–1,520 suite, plus taxes and resort fees). A recipient of many awards and accolades, the 58-room hotel encompasses a four-floor colonial structure with an enormous well-landscaped courtyard in the center. Common areas are filled with gorgeous Spanish antiques and reproductions. Rooms come with air-conditioning, cable TV, VCR, stereo, telephone, and refrigerator. Amenities include a fitness center, plunge pool, and whirlpool bath on the fourth floor, which overlooks Old San Juan and the bay. It has four restaurants.

Apartment Rentals

If you want make like a local and live in a residential setting, **(Caleta Balcony Rentals** (11 Caleta de las Monjas, 787/725-5347, fax 787/977-5642, reservations@thecaleta .com, www.thecaleta.com/guesthouse.html, $80–150) offers six cozy, modest units varying from studios to one-bedroom apartments in a three-story structure near the San Juan Gate. The property is a bit shabby, but it has a great location between Hotel El Convento and La Fortaleza, home of the governor. All apartments have balconies and a full kitchen or kitchenette; some have air-conditioning, TV, and telephones. Each room is different, and they all have character to spare, but the Sunshine Suite on the third floor is the best of the bunch. There's no reception desk or on-site management at this self-serve property.

PUERTA DE TIERRA
$150-250

Puerto de Tierra is a small bit of land between Condado and Old San Juan, just west of the bridge that connects those two communities. It includes a couple of small beaches, a very large park, and a commercial district of little interest to visitors. But it does contain one amazing hotel.

When you first see the **(Normandie Hotel** (499 W. Ave. Muñoz Rivera, 787/729-2929 or 877/987-2929, www.normandiepr.com, $219–239 s/d, plus 9 percent tax) you might think you're seeing things. The 1940s art deco hotel was built to look like a grand ocean liner complete with porthole windows. Even more remarkable, the Normandie has operated continuously as an independent hotel since its inception. Although it has seen shabbier times, it has recently been renovated with a hip eye toward minimalism. Decked out in cool shades of pale blues and greens, it's appointed with a circular porthole motif tastefully repeated in the carpets, lighting, and mirrors. There are 175 rooms, all with air-conditioning, cable TV, room safe, CD stereo system, mini-refrigerator, high-speed Internet, and concierge service. The property also has an atrium bar, an Italian restaurant, pool, beach access, spa, hair salon, and fitness center. Be sure to have a drink in the clever N Lounge, which looks like the coolest captain's quarters you've ever seen.

CONDADO
$100-150

Acacia Boutique Hotel (8 Calle Taft, 787/725-0668, 787/727-0626, or 877/725-0668, fax 787/268-2803, www.acaciaseaside inn.com, $105 s, $175–210 d) is a small, newish beachfront property from the folks at nearby Wind Chimes. Modern, modest rooms have air-conditioning and basic cable TV; some have balconies. Wireless Internet is available in common areas. Guests can use the bar and pool at Wind Chimes.

The pink oceanfront **Atlantic Beach Hotel** (1 Calle Vendig, 787/721-6900, fax 787/721-6917, www.atlanticbeachhotel.com, $115–149 s/d) serves a primarily gay clientele, but everyone is warmly welcomed. The exterior and lobby are a bit shabby, as are some of the 37 rooms, but there are some newly remodeled rooms that are more modern and comfortable. Each room has air-conditioning, satellite TV, and telephone. It has a rooftop terrace, a casual restaurant serving breakfast and lunch, and a popular ocean-side bar (happy hour 5–7 P.M.). On Sunday nights the bar hosts the Black Cat drag show. It starts at 9 P.M., but things don't really get going until around midnight.

It's at the far eastern end of Condado, several blocks from the nearest restaurant or shop, but **At Wind Chimes Inn** (1750 Ave. McLeary, 787/727-4159, fax 787/728-0671, reservations@atwindchimesinn.com, www .atwindchimesinn.com, $80–95 s, $109–150 d,

$155 suite) is just a block from the beach. Two Spanish-style haciendas have been combined to create a quaint, artful, 22-room boutique hotel. Each room has air-conditioning, cable TV, telephone, and wireless Internet; some rooms have kitchenettes. Rooms are tastefully decorated with high-quality furnishings and bright cheery bedspreads. Amenities include a small pool with jets and a waterfall, and a shady courtyard bar and grill.

Although it's about three blocks from the beach, **El Prado Inn** (1350 Calle Luchetti, 787/728-5925 or 800/468-4521, elpradoinn@ prtc.net, www.elpradoinn.net, $89–139 s/d, plus 9 percent tax and 6 percent service charge) has the benefit of being close to all the action on Avenida Ashford but with the quiet residential feel of Ocean Park. Each room is different, but they're all pleasant and comfortably decorated with a bohemian vibe. A modest continental breakfast is included, and there's a tiny pool in the courtyard. Another bonus is the lovely shaded Parque Luchetti across the street. Free parking.

The three **Canario** (800/533-2649, canario PR@aol.com, www.canariohotels.com) hotels in Condado offer small, clean, modern, no-frills accommodations at a budget rate. Rooms all come with air-conditioning, telephones, cable TV, and room safes. Service is minimal, continental breakfast is included, and all three properties are within walking distance of the beach, restaurants, shops, and bars. The one with the most attractive entrance and lobby is **El Canario Inn** (1317 Ave. Ashford, 787/722-3861, fax 787/722-0391, $115 s, $129–144 d, $144 t, $159 q, plus 9 percent tax and $5 in surcharges). Dramatic black-and-white floors and lots of plants provide a cheery welcome to its 25 units. **El Canario by the Sea** (4 Ave. Condado, 787/722-8640, fax 787/725-4921, $115 s, $129–144 d, $144 t, $159 q, plus 9 percent tax and $5 in surcharges) has 25 unremarkable rooms, a dull lobby, and lax service, but it's a mere half block from the beach. The largest property is **El Canario by the Lagoon** (4 Clemenceau, 787/722-5058, fax 787/723-8590, $119 s, $130–145 d, $145

t, $160 q, $150–180 penthouse suite, plus 9 percent tax and $5 surcharges), with 44 small basic rooms in a high-rise building beside Laguna del Condado. Rooms have balconies, and there's free parking on-site.

Over $200

◖ Caribe Hilton (1 Calle San Geronimo, 787/721-0303, fax 787/725-8849, sjnhi_sales@ hilton.com, www.hiltoncaribbean.com, $319 s/d, $845 one-bedroom villa, $1,216 two-bedroom villa, includes 12 percent resort tax) is proof that all Hilton hotels are not all alike. This stunning display of modernist architecture and design is a beloved blast from the past, a reminder of a time when the Condado was an epicenter of glamour. Built in the late 1940s, the sprawling hotel features an enormous lobby awash in curved lines and modular shapes that merge elegantly with blond woods, polished steel, and thick glass. Be sure to gaze up at the ceiling, a stunning wooden structure that mimics the swooping shape of ocean waves. There are seemingly countless bars, including a swim-up bar at the pool. The Caribe Hilton is one of two places in Puerto Rico (the other being Barranchina in Old San Juan) that claims to have invented the piña colada, so tourists often stop by to have one, whether they're staying at the hotel or not. And don't miss the hard-to-find Tropical Garden. Tucked away in a quiet corner is an oasis of lushly landscaped grounds built around a pond and gazebo where peacocks, geese, and black swans roam freely. There are 814 units in the hotel and nine restaurants, including Morton's the SteakHouse. There is also a spa and boutiques for shopping. Although the hotel is on the ocean, the only swimmable beach is a small public facility beside the hotel.

◖ Condado Plaza Hotel & Casino (999 Ave. Ashford, 787/721-1000 or 866/316-8934, www.condadoplaza.com, $199–259 s/d, $329–459 suites, plus taxes and resort fees) is an interesting bookend to the 1940s-era modernism of the Caribe Hilton. The Condado Plaza Hotel is a 21st-century modernist's dream with a minimalist aesthetic and a tastefully rendered nod to pop art sensibilities. The lobby is blindingly white with occasional touches of brilliant orange that draw the eye around the room, from the low-backed couches to the textured wooden wall treatments to the private nooks and crannies tucked behind beaded curtains. Modernist touches continue in the guest rooms, where billboard-size black-and-white photographs hang over the beds and the shower is a clear glass cube situated in the center of the spacious bathroom. The casino is open 24 hours a day, and there are multiple restaurants, including Tony Roma's and the dramatic Strip House, a steakhouse done up in red and black and appointed with black-and-white photographs of 1950s-era burlesque dancers. There is also a fitness center, a business center, and two pools, one of which is filled with salt water.

La Concha Renaissance Resort (1077 Ave. Ashford, 787/721-85000, fax 240/724-7929, www.lacencharesort.com, $309–369 s/d, $549 one-bedroom suite, plus tax and fees) was built in 1958 and is another huge, shimmering modernist hotel on the Condado. It closed and lay dormant for years, but a recent renovation has returned it to its former glory and beyond. Amenities include multilevel swimming pools with waterfalls and a sandy beach with food and beverage service, two lounges, and four restaurants, including Perla, an upscale restaurant serving contemporary American cuisine heavy on seafood in a stunning clamshell-shaped space right on the beach.

OCEAN PARK

Ocean Park boasts one of the better beaches in the metro area and some small, charming, gay-friendly guesthouses that pay a lot of attention to the kinds of details that can make an overnight stay memorable. Because this is primarily a residential neighborhood, there aren't a lot of restaurants, bars, or shops within walking distance. Also note that if you have a rental car, street parking can be scarce, especially on the weekends when locals flock to the beaches.

$100-150

You know you're in for something unique as

soon as you pass the tall contemporary waterfall and koi pond at the entrance to **Hostería del Mar** (1 Calle Tapia, 787/727-3302, fax 787/727-0631 or 787/268-0772, hosteria@caribe.net, www.hosteriadelmarpr.com, $89–199 s/d, $179–239 ocean view, $244–264 suites and one-bedroom apartment, plus 9 percent tax). This compact oceanfront hotel has a lot of pizzazz in its common areas. The small lobby features an artful mix of antiques and tropical-style decor that give way to a tastefully designed Polynesian-style bar and restaurant filled with warm woods and rattan furnishings. The wooden top-hinged windows open out from the bottom, revealing the sand and sea just a few steps away. The restaurant, Uvva, specializes in what it calls Nuevo Mediterranean cuisine and serves three meals a day. The small, basic guest rooms have air-conditioning, cable TV, and telephones. A second-floor room is recommended for those sensitive to noise that sometimes emanates from the bar at night.

$150-250

Numero Uno Guest House (1 Santa Ana, 787/726-5010 or 866/726-5010, fax 787/727-5482, info@numero1guesthouse.com, www.numero1guesthouse.com, $143–287 s, $277–287 suite, plus $25 for additional guests, plus 9 percent tax and 15 percent service charge; children under 12 stay with parents for free) is a small, well-maintained guesthouse with attentive service. There's no lobby to speak of, just a tiny reception office beside a petite black-bottomed pool. But the 11 rooms are newly furnished, tastefully decorated, and comfortable, if you don't mind the compactness. Amenities include air-conditioning, a minibar, and wireless Internet. The guesthouse also boasts the popular fine-dining restaurant Pamela's, serving internationally inspired cuisine.

ISLA VERDE

When it comes to accommodations, Isla Verde is mostly home to luxury chain hotels such as the Ritz-Carlton and the InterContinental. But there are a handful of small independent hotels and one swanky world-class boutique hotel for the glamour set.

$100-200

If paying bottom dollar is a primary concern, you can't do much better than **Coral by the Sea** (2 Calle Rosa, 787/791-6868, fax 787/791-1672, www.coralbythesea.com, $81–103 s/d). Its small, functional, slightly dreary rooms have air-conditioning and cable TV, but it's just two blocks from the beach. Bring some air freshener, as the rooms can have a funky odor. There are two restaurants on the first floor: Platos, serving Nuevo Puerto Rican cuisine, and Piu Bello, a deli.

It may be worthwhile to pay a little more and stay at **Hotel Villa del Sol** (4 Calle Rosa, 787/791-2600 or 787/791-1600, info@villadelsolpr.com, www.villadelsolpr.com, $100 s, $130 d, $180 minisuite). In a cheerful yellow faux hacienda-style building two blocks from the beach, the inn's 24 units have air-conditioning, cable TV, and mini-refrigerators. Some rooms are starkly furnished; others are a little nicer. Amenities include a tiny pool, restaurant, bar, free parking, and free Wi-Fi in common areas. Vias Car Rental service is on-site.

Hotel La Playa (6 Calle Amapola, 787/791-1115 or 787/791-7298, reservations@hotellaplaya.com, www.hotellaplaya.com, $215 s/d with terrace, $195 ocean view, $165 standard, $125 value, plus 9 percent tax and $5 energy surcharge) is under new management and has undergone a radical renovation. What was once a shabby budget hotel is now a sophisticated, moderately priced oasis in Isla Verde. Rooms have been updated with quality contemporary furnishings, tile floors, and new fixtures in the bathrooms. The kitschy boat bar in the lobby is no more, but a new full service restaurant, La Playita, has been added, serving casual and upscale creative cuisine with vegetarian options. Plans are underway to transform the neglected rooftop terrace into an open-air spa. And a new deck offers seaside sunbathing right on the water. Amenities include air-conditioning and satellite TV.

Over $200

The South Beach party crowd gravitates to **◖ The Water Club** (2 Calle Tartak, 787/728-3666 or 888/265-6699, fax 787/728-3610, info@waterclubsanjuan.com, www.waterclub.com, $179–399 s/d). The modern high-design boutique hotel offers super-luxurious accommodations for the young, trendy, and well-heeled crowd. The hotel's 75 rooms come with air-conditioning, satellite TV, CD players, two-line telephones, data ports, high-speed Internet, minibars, in-room safes, and superior beds topped with down comforters. Water is the theme of this stark white and aqua property: Bubbles float in Lucite countertops at the reception desk, and water features abound. Liquid, the lobby bar, has a corrugated tin wall with a constant flow of water trickling over it. Wet, the rooftop bar, features stunning views of the city and huge leather couches and beds—yes, beds—that spill out around the pool. The restaurant, Tangerine, serves American Asian cuisine.

Food

In recent years, San Juan's dining scene has experienced an evolution. More and more new restaurants have opened serving sophisticated international, Nuevo Latino, and Puerto Rican fusion cuisines in chic and trendy settings. But plenty of traditional restaurants serving authentic Puerto Rican cuisine can still be found, even in San Juan.

OLD SAN JUAN
Caribbean

The locally owned OOF! Restaurants group is in large part responsible for raising the dining standards in San Juan. The first of its four restaurants is (**The Parrot Club** (363 Calle Fortaleza, 787/725-7370, www.oofrestaurants .com, lunch Mon.–Fri. 11:30 A.M.–3 P.M., Sat.– Sun. 11:30 A.M.–4 P.M.; dinner Sun.–Wed. 6–11 P.M., Thurs.–Sat. 6 P.M.–midnight; bar Sun.–Wed. until midnight, Thurs.–Sat. until 1 A.M.; $17–32), which opened in 1996. At first

glance, this wildly popular restaurant might look like a prefab tourist attraction. It boasts a Disneyesque tropical-island theme, complete with faux palm trees and wooden parrots, and the din around the crowded bar can make conversation a challenge. But the reality is the Parrot Club serves some of the island's finest interpretations of Nuevo Latino cuisine. If you prefer a nice, quiet, leisurely served meal, bypass the bar and ask to be seated in the calm low-lit courtyard out back. The restaurant specializes in a smorgasbord of crisp, refreshing seviches, featuring a wide selection of seafood marinated in fresh citrus juices and served chilled. The shrimp, *chillo* (snapper), and *dorado* (mahimahi) are the best of the bunch. If you want something a little heartier, try the thick slab of blackened tuna steak served in a dark, slightly sweet sauce of rum and orange essence. It's an addictive dish that will have you coming back for more.

A pair of kids find a snack on Calle San Sebastían in Old San Juan.

Baru (150 Calle San Sebastían, 787/977-7107 or 787/977-5442, Mon.–Sat. 6 P.M.–midnight, Sun. 5:30 P.M.–midnight, $10–28) is a lovely, sensuous restaurant with a casually elegant atmosphere that melds classic architectural features with contemporary art, and then bathes it all in warm low lighting that makes you want to linger long after your meal is over. The cuisine is a creative combination of Caribbean and Mediterranean dishes, carefully prepared and artfully presented. Serving sizes are slightly bigger than an appetizer and smaller than an entrée, so order several and share with your tablemates. For an excellent starter, go with the goat cheese and almond spread drizzled with mango sauce and served with long fried yucca chips. Its satisfying combination of creamy and crunchy textures pairs beautifully with the blend of sweet and savory flavors. The asparagus risotto is appropriately creamy and nubby on the tongue, and it's studded with just the right amount of fresh chopped stalks and tips. Plump, slightly charred scallops are served each in their own tiny shell-shaped dish, drizzled with a delicate coconut curry sauce, and flecked with fresh mint. But skip the pork ribs. Although falling-off-the-bone tender, they're slathered in a supersweet guava sauce that overwhelms the flavor of the meat.

The atmospheric **El Asador Grill** (350 Calle San Francisco, 787/289-0489, Sun.–Thurs. 11 A.M.–midnight, Fri.–Sat. 11 A.M.–4 A.M., $13–37.50), located in a contemporary faux hacienda-style setting, specializes in grilled meats prepared in a courtyard kitchen. Cream-colored stucco walls, dark wood beams, terra-cotta tile floors, and dramatic archways create an inviting environment. And the menu is a carnivore's delight. Beyond the usual grilled steak, chicken, pork, and fish, you can get sausages, sweetbreads, and kidney too. Unfortunately the service was consistently abysmal on repeated visits. If the staff were more professional and welcoming, this place would come highly recommended.

Puerto Rican

Although it might seem like it at first glance, trendy upscale restaurants are not the only options in Old San Juan for traditional Puerto Rican cuisine. Fairly new on the scene is **Restaurante Raices** (315 Calle Recinto Sur, 787/289-2121, www.restauranteraices.com, daily 11 A.M.–11 P.M., $10–29), a casual, moderately priced spot for expertly prepared traditional Puerto Rican cuisine. Specialties include *mofongo* stuffed with *chimichurri* and mahi-mahi stuffed with shrimp. The original location is in Caguas.

Despite the dreadful service, **La Fonda El Jibarito** (280 Calle Sol, 787/725-8375, daily 11 A.M.–9 P.M., $5.50–18) is one of the best bets for authentic Puerto Rican cuisine, including codfish stew, fried pork, fried snapper, great rice and beans, and *mofongo,* cooked and mashed plantain seasoned with garlic. It's a major staple. Sometimes it's stuffed with meat or seafood. Patrons share tables in this casual restaurant designed to look like a traditional country house. Between the blaring TV and many families with small children, the noise level can be overwhelming. Thank goodness there's a full bar.

Café Puerto Rico (208 Calle O'Donnell, 787/724-2281, cafepr@coqui.net, Mon.–Sat. 11:30 A.M.–4:30 P.M. and 5:30–11 P.M., Sun. 11 A.M.–9 P.M., $9–20) has a whole new lease on life. The plain little café beside Plaza Colon that was there forever and never changed a bit is no more: The place has been outfitted in rich dark wood paneling and a new tile bar with tastefully lit contemporary artwork hanging on the walls. It's quite a transformation, but the coffee is still outstanding, and the Puerto Rican cuisine is still good solid fare. You can get everything from *asopao* and *mofongo* to paella and steak.

Several historic restaurants in Old San Juan have been serving customers for more than 100 years. One of the most venerable is **La Mallorquina** (207 Calle San Justo, 787/722-3261, Mon.–Sat. noon–10 P.M., $9–36), which has been in operation since 1848. This Old World white-linen restaurant serves traditional Puerto Rican cuisine, specializing in *asopao,* a hearty traditional rice stew served with a choice of meats or seafoods.

La Bombonera (259 Calle San Franciso, 787/722-0658, fax 787/795-2175, daily 6 A.M.–8 P.M., $7.25–14.45) was established in 1902. This huge dingy diner and bakery serves a large menu of fairly pedestrian Puerto Rican fare, including rice stews and sandwiches. But the best reason to go is for its famous *mallorca*, a light flaky piece of swirled pastry split lengthwise, stuffed with butter, smashed, heated on a grill press, and dusted with powdered sugar. The crispy breakfast sandwiches are also a good hearty way to start the day. But be prepared to wait: Service is excruciatingly slow, especially when you're waiting for the morning's first cup of coffee.

C Mallorca (300 Calle San Francisco, 787/724-4607, daily 7 A.M.–7 P.M., $5.95–17.95) offers a very similar dining experience to that at La Bombonera, complete with its namesake pastry, but with friendlier, more attentive service.

Barrachina (104 Calle Fortaleza, 787/721-5852, 787/725-7912, www.barrachina.com, Tues.–Sat. 11 A.M.–10 P.M., $14–45), located in the courtyard of a 17th-century building, is one of two places in Puerto Rico (the Caribe Hilton being the other) that claims to have invented the piña colada. They mix up a pretty good one. But the budget decor was looking pretty shabby on a recent visit, and the Puerto Rican cuisine was only adequate.

New American

Prepare yourself for an unforgettable dining experience at **C Marmalade** (317 Calle Fortaleza, 787/724-3969, fax 787/724-4001, www.marmaladepr.com, Mon.–Thurs. 6–11 P.M., Fri.–Sat. 6 P.M.–midnight, Sun. 6–10 P.M., bar daily 5 P.M. until late, $24.50–29). This lovely, romantic chef-owned restaurant serves an ever-changing eclectic seasonal menu. The fun starts with the creative cocktail menu: Cointreau jelly, kiwi puree, jasmine flowers, and Compari foam were among the ingredients featured on a recent visit. Appetizers included pan-roasted foie gras and prosciutto di Parma, served with grilled peaches. Among the entrées were duck breast stuffed with Roquefort cheese and apple slices, and lamb lasagna made with Persian feta cheese. For pure drama, dine in the bar area, where great sheaths of aqua, orange, and rose-colored silk organza drape from the high ceilings to the floor and marble-top tables are surrounded by deep plush couches with curved backs loaded with pillows. The sedate dining room in the back is more quietly elegant.

Located in the luxury Chateau Cervantes boutique hotel, **Panza** (329 Recinto Sur, 787/289-8900, www.cervantespr.com, daily 8 A.M.–noon, Mon.–Sat. 6–11 P.M., $26–35), is a new fine-dining restaurant serving creative interpretations of classic dishes. The lobster bisque with coconut is a specialty.

Spanish

In the historic Hotel El Convento, the focal point of **El Picoteo** tapas and paella bar (100 Calle Cristo, 787/723-9020, 787/721-2877, or 800/468-2779, elconvento@aol.com, www.elconvento.com, daily noon–11 P.M., $7–29) is the original woodstove of the former convent, which was built in the mid-17th century. Visitors are greeted at the entrance by an enormous wax-covered altar packed willy-nilly with whimsical ceramic roosters and half-melted candles. The main dining room is in the hotel courtyard, but there's also dining at the long tile bar overlooking the open kitchen. The traditional Spanish tapas include stiff planks of Manchego cheese, thin slices of buttery serrano ham, fresh sardines, and a variety of olives. Bypass the mushy, oily eggplant and roasted red-pepper salad, but definitely order the fiery bite-size chorizo sausages served in a pool of thin heady brandy sauce. Among the varieties of paellas is one prepared with nutty, earthy black rice and chock-full of shrimp, calamari, and chunks of *dorado*.

Italian

Fratelli (310 Calle Fortaleza, 787/721-6265, fax 787/729-2238, www.restaurantefratelli.com, Mon.–Sat. 6 P.M. until the place empties, $15–30) is another terrific restaurant from the owners of Baru, this one serving Italian cuisine in a classic Old World setting featuring high ceilings, a graceful archway, potted palms, a fresco on one wall, and a ceiling-high shelf lined with bottles of wine on another. As at Baru, the artful lighting creates a sumptuous ambiance that encourages you to linger long into the night. The food is superb, especially the fresh pasta made on the premises. Specialties include seafood linguine and risotto, beef and tuna carpaccios, and a *Caprese* salad that's almost too pretty to eat. It also has a full bar and extensive wine list.

Seafood and Steak

For a hip, hot restaurant where the gorgeous wait staff is attitude-free, the seafood is amazing, and the decor is evocative of dining in an aquarium, get thee to ◖ **Aguaviva** (364 Calle Fortaleza, 787/722-0665, www.oofrestaurants .com, daily 11:30 A.M.–4 P.M., Mon.–Thurs. and Sun. 6–11 P.M., Fri.–Sat. 6 P.M.–midnight, $17–30), another of the OOF! Restaurants' purveyors of contemporary cuisine. The space is drenched in bright white, chrome, and aqua, with glass jellyfish lights hanging from the ceiling. In addition to an oyster and seviche bar, dishes on a recent visit included grilled *dorado* with smoked shrimp salsa, grilled marlin with chorizo, and nueva paella with seared scallops. At the blue-lit bar, where seashells float in Lucite, sublime cocktails are prepared with fresh juices. Be sure to try the watermelon sangria.

Romance oozes from the patio of **Ostra Cosa** (154 Calle Cristo, 787/722-COSA—787/722-2672, Sun.–Wed. noon–10 P.M., Fri.–Sat. noon–11 P.M., $14–28). This lovely intimate restaurant in the back of Las Arcadas alley has just 11 tables on a red brick patio under a white tent surrounded by scores of tropical plants and orchids. The cuisine is mostly seafood, including grilled prawns, Alaskan crab legs, and cheesy crepes stuffed with your choice of fillings. For something unusual, try the smoked calamari salad, a refreshing combination of thin slices of tender pink calamari with bits of seaweed in a spritz of light ginger sauce. Accompany that with the house cocktail, the

Spinoza, a bracing mixture of white rum and fresh-squeezed lime juice. There's live mood-setting music on weekends.

Asian

Dragonfly (364 Calle Fortaleza, 787/977-3886, www.oofrestaurants.com, Mon.–Wed. 6–11 P.M., Thurs.–Sat. 6 A.M.–midnight, $12–26), another OOF! Restaurant establishment frequented by the young and beautiful party set, has recently been expanded from a tiny intimate space to encompass a lounge and second bar. Nevertheless, be prepared for the wait to get in, unless you go early in the night. The playful fusion menu offers delightfully creative cuisine combinations, such as Asian seared scallops and miso honey halibut. There's also a full-service sushi menu.

A fusion of Indian and Puerto Rican cuisine may seem an unusual combination, but ◖ **Tantra** (356 Calle Fortaleza, 787/977-8141, fax 787/977-4289, www.tantrapr.com, daily noon–midnight, late-night menu Mon.–Sat. midnight–3 A.M., $16–29) proves just how simpatico the dishes are. Sensual creations include crispy fried coconut sesame shrimp accompanied by a mango-peach salsa, and shredded tandoori chicken served over a platter of crispy fried plantain slices. The menu of eclectic small plates encourages sharing. If you can't decide, order one of the combo platters that serve 2–4 diners ($55–75). The bar serves a variety of fruity martinis ($10) garnished with fresh flower petals. Forgo dessert and have a coconut martini rimmed in chocolate and fresh grated coconut instead. After dinner, fire up a bowl of fruit-flavored tobacco in one of the hookahs that line the bar ($20 a bowl). When the kitchen closes, Tantra turns into a late-night hotspot popular with service-industry workers who flock there when their restaurants close.

French

For traditional French cuisine in a classic elegant setting featuring an enormous crystal chandelier and walls surrounded by long white flowing drapes, there's **Trois Cent**

Onze (311 Calle Fortaleza, 787/725-7959, www.311restaurantpr.com, Wed.–Fri. noon–3 P.M., Tues.–Thurs. 6:30–10:30 P.M., Fri.–Sat. 6:30–11:30 P.M., $22–35). This is the place to go for snails and foie gras. Check out their highly lauded wine-pairing dinners.

Eclectic

Carli Café Concierto (Banco Popular building, corner of Recinto Sur and Calle San Justo, 787/725-4927, carli@caribe.net, www.carlicafeconcierto.com, Mon.–Sat. 11:30 A.M.–2:30 P.M., 5–10 P.M., live music Mon.–Sat. 8–11:30 P.M., $16–34) is a romantic, sophisticated lounge and restaurant serving a variety of dishes, including risottos, raviolis, quesadillas, and Caribbean-inspired tapas. The owner, a jazz pianist, performs nightly with a changing array of guest musicians. It's also a great place to just sit at the bar and enjoy one of a large selection of specialty cocktails. There's alfresco dining on the sidewalk too.

OCEAN PARK

There are few restaurants in Ocean Park, but the ones that are there are top-notch. Despite its name, **Kasalta Bakery** (1966 Ave. McLeary, 787/727-7340 or 787/727-6593, fax 787/268-0864, www.kasalta.com, daily 6 A.M.–10 P.M.) is much more than a bakery. This large, professionally run operation sells piping hot *empanadillas, pastelillos,* and *alcapurrias* ($1.50), and super-thick toasted sandwiches ($4.50–8), including an exceptional Cubano, *media noche,* and a variety of breakfast sandwiches. There are also hot daily specials, including paella, seafood salads, and case after case of freshly made baked goods ($1.50) such as cheesecakes, jelly rolls, Danish, cookies, and more. It also sells whole cakes and has an excellent wine and liquor selection. Order at the counter and grab a seat on a short bar stool at shared tables to feast. Be prepared to wait for a parking space and stand in lines to order on the weekends.

In Numero Uno guesthouse, **Pamela's** (1 Calle Santa Ana, 787/726-5010, fax 787/727-5482, www.numero1guesthouse.com, lunch daily noon–3 P.M.; tapas daily 3–6 P.M.; dinner daily 6–10:30 P.M., $22–29) is the most popular restaurant in Ocean Park. This elegant fine-dining restaurant with excellent service features white linen tablecloths and mission-style furnishings inside, with casual seating outside right on the sandy beach. Specialties include grilled shrimp with tamarind sauce and rack of lamb with grilled pineapple and fresh mint chutney.

Uvva (at Hostería del Mar guesthouse, 1 Calle Tapia, 787/727-3302, fax 787/727-0631, www.hosteriadelmarpr.com, daily 8 A.M.–10 P.M., $20–36) is another popular fine-dining restaurant in Ocean Park. It features a tiny dining room decked out in warm woods and rattan furnishings. The cuisine is Mediterranean fusion, featuring several pasta dishes, fish, and lamb chops.

CONDADO
Puerto Rican

Ajili-Mójili (1006 Ave. Ashford, 787/725-9195, ajiligroup@yahoo.com, Mon.–Fri. 11:45 A.M.–3 P.M., Sat. noon–3:30 P.M., Sun. buffet noon–4 P.M., Sun.–Thurs. 6–10 P.M., Fri.–Sat. 6–11 P.M., $14–29) comes highly recommended for its upscale take on traditional Puerto Rican cuisine if you don't mind the Disneyfied ambiance. The large space is tricked out like a faux colonial-style hacienda, and the wait staff wears plantation garb, including suspenders and Panama hats. Dishes include *mofongo, arroz con pollo,* plantain-breaded snapper fillets, coconut shrimp with piña colada sauce, and stuffed Cornish hen. The clubby wood and glass-tile bar is a great place to meet for cocktails.

The late-night party crowd likes **Latin Star Restaurant** (1128 Ave. Ashford, 787/724-8141, $3.95–29.95) less for the food and more for the fact that it's open 24-7. It serves a huge menu, including authentic local dishes such as goat or rabbit stew, tripe soup, and brandied guinea. There's indoor and sidewalk dining, and if you want to keep the party going, Dom Perignon is on the wine list.

Orozco's Restaurant (1126 Ave. Ashford, 787/721-7669, daily 11 A.M.–11:30 P.M., $9.95–19.95) serves traditional Puerto Rican cuisine featuring *mofongo*, grilled steak, pork, and chicken, plus daily specials. There is a full bar; try the house-made sangria.

It's rare to find a true locals' place in Condado. That's what makes **Cafe Condado** (Ashford Medical Center, Ave. Ashford, 787/722-5963, Sun.–Fri. 5:30 A.M.–5:30 P.M., Sat. 7 A.M.–2 P.M.) so appealing. Little more than a drab crowded diner, this eatery is the perfect antidote to the corporate American chain restaurants that line the eastern end of Ashford Avenue. In the back of Ashford Medical Center, it serves good cheap Puerto Rican cuisine, including *carne guisada* (beef stew) and ham croquettes ($5.50–7.25), breakfast and sandwiches ($2.25–4.75), and an excellent cup of coffee ($0.50).

Seafood

For an unforgettable fine-dining experience, visit **《 Perla** (La Concha Renaissance Resort, 1077 Ave. Ashford, 787/977-3285, www.perla restaurant.com, Sun.–Thurs. 6–10 P.M., Fri.–Sat. 6–11 P.M., Sun. brunch noon–3 P.M., $25–39). The architecture is reason enough to go. The restaurant is nestled inside a 1958-era modernist interpretation of a clamshell located right on the beach. The seasonal menu leans mostly toward seafood and is ever-changing, depending on the availability of the freshest ingredients. Recent selections included frog's leg skillet chowder, skate wing poached in duck fat, and fennel-dusted diver scallops.

A casual option for good local cuisine is **《 Marisqueria La Dorada** (1105 Ave. Magdalena, 787/722-9583, daily 11 A.M.–10 P.M., tapas $5.95–9.95, entrées $16.95–29.95). The cute, cheerful little eatery serves terrific Puerto Rican cuisine, specializing in seafood. The bite-size *piononos*—balls of sweet plantain stuffed with spicy ground beef and deep-fried—make an excellent starter. Check the board for daily specials, including codfish in passion-fruit sauce and whole fried snapper.

Ikakos Restaurante Marisqueria (1108 Ave. Ashford, 787/723-5151, www.ikakos .com, Tues. and Thurs. noon–10 P.M., Wed. and Fri. noon–10 P.M., Sat. 5–11 P.M., Sun. noon–10 P.M., $10.95–28.95) is a casual but elegantly appointed seafood restaurant specializing in fresh local lobster and whole fish. Oysters, mussels, and *empanadillas* make up the tapas menu, while entrées feature *mofongo* and *mamposteao*, a sautéed rice dish served with your choice of meat or seafood.

Waikiki Caribbean Food & Oyster Bar (1025 Ave. Ashford, 787/977-2267, daily 11 A.M.–late, $12–35), a casual oceanfront restaurant, features a long pinewood bar, sidewalk dining, a stone grotto-style dining room inside, and a wood deck on the beach for alfresco dining. Dishes include mahimahi nuggets, crab-stuffed mushrooms, lobster tail, osso buco, and seafood *criolla*.

Cuban

A trendy take on Cuban cuisine can be found at **Ropa Vieja Grill** (1025 Ave. Ashford, 787/725-2665, Sun.–Wed. 11 A.M.–10:30 P.M., Thurs. 11:30 A.M.–11 P.M., Fri. 11:30 A.M.–midnight, Sat. 6 P.M.–midnight, $15–25). A modern space with a large cherrywood bar, tile floors, and a wall of windows that provides great people-watching, the restaurant serves risotto with pork rinds, filet medallions in Roquefort sauce, and grilled sea bass in pesto sauce.

Italian

In the heart of all the high-rises in Condado is a little seaside oasis called **Barlovento** (Plaza del Ancla on Ave. Ashford, 787/724-7286, Sun.–Wed. 5–11:30 P.M., Thurs.–Sat. 5 P.M.–midnight, $12–25). In a small park, the restaurant offers outdoor dining under a modernistic pavilion with purple awnings and chrome chairs. Like its counterparts in Old San Juan, Baru and Fratelli, it serves excellently prepared but less formal Mediterranean cuisine, including grilled chorizo, eggplant *rollatina,* and a variety of creative pizzas. Full bar.

Via Appia's Deli (1350 Ave. Ashford, 787/725-8711 or 787/722-4325, daily

11 A.M.–midnight, $12–30) serves standard red-sauce Italian dishes, including pasta, sandwiches, and pizzas. It has indoor and sidewalk dining.

Spanish

Don't be put off by the drab exterior of **Urdin** (1105 Ave. Magdalena, 787/724-0420, Mon.–Fri. noon–3 P.M. and 6–10:30 P.M., Sat. 6–10:30 P.M., $17.95–27.95). Inside is a shocking contrast: an elegant, contemporary dining room filled with thick carpets and dramatic paintings. The Spanish-influenced menu features several unusual dishes, including mussel croquettes, sweetbread cakes, wild boar chops, and roast duck in sour chocolate sauce. Take advantage of the valet parking.

Across the street from Urdin is a fine classic restaurant called **Ramiro's** (1106 Ave. Magdalena, 787/721-9056 or 787/721-9049, fax 787/722-6067, ramiros@caribe.net, http://premium.caribe.net/~ramiros, Mon. noon–4 P.M., Tues.–Fri. noon–9 P.M., $13–37). In a gorgeous green Spanish colonial mansion with enormous stained-glass windows, this chef-owned restaurant has exquisite table settings and tons of Old World style. The cuisine is international with an emphasis on Spanish interpretations, including halibut with banana chutney, yellowfin tuna in snail and chorizo sauce, and osso buco lasagna with foie sauce.

Mexican

On Avenida Magdalena is a pair of Mexican restaurants with the same name, **Cielito Linda** (1108 Ave. Magdalena, 787/723-5597 or 787/723-5597). The one on the left (Mon.–Fri. 11:30 A.M.–10 P.M., Sat. 6–11 P.M., Sun. 5–10 P.M., $4.95–17.95) is a tiny kitschy taqueria serving fajitas, enchiladas, tacos, and burritos. Two doors down is a slightly bigger, nicer eatery (Thurs. 5–11 P.M., Fri.–Sat. 6–11 P.M., Sun. 5–10 P.M., $7.95–19.95) serving beef tenderloin, marinated pork, and shrimp in tequila sauce, in addition to the typical taco, enchilada, and burrito fare. Both have full bars and specialize in frozen drinks.

Hacienda Don Jose (1025 Ave. Ashford,

787/722-5880, daily 7 A.M.–11 P.M., $12.95–32.95. A casual spot serving Puerto Rican and Mexican cuisine, including tacos, enchiladas, and burritos.

SANTURCE

One of San Juan's most exclusive restaurants is **☾ Pikayo** (Museo de Arte de Puerto Rico, 299 Ave. José de Diego, 787/721-6194, fax 787/724-8280, www.wilobenet.com, Tues.–Fri. noon–3 P.M., Mon.–Sat. 6–11 P.M., $32–70), just a few blocks south across Highway 26 from Condado. This is expense-account dining at its most lavish, and don't expect to save money by going for lunch—it's the same menu as for dinner. The seasonal menu changes, but dishes during a recent visit included octopus carpaccio and rack of lamb with shiitake mushroom stuffing. The food is superb. Reservations are recommended for dinner.

At the opposite end of the cost spectrum is **Plaza del Mercado,** at the end of Calle Roberts off Calle Canals. If the tourist scene along the Condado gets to be too predictable, venture just eight blocks inland for an authentic Puerto Rican experience. At this small historic market built in 1910, vendors sell fresh fruit, vegetables, and cut-to-order meat for far less than you'd pay at the local grocery store. You can also find herbs and roots from the *botanicas,* pick up a few sundries, and have a fresh blended fruit shake, with or without rum. Packed around the market are a number of bars and restaurants serving Puerto Rican cuisine. This is a popular place for working-class locals to congregate on Friday afternoons to get their weekends started, and the partying lasts well into the night. A convenient ATM is on Calle Roberts just before the market entrance.

ISLA VERDE
Puerto Rican

Platos Restaurant (below Coral by the Sea hotel, 2 Calle Rosa, 787/791-7474 or 787/721-0396, Sun.–Thurs. 11 A.M.–11 P.M., Fri.–Sat. 11 A.M.–midnight, $17–23) is not named after the Greek philosopher but rather the Spanish word for "plates." This trendy, touristy restaurant is decorated in moss green and burned orange with a large steel counter and big-screen TV in the bar. Tropical-drink specials are tall, but weak and pricey at $12 a pop. The formerly froufrou menu has been replaced with streamlined traditional dishes including *mofongo*, steaks, pork chops, and fettuccine. Creativity reigns among the seafood dishes, which include mahimahi in coconut-passion fruit sauce.

Casa Dante (39 Ave. Isla Verde, 787/726-7310, Mon.–Thurs. 11:30 A.M.–1 A.M., Fri.–Sat. 11:30 A.M.–midnight, Sun. 11:30 A.M.–10:30 P.M., $8–30) is a casual, low-key locals' restaurant serving authentic Puerto Rican cuisine, specializing in a variety of *mofongos* with choice of fish, seafood, beef, chicken, or pork. There are also a few pasta dishes available.

Seafood and Steak

Locals and tourists alike flock to **C̱ Che's** (corner of Calle Caoba and Calle Laurel, 787/726-7202 or 787/268-7507, Sun.–Thurs. noon–11 P.M., Fri.–Sat. noon–midnight, $12.95–28.95), a large casual restaurant serving excellent Argentine cuisine. Grilled meats are the specialty—veal, lamb, *churrasco,* veal kidneys, and so on. There are also some unexpected offerings—a Greek-style spinach pie with a whole boiled egg buried inside and an apple and celery salad. Che's has good service and a full bar.

Cuban

Decor is secondary at the crowded casual Cuban restaurant **C̱ Metropol** (Ave. Isla Verde, beside Club Gallistico cockfight arena, 787/791-4046, www.metropolpr.com, daily 11:30 A.M.–10:30 P.M., $8.95–34.95, although most dishes are $10–15). The house specialty is *gallinita rellena de congri*—succulent roasted Cornish hen stuffed with a perfectly seasoned combination of rice and black beans. The presentation is no-nonsense and the service expedient, designed to get you in and out so the folks lining up outside can have your table.

Italian

Despite its modest location on the busy thoroughfare, **Il Nonno** (41 Ave. Isla Verde, 787/728-8050, Sun.–Thurs. 11:30 A.M.–10 P.M., Fri.–Sat. 11:30 A.M.–11 P.M., $14–29) is a small fine-dining restaurant with a lovely setting. Pale green walls and walnut accents are complemented by an excellent selection of contemporary paintings. The restaurant serves Italian cuisine from gnocchi Gorgonzola to osso buco.

The casual modern Argentine-Italian restaurant **Ferrari Gourmet** (51 Ave. Isla Verde, 787/982-3115, Ferrari@caribe.net, Sun.–Thurs. noon–10 P.M., Fri.–Sat. noon–11 P.M., delivery after 6 P.M., $9.95–21.95) specializes in a wide variety of tasty creative pizzas. Selections include black olive and blue cheese; asparagus, parmesan cheese, and fresh tomato; and ham, roasted red peppers, and green olives. Entrées include *churrasco,* veal saltimbocca, and lasagna.

Deli

Piu Bello (2 Calle Rosa, 787/791-0091, fax 787/791-0092, Mon.–Thurs. 7 A.M.–11 P.M., Fri.–Sun. 7 A.M.–midnight, $6.99–12.99) is a large, modern retro-style diner with indoor and outdoor dining. The enormous menu includes every sandwich imaginable, including wraps, Italian focaccias, flatbreads, paninis, burgers, and clubs. It also serves breakfast, pasta dishes, and gelato. A second location is on Avenida Ashford in Condado. There's free Wi-Fi.

Information and Services

TOURIST INFORMATION

Puerto Rico Tourism Company (La Casita, Plaza de la Dársena, Old San Juan, 787/722-1709, fax 787/722-5208, www.goto puertorico.com, Sat.–Wed. 8:30 A.M.–8 P.M., Thurs.–Fri. 8:30 A.M.–6:30 P.M.) is in a small yellow colonial building near San Juan Bay, conveniently located near the cruise ship piers. It's a good place to pick up promotional brochures on various tourist sites, hotels, and tours, as well as a free rum cocktail.

Tourism Office of San Juan (250 Calle Teután at Calle San Justo, Old San Juan, 787/721-6363, Mon.–Sat. 8 A.M.–4 P.M.) offers self-guided audio tours of Old San Juan in English and Spanish for $9.99 per person. There's also a random selection of promotional materials for local tourist sites, hotels, and tours.

NEWSPAPERS AND MAGAZINES

El Nuevo Dia (www.endi.com) is the island-wide Spanish-language daily newspaper.

There are two English-language travel magazines devoted to Puerto Rico. The free bimonthly *Qué Pasa?* (www.qpsm.com) published by Travel and Sports (www.travel andsports.com) for the Puerto Rico Tourism Company. The magazine's current issue is available online, and the publishing company's website is an exhaustive source of information about the entire island. *Travel and Tourism Puerto Rico* is a quarterly publication available for purchase at magazine stands. Both are good sources for general tourist information, but they tend to be promotional and not very subjective.

EMERGENCY SERVICES

The central hospital serving San Juan's tourist areas is **Ashford Medical Center** (1451 Ave. Ashford, Condado, 787/721-2160). The clinic is open Monday–Friday 7 A.M.–7 P.M., Saturday 7 A.M.–noon. The emergency room is open 24 hours a day. Call 911 for ambulance service. There's a pharmacy on the first floor.

There are several **Walgreens** pharmacies (201 Calle de la Cruz at Calle San Francisco, Old San Juan, 787/722-6290; 1130 Ave. Ashford, Condado, 787/725-1510; 5984 Ave. Isla Verde, Isla Verde, 787/982-0222). Another option is **Puerto Rico Pharmacy** (157 Calle San Francisco, Old San Juan, 787/725-2202).

Dial 911 to reach the fire or police departments in case of emergency.

OTHER SERVICES

There is no shortage of banks and ATMs in San Juan, the most popular being **Banco Popular** (206 Calle Tetuán, Old San Juan, 787/725-2636; 1060 Ave. Ashford, Condado, 787/725-4197; 4790 Ave. Isla Verde, Isla Verde, 787/726-5600).

Convenient **post office** facilities are at 153 Calle Fortaleza, Old San Juan, 787/723-1277; and 1108 Calle Magdalena, Condado, 787/723-8204.

Self-service laundries are available at **Coin Laundry** (1950 Calle Magdalena, Condado, 787/726-5955) and **Isla Verde Laundromat** (corner of Calle Emma and Calle Rodríguez, Isla Verde, 787/728-5990).

Getting There and Getting Around

GETTING THERE
By Air
Aeropuerto Internacional Luis Muñoz Marín (SJU, Isla Verde, 787/791-4670 or 787/791-3840, fax 787/253-3185 or 787/791-4834) is nine miles east of San Juan. It is a full-service airport with three terminals. There are a bank, restaurants, bars, and shops on the second floor alongside the departure gates. A tourist-information office (787/791-1014) is in Terminal C, and a ground-service desk is on the first level by the baggage claim.

For transportation into the city from the airport, there are several car-rental agencies on the first level, including **Wheelchair Getaway Rent A Car** (787/726-4023), which provides vehicles for drivers with disabilities. The first level is also where you can catch a taxi or bus into town. From the airport, take Baldorioty de Castro Avenue west toward Isla Verde, Ocean Park, and Condado and into Old San Juan.

The airport also is the site of the Luis Muñoz Marín International Airport Hotel (787/791-1700), which can be found in Terminal D on the second level.

Airline ticket prices fluctuate throughout the year, but the cheapest rates can usually be secured during the off-season, May–September, which is the rainy season. Note that late summer and early fall are also hurricane season.

The following airlines service San Juan from the United States:

- **AirTran** (800/247-8726, www.airtran.com)
- **American Airlines** (800/433-7300, www.aa.com)
- **Continental Airlines** (800/231-0856 or 800/523-3273, www.continental.com)
- **Delta Air Lines** (800/221-1212 or 800/325-1999, www.delta.com)
- **JetBlue Airways** (800/538-2583, www.jetblue.com)

- **Northwest** (800/225-2525, www.nwa.com)
- **Spirit Airlines** (800/772-7117, www.spiritairlines.com)
- **United** (800/864-8331, www.united.com)
- **U.S. Airways** (800/428-4322, www.usairways.com)

Aeropuerto de Isla Grande (End of Ave. Lindberg, Puerta de Tierra near Old San Juan, 787/729-8790, fax 787/729-8751) is a regional airport that services flights throughout the island and the Caribbean.

By Cruise Ship
San Juan is the second-largest port in the western hemisphere, and it is a port of call or point of origin for nearly two dozen cruise-ship lines. The cruise-ship docks are at the piers along Calle La Marina in Old San Juan.

Some of the most popular cruise-ship lines serving San Juan include:

- **Carnival Cruise Lines** (866/299-5698, 800/327-9501, www.carnival.com)
- **Celebrity Cruises** (800/647-2251, 800/722-5941, 800/280-3423, www.celebritycruises.com)
- **Holland America Line** (877/724-5425, www.hollandamerica.com)
- **Norwegian Cruise Line** (800/327-7030, www.ncl.com)
- **Princess Cruises** (800/PRINCESS— 800/774-6237, 800/421-0522, www.princess.com)
- **Radisson Seven Seas Cruises** (877/505-5370, 800/285-1835, www.rssc.com)
- **Royal Caribbean International** (866/562-7625, 800/327-6700, 305/539-6000, www.royalcaribbean.com)

GETTING AROUND

Taxi

Taxis are a terrific way to get around San Juan because you can catch them just about anywhere. In Old San Juan, there are taxi stands at Plaza de Colón, Plaza de Armas, and the Sheraton near the cruise-ship piers. In Condado, you can flag them down on Avenida Ashford or at the Marriott hotel. In Isla Verde, flag one down on Avenida Isla Verde or find them congregating at the Hotel InterContinental. In outlying areas such as Santurce, Bayamón, Hato Rey, or Río Piedras, you can sometimes flag one down on the major thoroughfares, but you might be better off calling one.

There are a number of licensed taxi services that are well regulated. Operators include **Metro Taxi** (787/725-2870), **Major Taxi** (787/723-2460), **Rochdale Radio Taxi** (787/721-1900), and **Capetillo Taxi** (787/758-7000).

Fares between the airport and the piers in Old San Juan are fixed rates. From the airport, the rates are $10 to Isla Verde, $14 to Condado, and $19 to Old San Juan. From the piers, the rates are $12 to Condado and $19 to Isla Verde. Metered fares are $3 minimum, $1.75 initial charge, and $0.10 every 19th of a mile. The first three pieces of luggage are $0.50; additional luggage is $1 a piece. Customers pay all road tolls.

Bus

Autoridad Metropolitana de Autobuses (787/250-6064 or 787/294-0500, ext. 514, www.dtop.gov.pr/ama/mapaindex.htm) is an excellent public bus system that serves the entire metropolitan San Juan area. It's serviced by large air-conditioned vehicles with access for those with disabilities, and the cost is typically a low $0.75 per fare (exact change required). Bus stops are clearly marked along the routes with green signs that say "Parada," except in Old San Juan, where you have to catch the bus at **Covadonga Bus and Trolley Terminal,** the large terminal near the cruise-ship piers at the corner of Calle la Marina and Calle J. A. Corretjer. When waiting for a bus at a Parada,

it is necessary to wave at the driver to get him to stop. Operating hours are Monday–Friday 4:30 A.M.–10 P.M., Saturday–Sunday and holidays 5:30 A.M.–10 P.M.

The most commonly used routes for tourists are B-21 and A-5. Route B-21 starts at the terminal in Old San Juan and travels down Avenida Ashford in Condado and then south along Avenida Muñoz Rivera through Hato Rey to Plaza Las Americas, the island's largest shopping mall. B-21 runs every 20 minutes Monday–Saturday and every 30 minutes on Sunday and holidays.

Route A-5 connects Old San Juan and Isla Verde. The route travels along Avenida Isla Verde, Calle Loíza, Avenida de Diego, and Avenida Ponce de León into Old San Juan. A-5 does not go to Condado. It is possible to get to Condado from this route by transferring to B-21 at Parada 18 by Avenida De Diego, but keep in mind this stop is near a public-housing project in Santurce, which has been the site of violent crime. A-5 runs every seven minutes Monday–Friday, every 15 minutes Saturday, and every 30 minutes Sunday and holidays.

From the airport, visitors can take the C-45 bus to Isla Verde. To get to other parts of the city, it will be necessary to transfer to another route.

There are many other bus routes in San Juan. To obtain a free, detailed map of all routes, visit the bus terminal in Old San Juan. Riders should be aware, though, that buses serve tourist districts as well as housing projects, and some stops are in places where visitors who are unfamiliar with the lay of the land may not want to be. Make sure you know where you are before you disembark.

Trolley

Although Old San Juan is best experienced by foot, a free trolley service runs daily 8 A.M.–10 P.M. throughout the walled town. The south route goes to Plaza de Armas and the piers. The north route goes to both forts and other major sights. You can catch the trolley at the Covadonga Bus and Trolley Terminal by Plaza de Colón, at La Puntilla parking lot on Calle Puntilla, or at marked stops throughout Old San Juan.

Ferry

Agua Expreso (787/729-8714) provides ferry service from Pier 2 in Old San Juan to Cataño across the San Juan Bay daily 6 A.M.–10 P.M. The 10-minute ride costs $0.50 one way. You can also take a commuter car ferry down the Marin Pena Channel south of Santurce, which connects with the Nuevo Centro station of the Tren Urbano.

Train

In 2005, San Juan launched **Tren Urbano** (866/900-1284, www.dtop.gov.pr/ama/rutas/rutas.htm), its first, long-awaited commuter train service. The system runs 10.7 miles, mostly aboveground, and has 16 stations, many of which house a terrific collection of specially commissioned public art. The train connects the communities of Bayamón, the University of Puerto Rico in Río Piedras, Hato Rey, and Santurce at Sagrado Corazón University. The train runs daily 5:30 A.M.–11:30 P.M. Fares are $1.50.

Publico

Publicos are privately owned transport services that operate passenger vans along regular routes from San Juan to areas around the island. This is a very slow but inexpensive way to see the island. Providers include **Blue Line** (787/765-7733) to Río Piedras, Aguadilla, Aguada, Moca, Isabela, and other areas; **Choferes Unidos de Ponce** (787/764-0540) to Ponce and other areas; **Lina Boricua** (787/765-1908) to Lares, Ponce, Jayuya, Utuado, San Sebastián, and other areas; **Linea Caborrojeña** (787/723-9155) to Cabo Rojo, San Germán, and other areas; **Linea Sultana** (787/765-9377) to Mayagüez and other areas; and **Terminal de**

Transportación Pública (787/250-0717) to Fajardo and other areas.

Car

Driving a car in San Juan can be a nerve-rattling experience for drivers not accustomed to inner-city traffic. The sheer volume of cars on the road at any given time can be daunting, and parking on sidewalks or driving up expressway shoulders are not atypical habits of Puerto Rican drivers. But renting a car is one of the best ways to explore the city and its outlying areas. In addition to most major car-rental agencies, there are several local companies that provide comparable services.

Charlie Car Rental (6050 Ave. Isla Verde and 890 Ave. Ashford, 787/728-2418 or 800/289-1227, www.charliecars.com) is a cheap, reliable alternative to the national agencies. Drivers must be at least 21, and those younger than 25 must pay an additional $10 per day surcharge. Free pickup and drop-off at the airport, hotels, and the cruise-ship port is available.

Vias Car Rental (Hotel Villa del Sol, 4 Calle Rosa, Isla Verde, 787/791-4120 or 787/791-2600; Carr. 693, km 8.2, Calle Marginal in Dorado, 787/796-6404 or 787/796-6882; and Carr. 3, km 88.8, Bo. Candelero in Humacao near Palmas del Mar, 787/852-1591 or 787/850-3070; info@viascarrental.com, www.viascarrental.com, daily 8 A.M.–5 P.M.).

Scooter and Motorcycle

San Juan Motorcycle Rentals (102 Verde Mar, Ave. Isla Verde, 787/722-2111 or 787/791-5339) provides an alternative to renting a full-size car with its Vespa-style motor scooters available for rent by the hour. Free pickup and delivery service is provided.

EAST COAST

Puerto Rico's east coast is rich in natural wonders, making it the most popular destination for day-trippers from San Juan. Less than an hour's drive from the island's capital are three quintessential Puerto Rican sights: El Yunque Caribbean National Forest, Balneario La Monserrate (Playa Luquillo), and Bosque Estatal de Piñones, all on the north end of the east coast. Farther east is Fajardo, the island's boating center renowned for its water sports, and Laguna Grande, a bioluminescent lagoon. Fajardo is also the point of departure for the ferry to the islands of Vieques and Culebra.

The southern side of the east coast is less developed and lacks the big-draw tourist sights found farther north, but its sleepy towns and beaches offer a quiet getaway for those wanting to escape the bustle and crowds.

The east coast is also home to several spectacular resorts, including El Conquistador in Fajardo and Palmas del Mar in Humacao, and the whole area is rich in outstanding golf courses.

There are two officially designated scenic drives in the east coast. The **Ruta Flamboyan** (along Carr. 30 from Carr. 52 to Humacao) affords a lovely view of the spectacular *flamboyan* trees that bloom throughout the summer. These huge trees, also known as royal poinciana, have a broad, umbrella-shaped canopy that blooms a brilliant orange-red from June to early August. The **Ruta Coqui** doesn't necessarily get you any closer to its namesake, the *coqui* tree frog, than does a walk through any other forested part of the island. Instead the route (along Carr. 3 from San Juan

HIGHLIGHTS

◖ Bosque Estatal de Piñones: Between the San Juan airport and the town of Loíza, this untouched parcel of natural beauty features several long stretches of wilderness beach, salt flats, mangroves, lagoons, and tropical forest, as well as six miles of bike path and a cluster of food kiosks serving some stellar Puerto Rican fast-food fare (page 70).

◖ El Yunque Caribbean National Forest: Puerto Rico's crowning jewel of natural treasures, the Caribbean National Forest is a 28,000-acre reserve that encompasses a rain forest, hiking trails, observation towers, waterfalls, and natural pools (page 72).

◖ Las Pailas: This natural water slide is formed by a mountain stream cascading over a smooth but rocky descent that bottoms out in a chest-deep pool of crystal-clear water (page 79).

◖ Balneario La Monserrate: Considered by many to be the main island's most beautiful beach, this publicly maintained facility, commonly called Playa Luquillo, features gentle waters, a wide crescent-shaped strip of sand, and a palm grove, which create the picture-perfect idyll of tropical paradise (page 79).

◖ Reserva Natural Las Cabezas de San Juan: Despite its small 300-acre size, the Fajardo nature reserve features seven different ecosystems, including coral reef, turtle grass, sandy beach, rocky beach, lagoon,

dry forest, and mangrove forest. Its man-grove-enveloped Laguna Grande is bioluminescent − kayak here on a moonless night to see the water glow green, thanks to the harmless microscopic organisms that live here. It also boasts an 1880 lighthouse (page 82).

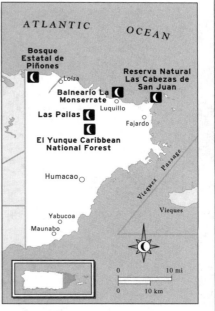

LOOK FOR ◖ TO FIND RECOMMENDED SIGHTS, ACTIVITIES, DINING, AND LODGING.

to Humacao) passes by the east coast's most popular attractions—Playa Luquillo and El Yunque—and the town of Fajardo.

PLANNING YOUR TIME

It's actually possible to take a drive-by tour of the east coast's triumvirate of spectacular natural sights—Piñones, El Yunque, and Playa Luquillo—in a single day if you're pressed for time. But a better option is to spend a full day exploring each one. The attractions are less than an hour's drive from San Juan, and only minutes apart from one another.

When it comes to natural treasures, **El Yunque Caribbean National Forest** is Puerto Rico's shining jewel. One of the world's most accessible rain forests, it offers hours of hiking, swimming, and bird-watching in a lush, tropical setting.

Coming in a close second as Puerto Rico's most popular attraction is Playa Luquillo, officially named **Balneario La Monserrate.** This is

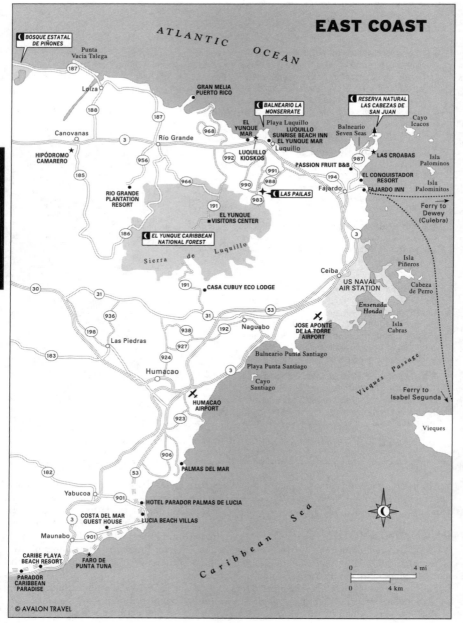

EAST COAST

ATLANTIC OCEAN

BOSQUE ESTATAL DE PIÑONES
Punta Vacia Talega
187
Loíza
188
187
Canovanas
3
Río Grande
968
HIPÓDROMO CAMARERO
956
185
966
RIO GRANDE PLANTATION RESORT
191
186
EL YUNQUE VISITORS CENTER
EL YUNQUE CARIBBEAN NATIONAL FOREST
Sierra de Luquillo

GRAN MELIA PUERTO RICO
BALNEARIO LA MONSERRATE
EL YUNQUE MAR
Playa Luquillo
LUQUILLO SUNRISE BEACH INN
EL YUNQUE MAR
Luquillo
LUQUILLO KIOSKOS
992
991
PASSION FRUIT B&B
990
988
983
LAS PAILAS
194
Fajardo

RESERVA NATURAL LAS CABEZAS DE SAN JUAN
Balneario Seven Seas
Cayo Icacos
987
LAS CROABAS
Isla Palominos
EL CONQUISTADOR RESORT
FAJARDO INN
Isla Palominitos
Ferry to Dewey (Culebra)
3
Ceiba
US NAVAL AIR STATION
Ensenada Honda
Isla Piñeros
Cabeza de Perro
Isla Cabras

30
31
936
198
Las Piedras
183
31
938
192
Naguabo
JOSE APONTE DE LA TORRE AIRPORT
53
191
CASA CUBUY ECO LODGE
927
924
Humacao
3
Balneario Punta Santiago
Playa Punta Santiago
Cayo Santiago
HUMACAO AIRPORT
923
906
PALMAS DEL MAR
182
53
Yabucoa
901
HOTEL PARADOR PALMAS DE LUCIA
3
COSTA DEL MAR GUEST HOUSE
LUCIA BEACH VILLAS
Maunabo
901
CARIBE PLAYA BEACH RESORT
FARO DE PUNTA TUNA
PARADOR CARIBBEAN PARADISE

Vieques Passage
Ferry to Isabel Segunda
Vieques

Caribbean Sea

0   4 mi
0   4 km

© AVALON TRAVEL

what picture postcards are made of: a long crescent of pristine sand gently lapped by the Atlantic Ocean and shaded by a thick palm grove.

Despite its proximity to San Juan, **Bosque Estatal de Piñones** is one of the most beautiful spots of coastal wilderness to be found on the island. It's easy to spend a day hiking or biking through the mangrove forest along the newly constructed bike path, kayaking through its lagoons, and swimming in the Atlantic surf beside palm-lined beaches.

Spending at least a long weekend in Fajardo is recommended for sports enthusiasts who want to enjoy all the boating, diving, fishing, and golfing to be had here. **Reserva Natural Las Cabezas de San Juan** is home to a diversity of ecosystems, as well as **Laguna Grande,** a bioluminescent lagoon that must be experienced at night.

Loíza and Piñones

Loíza holds a special place in Puerto Rican history because it was settled primarily by Yoruba slaves from Nigeria, who were brought over by the Spanish to work the island's sugar and coffee plantations. Emancipated slaves were relocated to Loíza, possibly because the east coast lacked much defense and it was hoped they could help repel foreign intruders. The town also served as a haven for escaped slaves who fled here in increasing numbers. Together they assimilated with the local Taíno Indians.

Loíza is a highly individual, tight-knit community rich in African-Caribbean culture where traditional customs and art forms are preserved and cultivated. Unfortunately, Loíza is also severely economically depressed. There's virtually no industry, and many residents receive some form of public assistance. Not surprisingly, the crime rate is high, with the majority of offenses revolving around the thriving local drug trade.

Loíza's best option for economic viability may be in developing its tourism, because of its proximity to some of the island's most wonderfully unique cultural and natural gems. But that would undoubtedly change the nature of the municipality forever. For now, there's little American influence or tourist industry in Loíza, which makes it the kind of place you should experience sooner rather than later.

Loíza's big claim to fame is its annual weeklong festival, **Fiestas Tradicionales de Santiago Apóstol (St. James Carnival),** a not-to-be-missed celebration for young and old in late July. The festival's complex history, which dates to the Spanish Inquisition, is feted with parades, music, dance, food, and elaborately costumed street theater.

A big part of St. James Carnival is *bomba* and *plena* music, traditional drum-heavy styles of music and dance with African roots that originated in Loíza and thrive there today. Some of *bomba* and *plena's* most celebrated artists are from Loíza.

Among Loíza's greatest charms is its proximity to Piñones, the site of the most gorgeous pristine pieces of natural beauty on the island, **Bosque Estatal de Piñones.** This forest reserve features miles of wild coastline thick with palm groves, mangrove forests and canals, lagoons, sand dunes, and stretches of uninhabited beach as far as the eye can see.

Accommodations are limited to privately owned vacation rentals in Loíza, and dining options are best found in Piñones, which has a dizzying array of terrific roadside food kiosks and several decent restaurants specializing in seafood. It's an ideal day trip from San Juan, 19 miles away.

SIGHTS
Iglesia San Patricio

Iglesia San Patricio (Calle Espíritu Santo, Loíza, 787/876-2229, Mon.–Fri. 8 A.M.–4 P.M.) is claimed to be Puerto Rico's oldest church in continuous use, founded in 1670. It is also known as Espíritu Santo.

BOMBA Y PLENA MUSIC

Bomba y plena refers to two distinctive styles of music that originated with the Nigerian slaves who were captured and shipped to Puerto Rico to work on sugar and coffee plantations.

Bomba is a percussive, call-and-response form of music. The primary instrument is a *barril*, a drum similar to the conga, originally made by stretching animal skins over discarded wooden barrels. The drums are accompanied with sticks, *güiros* (a washboard-style percussion instrument made from a gourd) and maracas (one, never two). The call-and-response vocals are secondary in importance to the dance, which is an integral part of *bomba*. The dancers match each beat of the drums, which goes at a very fast clip, sending the dancers into a frenzy of movement. Performances become a test of endurance between drummers and dancers as they each try to best the other.

Many believe *bomba* originated in Loíza, while others believe it was brought to Loíza by slaves who were already performing it in West Africa. Nevertheless, Loíza is considered the epicenter of *bomba*, although Ponce, Mayagüez, Guayama, and Santurce are also important sources of the music.

There are two celebrated families of *bomba* musicians in Puerto Rico today that reflect two different philosophical approaches to the music. Los Hermanos Ayala, sons of the legendary *bomba* musician and mask-maker Castor Ayala, are based in Loíza, and their style is strictly traditional, consistently fast-paced, and drum-heavy. Their cousins, the Cepedas, are based in Santurce and make what is called Congrejas *bomba*, a more contemporary evolution of the form influenced by its more urban roots and other musical styles, such as flamenco.

Plena shares features with *bomba*, but it adds horns and stringed instruments such as the *cuatro* (a double-stringed guitar-like instrument) to the mix, and the percussive emphasis is less on the *bomba* drum and more on the *pandereta*, a small handheld drum similar to a tambourine but without the cymbals. In *plena*, dance is secondary to the vocals, which consist of a kind of oral record that usually comments on topical subjects such as scandals, politics, or natural disasters. It is believed to have originated in Ponce, but like *bomba*, its roots are in Puerto Rico's African culture.

Although *plena*'s popularity has abated through the years, there is a renewed interest in preserving and cultivating the form, and strains of it can be heard in salsa music.

◖ Bosque Estatal de Piñones

There's no other place in Puerto Rico like the spectacular Bosque Estatal de Piñones (along Carr. 187 between San Juan and Loíza, 787/791-7750, office Mon.–Fri. 7 A.M.–3:30 P.M.). Stretching from the eastern tip of Isla Verde, San Juan, to the town of Loíza, this pristine reserve is a natural wonderland of deserted beaches; mangrove, pine, and palm forests; sand dunes; coral reefs; bays; salt flats; and lagoons. An important part of the island ecosystem, Piñones is home to 46 species of birds, including a variety of herons and pelicans.

Boca de Congrejas (just east of the Aeropuerto Internacional Luis Muñoz Marín in San Juan and the Congrejas Yacht Club) is the gateway to Piñones from San Juan. At first glance, it looks like a shantytown of wooden shacks and concrete sheds barely clinging to a rocky point that juts into the sea. But you shouldn't bypass Boca de Congrejas. It contains some of the best and cheapest local food you'll find, from stuffed fritters to all varieties of seafood. Walk from kiosk to kiosk and try a little bit of everything. Many items cost only $1. Expect crowds and a party atmosphere on weekends and holidays. Just east of Boca de Congrejas along Carretera 187 are also several bars and nightclubs that keep the place hopping, day and night. Some people caution against venturing here at night, but it can be a fun, adventurous immersion into the local scene if you keep your wits about you. And definitely stop here during the day to stock up on provisions before entering the forest.

Carretera 187 is a narrow two-lane road that winds through Piñones to Loíza from San Juan. Tucked between the thick clusters of palms along the coastal side of the road are unmarked sandy turn-ins that lead to the beach where you can park and walk down the dunes into the water to swim. You'll start to encounter the best swimming beaches around km 9, where the reef recedes from the beach. Another option for a good swimming spot is **Vacia Talega,** a small unmarked crescent beach visible from the road on Carretera 187 just before you cross the river into Loíza. It has a small sandy parking lot but no facilities. This is also a good fishing spot. Piñones is also a popular place for surfing, especially at **Aviones,** just past Boca de Congrejas.

In addition to swimming, surfing, and fishing, a major draw for Piñones is the **Paseo Piñones Bike Path,** a six-mile-long system of paved trails and boardwalks, which provides an excellent way to explore the forest. Bikes are available for rent at the restaurant **El Pulpo Loco** (Carr. 187, km 4.5, 787/791-8382, 10 A.M.–6 P.M.) for about $25 a day.

Venture away from the coast into the forest's interior and you encounter two lagoons, **Laguna de Piñones** and **Laguna la Torrecilla.** The best way to explore these rich mangrove ecosystems is by kayak. To reach the launch site, turn inland off Carretera 187 at km 9 and follow the sign pointing to the Bosque Estatal de Piñones office. A couple of tour operators in the area offer kayak tours of the lagoons and hiking tours of the forest.

It is possible to take a bus (B-40 or B-45) from Isla Verde to Boca de Congrejas or catch a taxi, but the best option for exploring Piñones is to drive there. Just be sure to lock your car, keep it in sight as much as possible, and don't leave anything of value visible inside.

SPORTS AND RECREATION

Piñones Ecotours (Carr. 187 at Boca de Congrejas Bridge, 787/272-0005, fax 787/789-1730, ecotours@caribe.net) offers biking, hiking, and kayak tours in Bosque Estatal de Piñones. Gear rental is also available.

ENTERTAINMENT AND EVENTS

Fiestas Tradicionales de Santiago Apóstol (St. James Carnival) is one of Puerto Rico's liveliest and most colorful festivals, spanning about six days around July 25. Based in Plaza de Recreo de Loíza, the festival features lots of costumed parades, dances, street pageants, concerts, and traditional food vendors. Ostensibly a celebration of the town's patron saint, St. Patrick, religion takes a back seat to this raucous street party that has origins in 13th-century Spain but is heavily influenced by African traditions. At the center of the celebration is a street pageant in which costumed caballeros (Spanish knights), masked *vejigantes* (Moors), and *locas* (trickster men dressed as old women) reenact Spain's defeat of the Moors. The colorful *vejigante* mask, made from coconut shell, wire, and papier-mâché and featuring protruding horns, has become a highly collectible, iconic symbol of the festival and Puerto Rico as a whole, and there are several local artisans in the area who produce them. St. James Carnival is also a prime place to revel in the African-influenced *bomba* music, which is performed late into the night.

SHOPPING

Estudio de Arte Samuel Lind (Carr. 187, km 6.6, Loíza, 787/876-1494, fax 787/876-1499, loizano@prtc.net, www.studioporto.com/guestsamuellind, Wed.–Sun. 10 A.M.–5 P.M.) is open to the public for the sale of paintings, prints, and sculptures by artist Samuel Lind.

Artesanías Castor Ayala (Carr. 187, km 6.6, 787/876-1130, rayala@caribe.net, daily 9 A.M.–6 P.M.) sells highly collectible *vejigante* masks made by second-generation master mask-maker Raul Ayala.

ACCOMMODATIONS

The best option for accommodations in Loíza and Piñones is an **apartment rental** in one of the many new, modern, gated condominium developments that have cropped up. Several are on the beach. For information, visit www.vacationrentals411.com, www.rentalo.com, and www.vrbo.com.

FOOD

The casual no-frills dining options are endless at Boca de Congrejas in Piñones and a little farther eastward along Carretera 187. In addition to dozens of kiosks selling fritters and *coco frio* (chilled coconut milk served straight from the shell), there are several casual restaurants selling traditional Puerto Rican cuisine, mostly seafood, for a pittance. Options include **Pulpo Loco by the Sea** (Carr. 187, km 4.5, Piñones, 787/791-8382) and **The Reef** (Carr. 187, km 1, Piñones, 787/791-1973).

Soleil Beach Club (Carr. 187, km 4.6, Piñones, 787/253-1033, www.soleilbeachclub.com, Sun.–Thurs. 11 A.M.–11 P.M., Fri.–Sat. 11 A.M.–2 A.M., $10–39) is the closest thing Piñones has to fine dining, but the atmosphere is still appropriately casual, considering its beachfront location. The two-level restaurant serves traditional Puerto Rican cuisine, including pumpkin soup and crab stew, as well as creative Caribbean cuisine like pan-roasted *dorado* and rock lobster. On weekend nights the place turns into a nightclub when salsa bands and DJs provide the entertainment. The restaurant also offers free transportation to and from your hotel.

PRACTICALITIES

The Loíza **tourist office** (787/886-3628 or 787/876-3570, fax 787/256-2570, Mon.–Fri. 8 A.M.–noon and 1–4:30 P.M.) isn't often open, but it's across the street from Iglesia San Patricio on the plaza. **Juan Carlos Transportation** (787/876-3628 or 787/374-1056, daily 8 A.M.–5 P.M.) offers taxi service and tours around Loíza.

Río Grande

The area that comprises Río Grande saw much fighting between Spanish settlers and the Taíno and Carib Indians. Once the Indian populations dwindled, it became an important agricultural area thanks to the many rivers (Herrera, Espíritu Santo, Mameyes, Sonador, Grande, La Mina) that run through it. Many plantations growing sugarcane and coffee were established here.

Today Río Grande is best known as "The City of El Yunque" because 45 percent of the Caribbean National Forest, as well as the popular El Yunque Recreation Area, is here. It's also a popular golf destination.

◖ EL YUNQUE CARIBBEAN NATIONAL FOREST

It is commonly called El Yunque rain forest, but the official name of this spectacular natural preserve is the Caribbean National Forest. The name El Yunque technically refers to the forest's second-highest peak (3,469 feet), and

a waterfall in El Yunque

it's also the name of the forest's recreational area. But regardless of its moniker, it is without a doubt Puerto Rico's crowning jewel of natural treasures.

The only tropical forest in the U.S. National Forest System—not to mention the smallest and most ecologically diverse—the Caribbean National Forest is a must-see for visitors to Puerto Rico. Nearly half of the 28,000-acre area contains some of the only virgin forest remaining on the island, which was completely covered in forest when Columbus arrived in 1493. It also contains one of the world's most accessible rain forests.

El Yunque is about 35 minutes east of San Juan off Carretera 3. Go south on Carretera 191 and it will take you into the forest and to El Portal Tropical Forest Center.

History

The name El Yunque is believed to be a Spanish derivation of the Taíno Indian name for the area, Yuke, which means "white earth" because the mountaintops are often covered in clouds. The Taíno believed that El Yunque was a sacred place and home to their gods, the most powerful and revered being Yuquiyu, who protected mortals from evil. The Taíno visited the forest to cut trees, vines, and palm fronds to make canoes, baskets, and roofing thatch, and to gather its abundance of fruits, roots, and medicinal plants. It is also believed that religious ceremonies and rituals were held here. Many petroglyphs can be found carved into rocks and boulders throughout the forest.

Upon the arrival of Spanish settlers, attempts were made to exploit the forest's resources. The timber industry initiated forestation, and copper mining was pursued. But in 1876, King Alfonso XII of Spain decreed 12,300 acres of the forest a preserve, making it one of the oldest forest reserves in the western hemisphere. In 1903, after the United States gained control of Puerto Rico following the Spanish-American War, President Theodore Roosevelt designated the area the Luquillo Forest Reserve, and it was eventually expanded to its current size. Further securing its safekeeping, the United Nations

EAST COAST

designated it as part of the international network of biosphere reserves in 1976.

Flora and Fauna

More than 240 inches of rain—100 billion gallons!—falls annually in the forest, making it a rich habitat for moisture-loving flora and fauna. It is home to more than 1,000 plant species, including 50 types of orchids, 150 ferns, and 240 species of trees, 23 of which are endemic only to El Yunque.

The Caribbean National Forest is in the Sierra de Luquillo, with mountains ranging in height from 600 feet to more than 3,500 feet above sea level, and it contains four distinct forests. Most of the area is covered in the **Tabonuco Forest,** found in areas up to 2,000 feet above sea level. This is the most dramatic part of the forest and site of the true rain forest. The dominant tree species is the *tabonuco,* which grows up to 125 feet in height and is distinguished by its huge dark-green canopy and straight trunk, which has a smooth whitish bark.

The **Sierra Palm Forest** is found along steep slopes and near rivers and creeks more than 1,500 feet above sea level. Its dominant tree, the sierra palm, is easily identified by the thick skirt of exposed roots around its base, which is an adaptation that allows it to thrive in the wet soil. The **Palo Colorado Forest** is found in valleys and slopes at an altitude between 2,000 feet and 3,000 feet. The dominant tree is the *palo colorado,* also known as swamp cyrilla, which is characterized by its thick twisted trunk and red bark. Most of these trees have been around for ages—some reportedly more than 1,000 years.

On the uppermost peaks of El Yunque, between 2,500 and 3,500 feet above sea level, is the **Cloud Forest,** also known as the Dwarf or Elfin Forest. This is a nearly mystical, otherworldly place where constant wind and moisture have stunted and twisted the dense vegetation. Roots snake across the windswept ground in thick tangles, and the trees, which don't exceed 12 feet in height, are covered with moss and algae. Here you also find many species of ferns and bromeliads, which bloom with brilliant red flowers. The air is cool, and visibility is often obscured by misty cloud covering.

Wildlife

The majority of El Yunque's wildlife falls into three categories: birds, reptiles, and amphibians. There are more than 50 species of birds in the forest; the rarest and most beloved is the Puerto Rican parrot, which is classified as endangered. In 1987 an extensive program was initiated to try to bolster the population, though its success has been limited so far. Today there are about 35 Puerto Rican parrots living in the Caribbean National Forest. You're highly unlikely to spot one, but just in case, keep your eyes peeled for a foot-long, bright green Amazon parrot with blue wing tips, white eye rings, and a red band above its beak. When in flight, it emits a repetitive call that sounds like a bugle.

Other species of birds found in El Yunque include the sharp-skinned hawk, the broadwing hawk, the bananaquit, the Puerto Rican tody, the red-legged thrush, the Puerto Rican lizard-cuckoo, the green mango, the Puerto Rican emerald, the Puerto Rican woodpecker, the elfin woods warbler, the Puerto Rican bullfinch, and the stripe-headed tanager.

Even more beloved than the Puerto Rican parrot is the tiny *coqui* tree frog. There are 16 varieties of the species on the island, 13 of which live in El Yunque. You're only slightly more likely to see a *coqui* than a Puerto Rican parrot, but you're sure to hear its distinctive "co-QUI" call, particularly after a rain or at dusk. Even more elusive is the Puerto Rican boa, a nonpoisonous snake that reaches lengths exceeding six feet.

Probably the most likely creature to be spotted in El Yunque is one of its many species of lizards. They are as common as ants at a picnic. The large Puerto Rican giant green lizard, which can grow as big as a cat, is commonly found along the limestone hills, and the smaller *anoli,* of which there are eight species, are ubiquitous.

The only mammals native to Puerto Rico are bats, of which there are 11 species in El Yunque. But rats and mongooses have been introduced to the island and now live in the forest. The rats were inadvertently brought over on trade ships and thrived on the island's sugar plantations. The mongooses were imported in a misguided attempt to control the rat population. They are vicious creatures and carriers of rabies, so give them a wide berth if you encounter them.

Recreation

The main thoroughfare through El Yunque is Carretera 191, which once completely bisected the forest from north to south, but recurrent landslides convinced engineers that the soil was too unstable to sustain a roadway at the forest's highest peaks. The forest is still accessible from the north and south on Carretera 191, but its midsection has been permanently closed. Most visitors to El Yunque drive in from the north end of Carretera 191 because it passes through the El Yunque Recreation Area. But there are efforts under way to close the north end of Carretera 191 and replace car traffic in the forest with a public transportation system to reduce the damaging effects of auto emissions.

The official entrance to the forest is **El Portal Tropical Forest Center** (Carr. 191, km 4, 787/888-1880, daily 9 A.M.–5 P.M., $3 adults, $1.50 children 4–12, free children under 4), a striking piece of architecture designed by the local firm Sierra Cardona Ferrer. Built in 1996, the bright white building is a modern interpretation of the traditional pavilion-style structure seen throughout the island. An elevated walkway leads visitors to its open-air interior filled with interactive educational displays. There are also an excellent gift shop heavy on educational materials, bathroom facilities, and a small screening room that continuously shows a film about the forest alternately in English and Spanish. This is also the place to obtain camping permits and arrange guided tours.

Travel farther south into the forest and you enter **El Yunque Recreation Area,** which encompasses El Yunque peak and the surrounding

area, and which contains the forest's major tourist sights. The first stop you encounter is **La Coca Falls** (Carr. 191, km 8.1), the most accessible and photographed waterfall in the forest. It has an 85-foot drop and a constant flow of rushing water. There's plenty of parking space and a small snack bar nearby because this is also the trailhead for La Coca Trail. The next stop on the route is **Yokahu Tower** (Carr. 191, km 8.8), a 69-foot-high observation tower built in 1963 from where you have terrific views of the forest and the Atlantic Ocean. Farther south is **Sierra Palm Recreation Area** (Carr. 191, km 11.3), offering more food concessions, restrooms, and a picnic area. Across the street is the Caimitillo Trailhead. The last stop is **Palo Colorado Visitors Center** (Carr. 191, km 11.8), an information center with still another snack bar and picnic area. Across the street is a short hike to **Baño Grande,** a picturesque stone pool built in the 1930s by the Civilian Conservation Corps. Slightly south of Palo Colorado is another pool, **Baño de Oro,** also built by the CCC. Although visitors are no longer allowed to swim in the pools, they're lovely spots that provide great photo opportunities. Palo Colorado is also the site of La Mina Trailhead and the Baño de Oro Trailhead.

Just before your reach the end of Carretera 191, the road intersects at kilometer 12.6 with a small loop road called Carretera 9938. This road takes you to the trailhead for Mount Britton Trail, which leads to **Mount Britton Tower,** built by the CCC. If visibility is good, you can see the south coast from here. From Mount Britton Trail, you can pick up the Mount Britton Spur Trail to the observation deck on the peak of El Yunque and **Los Picachos Tower,** another CCC tower.

Despite what many visitors might think, there is more to the Caribbean National Forest than El Yunque Recreation Center. In fact, the forest stretches way beyond Río Grande into the municipalities of Ceiba, Canóvanos, Fajardo, Naguabo, Luquillo, and Las Piedras. Many locals actually prefer the southern and western sides of the forest because they're less likely to attract busloads of tourists and they feature plenty of waterfalls and natural pools for swimming. To explore the western side, take Carretera 186 south from Carretera 3. To explore the southern side from Naguabo, proceed west on Carretera 31, and go north on Carretera 191.

Trails

Although it's possible to do a quick drive-by tour of El Yunque, the only way to fully appreciate its beauty and majesty is to park the car and hike into the jungle. It doesn't take more than a couple of dozen steps to become completely enveloped by the dense lush foliage. One of the greatest joys of hiking in El Yunque is the sound. Here the aural assault of the 21st century is replaced by a palpable hush and the comforting, sensual, eternal sounds of water—dripping, gurgling, rushing, raining. It's more restorative than a dozen trips to the spa.

There are 12 trails spanning about 14 miles in El Yunque. Many of the trails are paved or covered in gravel because the constant rain and erosive soil would require continuous maintenance to keep them passable. Nonetheless, hiking boots with good tread are a necessity. Even paved trails can be slippery and muddy. The warm air and high humidity also require frequent hydration, so bring plenty of water. And naturally, it rains a lot, so light rain gear is recommended. Avoid streams during heavy rains as flash floods can occur. Primitive camping is permitted in some areas. Permits are required and can be obtained at El Portal Tropical Forest Center.

The following trails are found in El Yunque Recreation Area. All trail lengths and hiking times are approximate.

Angelito Trail (0.5 mile, 15 minutes, easy, clay and gravel) crosses a stream and leads to Las Damas, a natural pool in the Mameyes River. To get to the trailhead, proceed south on Carretera 191 just past El Portal and turn left on Carretera 988, 0.25 mile past Puente Roto Bridge.

La Coca Trail (2 miles, 1 hour, moderate to strenuous, gravel) starts at La Coca Falls and requires navigating over rocks to cross a couple of streams.

La Mina Trail (0.5 mile, 25 minutes, moderate, paved and steps) starts at Palo Colorado and follows the La Mina River, ending at La Mina waterfall, where it connects with Big Tree Trail.

Big Tree Trail (1 mile, 35 minutes, moderate, paved and steps) is an interpretive trail with signs in Spanish and English. It passes through Tabonuco Forest, over streams, and ends at La Mina waterfall, where it connects to La Mina Trail. The trailhead is by a small parking area at Carretera 191, km 10.2.

Caimitillo Trail (0.5 mile, 25 minutes, easy, paved and steps) begins at Sierra Palm Recreation Area and crosses a stream. Along the way are a picnic area and structures used by the Puerto Rican parrot recovery program. It connects to the Palo Colorado Visitors Center and El Yunque Trail.

Baño de Oro Trail (0.25 mile, 20 minutes, moderate, paved and gravel) starts just south of the Palo Colorado Visitors Center and passes by Baño de Oro before connecting with El Yunque Trail.

El Yunque Trail (2.5 miles, 1 hour, strenuous, paved and gravel) is one of the forest's longest and most strenuous hikes. It starts a little north of the Palo Colorado Visitors Center and climbs to an altitude of 3,400 feet. Along the way it passes several rain shelters, through the Cloud Forest, and ends at the peak of El Yunque. The lower part of the trail is accessible from Caimitillo Trail and Baño de Oro Trail. The higher reaches of the trail connect with Mount Britton Trail and Los Picachos Tower Trail.

Mount Britton Trail (1 mile, 45 minutes, strenuous, paved) starts at Carretera 9938, a loop road at the end of Carretera 191. It is an uphill hike through the Tabonuco, Sierra Palm, and Cloud Forests. The trail crosses two streams and runs along a service road for a short distance—if you're not sure which way to go, just keep heading straight up. It ends at the Mount Britton Tower, built in the 1930s by the Civilian Conservation Corps.

Mount Britton Spur (1 mile, 30 minutes, moderate, paved) connects Mount Britton Trail to El Yunque Trail.

Los Picachos Trail (0.25 mile, 25 minutes, strenuous, unpaved and steps) is a steep ascent from El Yunque Trail to an observation deck built by the CCC.

The forest's remaining two trails are outside El Yunque Recreation Center on the western side of the forest. The trails are unpaved, muddy, not maintained, and often overgrown in parts. Long sleeves and pants are recommended for protection against brush, some of which can cause skin irritation on contact. These trails are for adventurous hikers who really want to get away from it all.

Trade Winds Trail (4 miles, 4 hours, strenuous, primitive) is the forest's longest trail. To reach the trailhead, drive all the way through El Yunque Recreation Area to the end of Carretera 191 where the road is closed. Be mindful not to block the gate. Walk past the gate 0.25 mile to the trailhead. The trail ascends to the peak of El Toro, the highest peak in the forest, where it connects with the El Toro Trail.

El Toro Trail (2 miles, 3 hours, difficult, primitive) starts at Carretera 186, km 10.6, and traverses Tabonuco, Sierra Palm, and Cloud forests. It connects with the Trade Winds Trail.

SPORTS AND RECREATION
Golf
What made Río Grande a fertile, well-hydrated place for growing sugarcane and coffee has made it an excellent place for golf courses today. A new course designed by Robert Trent Jones Jr. is slated to open in 2010 at the St. Regis Resort, currently under development at Bahía Beach Plantation.

Río Mar Beach Resort (Carr. 968, km 1.4, 787/888-8811, www.wyndhamriomar .com, 6:30 A.M.–6:30 P.M., greens fees $150–175 for resort guests, $185–200 nonguests, call 24 hours in advance) has two courses. Ocean Course, built in 1975 by George and Tom Fazio, offers excellent views of the Atlantic Ocean and one of the best-rated holes (No. 16) on the island. River Course, an 18-hole grass course with water in play built in 1997 by Greg Norman, runs along the Río Mameyes. There's

also a 35,000-square-foot clubhouse. Golf club rentals are available.

Trump International Golf Club (100 Club House Dr., Rio Grande, 787/657-2000, www .trumpgolfclubpuertorico.com, daily dawn–dusk), formerly the Coco Beach Golf and Country Club, offers 36 holes of ocean-side golf on courses designed by Tom Kite and Bruce Besse. Food and beverage service is provided on the course and in the clubhouse, which also has a pro shop. There is a putting green and driving range as well. In 2008 it hosted the PGA Tour's Puerto Rico Open.

Hiking
AdvenTours (787/889-0251, www.adventours pr.com) is an ecotourism operator offering expeditions throughout the island, including night hikes and bike tours of El Yunque. Expeditions depart from La Castia in Old San Juan. Reservations are required.

ENTERTAINMENT
Casinos
There are two casinos in Río Grande. **Gran Melia Puerto Rico** (1000 Coco Beach Blvd., Carr. 3 at Carr. 955, 787/809-1770, www .gran-melia-puerto-rico.com, 5 P.M.–2 A.M.) has a small casino with 130 slot machines, blackjack, progressive blackjack, roulette, craps, poker, and Texas hold 'em. **Río Mar Beach Resort** (Carr. 968, km 1.4, 787/888-6000, www.wyndhamriomar.com, Sun.–Thurs. 10 P.M.–2 A.M., Fri.–Sat. 10 A.M.–4 A.M.) is even smaller space-wise, but it has 190 slots, blackjack, roulette, craps, Caribbean poker, Texas hold 'em, and three-card poker.

Horse Racing
Hipódromo Camarero (Carr. 3, km 15.3, Canóvanas, 787/876-2450, www.hipodromo camarero.com, Mon., Wed., and Fri.–Sun.; first race begins 2:45 P.M. except Sun., when it begins at 2:15 P.M.; last race 6 P.M.; admission free) is technically in the municipality of Canóvanas, just east of Río Grande. Watch the races with food and beverage service from the grandstand, the clubhouse, or the Terrace Room restaurant.

You can also watch the action on live monitors in the Winners Sports Bar.

SHOPPING

Coqui International (54 Calle Principal, Palmer, off Carr. 191 on the way to El Yunque, 787/887-0770, www.coquistores.com, Mon.–Sat. 10 A.M.–6 P.M., Sun. noon–6 P.M.) is a huge gallery selling a wide selection of crafts by local artisans as well as artisans from Haiti and the Dominican Republic. It's a great place to buy contemporary and traditional *vejigante* masks, plus paintings, hammocks, food items, candles, and jewelry. Technically it is located in the community of Palmer, but it's on the way to the El Yunque rain forest. If you're traveling east on Carretera 3 from San Juan, turn right on Carretera 191 then left on Calle Principal; the store is on the left.

ACCOMMODATIONS

Río Grande Plantation Eco Resort (Carr. 956, km 4.2, Guzmán Abajo, 787/887-2779 or 787/887-5822, fax 787/888-3239, info@riograndeplantation.com, www.riograndeplantation.com, $136 s, $163–272 one-room villa, $272 two-room villa, plus 9 percent tax) is a unique, rustic property at the base of the Caribbean National Forest. It features 22 accommodations that run the gamut from single rooms to two-level villas with balconies overlooking the Río Grande. The buildings are a tad shabby and the furnishings a bit worn, but most rooms are large and comfortable and feature modern bathrooms, satellite TV, VCRs, air-conditioning, and kitchenettes. Amenities include a swimming pool, a basketball court, a game room, a business office, and several large event pavilions. What really makes this property interesting is its massive grounds, which have been left in their natural wooded state and feature several hiking trails. Las Tasqueria serves a modest menu daily 11 A.M.–11 P.M. This is a popular family vacation spot for Puerto Rican families.

Gran Melia Puerto Rico (1000 Coco Beach Blvd., Carr. 3 at Carr. 955, 787/809-1770 or 866/436-3542, fax 787/807-1785, www.gran-melia-puerto-rico.com, $169–350 s/d, plus taxes and resort fees) is a large 500-unit luxury resort, formerly known as Paradisus Puerto Rico. All accommodations are suites or villas and come with balconies or terraces, marble baths, air-conditioning, hair dryers, room safes, minibars, satellite TV, high-speed Internet, and room service. It has three restaurants serving Puerto Rican, Asian, and Italian fare, as well as two bars. Amenities include a lovely lagoon-style swimming pool, a spa and health club, three lighted tennis courts, and access to Trump International Golf Clubs. Guests can upgrade to what's called Royal Service to receive butler service and access to a private lounge and adults-only pool.

FOOD

Most of the notable dining options in Río Grande are limited to the restaurants at the Gran Melia Puerto Rico and Río Mar resorts. But there is one local nonhotel option worth checking out: **Antojitos Puertorriqueños** (No. 60, Carr. 968, Barrio Las Coles, 787/888-7378, daily 10 A.M.–9 P.M.) serves excellent local cuisine, including stuffed *mofongo* and *tostones,* rice and crab, *chillo* in garlic sauce, and salmon. Check out the changing exhibits of work by local artists.

And if you want to try some excellent Caribbean-style sangria, pay a visit to **Los Paraos Liquors** (54 Calle Pimentel, off Carr. 3, Río Grande, 787/888-3320, daily noon–2 A.M.), a modest-looking roadside liquor store with a popular outdoor stand-up bar. Those in the know flock here to buy the outstanding homemade sangria, a delicious pale-pink concoction packed with fresh fruit juices and sold in recycled liquor bottles for $7.50 apiece. Stock up! Once you try it, you'll want more. If traveling east on Carretera 3, turn left by the giant parrot sculptures onto Carretera 187R, and then take an immediate left on the one-way street. It's on the right—look for the large sign above the awning.

Luquillo

Luquillo is renowned for its breathtakingly beautiful public beach, most commonly referred to as Playa Luquillo, although its proper name is Balneario La Monserrate. Many consider this the finest beach on the main island, and its proximity to San Juan makes it one of the most popular among visitors.

Unfortunately, Luquillo's town center has undergone a recent renovation that has transformed its uncommonly large plaza into a modernist concrete pad with nary a tree in sight. There's little reason to tarry here, except to stop by Victor's Place for a stellar seafood meal. Instead, head over to the coastal side of town, where you'll find great swimming, surfing, and the island's popular array of kiosks selling fabulous fried fare for a pittance.

◖ LAS PAILAS

Las Pailas (Carr. 983, Barrio Yuquiyu, Luquillo) is about as off the beaten path as you can get. This natural waterslide is formed by a mountain stream cascading over a smooth but rocky descent that bottoms out in a chest-deep pool of crystal-clear water. Locals come here on weekends to mount the "horse," a saddle-shaped rock at the top of the descent, and slide down the rocks, landing in the natural pool below. If you're lucky, you'll see expert showboaters slide down on their bellies, face first, or even on foot. This is not an official tourist site. There are no signs, facilities, parking, or rules, although visitors should be mindful of respecting the property and not leave any trash behind. Although it's primarily a locals' spot, visitors are welcome, especially if they prove their mettle by taking a ride. To get here from San Juan, take Highway 3 east. Turn right on Carretera 992 and go toward Sabana, and then turn right on Carretera 983. Las Pailas is behind the homes that line the right side of the road. The best access is behind house No. 6051, distinguished by a cyclone fence. Homeowners along this stretch allow visitors to park for $5 and will point you toward a well-worn path

that takes you to the nearby shoals. If you get lost, just ask.

BEACHES
◖ Balneario La Monserrate

Balneario La Monserrate, or Playa Luquillo (Carr. 3, east of San Juan, 787/889-5871, daily 8:30 a.m.–5:30 p.m.), is the kind of place people dream of when they envision an island paradise. A thick grove of tall, shady coconut palm trees sways in the breeze over a mile-long wide crescent of pristine sand gently lapped by the Atlantic Ocean. The only signs of civilization are a clean modern complex of bathrooms and showers, some covered picnic shelters, and a couple of snack bars serving fritters and piña coladas. Camping is permitted in a grassy area with picnic tables and grills on the western side. Rates are $13, $17 with electricity. Call 787/889-5871 for reservations.

The only drawback to this idyllic spot is

taking a ride down Las Pailas in Luquillo

that it gets packed with beachgoers on weekends, holidays, and during the summer, when beach chairs and umbrellas are available for rent and lifeguards keep an eye on things. If you want solitude, visit on a weekday during the low season, and you'll practically have the place to yourself.

On the far eastern side of the beach is **Mar Sin Barreras** (Sea Without Barriers), a staffed, wheelchair-accessible beach that caters to visitors with disabilities. In addition to a system of ramps that permits those in wheelchairs to roll right into the water, there are accessible bathrooms, showers, parking, and picnic shelters. The facility also rents special wheelchairs for entering the water.

Other Beaches

Although Balneario La Monserrate gets all the accolades and attention, it isn't the only beach in Luquillo. A newly designated nature preserve, **La Selva Natural Reserve** (Carr. 193, just east of Luquillo) is a 3,240-acre tract of land comprised of wetlands, mangroves, coastal forest, and pristine beaches ideal for swimming and surfing—just beware of the reefs. This is an important nesting site for leatherback turtles.

In the town of Luquillo along Carretera 193 is **Playa Azul,** a sandy crescent beach great for swimming and snorkeling. Parking is limited, and there are no facilities besides a few street vendors selling snacks. Farther eastward on Calle Herminio Diaz Navarro is **La Pared,** a great surfing spot adjacent to a picturesque seawall just one block from Luquillo's central plaza.

SPORTS AND RECREATION

La Selva Surf Shop (250 Fernandez Garcia, one block south of the plaza, 787/889-6205, daily 9 A.M.–5 P.M.) is a great source for tips on surfing in the area. In addition to selling a variety of beach and surfing accessories, it rents surfboards ($30 per day) and boogie boards ($10 per day).

Hacienda Carabalí (Carr. 992, km 3, 787/889-5820 or 787/889-4954, www

.haciendacarabalipuertorico.com) is a 600-acre ranch offering guided horseback-riding tours on Paso Finos along mountainside and beachfront trails, along with ATV tours, mountain biking, and go-karts.

ACCOMMODATIONS

Despite Luquillo's popularity as a tourist destination for locals and international travelers alike, it has a dearth of overnight accommodations.

Luquillo Sunrise Beach Inn (A3 Ocean Blvd., 787/409-2929, info@luquillosunrise .com, www.luquillosunrise.com, $115–135 s/d, $210 suite, $195 two-bedroom casita, plus 9 percent tax) is a spiffy new 15-unit property right across the street from La Pared beach at Calle Herminio Diaz Navarro. Rooms are neat, modern, and comfortable. A restaurant on-site serves breakfast only.

El Yunque Mar (6 Calle 1, 787/889-5555, hotel@yunquemar.com, www.yunquemar.com, $95–110 s/d, suites $225–250, plus 9 percent tax) is a small hotel in a residential area right on Playa Fortuna. This modest, faux Spanish-style hacienda offers 15 clean modern units with air-conditioning and cable TV. Suites come with mini-refrigerators and microwaves. There's no restaurant or bar, but there is a small pool.

FOOD

❰ Luquillo Kioskos (Carr. 3) is nearly as popular an attraction in Luquillo as Balneario La Monserrate. Along Carretera 3 just before you approach Luquillo from San Juan, this long stretch of 80-plus side-by-side shacks is one of the best places to experience Puerto Rico's array of traditional fritters. Shaped like discs, half moons, cigars, boats, and balls, these crispy deep-fried goodies come stuffed with a varied combination of meat, crab, cheese, plantain, coconut, and more. Each kiosk serves nearly identical fare at stand-up bars where you can eat on your feet or seated at a table nearby. Pick one of each (they're only $1–3 apiece) and wash it all down with a cold beer, a cocktail, or *coco frío,* ice-cold coconut juice served from the shell. Be sure to buy a bag of *coco dulce,*

KIOSK CUISINE

© SUZANNE VAN ATTEN

one of many food kiosks in Luquillo

The roadways all over Puerto Rico are dotted with countless lean-tos, shacks, pavilions, tents, and trucks where enterprising cooks sell a variety of mostly fried local delicacies. For the uninitiated, the assortment of fried blobs, discs, and turnovers can be daunting. But if you want a truly traditional Puerto Rican experience, muster your courage, pop an antacid, and dive into an adventurous array of some of the freshest, tastiest dining on the island.

Most items sell for as little as a dollar apiece, are served not on plates but wrapped in napkins, and are eaten standing up. A variety of hot sauces is usually on hand to spice things up if desired, and nothing washes it all down better than an ice-cold Medalla beer.

Some of the most common items served include:

· **Alcapurria:** Grated, mashed plantain and/or *yautia* (taro root) stuffed with crab or beef and deep-fried. They look like small fried sweet potatoes, fat in the middle, tapered on the ends.

· **Arepa coco:** South American in origin, it's made from mashed or grated coconut mixed with corn flour, formed into a small round patty, and fried. It looks like a small fried disc.

· **Bacalaito:** Mashed codfish mixed into a flour batter and deep-fried. Looks like a big, irregularly shaped funnel cake or "elephant ear" like the kind sold at amusement parks.

· **Barcazas:** Whole plantains sliced length-wise, stuffed with ground beef, topped with cheese. They look like banana boats.

· **Coco dulce:** An immensely sweet confection of fresh, coarsely grated coconut and caramelized sugar. Looks like a brown craggy praline.

· **Coco frio:** Chilled coconuts still in their green husks. A hole is cut in the top and a straw stuck through it. Inside is a refreshing thin coconut milk. After you drink all the liquid, ask your server to chop it in half and scoop the coconut out with a spoon if it's unripe and soft, or you can chunk it out with a knife if it's ripe and hard.

· **Empanada:** Savory circle of pastry stuffed with meat, crab, lobster, shrimp, or fish, folded into a half moon, thickly crimped along the rounded side, and deep-fried. Looks like a giant apple turnover.

· **Papas rellenas:** A big lump of mashed potatoes stuffed with meat and deep-fried. Looks like a fried baseball.

· **Pastele:** Traditionally eaten around the Christmas holidays, the *pastele* is a Puerto Rican version of a tamale featuring mashed plantain, green banana, yucca root, and pork or chicken, wrapped in a banana leaf and steamed. Don't eat the leaf!

· **Pastilillo:** Smaller version of the empanada with a thinner, airier crust. Looks like a small apple turnover.

· **Pinchos:** Chunks of chicken, pork, or fish threaded on a skewer and grilled. Looks like a shish kebab.

· **Pionono:** A thin, lengthwise slice of plantain lightly fried and then wrapped around a patty of meat and egg and deep-fried. Looks like a giant deep-fried crab cake.

· **Taquitos:** Chicken, ground beef, crab, or fish rolled up in a piece of dough and deep-fried. They look like big fat cigars and are sometimes called tacos, but they're nothing like the Mexican version.

sinfully rich patties of sugary coconut, for later. This place can get packed on the weekends and holidays, and the atmosphere can get rowdy at night. Despite the area's rustic nature, most kiosks accept credit and debit cards.

Cafeteria La Exquisita (corner of Calle L. Calzada and Ave. 14 de Julio, on the plaza, 787/633-5551 or 787/370-3537, daily 10 A.M.–2 P.M., $5–8) serves traditional Puerto Rican cuisine, including *arroz con pollo,* rice and beans, pork, *tostones,* and more.

€ Erik's Gyros and Deli (352 Calle Fernandez Garcia, at the intersection of Carr. 992 and Carr. 193 right by Carr. 3, 787/889-0615, Mon.–Sat. 7 A.M.–5 P.M., $4–10) is an excellent place to get a cheap Greek-, American-, or Puerto Rican–style breakfast or lunch. This little corner deli serves gyros, burgers, lamb barbecue, Cuban sandwiches, tortilla-style omelets, French toast, and more. It also sells chorizo and serrano ham by the pound.

Fajardo

Fajardo is a bustling little seaside town notable for its many marinas and plethora of sports and recreation opportunities. It's also an excellent seaborne transportation hub to Caribbean points east, where you can catch a ferry or sailboat to Vieques, Culebra, St. Thomas, and beyond.

Although it has a town proper with the requisite plaza and church, the heart of Fajardo can be found along the coast, where hundreds of vessels dock and dozens of seafood restaurants vie to serve fresh fish and Puerto Rican fare to the day-trippers and sports enthusiasts who flock here for the superb diving, fishing, sailing, and golf.

Fajardo is also home to one of the island's bioluminescent lagoons, Laguna Grande, in Reserva Natural Las Cabezas de San Juan. Here you can kayak at night and marvel at the phosphorescent microorganisms that light up the water with a sparkling green glow.

SIGHTS
Balneario Seven Seas

Balneario Seven Seas (Carr. 987, beside Las Cabezas de San Juan, Las Croabas, 787/796-1052, daily 6 A.M.–6 P.M., $3) is a great beach for swimming and snorkeling. For underwater action, check out the reef on the far eastern end of the beach. Camping for RVs and tents is also available, although quarters are close so don't expect much privacy. Call 787/863-8180 for reservations.

Parque Las Croabas

Parque Las Croabas (Carr. 987) is a pleasant waterside park overlooking Bahía Las Croabas, dotted with moored fishing boats. From here you can see the island of Vieques. There are several concrete picnic shelters, poorly maintained bathroom facilities, and a small boat launch. Across the street are several bars and restaurants serving seafood.

Reserva Natural La Cordillera

Reserva Natural La Cordillera, comprised of Icacos, Diablo, Palomino, and Palominitos, is a protected string of small sandy islands just north and east of Fajardo with lots of great snorkeling and diving spots around them. Bring plenty of water and sunscreen—there are no facilities or stores on the islands. To get there, go to the dock in Las Croabas and arrange a ride with one of the boat operators there. They'll drop you off and return later to pick you up. The cost is typically $10 each way. The islands can get crowded on weekends and holidays.

€ Reserva Natural Las Cabezas de San Juan

Reserva Natural Las Cabezas de San Juan/ El Faro (Carr. 987, km 6, 787/722-5882, guided tours Wed.–Sun. 9:30 A.M., 10 A.M., 10:30 A.M., 2 P.M., $7 adults, $2 children 11 and younger) is a unique and treasured piece of island property that has been protected from encroaching development. This 316-acre piece of land contains examples of all the island's natural habitats except for the rain forest: coral reefs, turtle grass, sandy and rocky beaches, lagoons, a dry forest, and a mangrove forest. It is home to many endangered wildlife species, including the osprey and the sea turtle, and artifacts of the Igneri Indians, precursors to the Taínos, have been excavated here.

Two main points of interest are found at Las Cabezas de San Juan. One is the neoclassical lighthouse *(el faro),* built by the Spanish in 1880, making it the island's second-oldest lighthouse. Today it houses facilities for scientific research in the areas of ecology, marine biology, geology, and archaeology.

The other highlight of Las Cabezas de San Juan is **Laguna Grande,** a mangrove lagoon filled with microscopic bioluminescent organisms that glow green at night when they sense motion. Several outfitters in the area offer canoe or kayak rides into the lagoon after dark on moonless nights so visitors can witness the biological phenomenon. Swimming in the lagoon is no longer permitted.

This rich nature reserve also features a nature center, hiking trails, a boardwalk, and an observation tower from which you can see El Yunque and nearby islands as far away as Tortola.

Entrance into Las Cabezas de San Juan is by guided tour only. Call for reservations. To get here, take Carretera 3 to the Conquistador Avenue exit and turn left on Carretera 987. The reserve is on the left after Balneario Seven Seas recreation area.

SPORTS AND RECREATION
Snorkeling, Diving, and Sailing

Most water-sports outfitters offer a variety of snorkeling, diving, and sailing opportunities to the northeast coast's natural attractions, as well as to Vieques and Culebra.

Sea Ventures Dive Center (Carr. 3, km 51.2, Fajardo, www.divefajardo.com; and Palmas del Mar Resort, Humacao, www.palmasdel mar.com, 787/863-3483 or 800/739-3483,

fax 787/863-0199) operates three dive centers on the east coast, one in Fajardo, one in Guanica, and the other at Palmas del Mar, offering dive and snorkel trips to local reefs, Vieques, Culebra, and Cayo Santiago (Monkey Island) in Naguabo. Rent equipment or bring your own. The company also operates a dive center at the Copamarina Beach Resort in Guanica. Reservations are required.

Las Tortugas Adventures (4 Calle La Puntilla, San Juan, 787/725-5169, info@kayak-pr.com, www.kayak-pr.com) offers a variety of half- and full-day snorkeling and kayak tours on the east coast, launching from Bahía Las Croabas in Fajardo. Tours include Las Cabezas de San Juan in Fajardo, the bioluminescent lagoon, the mangrove forest in Piñones, and excursions to Cayo Icacos, Cayo Diablo, and Monkey Island. No experience is necessary, and all equipment is provided. Reservations are required.

East Island Excursions (Puerto Del Rey Marina, Fajardo, 787/860-3434 or 877/937-4386, fax 787/860-1656, www.eastwindcats .com) offers sailing and snorkeling trips aboard a 62-foot sailing catamaran with a glass bottom and a slide, a 65-foot power catamaran, or a 45-foot catamaran. Excursions are available to Vieques, Culebra, Culebrita, and St. Thomas. Reservations are required.

Caribbean School of Aquatics (Villa Marina, Fajardo, 787/728-6606, www.sail diveparty.com) advertises itself with the slogan "Sail Dive Party" despite the scholarly name of its operation. It offers snorkeling, diving, and sailing trips to Vieques and Culebra aboard catamarans and sailing sloops. Reservations are required.

Traveler (Carr. 987, km 1.3, Villa Marina, Fajardo, 787/863-2821 or 787/396-0995, fax 787/801-0608, puertoricotraveler@hotmail .com, www.travelerpr.com) offers snorkeling and sailing on a 54-foot Catamaran. Trips depart from Villa Marina at 1 P.M., and transportation can be arranged from San Juan. Group rates and charter packages are available.

Kayaking Puerto Rico (787/435-1665 or 787/564-5629, info@kayakingpuertorico.com, www.kayakingpuertorico.com) offers combination kayaking and snorkeling expeditions, as well as bioluminescent plankton tours in Laguna Grande.

Kayaking

Yokahu Kayaks (Carr. 987, km 6.2, Las Croabas, Fajardo, 787/863-5374 or 787/604-7375, yokahukayaks@hotmail.com) offers kayak tours to Laguna Grande in Las Cabezas de San Juan with licensed guides and equipment included. Reservations are required.

Kayaking Puerto Rico (787/435-1665 or 787/564-5629, info@kayakingpuertorico.com, www.kayakingpuertorico.com) offers bioluminescent plankton tours in Laguna Grande, as well as combination kayaking and snorkeling expeditions.

Las Tortugas Adventures (4 Calle La Puntilla, San Juan, 787/725-5169, info@kayak-pr.com, www.kayak-pr.com) offers kayak tours from Bahía Las Croabas to Las Cabezas de San Juan in Fajardo and the mangrove forest in Piñones. No experience is necessary, and all equipment is provided. Reservations are required.

Fishing

Light Tackle Paradise (Marina Puerto Chico, Carr. Road 987, km 2.4, 787/347-4464, $350–450 half-day for 4 or 6 people) offers fishing excursions on 22-foot and 26-foot catamarans or 17-foot skiffs.

Tropical Fishing Charters (787/379-4461 or 787/266-4524, tropicaldeepsea@aol.com, www.tropicalfishingcharters.com) offers year-round big-game fishing, specializing in blue marlin May–October.

Golf and Tennis

El Conquistador Resort (1000 Conquistador Ave., 787/863-1000, www.elconresort.com) boasts the Arthur Hills Golf Course (daily 6:30 A.M.–6:30 P.M.), a 72-par hilly course overlooking the Atlantic Ocean and El Yunque rain forest. There are more than 50 bunkers and five water hazards, including a waterfall on the 18th hole. There are also a driving range and a putting green. It is home to the Ambassador's Cup golf tournament in December. There are also seven tennis courts, four clay and three hard. Four are lit for 24-7 play.

Spa

Golden Door Spa (El Conquistador Resort, 1000 Conquistador Ave., 787/863-1000, www.elconresort.com) offers a wide variety of massages, hydrotherapy treatments, facials, reflexology, and energy-balancing treatments, including Reiki and craniosacral.

ENTERTAINMENT AND EVENTS

Carnaval de Fajardo (787/863-1400) is held in early August on Plaza de Recreo, featuring an artisans fair, a carnival, music, food, and arts and crafts.

The Casino at El Conquistador (El Conquistador Resort, 1000 Conquistador Ave., 787/863-1000, www.elconresort.com) features two Caribbean stud poker tables, five roulette wheels, three craps tables, 12 blackjack tables, and 224 slot machines.

ACCOMMODATIONS
$50-100

Anchor's Inn (Carr. 987, km 2.7, 787/863-7200, Frenchman@libertypr.net, $62 s, $73 d, $97 t, includes tax) is a good option if you just need a cheap place to crash. The inn is tacked on behind the Anchor's Inn restaurant and is in a parking lot near a fairly busy intersection. Amenities and aesthetics are nil.

$100-150

◖ **The Fajardo Inn** (52 Parcelas Beltrán, 787/860-6000, fax 787/860-5063, info@fajardoinn.com, www.fajardoinn.com, $110–120 s, $132 d, $160 t, $132 junior suite, $175–300 luxury suite, plus 9 percent tax) is a large, bright white complex with 97 units high on a hill, affording gorgeous views of the ocean from one side and the mountains from the other. Formerly a property belonging to the U.S. military, this hotel has undergone a complete overhaul, making it a very pleasant family-friendly place to stay. The rooms are modern, well-maintained, and simply furnished. They all have air-conditioning, cable TV, and telephones, and some have kitchenettes, balconies, mini-refrigerators, and whirlpool baths. On the property are two pools, a playground, miniature golf, laundry facilities, and two restaurants.

Passion Fruit Bed & Breakfast (Carr. 987, Las Croabas, 787/801-0106, gladys@passionfruitbb.com, www.passionfruitbb.com, $93–114 d, $136 suite, $141 quad, plus taxes, includes full breakfast) offers comfortable, modern accommodations in a brightly colored, three-story structure that houses 11 units named after famous Puerto Ricans. Amenities include air-conditioning, satellite TV, and a pool. Wi-Fi is available in common areas.

Over $250

El Conquistador Resort and Golden Door Spa (1000 Conquistador Ave., 787/863-1000, www.elconresort.com, $319–494 s/d), now a Luxury Resorts & Hotels property, is one of Puerto Rico's best-known and most highly regarded luxury resorts. A behemoth property perched atop a dramatic cliff with a stunning panoramic view of the ocean, El Conquistador is more like a small town than a hotel. It boasts 750 rooms in five separate white stucco and terra-cotta complexes set amid beautifully landscaped cobblestone streets, plazas, and fountains. There are a whopping 23 restaurants and bars on-site, as well as a casino, fitness center, full-service spa, seven swimming pools, an ocean-side water park, seven tennis courts, an 18-hole golf course, and a 35-slip marina. Every room has air-conditioning, satellite TV, telephone, minibar, marble bathroom, CD player, VCR, computer and fax connections, coffeemaker, and a sitting area. Snorkeling, scuba diving, and fishing tours and equipment are available on-site. There's also transportation available to the more secluded beaches on nearby Palomino Island.

FOOD
Puerto Rican and Seafood

La Estacion (Carr. 987, km 3.5, next to Hotel Conquistador, Las Croabas, Fajardo, 787/863-4481, www.laestacionpr.com, Wed.–Sun. 5 P.M.–midnight, $9–22), owned and operated by Kevin Roth from Brooklyn, New York, and Idalia Garcia from Puerto Rico, is a super-casual oasis of convivial fun and outstanding, freshly prepared cuisine. The kitchen is located in a converted gas station, but the sprawling dining areas are on open air patios appointed with awnings, padded lawn furniture, butterfly chairs, and tabletops surrounded by tiki torches and festive strings of lights. There's also a partially enclosed bar with a juke box filled with contemporary Latino rock and reggaetón tunes and a pool table. The vibe is akin to hanging out in your coolest friend's basement. But it's the food that really puts this place on the map. Everything is charcoal grilled, right outside where you can watch the action—fresh fish of the day, shrimp, *churrasco,* strip steaks, chicken, and burgers. The green papaya salad makes for a refreshing starter. And many of the ingredients are locally sourced. Be sure to order the house cocktail, called the Low Tide. It features rum, Triple Sec, and fresh pineapple and tamarind juices.

Rosa's Sea Food (536 Calle Tablado, Marina Puerto Real, 787/863-0213, Thurs.–Tues. 11 A.M.–10 P.M., $12–30) is a highly recommended spot for traditional Puerto Rican cuisine, especially the grilled fish and lobster.

Restaurante Ocean View (Carr. 987, km 6.8, 787/863-6104, Thurs.–Mon. 11 A.M.–midnight, $10–40) is right across the street from Parque Los Croabas and is a festive casual place to dine on fresh seafood under an open-air pavilion. It serves excellent combination seafood platters, *mofongo,* and paella, and it has a full bar.

Anchor's Inn (Carr. 987, km 2.7, 787/863-7200, Sun.–Mon. and Wed.–Thurs. noon–10 P.M., Fri.–Sat. noon–11 P.M., $8–30) is a whimsical black, white, and red wooden structure that looks something like an old

English seaside inn. The menu primarily comprises steak and seafood, its specialties being paella, stuffed seafood *mofongo,* and *chillo* tropical, featuring boneless red snapper in plantain leaves. For a change of pace, there are two French dishes: escargot and crepes stuffed with lobster. There's also a full bar with a long list of drink specials. On-site is a small budget guesthouse with 13 rooms.

Cuban

⟨ Metropol (Punta del Este Sur Court at the intersection of Carr. 3 and Carr. 194, 787/801-2877 or 787/801-2870, www.metropolpr.com, daily 11:30 A.M.–10:30 P.M., $9.95–35.95) is a modest casual restaurant serving excellent Cuban cuisine. The house special is *gallinita rellena de congri*—succulent roasted Cornish hen stuffed with a perfectly seasoned combination of rice and black beans. The presentation is no-nonsense and the service expedient.

INFORMATION AND SERVICES

Bank service is available at **Banco Popular** (Calle Garlinda Morales, between the central plaza and Carr. 3, 787/863-0101), which has an ATM. **Hospital San Pablo del Este** (Carr. 194 off Conquistador Ave., 787/863-0505) offers 24-hour emergency-room services. For pharmacy needs, there is a **Walgreens** (4302 Calle Marginal, 787/860-1600).

GETTING THERE AND GETTING AROUND

Although its airport has closed and relocated about 4 miles south to Ceiba, Fajardo is still a gateway to the nearby islands of Vieques and Culebra, thanks to daily ferry service and boats operating out of its seven marinas. Nevertheless, all the transportation options in Fajardo point in one direction: to Vieques, Culebra, or the Virgin Islands. Getting to Fajardo requires a flight into San Juan and either renting a car and driving there or taking a *publico,* a privately operated van transport service. **Padin** operates 24-hour transportation service between Fajardo and

the Luis Muñoz Marín International Airport in San Juan. Call Mrs. Rivera at 787/644-3091 (day) or 787/889-6202 (after 6 P.M.), or José Padin at 787/644-3091. The drive is about an hour.

By Air

The Fajardo airport has closed, and all operations have relocated about 4 miles south to the **Jose Aponte de la Torre Airport** (787/863-4447) on the former Roosevelt Roads Naval Base in Ceiba. It is a small operation devoted to servicing transportation to the coast's neighboring islands. **Isla Nena Air Service** (787/741-1577, www.islanena.8m.com) flies to Vieques, Culebra, and St. Thomas. **Vieques Air Link** (888/901-9247, www.viequesairlink.com) flies to Vieques, Culebra, and St. Croix. Charter air service is available through **Air Flamenco** (787/901-8256).

By Ferry

The Puerto Rican Port Authority operates daily ferry service to Vieques and Culebra from the Fajardo ferry terminal at Puerto Real (Carr. 195, 787/863-0705, or 787/863-4560).

The **passenger ferry** is primarily a commuter operation during the week and can often be crowded—especially on the weekends and holidays. Reservations are not accepted, but you can buy tickets in advance. Arrive no later than one hour before departure. Sometimes the ferry cannot accommodate everyone who wants to ride. The trip typically takes about an hour to travel to Vieques ($4 round-trip) and 1.5 hours to Culebra ($4.50). There is no ferry service between Vieques and Culebra.

Note that ferry schedule is subject to change.

- **Fajardo to Vieques:** Monday–Friday 9:30 A.M., 1 P.M., 4:30 P.M., 8 P.M.; Saturday–Sunday and Monday holidays 9 A.M., 3 P.M., 6 P.M.

- **Vieques to Fajardo:** Monday–Friday 6:30 A.M., 11 A.M., 3 P.M., 6 P.M.; Saturday–Sunday and Monday holidays 6:30 A.M., 1 P.M., 4:30 P.M.

- **Fajardo to Culebra:** Daily 9 A.M., 3 P.M., 7 P.M.

- **Culebra to Fajardo:** Daily 6:30 A.M., 1 P.M., 5 P.M.

There is also a weekday **cargo/car ferry** from Fajardo that goes between Culebra and Fajardo, for which reservations are required. But be aware that most car-rental agencies in Puerto Rico do not permit their automobiles to leave the main island. The best option is to leave your car in Fajardo and rent another car on Culebra. The trip usually takes about 2.5 hours, and the cost is $15 for small vehicles and $19 for large vehicles. The schedule is as follows:

- **Fajardo to Vieques:** Monday–Friday 4 A.M., 9:30 A.M., 4:30 P.M.

- **Vieques to Fajardo:** Monday 6 A.M., 1:30 P.M., 6 P.M.

- **Fajardo to Culebra:** Monday, Tuesday, and Thursday 4 A.M. and 4:30 P.M.; Wednesday and Friday 4 A.M., 9:30 A.M., 4:30 P.M.

- **Culebra to Fajardo:** Monday, Tuesday, and Thursday 7 A.M. and 6 P.M.; Wednesday and Friday 7 A.M., 1 P.M., 6 P.M.

Marinas

Fajardo's main commercial marina is **Marina Puerto Real** (Carr. 195, 787/863-2188). This is where the Puerto Rican Port Authority operates daily ferry service to Vieques and Culebra.

Other marinas include the tony **Villa Marina Yacht Harbour** (Carr. 987, km 1.3, Fajardo, 787/863-5131, fax 787/863-2320, gerente@villamarinapr.com, www.villa marinapr.com); **Puerto Del Rey** (Carr. 3, km 51.4, Fajardo, 809/860-1000 or 809/863-5792); and **Inversiones Isleta Marina** (787/643-2180, luisdiaz@coqui.net), offshore at Puerto Real Plaza, a startling high-rise development surrounded by ocean.

EAST COAST

Naguabo and Humacao

Check out the petite plaza with the umbrella-shaped trees in the town proper of Nagaubo, then go straight to its seaside community off Carretera 3. There's a slightly Mediterranean feel to this friendly little town, which overlooks a large bay and a hilly peninsula dotted with houses that cling to its sides. A long, wide *malécon,* a seawall with a balustrade, lines the ocean side of the road; shops, restaurants, and bars line the other side. Downtown Humacao is much more bustling with shops and restaurants clustered around a shady plaza flanked by a church and *alcadia* (town hall). But the main reason to go is to catch some rays at Balneario Santiago or to pamper yourself in the luxury of Palmas del Mar resort.

SIGHTS

Balneario Santiago (Carr. 3, km 72.4, Humacao, 787/852-1660 or 787/852-3066,

Mon.–Fri. 7:30 A.M.–3:30 P.M., Sat.–Sun. and Mon. holidays 7:30 A.M.–5 P.M., $3 cars, $2 motorcycles, $4 vans, $5 buses, camping $25–40) is a great stretch of publicly maintained beach and vacation center with a swimming pool featuring a big waterslide, modest overnight accommodations, camping facilities, bathrooms, and picnic shelters. Adjacent to the balneario, along about km 68.3, is a large shady **wilderness beach** that is unfortunately heavily littered and crawling with feral dogs. On the weekends you can find vendors there selling beverages, trinkets, oysters, and other food items. From here you can see **Cayo Santiago,** also known as Monkey Island because of the large population of rhesus monkeys placed there for safekeeping by animal researchers. Visitors are not allowed on the island, but they're welcome to dive and snorkel around its edges and watch the primates from a distance.

Reserva Natural de Humacao (Carr. 3, km 74.3, Humacao, 787/852-6058, Mon.–Fri. 7:30 A.M.–3:30 P.M.; Sat.–Sun. and Mon. holidays 7:30 A.M.–6 P.M. May–Aug.; Sat.–Sun. and Mon. holidays 7:30 A.M.–5:30 P.M. Sept.–Apr., free) is a lovely natural reserve containing 3,186 acres of swamps, marshes, channels, and an interconnected lagoon system perfect for kayaking. There are also six miles of walking and bike trails. Sights along the way include an antique water-pumping station and bunkers constructed during World War II. Tour outfitters Water Sports & Ecotours operates out of the reserve, offering walking tours for $3.50 per person and kayak rentals for $10 per hour per person.

Iglesia Dulce Nombre de Jesus (3 Ave. Font Martelo, Humacao, 787/852-0868), located on the main plaza in downtown Humacao, is a Spanish colonial–style church built in 1793.

Museo Casa Roig (66 Calle Antonio Lopez, Humacao, 787/852-8380, fax 787/850-9144, www.uprh.edu/~museocr, Wed.–Fri. and Sun. 10 A.M.–4 P.M.) is a museum and cultural center operated by the University of Puerto Rico in Humacao. It was originally a private home built in 1919 by Antonin Nechodoma, a student of the Frank Lloyd Wright style of architecture.

SPORTS AND RECREATION

Palmas del Mar Country Club (Palmas del Mar, Country Club Dr., Humacao, 787/285-2255, www.palmasdelmar.com) has two 18-hole, 72-par courses: Golf Club was built in 1974 by Gary Player, and Flamboyan, considered one of the island's most challenging, is a newer course designed by Rees Jones. There are also tennis courts, an equestrian center, an enormous pool, a fitness center, and a modest spa.

Sea Ventures Palmas Dive Center (110 Harbour Dr., Palmas del Mar, Humacao, 787/781-8086 or 787/739-3483, seaventures@ divepuertorico.com, www.divepalmasdelmar .com) offers daily two-tank dives in the morning and snorkeling trips in the afternoon. There are more than 35 dives sites in the area,

including overhangs, caverns, reefs, and tunnels. It also goes to Cayo Santiago.

Rancho Buena Vista (Palmas Dr., Palmas Del Mar Resort, Humacao, 787/479-7479, www.ranchobuenavistapr.com) is an equestrian center offering horseback riding on the beach and pony rides for children.

Water Sports & Ecotours (Reserva Natural de Humacao, Carr. 3, km 74.3, Humacao, 787/852-6058, Mon.–Fri. 7:30 A.M.–3:30 P.M.; Sat.–Sun. and Mon. holidays 7:30 A.M.–6 P.M. May–Aug.; Sat.–Sun. and Mon. holidays 7:30 A.M.–5:30 P.M. Sept.–Apr.) offers walking tours for $3.50 per person and kayak rental for $10 per hour per person in the 3,186-acre reserve.

ENTERTAINMENT

Casino Real at Palmas de Mar (Four Points By Sheraton, 170 Candelero Dr., Palmas del Mar, 787/850-6000, daily 10 A.M.–2 A.M.) is a modest 7,000-square-foot casino with slot machines, blackjack, roulette, and Texas hold 'em.

ACCOMMODATIONS

Palmas del Mar (Carr. 3, km 86.4, Humacao, 787/852-8888, www.palmasdelmar.com) is a 2,700-acre planned community that includes residential and resort developments.

Sheraton Four Points Hotel & Casino (170 Candelero Dr., Humacao, 787/850-6000, fax 787/850-6001, www.starwoodhotels.com, $240–314 s/d) operates the 107-room hotel, featuring all the amenities one would expect from a Sheraton. Attractions include more than three miles of beach, a casino, an 8,000-square-foot pool, a 200-slip marina, two golf courses, tennis courts, a fitness center, a spa, an equestrian center, and 18 restaurants. For vacation rentals in Palmas del Mar, visit www.prwest.com. Police, fire, postal, banking, and medical services are all available at Palmas del Mar.

◀ **Casa Cubuy Eco Lodge** (Carr. 191, km 22, Naguabo, 787/874-6221, fax 787/874-4316, www.casacubuy.com, $90–115 s/d plus 9 percent tax, includes breakfast, 2-night minimum) is a small low-key lodge on the quiet, less visited southern side of El Yunque. Perched on a hill above a gurgling stream, this is definitely the place to go to get away from it all. Amenities are few (no TV!) beyond balconies and hammocks. But you're a short hike away from waterfalls and a natural pool where you can take an invigorating dip. You can buy sack lunches for $7, and dinner is served if six or more guests request it by 1 P.M. ($18 per person). In-room massages are available.

Centro Vacacional de Humacao Villas Punta Santiago (Carr. 3, km 72.4, Punta Santiago, Humacao, 787/622-5200, www.parquesnacionalespr.com, $65–71 cabanas, $109–115 villas, 2-night minimum) is a government-maintained and operated vacation center patronized almost exclusively by Puerto Ricans but open to anyone looking for basic economical accommodations on the ocean. The gated property features a yellow-and-adobe-colored complex containing 99 cabanas and villas. Only the villas are air-conditioned, but both cabanas and villas have full kitchens. Linens, towels, and cooking utensils are not provided. Amenities include tennis courts, a playground, a pool with a waterslide, and lovely shady grounds featuring almond trees, palms, and *flamboyans*.

FOOD

Chez Daniel (Palmas del Mar, Anchor's Village Marina, Humacao, 787/850-3838, fax 787/285-2330, chezdaniel@libertypr.net, www.chezdanielpalmasdelmar.com, Wed.–Sun. 6:30–10 P.M., closed June, $27–35) is an award-winning upscale fine-dining restaurant serving French cuisine with a Caribbean twist. Grilled duck breast, bouillabaisse, and Dover sole are among its specialties. It also has an extensive wine list. Dine inside or outside overlooking the marina. Check out the massive Sunday brunch buffet ($42 per person).

Los Makos Restaurant (Carr. 3, Nagaubo Playa, Naguabo, 787/874-2353, Tues.–Wed. 11:30 A.M.–8 P.M., Thurs. and Sun. 11 A.M.–10 P.M., Fri.–Sat. 11 A.M.–midnight, $10–40) is a large modern restaurant with dining indoors and out, and a separate bar. It specializes in seafood, and its big seller by far is the local lobster, served in salads, soups, creole sauce, charbroiled, in garlic butter, or "Makos" style, accompanied by octopus, conch, and shrimp.

Yabucoa, Maunabo, and Patillas

Often bypassed by visitors, Yabucoa, Maunabo, and Patillas are quiet, low-key, seaside municipalities in the southeastern corner of Puerto Rico that offer a tranquil getaway from the crowds, traffic, and American influence found elsewhere on the island. Nevertheless, the area is home to several small well-maintained hotels and restaurants that serve travelers who aren't looking for a lot of excitement or nightlife.

Unlike the island's southwestern corner, the vegetation here is emerald-green thanks to the convergence of several rivers from the Cordillera Central. In Maunabo, the Cordillera Central descends into the Caribbean Ocean, creating lovely views where the mountains meet the sea. Maunabo was once the domain of Carib Indians and pirates, but along with Patillas, it is primarily an agricultural community today, producing everything from cattle to grapes. Yabucoa was once integral to Puerto Rico's sugar production during the industry's heyday. At one time it had six sugar mills in operation. Today it is a manufacturing center, producing electronics, clothing, and cigarettes. Unfortunately, it's also home to an unsightly oil refinery that mars the view of its coast.

SIGHTS

The primary reason to visit the area is for its long stretches and private pockets of deserted beaches gently lapped by the Caribbean Sea. The most popular one is **Playa Punta Tuna**

(Carr. 760, km 3, Maunabo), where the low-lying hills of the Cordillera Central kiss the sea. In addition to a nice wide mile-long beach and great surfing, this is where you'll find picturesque Faro de Punta Tuna, a lighthouse perched atop a hilly point that juts into the water.

Other beaches in Maunabo are **Los Bohios** (Carr. 760, Bordaleza), which offers a wonderful view of the Punta Tuna lighthouse and great surfing, and **Los Pinos** (Carr. 901), northwest of Playa Punta Tuna. **Playa Lucia** (Carr. 901, km 4) is a small beach in Yabucoa.

Faro de Punta Tuna (follow the signs from Carr. 760, Maunabo, 787/861-0301, Wed.–Sun. 9 A.M.–4 P.M., free) is a neoclassical-style lighthouse built in 1863. Stop by the office for information on the history of the lighthouse and the surrounding community, available in English and Spanish, then stroll the shady 0.25-mile path toward the octagonal tower high on a cliff offering 180-degree views of the ocean and mountains.

ENTERTAINMENT AND EVENTS

If you want something to do besides loll around on the beach all day, visit during festival time when things get lively. In Maunabo, the big draw is **Festival Jueyero,** a celebration that fetes the land crab, held in late September in the town plaza on Calle Santiago Iglesia. All sorts of crab dishes are on the menu, as are a parade, crab races, and more. Maunabo is also home to **Fiestas del Pueblo,** a town celebration held in late June in the plaza featuring music, dance, rides, games, and food kiosks. Yabucoa has a **Patron Saint Festival,** held in late September through early October in Parque Felix Millan, to commemorate Saint Angeles Custodios.

ACCOMMODATIONS

Hotel Parador Palmas de Lucia (Carr. 901 at Carr. 9911, Playa Lucia, Yabucoa, 787/893-4423, www.tropicalinnspr.com, $119 s/d, includes breakfast and snacks) is a modern motel-style property with a petite pool and a small

sandy beach half a block away. It has 34 simple, comfortable rooms featuring air-conditioning, satellite TV, refrigerators, microwaves, coffee-makers, and balconies. There's a restaurant on-site serving breakfast, lunch, and dinner.

Lucia Beach Villas (Carr. 99011 at Carr. 901, Yabucoa, 787/266-1111 or 787/266-1716, www.luciabeachvillas.com, $152 for 2 people, $185 for 4, $250 for 6) is a newly constructed, modern townhouse-style complex of 15 connected units located in a remote spot where you can see the mountains meet the sea. The two-story units with loft-style bedrooms feature air-conditioning, satellite TV, Wi-Fi, full kitchens, 1.5 baths, and a pool with a dramatic backdrop that features a natural waterfall that trickles down the mountain behind it. Each unit sleeps up to six people. There's no restaurant on-site, but a secluded public beach is located right across the street.

Costa del Mar Guest House (Carr. 901, km 5.6, Yabucoa, 787/266-6276 or 787/893-6374, fax 787/893-6374, www.tropicalinnspr.com, 2-night stay $359 for 2 people, $55 for 3, and $570 for 4, includes breakfast) is a new property with 16 units, 12 of which overlook the ocean (although there is no beach access). Amenities include air-conditioning, satellite TV, balconies, a pool, and a basketball court.

Caribe Playa Beach Resort (Carr. 3, km 112, Patillas, 787/839-6339, fax 787/839-1817, www.caribeplaya.com, $130 s/d plus tax) is a bit of a misnomer. It's too small, modest, and low-key to qualify for what most people think of when they think of a resort. Instead, it is quaintly old-fashioned, intimate, casual, and quiet. The pale yellow and white motel-style structure hugs the coastline so closely that you can practically hear the waves lapping the beach from the bed. The 27 units are simply furnished and come with air-conditioning, satellite TV, refrigerators, and coffee makers. Wi-Fi is available in common areas. The grounds are lushly landscaped and appointed with grills, shady hammocks, umbrella tables, and lounge chairs. The seaside Ocean View Terrace serves three meals a day.

Parador Caribbean Paradise (Carr. 3, km

114.3, Patillas, 787/839-5885, fax 787/271-0069, www.caribbeanparadisepr.com, $80–99) is a motel-style facility with 24 rooms. Rooms come with air-conditioning, cable TV, and a coffeemaker. Amenities include a swimming pool, tennis courts, and basketball courts.

FOOD

Gemelo y Su Rumba (Carr. 981, km 4.3, Yabucoa, 787/585-6284, Mon.–Thurs. 9 A.M.–9 P.M., Fri.–Sun. 9 A.M.–midnight, $1–18) is a casual open-air bar and restaurant serving exceptional empanadas during the week and fresh fish specials Thursday through Sunday. The owner, Leftie, is a musician, and he turns the place into a lively music venue on Sundays when crowds flock there for the live salsa music and dancing that goes on throughout the day.

Restaurante El Nuevo Horizonte (Carr. 901, km 8.8, Yabucoa, 787/893-5492, fax 787/893-3768, Wed.–Thurs. 11 A.M.–8 P.M., Fri.–Sat. 11 A.M.–10 P.M., Sun. 11 A.M.–8 P.M., $12.95–28.95) offers inside dining on seafood and Puerto Rican cuisine while enjoying the ocean view from high up on a mountain peak. Outside is a kiosk serving empanadas and other Puerto Rican–style fritters and beers.

Palmas de Lucia (Hotel Parador Palmas de Lucia, Carr. 901 at Carr. 9911, Playa Lucia, Yabucoa, 787/893-4423, www.tropicalinnspr.com, Sun.–Thurs. 8 A.M.–9 P.M., Fri.–Sat. 8 A.M.–10 P.M., $11–17) serves three meals a day. Lunch consists of burgers, ribs, and chicken fingers, but dinner specializes in a variety of fresh seafood, including halibut, shrimp, and lobster, as well as Puerto Rican dishes such as *mofongo* and *asopao*.

AquaMar Steakhouse & Seafood (Carr. 901, km 1.7, Maunabo, 787/861-1363, Mon.–Wed. 11 A.M.–10 P.M., Thurs.–Sun. 11 A.M.–11 P.M., $12–34) is a contemporary, dressy-casual restaurant serving Angus and Kobe beef, seafood, pasta, and exotic meats, including ostrich, buffalo, and boar. It also boasts a large selection of wines.

Café Terraza Panaderia y Respoteria (11 Ave. Calimano, Maunabo, 787/861-3375, daily 7 A.M.–11 P.M., $2–5) serves everything you could want, from whole baked chickens and Puerto Rican cuisine to pastries and sandwiches. There is also a small market selling cold drinks and dry goods.

Los Bohios (Carr. 760, km 2.3, Maunabo, 787/861-2545, Wed.–Sun., $10–18) is a casual open-air restaurant overlooking the ocean that serves Puerto Rican cuisine, seafood, and steaks.

Open daily and serving three meals a day is the small seaside **Ocean View Terrace** (at Caribe Playa Beach Resort, Carr. 3, km 112, Patillas, 787/839-6339, fax 787/839-1817, www.caribeplaya.com, daily 8 A.M.–10:30 A.M., noon–3 P.M., and 6–9:30 P.M., reservations required for dinner, $14–19), which specializes in continental and Puerto Rican cuisine. The menu includes pasta, whole fried snapper, and *mofongo*.

EAST COAST

SOUTH COAST

The south coast stands in stark contrast to Puerto Rico's north coast. Instead of lush, rocky coastlines, rough Atlantic waters, mountainous karst country, and a dense population, the south coast features a flat, dry topography, the calm waters of the Caribbean, and considerably less development. It's a great place to go if you want to escape the traffic and American influence found elsewhere on the island. And there are many great historic and cultural sights to explore.

Historically, the south coast was a major player in the island's sugar industry. It was once dotted with enormous sugarcane plantations, as well as sugar refineries, rum distilleries, and shipping operations. As that industry died out, the south coast turned its economic development toward the manufacturing of goods,

although it hasn't come close to restoring the area to the level of wealth it once enjoyed.

Ponce is the south coast's biggest city, and what a city it is. It has a large, lovely central plaza that bustles with activity night and day, and it rivals San Juan as the island's cultural, historical, and architectural center. Home to the founders of Don Q rum, Ponce was once a very wealthy city, which is apparent in its many beautiful buildings, museums, and elaborate festivals.

The natural jewel of the south coast is undoubtedly Bosque Estatal de Guánica, on the western end. The 10,000-acre subtropical dry forest is reminiscent of the American Southwest, with its dry, sun-bleached soil and plenitude of cacti that create a stark but lovely landscape on the Caribbean. It is also home to a couple of beautiful beaches and some great

© SUZANNE VAN ATTEN

HIGHLIGHTS

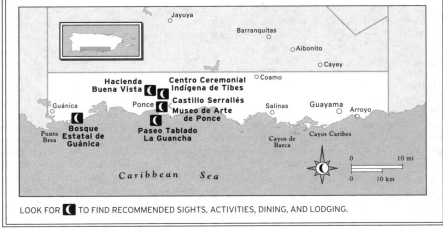 **Bosque Estatal de Guánica:** The 10,000-acre subtropical dry forest and United Nations Biosphere Reserve features hiking trails, caves, beaches, the ruins of a Spanish fort, and great bird-watching opportunities (page 95).

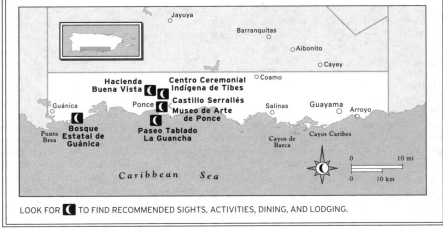 **Centro Ceremonial Indígena de Tibes:** Discovered in 1975, this site just a couple of miles north of the city of Ponce was once the ceremonial grounds to two indigenous groups, the Igneri, who lived in the region from 300 B.C. to A.D. 600, and the Pre-Taínos, who inhabited the island from A.D. 600 to 1200. The site contains several ceremonial *bateyes* (ball fields), plazas, and petroglyphs (page 101).

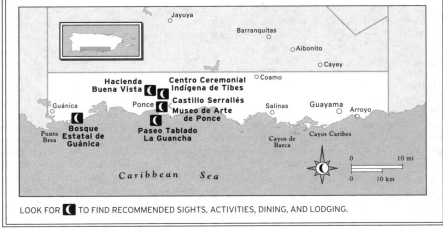 **Museo de Arte de Ponce:** In addition to its impressive collection of Italian baroque and British pre-Raphaelite work, the museum contains a solid collection of work by Puerto Rican artists (page 102).

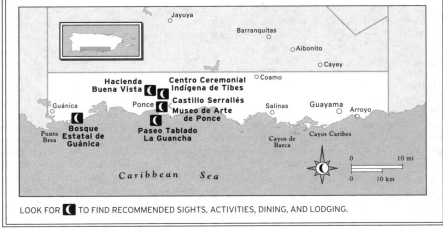 **Castillo Serrallés:** An elaborate Spanish Revival mansion built in 1934 atop El Vigía Hill overlooking the city of Ponce and the Caribbean Sea. It was built for Eugenio Serrallés, a major player in the local sugar-cane industry and founder of Serrallés Rum Distillery, maker of Don Q rum (page 102).

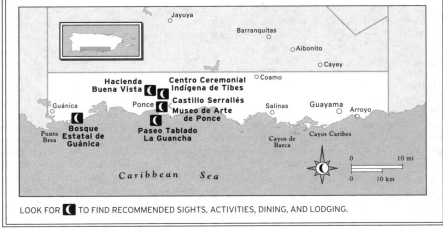 **Hacienda Buena Vista:** Reservations are required to take the two-hour tour of this restored 19th-century coffee plantation in the municipality of Ponce (page 104).

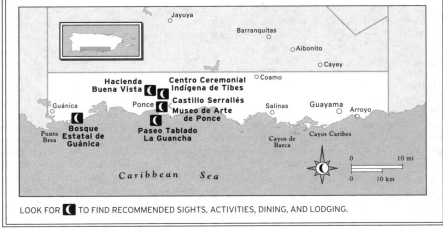 **Paseo Tablado La Guancha:** This modern new waterfront development in Ponce features a panoramic seaside boardwalk, lots of bars and restaurants, and a huge playground for children (page 105).

LOOK FOR 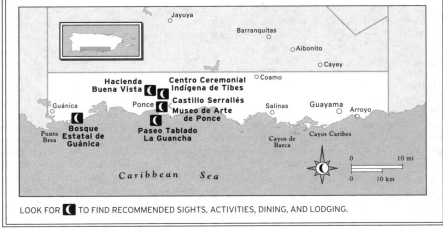 TO FIND RECOMMENDED SIGHTS, ACTIVITIES, DINING, AND LODGING.

snorkeling sites. Although there is some dispute as to where Christopher Columbus first set foot on the island in 1493, the majority of experts agree that it was probably in Guánica.

The south coast's other well-known natural site is Baños de Coamo, a natural hot springs near the center of the region. Believed to contain restorative powers, Baños de Coamo has been a tourist attraction since colonial times. Despite the fact the south coast is on the Caribbean, it's not particularly known for its beaches, but there are a couple of noteworthy ones, particularly Gilligan's Island and Balneario Caña Gorda in Guánica.

The south coast was home to a significant Taíno Indian community, established in the 1200s, that stretched from Guánica to Ponce. At the time of Columbus's arrival, its chief was

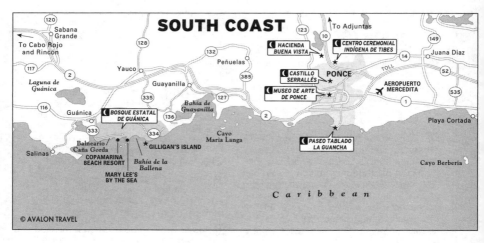

SOUTH COAST

Cacique Agüeybaná, who is believed to have been the island's most powerful leader at that time. But the south coast's indigenous history predates the Taíno culture. Just north of Ponce, Centro Ceremonial Indígena de Tibes is one of Puerto Rico's most significant historical sites. Many ceremonial ball fields, plazas, and petroglyphs have been discovered on this site, which archaeologists have attributed to Pre-Taíno and Igneri cultures that date back as far as 300 B.C.

The southeastern corner of Puerto Rico is the least populated part of the island. Aside from a couple of nice beaches, its sights are few. But it's a good place to go if you want to get away from it all, and you can find some terrific seafood restaurants in the fishing village of Salinas.

PLANNING YOUR TIME

Most of the south coast is conveniently connected by multilane divided highways—Highway 2 west of Ponce, and toll roads Highway 52 and Highway 53 east of Ponce. Highway 52 also connects San Juan to the south coast near Salinas. Traffic along the south coast is generally pretty light, so all in all, getting around the area is fairly easy.

The farthest point from San Juan is Guánica, which is 94 miles away and takes about two hours to drive. Although doable as a day trip, you'll want to get an early start so you can spend as much time as possible at **Bosque Estatal de Guánica,** a beautiful and unique wilderness preserve with great hiking trails, beaches, and snorkeling spots. Better yet, stay in one of several unique accommodations in the area and spend the weekend to get the most out of your visit.

The same can be said of Ponce, which is 79 miles away from San Juan and takes about 1.5 hours to drive. You can get there and back in a day, but you'd be hard-pressed to see it all. Better to stay a weekend or longer, so you're sure to have time to visit the Indian grounds at **Centro Ceremonial Indígena de Tibes;** the city's impressive **Museo de Arte de Ponce;** the castle-like former home of the Don Q founder, the **Castillo Serrallés;** the former coffee plantation **Hacienda Buena Vista;** and the new waterfront development, **Paseo Tablado La Guancha.**

Salinas, on the other hand, is close enough to drive down from San Juan just for dinner at one of its many stellar seafood restaurants.

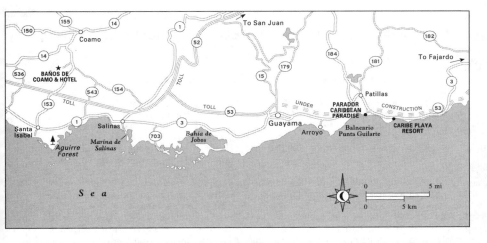

Guánica

Christopher Columbus is believed to have first disembarked on the island of Puerto Rico at Bahía de Guánica in 1493. At that time, Guánica was the indigenous capital of the island, led by the culture's most powerful Taíno Indian, Cacique Agüeybaná. Guánica also played a role in the Spanish-American War when it was fired on by the USS *Gloucester* and surrendered to U.S. troops in 1898.

Guánica is so completely different from the rest of Puerto Rico that you'd think you were on a whole other island. The flat, dry, desert-like landscape is so unusual, in fact, that a large part of the municipality has been designated a United Nations Biosphere Reserve in an effort to preserve and study its unique environment. Called Bosque Estatal de Guánica, the 10,000-acre reserve contains hiking trails, caves, beaches, and the ruins of a Spanish fort, among other sights. There are also great snorkeling and diving along its coast.

Guánica also has a burgeoning tourism infrastructure featuring several interesting accommodations varying from a quaint, funky B&B to an all-luxury resort.

◖ BOSQUE ESTATAL DE GUÁNICA

The primary draw for visitors to Guánica is the astounding landscape of Bosque Estatal de Guánica (Carr. 334, 787/821-5706, 787/724-3724, or 787/721-5495, Mon.–Fri. 7 A.M.–4 P.M., Sat.–Sun. 8:30 A.M.–4 P.M., free). This 10,000-acre subtropical dry forest sits atop petrified coral reefs millions of years old and features a variety of environments. On the southern side you'll find the dry scrub forest, featuring sun-bleached rocky soil, cacti, and stunted, twisted trees. There are also patches of evergreen forest along the upper eastern and western parts of the forest, where you can find Spanish moss, mistletoe, bromeliads, and orchids.

The rest of the forest has deciduous growth, where 40 percent of the trees lose their leaves between December and April. Agave and *campeche* trees, a source of red and black dye once exported to Europe for hundreds of years, are common to the area. Other flora among the forest's 700 species includes prickly pear cactus, sea grape, milkweed, mahogany, and yucca. Be sure to avoid the poisonous *chicharron,* a shrub

NATIONALIST HERO: DON PEDRO ALBIZU CAMPOS

Dr. Pedro Albizu Campos has been dead since 1965, but the beloved nationalist leader lives on in the memory of Puerto Ricans everywhere. Nearly every town in Puerto Rico has a street or school named after him, and on the side of a building on Calle San Sebastían in Old San Juan, local artist Dennis Mario Rivera has memorialized him with a stunning graffiti portrait, helping make Campos a pop-culture icon among Puerto Ricans akin to Che Guevara in other Latin American countries.

Born in Ponce in 1891, Campos was a brilliant man who was fluent in eight languages and earned five degrees at Harvard University – in law, literature, philosophy, chemical engineering, and military sciences. So how did a man with such a promising future end up spending the last 25 years of his life in and out of prison? By leading the charge for Puerto Rico's independence from the United States.

Campos was reportedly not anti-American, nor was he communist. But he passionately believed that the 1898 Treaty of Paris, which ended the Spanish-American War, wrongfully gave the United States sovereignty over Puerto Rico. After all, Spain had granted autonomy to Puerto Rico in 1897. The island had established its own currency, postal service, and customs department. It's hard to deny Campos's belief that Spain had no authority to bequeath the island to the United States.

Nevertheless, the island did become a property of the United States, and Campos even went on to serve as a first lieutenant in the U.S. Infantry during World War I. After he was discharged, he completed his studies at Harvard and returned to Puerto Rico, where he joined the Nationalist Party in 1924.

A gifted orator, Campos traveled throughout the island, as well as the Caribbean and Latin America, seeking support for the independence movement with such eloquent speeches that he was nicknamed El Maestro. And he was eventually elected president of the Nationalist Party. Although the Nationalist Party fared poorly in local elections, during the next six years Campos kept the movement in the forefront of political discourse by staging a protest at the San Juan capitol, implicating the U.S.-based Rockefeller Institute in the deaths of patients who were the subject of medical testing without their consent, and by serving as legal representation for striking sugarcane workers.

The beginning of Campos's downfall came in 1935, when four Nationalists were killed by police under the command of Colonel E. Francis Riggs in an event referred to as the Río Piedras Massacre. The next year, two nationalists killed Riggs, a crime that resulted in their being arrested and executed without trial. That same year, the federal court in San Juan ordered the arrest of Campos and several other Nationalists on the grounds of seditious conspiracy to overthrow the U.S. government in Puerto Rico. A jury trial found him innocent, but a new jury was ordered and Campos was found guilty. The verdict was upheld on appeal, and Campos was sent to the federal penitentiary in Atlanta.

Campos returned to Puerto Rico in 1947 and is believed to have become involved in a plot to incite armed struggle against the United States. Three years later, two nationalist attacks – one on La Fortaleza, the governor's residence in San Juan, and one on Blair House, the temporary home of President Harry Truman – led to Campos's rearrest, conviction, and imprisonment for sedition. His imprisonment at La Princesa in Old San Juan was marked by a serious decline in his health, which he attributed to radiation experiments performed on him without his consent.

Governor Luis Muñoz Marín pardoned Campos in 1953, but the pardon was overthrown when there was another attempted attack made on the U.S. House of Representatives. In 1964, Marín successfully pardoned Campos, who was by then a sick and broken man. A year later he died of a stroke in Hato Rey. More than 75,000 Puerto Ricans reportedly joined the procession that carried Campos's body to his burial in Cementerio de Santa María Magdalena de Pazzis, Old San Juan's historic cemetery.

Although the independence movement still has little political clout in Puerto Rico today, Campos is revered as a man who gave his life for liberty – an ideal the island has never fully achieved.

with reddish piney leaves that can irritate the skin on contact.

Guánica is of special interest to bird-watchers. More than 80 species have been identified here, including the pearly-eyed thrasher, a variety of hummingbirds, the Puerto Rican mango, and the Puerto Rican nightjar, a bird that nests on the ground and remains nearly motionless all day until dusk. Other species of wildlife include the crested toad, a variety of geckos and lizards, land crabs, and green and leatherback turtles. Mongooses are also present in the area, having been introduced to the island many years ago to kill rats on the sugar plantations. The vicious little varmints are to be avoided at all costs.

There are 36 miles of trails in the forest. From the main entrance off Carretera 334, follow the long narrow road to the information center, where you'll find the trailheads and where you can obtain trail maps and tips from the helpful English-speaking rangers. Among the most popular hikes are a 3-mile, 1.5-hour hike to the ruins of **Fuerte Capron**, once a lookout tower for the Spanish Armada and the site of an observation tower built by the Civilian Conservation Corps in the 1930s; a 40-minute loop trail ideal for bird-watching; a 35-minute hike to see the ancient Guayacán tree (300 or 1,000 years old, depending on the source); and a 2-hour hike to underground caves, which requires special permission from the information center and accompaniment by a guide.

If you're planning to hike in the forest, be sure to wear sturdy shoes or hiking boots and bring a hat, insect repellent, sunscreen, and plenty of fresh drinking water.

Should you prefer a drive-by tour of Bosque Estatal de Guánica, take the breathtakingly beautiful **scenic route Carretera 333,** which starts in the town of Guánica and traverses eastward along the southern rim of the forest. The curvy road snakes up the side of a steep incline that grows thick with cactus and bougainvillea. When the road crests, prepare yourself for a stunning bird's-eye view of the ocean and Bahía de Guánica. Continue eastward and

you pass the ruins of a Spanish lighthouse on the left, and on the right is **Area de Pesca Recreativa,** a shady remote patch of beach and a fishing spot with no facilities except for one picnic shelter. The road leading to the recreation area is bumpy and deeply rutted, but it is possible to travel without a four-wheel drive if you proceed with caution.

Continue eastward along Carretera 333 and you encounter **Balneario Caña Gorda** (Carr. 333, km 5.8), a large, modest, shady public beach with bathrooms, covered picnic shelters, a roped-off swimming area, and a wheelchair-accessible area. The facilities are fairly worn but well maintained. There are also a basketball court and lots of parking.

Next on the route is Punta San Jacinto, where you can catch a **ferry** (Carr. 333, 787/821-4941, Tues.–Sun. during high season and Fri.–Sun. during low season, 9 A.M.–5 P.M., every hour on the hour, $5) to **Gilligan's Island,** a small *cayo* just a few hundred yards offshore featuring a huge shallow lagoon of aquamarine water perfect for swimming and lots of great snorkeling and diving spots. It was tagged Gilligan's Island by the local tourist trade as a marketing gimmick, and the name caught on.

Carretera 333 ends at **Bahía de la Ballerna,** a lovely sandy beach area and a great snorkeling and diving spot known as Submarine Gardens.

SPORTS AND RECREATION

Sea Ventures Dive Copamarina (Copamarina Beach Resort, Carr. 333, km 6.5, 800/468-4553 or 877/348-3267, www.divecopamarina .com, daily 9 A.M.–6 P.M.) runs day and night dive excursions ($65–119) to sites including the 22-mile-long Guánica Wall, the Aquarium, and the Parthenon, a coral formation featuring a variety of sponges. Daily snorkeling excursions go to Gilligan's Island, Cayo Coral Reef, and Bahía de la Ballerna ($55 including equipment). Certification courses are offered. Also available are kayak, catamaran, and paddleboat rentals.

San Jacinto Boats and Seafood (Carr. 333, 787/821-4941) rents sea kayaks and equipment for diving and snorkeling. It also operates a ferry to Gilligan's Island every hour on the hour Tuesday–Sunday (high season) 9 A.M.–5 P.M. or Friday–Sunday (low season) for $5. Dine on fresh seafood dishes while you're there.

ACCOMMODATIONS
$100-150

€ **Mary Lee's by the Sea** (off Carr. 333, first road on right just past the Copamarina Beach Resort tennis courts, 787/821-3600, fax 787/821-0744, www.maryleesbythesea.com, $100–250 plus $10 per additional person) is unlike any guesthouse in Puerto Rico—maybe the world! This bright, cheerful, sprawling guesthouse has a distinctive bohemian style reflective of its unique owner, Mary Lee, who came to Puerto Rico 50 years ago on a diving trip and never left. Each of the 11 rooms is different, but they all share two things: wall-to-wall thick straw mats and tons of hand-sewn curtains, bedspreads, and furniture upholstery made by the owner and her daughters, which gives the place a pleasant 1970s-era Southern California vibe. Rooms vary from small single units that sleep four ($100) to an enormous three-bedroom apartment with a living room, dining room, and furnished porch ($250). Each unit has some form of kitchen, whether it's a cleverly efficient "closet kitchen," a kitchenette, or a full kitchen. The grounds are basically a series of funky, small courtyards and seating areas with a lovely a view of Gilligan's Island. There is a small dock, kayak rentals, and boat rides to Gilligan's Island, as well as swimming at the beach at Bahía de la Ballena. Rooms have air-conditioning, but no phones; small TVs are available for rent. There is weekly maid service and laundry facilities on-site. Be sure to book early: Mary Lee's by the Sea has a high return rate of regulars who come here every year.

Guánica Parador 1929 (Carr. 3116, km 2.5, Ave. Las Veteranos, 787/821-0099, www.Guanica1929.com, $102 s/d, plus $20 per additional guest, plus 7 percent tax) is a two-story Spanish colonial–style structure built in 1929 as Hotel Americano. Recently restored and reopened, Guánica Parador feels brand-new despite its history. What it lacks in landscaping, it makes up for in bright comfortable furnishings and modern facilities. Rooms come with cable TV and air-conditioning, but no phone. There are a small pool and restaurant on the grounds, but no bar. The property is part of a small, locally owned and well-run chain.

Over $200

€ **Copamarina Beach Resort** (Carr. 333, km 6.5, 787/821-0505 or 800/468-4553, fax 787/821-0070, info@copamarina.com, www.copamarina.com, $235–285 s/d, $400 suite, $1,000 villa, plus 9 percent tax and 7 percent resort fees) is a secluded full-service luxury resort featuring large comfortable rooms appointed with lovely, thick pine furniture, Dutch doors, and plantation windows that look out over the water. There is an excellent white-linen restaurant, Alexandra's, serving seafood and Puerto Rican cuisine, as well as a casual waterside eatery and bar, Las Palmas. The beautifully landscaped beachfront grounds feature two pools, two children's pools, two whirlpool baths, lighted tennis courts, and a lovely white-sand beach with a pier and a small boat dock. Other amenities include a spa and a fitness room. Sea Ventures Dive Copamarina is an on-site snorkeling and dive operator, which also offers water taxi service taking guests to nearby Gilligan's Island. All-inclusive packages are available starting at $398 a night.

FOOD

Restaurante Alexandra (Copamarina Beach Resort, Carr. 333, km 6.5, 800/981-4676, U.S. tel. 800/468-4553, daily 6–10 P.M., $19–32) is that rare thing in Guánica: an upscale fine-dining establishment. The lovely enclosed ocean-side restaurant features floor-to-ceiling windows hung with long sheer white curtains that set an elegant, romantic mood for your meal. The menu serves classic continental and New American cuisine, including osso bucco and pan-seared duck breast in port wine mango sauce.

San Jacinto Boats and Restaurant (Carr.

333, 787/821-4941, daily 3–10 P.M., $8–25) is a rustic fish-camp kind of establishment in a rambling old two-story white clapboard building overlooking the water. The restaurant serves seafood Puerto Rican–style, including *mofongo* stuffed with lobster or shrimp, octopus salad, and fried whole fish, as well as steak and pork chops. Outside there is a small walk-up kiosk where water-sports enthusiasts can grab an *empanadilla* on their way to Gilligan's Island.

Festival del Juey, held in mid- to late June in the town of Guánica, celebrates the crab with a variety of local dishes made from the crustacean.

Ponce

Ponce is like a grand dame who has deteriorated a bit through the years but still maintains a shabby elegance that harks back to a gilded past when wealth, culture, and social graces were the glue that held society together.

An economic and cultural rival to San Juan, Ponce experienced great growth and wealth during the 18th and 19th centuries thanks to its international shipping trade, which brought in an influx of European immigrants who established lucrative rum distilleries and many coffee and sugar plantations in the area. All that wealth translated into the construction of hundreds of gorgeous, ornate homes and buildings that combine rococo, neoclassical, and Spanish Revival architectural elements with traditional *criolla* building styles, distinguished by broad balconies, large doorways, and open-air patios. At the city's core was built Plaza de Las Delicias, an enormous plaza anchored by a massive fountain, Fuentes de Leones, and the impressive Catedral de Nuestra Señora de Guadalupe.

HISTORY

Ponce's rich cultural life gave birth in the mid-1800s to a unique form of romantic classical music called *danza*. A melding of Caribbean and European styles, the formally structured musical style is often described as an Afro-Caribbean waltz and was typically performed on piano and *bombardino* (similar to a trombone) to accompany dance. As with early rock and roll, conservatives disapproved of the new style because it encouraged couples to dance too closely. But it was eventually embraced by the whole island. In fact, Puerto Rico's national anthem, "La Borinqueña," was originally written as a *danza*. The form is still celebrated today with Ponce's annual Semana de la Danza festival.

The good times continued to roll for a while in Ponce. In 1882 the much ballyhooed Exposition-Fair was held in Plaza de Las Delicias to celebrate and cultivate the city's standing as a cultural and agricultural center. Several pavilions were built, including a Moroccan-style structure, no longer standing, that contained a bazaar and hosted children's dances. Another structure built for the fair was the startling black-and-red-striped structure known today as the Parque de Bombas, which later became the city's fire station and now houses the local tourism office. Many more tents and stalls filled the plaza displaying local produce, flora, and fauna. Horse races were held in the streets, and concerts, plays, and literary readings were held at Teatro La Perla.

But by the turn of the 20th century, the tides began to turn for Ponce. When the United States took control of the island in 1898, new trade restrictions choked the city's shipping industry. Sugar prices fell, sending that industry into decline, and hurricanes destroyed the coffee plantations. By the time the Depression rolled around, Ponce began to spiral into a severe economic decline from which it has never fully recovered.

Further demoralizing the social fabric of the city was an event in 1937 referred to as the Ponce Massacre, in which 19 people were gunned down during a demonstration by

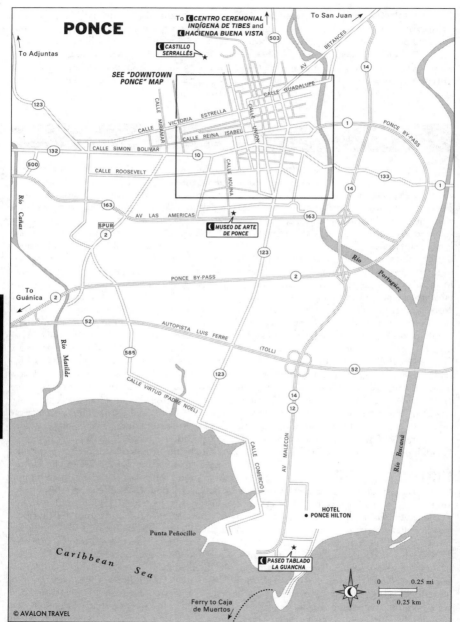

PONCE

To ((*CENTRO CEREMONIAL INDÍGENA DE TIBES* and ((*HACIENDA BUENA VISTA*

To San Juan

((CASTILLO SERRALLÉS ★

To Adjuntas

SEE "DOWNTOWN PONCE" MAP

123

132

500

Río Cañas

Calle Mirkmar

Calle Victoria Estrella

Calle Reina Isabel

Calle Simon Bolivar

Calle Roosevelt

Calle Union

Calle Guadalupe

Calle Molina

10

AV BETANCES

14

1

PONCE BY-PASS

133

1

SPUR
2

163

AV LAS AMERICAS ★

((*MUSEO DE ARTE DE PONCE*

163

123

14

2

PONCE BY-PASS

2

Río Portugués

To Guánica

2

Río Matilde

52

585

AUTOPISTA LUIS FERRE

123

(TOLL)

52

14
12

CALLE VIRTUD (PADRE NOEL)

Calle Comercio

AV Malecon

Río Bucaná

HOTEL
● PONCE HILTON

Punta Peñocillo

Caribbean   Sea

★
((*PASEO TABLADO LA GUANCHA*

Ferry to Caja
de Muertos

0   0.25 mi

0   0.25 km

© AVALON TRAVEL

SOUTH COAST

members of the island's Nationalist Party seeking independence from the United States. Two hundred people were injured in the melee, including many women and children.

Today Ponce is still an economically depressed city, and many of its fabulous buildings are vacant, abandoned, and falling into serious disrepair. But steps are being taken to turn things around. In the early 1990s, millions of dollars were earmarked to revitalize the city, and much of the area around Plaza de Las Delicias has been restored. The plaza is lined with many thriving businesses, including banks, hotels, bars, tourist shops, cafés, and fast-food restaurants. During the day, sidewalks are filled with shoppers, tourists, and street vendors selling everything from fresh flowers to hot dogs. At night there are often live concerts and lots of teenagers and lovers sitting on park benches, eating ice cream and parading along the sidewalks. In addition, a new recreational facility called La Guancha was recently built near the harbor, and it has infused the tourist industry with some much-needed enthusiasm. And in 2005, JetBlue began flying direct from New York City's JFK airport into Ponce's Aeropuerto Internacional Mercedita.

Unfortunately, Ponce is plagued with a high level of street crime; therefore armed police in flak jackets can be seen patrolling the plaza at night, and venturing on foot beyond a two-block radius outside the plaza after dark is ill-advised. Dark vacant streets and homeless people asking for handouts are what you'll find there. Asked how best to keep on the safe side when in Ponce, a knowledgeable source advises to avoid the illegal drug trade and take care not to romance someone who's already spoken for.

Another word of caution: If you're traveling by car, beware of Ponce drivers. They're arguably the worst on the island. They roll through stop signs, run red lights, cut off merging traffic, block intersections, pass illegally, and blow their cars horns continuously.

Nevertheless, Ponce is full of many charms that are well worth taking a few extra precautions to enjoy.

SIGHTS
◖ Centro Ceremonial Indígena de Tibes

In 1975 the remains of two native civilizations were discovered a couple of miles north of Ponce on what is now called the Centro Ceremonial Indígena de Tibes (Carr. 503, km 2.5, 787/840-2255, www.nps.gov/nr/travel/prvi/pr15.htm, Tues.–Sun. 9 A.M.–4 P.M., except when holidays fall on Mon., then Wed.–Mon., $2, $1 children and seniors, $3 parking). The Igneri reigned over the region from 300 B.C. to A.D. 600. On the same location, a Pre-Taíno culture thrived from A.D. 600 to 1200. Excavation of the site is still under way, but among the structures uncovered and restored are seven *bateyes,* or ball fields, and two rectangular stone-rimmed ceremonial plazas, around which you can spot faint petroglyphs carved into the rock.

The vegetation is rich with many of the same plants used by native cultures for medicinal and other purposes, including the *cohoba* tree (its red berries were used to induce hallucination and communication with the gods), the calabash tree (its gourd-like fruit was hollowed out and dried to make bowls), and the *mavi* tree (its bark was used to make a fermented drink).

A small museum contains artifacts from both cultures found on the site, including *cemis,* amulets, vomit spatulas, *dujos* (stools), idols, necklaces, a mortar and pestle, flints, blades, and stone collars. In addition, there are the human remains of a woman, possibly sacrificed, found among 187 bodies discovered buried under one of the *bateyes.* There's also a gift shop selling literature about the native cultures and traditional crafts made by local artisans.

Don't be misled by the re-creation of a Taíno village on the site. That culture is not known to have inhabited this land, but it's interesting to see how the *bohío* (a conical wood and straw hut inhabited by commoners) and *caney* (a rectangular wood and straw structure where the cacique leaders lived) were constructed.

© SUZANNE VAN ATTEN

re-creation of a Taíno village at the Centro Ceremonial Indígena de Tibes near Ponce

◖ Museo de Arte de Ponce

It's closed until mid-2010 for expansion and renovation, but Museo de Arte de Ponce (2325 Ave. Las Americas, 787/848-0505 or 787/840-1510, map@museoarteponce.org, www.museoarteponce.org, hours and admission TBA) is a major player among Puerto Rico's cultural attractions. It contains an impressive collection of more than 3,000 pieces of European, North American, and Puerto Rican art from the 14th century to the present. In addition to its renowned collection of Italian baroque and British Pre-Raphaelite work, Puerto Rican artists are also represented with works by painters José Campeche (1759–1809) and Franciso Oller (1822–1917), as well as photographer Jack Delano (1914–1997), a member of a distinguished group of photographers who worked for the Farm Security Administration during the Depression and documented the island's people and places for more than 50 years.

The most celebrated piece in its collection is *Flaming June,* an 1895 classicist painting of a slumbering woman in a brilliant orange gown

by Briton Lord Fredric Leighton. It may seem an unlikely symbol of Ponce's cultural heritage, but once you witness the power of the large gilt-framed painting in the Museo de Arte de Ponce, you can begin to understand why the image has not only been plastered on coffee cups, T-shirts, and mouse pads in the museum store but has been appropriated by local contemporary artists who've taken the liberty of altering her image in various ways, including wrapping her in the Puerto Rican flag.

While the museum is closed, portions of its permanent collection are on view in rotating exhibitions at MAP@PLAZA (Plaza Las Americas, 525 Ave. F. D. Roosevelt, Hato Rey, San Juan, 787/200-7090, Wed.–Fri. 9 A.M.–1 P.M., $5 adults, $2.50 seniors, students, and children under 12). *Flaming June* is temporarily on exhibit in Europe until the renovations are complete.

◖ Castillo Serrallés

Set high on a hill overlooking Ponce is a startling reminder of the height of the city's flourishing sugar industry, when its port was the

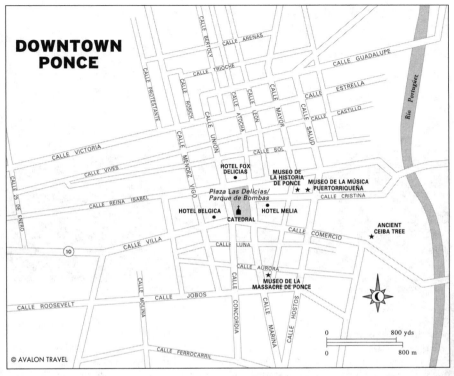

DOWNTOWN PONCE

CALLE BERTOLY
CALLE ARENAS
CALLE TRIOCHE
CALLE GUADALUPE
CALLE PROTESTANTE
CALLE ROSICH
CALLE UNION
CALLE LEON
CALLE ATOCHA
CALLE MAYOR
CALLE SALUD
ESTRELLA
CALLE CASTILLO
Río Portuguét
CALLE VICTORIA
CALLE VIVES
MENDEZ VIGO
CALLE SOL
HOTEL FOX DELICIAS ●
MUSEO DE LA HISTORIA DE PONCE ★
MUSEO DE LA MÚSICA PUERTORRIQUEÑA ★
CALLE REINA ISABEL
Plaza Las Delicias/ Parque de Bombas
CALLE CRISTINA
CALLE 25 DE ENERO
HOTEL BELGICA ●
CATEDRAL
HOTEL MELIA ●
ANCIENT CEIBA TREE ★
CALLE COMERCIO
CALLE VILLA
(10)
CALLE LUNA
CALLE AURORA
★ MUSEO DE LA MASSACRE DE PONCE
CALLE ROOSEVELT
CALLE MOLINA
CALLE JOBOS
CALLE CONCORDIA
CALLE MARINA
CALLE HOSTOS
0   800 yds
0   800 m
CALLE FERROCARRIL
© AVALON TRAVEL

busiest on the island. Castillo Serrallés (17 Calle El Vigía, 787/259-1774, 787/259-1775, or 800/981-2275, fax 787/259-3463, castserr@ coqui.net, www.castilloserralles.org, Tues.– Thurs. 9:30 A.M.–5 P.M., Fri.–Sun. 9:30 A.M.– 5:30 P.M., gardens $2, $1 students and seniors; gardens and castle $5, $2.50 students and seniors) was built in 1934 for Eugenio Serrallés, a leader in the local sugarcane industry and founder of the still-operating Serrallés Rum Distillery, maker of the island's premier rum, Don Q.

Designed by architect Pedro Adolfo de Castro, the four-story Spanish Moroccan– style mansion was last inhabited in 1979 by Serrallés's daughter. It became a museum in 1991.

The house contains many of the Serrallés family's original furnishings, many of them made by Puerto Rican craftsman or imported from Europe, the oldest piece being a small 16th-century table in the foyer. No cost was spared in the construction of the house. The parquet wood floor in the parlor was imported from Brazil, and the dining room, which took 18 months to build, features a painted, hand-carved ceiling made of oak, mahogany, and ceiba woods, and the black-and-cream bathrooms are designed in an art deco style. The building was technologically advanced for the times: It even has an intercom system with 14 receivers as well as an elevator. In the kitchen is a 1929 GE side-by-side refrigerator that still works. One room in the house has been converted into an exhibition space that explains and illustrates sugarcane processing and rum-making.

Across the street from Castillo Serrallés is

© SUZANNE VAN ATTEN

Castillo Serrallés, a Spanish Revival mansion on a hill overlooking Ponce

Cruceta del Vigía ($6, $3 students and seniors, includes admittance to Castillo Serrallés and the gardens), an enormous concrete cross with an observation deck built in 1984. It marks the site of a Spanish lookout station established in 1801 to watch over the Ponce harbor. At that time, a crude wooden cross was erected on the site that remained there until it was destroyed in 1998 by Hurricane Georges. The cross was used as a flag-signaling system to alert troops to the arrival of merchant ships in the harbor. If a white flag was raised, it meant the harbor was under possible attack.

◖ Hacienda Buena Vista

Hacienda Buena Vista (Carr. 10, km 16.8, 787/722-5882 or 787/284-7020, fax 787/722-5872, www.fideicomiso.org, Fri.–Sun. except holidays, two-hour tours start at 8:30 A.M., 10:30 A.M., 1:30 P.M., and 3:30 P.M., reservations required, $7 adults, $4 children under 12) is a carefully restored 19th-century coffee plantation just north of Ponce and part of the network of historic sites operated under the auspices of the Conservation Trust of Puerto Rico.

Established in 1833, Hacienda Buena Vista was one of the most successful of the 50 plantations around Ponce. It was founded by a Venezuelan, Salvador de Vives, who started out as a small cash-crop farmer growing corn, plantains, yams, pineapples, and coffee. Eventually he added a corn mill, a rice husker, a cotton gin, and a coffee depulper to the operation. As Puerto Rico's coffee industry boomed, so did Hacienda Buena Vista, due in large part to the labor of as many as 57 slaves.

When the island's coffee industry went bust in 1897, the plantation was converted into orange groves and remained operational until the 1950s, when the land was expropriated by the Puerto Rican government and distributed in small lots to local farmers. Termites destroyed most of the original buildings, and the farm machinery was left to rust for many years, but in 1984 the Conservation Trust of Puerto Rico began an extensive restoration project using 19th-century construction techniques.

In addition to the restored structures, mill, and machinery, the plantation's lush natural setting is worth a visit. On the Canas River, the property features mature vegetation filled with a variety of birds, including the mangrove cuckoo and Puerto Rican screech owl, as well as plenty of *coqui* and lizards.

◖ Paseo Tablado La Guancha

Commonly called La Guancha (end of Carr. 14 south), this brand-new waterfront facility compensates for the fact that although Ponce is on the coast, little of it is suitable for recreational use.

At first glance, the development isn't too welcoming. There are acres of asphalt parking and an enormous characterless park with tons of playground equipment and picnic tables yet not a lick of shade. Venture farther seaward, though, and you'll find a lovely wide boardwalk along the water that is lined with large pink-and-green matching pavilion-style buildings that house a variety of restaurants and bars. There are also an observation tower and clean, well-maintained bathroom facilities.

Things get particularly lively on the weekends. During the day you can catch a ferry to Caja de Muertos, five miles offshore, for swimming and snorkeling. And at night, families, teenagers, and couples flock here to parade up and down the boardwalk, feeding the fish and stopping in one of the many establishments for some refreshment.

Plaza de Las Delicias

Plaza de Las Delicias (bounded by Calles Isabel, Atocha, Union, and Simon Bolívar) is a bustling Spanish colonial plaza surrounded by many lovely 19th-century buildings, many of them containing banks, but there are also a couple of bars and lots of fast-food joints. Although it looks like one large plaza, Plaza de Las Delicias is in fact composed of two smaller plazas: Plaza Degetau and Plaza Luis Muñoz Rivera. Together they create what appears to

SOUTH COAST

© SUZANNE VAN ATTEN

Paseo Tablado La Guancha, Ponce's new waterfront development

be the central gathering spot for all of Ponce, especially on the weekends.

During the day the sidewalks along Calle Isabel and Calle Atocha are lined with dozens of brightly colored umbrellas, under which vendors sell hot dogs, silk flowers, lottery tickets, gift wrap by the yard, electronics, sneakers, jewelry, and more. At night, live bands give concerts, attracting multigenerational families, troupes of preening teenagers, and love-struck couples who stake out cuddling corners on park benches.

The plaza contains two enormous fountains, including the elaborate Fuentes de Leones (Fountain of Lions). This is also where you'll find the stunning **Catedral de Nuestra Señora de Guadalupe** (787/842-0134, office Mon.–Fri. 9 A.M.–1:30 P.M., services Mon.–Fri. 7 A.M., 9 A.M., 12:05 P.M., Sat. 7 A.M., 4 P.M., 7 P.M., Sun. 7 A.M., 9 A.M., 11 A.M., 4 P.M., 7 P.M.), a gorgeous French neoclassical–style edifice reconstructed in the 1930s and featuring two bell towers, stone tile floors, and a sky-high arched ceiling painted a robin's-egg blue and hung with 20 crystal chandeliers. Check out the stunning religious statuary, including one of Mary dressed in a pale blue robe with a gold halo above her head, and the bloodied body of Christ in a glass coffin.

But by far the most exceptional structure in Plaza de Las Delicias is **Parque de Bombas** (787/284-3338 or 787/284-4141, daily 9 A.M.–5 P.M., free), a startlingly whimsical black-and-red-striped pavilion built in 1882 to provide exhibition space for the Exposition-Fair of Ponce. A year later it became home to the city's fire station. Today it is a museum honoring the history of the city's firefighters. It contains portraits of past fire chiefs, exhibits of fire helmets, hats, axes, and hose nozzles, and it also serves as the tourism office for the city. Lots of travel brochures on sights in the area and an interactive electronic display board provide directions and hours of operation for many of the city's sights.

Hanging around Plaza de Las Delicias at night is probably not a good idea, if the armed police in bulletproof jackets who patrol it after dark are any indication.

Museums

Museo de la Música Puertorriqueña (Calle Isabel at Calle Salud, 787/290-6617 or 787/848-7016, www.icp.gobierno.pr/myp/museos/m15.htm, Tues.–Sun. 8:30 A.M.–4:20 P.M., $1) is a tribute to the rich history of Puerto Rican music in a lovely neoclassical home built in 1912 for the Serrallés family, founders of the Serrallés Rum Distillery. Designed by architect Alfredo Wiechers Pieretti of Ponce, the home's stained-glass windows, stone tiles, and brass-embossed walls are reason enough to tour the museum.

Each room is dedicated to a different musical style and the vintage instruments used to create it. In the *danza* room are cellos, violins, and French horns; in the salsa room are bongos, bells, maracas, trumpets, trombones, timbales, and *güiros* (gourds); in the *bomba y plena* room are tambourines, *güiros,* and accordions. There's also a room devoted to Taíno ceremonial instruments, including a drum made from a tree trunk, wooden maracas, conch shell horns, flutes made of royal palm and bamboo, and ocarinas (seeds made into flutes). Another room is devoted to the art of making bongos from wooden barrels. Free classes in bongo-making are held in June and July.

Museo de la Historia de Ponce (53 Calle Isabel, corner of Calle Mayor, 787/844-7071 or 787/842-7042, Tues.–Sun. 9 A.M.–5 P.M., free) is more than just a monument to the city's history. Its construction served to preserve and adapt two historic neoclassical homes, Casa Salazar and Casa Zapater, and thanks to the addition in 1998 of the Ernesto Ramos Antonini auditorium, it is a cultural center for the local arts community. Permanent exhibits focus on ecology, pre-Hispanic times, politics, economic development, and architecture. Wall text and information are in Spanish only. A separate museum, **Museo de la Massacre de Ponce** (corner of Calle Marina and Calle Aurora, 787/844-9722, Tues.–Sun. 8 A.M.–4:30 P.M., free), has a very modest exhibit in Spanish dedicated to the memory of a bloody incident on Palm Sunday in 1937 when local police were ordered to fire on Puerto

Rican Nationalists demonstrating for Puerto Rico's independence from the United States. Nineteen people were killed and more than 200 were injured.

Ancient Ceiba Tree

Puerto Rico's national tree, the ceiba, plays an important role in Puerto Rico's environment. Its massive ridged trunks were carved into canoes by the Taíno Indians, and its tall umbrella-shaped branches rise to 150 feet, high above the forest canopy, where it provides a habitat for birds, tree frogs, and insects. It is also host to many aerial plants, including bromeliads.

To see Ponce's 300-year-old ceiba tree, travel west from Plaza de Las Delicias on Calle Comericio (Carr. 133) and turn left on Avenida La Ceiba just before you get to Highway 12. The massive gnarled trunk and thick canopy stand in majestic defiance of the surrounding urban blight that threatens to crowd it out.

Isla Caja de Muertos

Isla Caja de Muertos is a small uninhabited island five miles south of Ponce accessible by ferry (Sat.–Sun. and holidays 9 A.M.–5 P.M.) from La Guancha in Ponce. There are hiking trails through the island's interior, which is a semiarid forest containing a variety of cactus. There are also a cave to explore, a lighthouse built in 1887, and a one-of-a-kind underwater snorkeling trail.

SPORTS AND RECREATION

Island Venture Water Excursions (La Guancha, 787/842-8546, www.islandventure pr.com) offers transportation to Caja de Muertos for $20, $25 with lunch; two-tank diving excursions for $65 with lunch; and snorkeling excursions for $35 with lunch). On Friday and Saturday nights it offers sunset tours of the bay from La Guancha.

If you've got your own boat, **Ponce Yacht and Fishing Club** (787/842-9003 or 787/840-4388, fax 787/844-1300, nautico@ coqui.net) is a full-service marina with an enormous activities pavilion, including a bar and restaurant (seafood and Puerto Rican cuisine,

daily noon–10 P.M.). Visiting boaters who pay a dockage fee can use the facilities (showers, cafeteria, restaurant, bar). Registration at the office (Mon.–Fri. 8 A.M.–5 P.M., Sat. 8 A.M.–3 P.M.) is required.

Acampa Adventure Tours (1211 Ave. Piñero, San Juan, 787/706-0695, info@acampa pr.com, www.acampapr.com) offers tours to Isla Caja de Muertos on a 37-foot sailing catamaran that include hikes and snorkeling. It departs from La Guancha pier in Ponce.

Costa Caribe Golf and Country Club (Ponce Hilton Golf and Casino Resort, 1150 Ave. Caribe, 787/812-2675, 787/848-1000, or 787/259-7676, www.costacaribe-resort.com, www.ponce.hilton.com) is a 27-hole course designed by Bruce Besse on what was once sugarcane fields. It offers spectacular views of the Caribbean and Puerto Rico's central mountain region. The signature hole is number 12, featuring an island green.

Complejo Turistico El Tuque (3330 Ponce Bypass, Carr. 2, km 220.1, 787/290-2000, fax 787/290-2002, administration@eltuque.com, www.eltuque.com,) is a one-stop spot for family fun. The **Speed and Splash Water Park** (June–Aug., $15 adults, $13 children under 12) has a variety of water rides and a wave pool, complete with lifeguards, plus there are a surf shop, a video-game arcade, tube and locker rentals, and a food court. This is also the site of the newly opened **Ponce International Speedway Park** (open Tues. and Thurs.), commonly called La Pista's Tuque, where drivers in the local drag racing circuit compete. The on-site **Hotel El Tuque** (787/290-2000, hotel@ eltuque.com, www.eltuque.com, $65 and up plus tax) is a modern budget motel with a pool and sports bar.

ENTERTAINMENT AND EVENTS
Festivals

Río de Janeiro's celebration may be the world's most famous, but Ponce's **Carnaval** is no slouch. In February, during the five days preceding the first day of Lent, Plaza de Las Delicias is filled with festivities. Elaborate masquerade dances and parades are held each day, during which revelers show off their elaborate costumes and play out a symbolic battle between the Christians and the Moors. Traditional costumes include caballeros, who represent Spanish knights, *vejigantes* (horned entities), who represent the Moors, as well as the evil trickster spirits of the *viejos* (old men) and *locas* (crazy women).

In dramatic contrast to the frivolity of Carnaval is **Las Mañanitas** (787/841-8044). Every December 12 beginning at 5 A.M. a religious procession marches from Calle Lolita Tizol to Plaza de Las Delicias. Leading the way are a band of mariachis who sing songs honoring the city's patron saint, Our Lady of Guadalupe.

Semana de la Danza (787/841-8044) features a weeklong series of events celebrating *danza*, a turn-of-the-20th-century ballroom dance that originated in Ponce, and one of its most beloved composers, Juan Morel Campos. Held mid- to late May, the festival features conferences, concerts, parades, and dance competitions.

Feria de Turismo de Puerto Rico (787/287-0140) is an annual tourism fair held in late April at Paseo Tablado La Guancha from noon until midnight. Municipalities around the island represent themselves with their traditional foods, music, and crafts. There are also exhibits representing the island's hospitality industry.

In early April, Ponce hosts **Las Justas,** a massive athletic event that started as an intercollegiate track and field competition but now embraces all varieties of sporting events, including swimming, baseball, basketball, judo, table tennis, and cheerleading. Each year the event attracts more than 100,000 people, drawn as much by the athletic competition as by the nightly concerts featuring the island's biggest reggaetón stars. If this isn't your thing, stay far away from Ponce during Justas. Many businesses, including restaurants and hotels, not only close down but board up their windows; the heavy-drinking crowds are known to get rowdy.

Nightlife

The nightlife in Ponce appears to be pretty limited. There are two casinos in Ponce. **Ponce Hilton and Casino Resort** (1150 Ave. Caribe, 787/259-7676, fax 787/259-7674, www.ponce.hilton.com, 10 A.M.–4 A.M.) is a 7,000-square-foot casino with 230 slot machines plus blackjack, craps, roulette, Caribbean stud poker, Texas hold 'em, and three-card poker.

Holiday Inn and Tropical Casino (3315 Ponce Bypass, 787/844-1200, open 24 hours) is a 9,800-square-foot casino with 339 slot machines plus blackjack, craps, roulette, let it ride, poker, three-card poker, and triple shot.

A restaurant by day, **Restaurante Rincon Argentino** (69 Calle Salud at Calle Isabel, 787/284-1762, rinconargentinoponce@hotmail.com, daily) turns into an impromptu party spot for the young professional set later in the night. You can get some pretty good food too.

Hollywood Café (Carr. 1, km 125.5, 787/843-6703, Wed.–Mon. 6 P.M.–late) is a popular upscale sports bar and restaurant for the young meet-and-greet party set serving wings and other typical pub fare and a full bar. Inside are pool tables and loud music, and outside there's a patio. There is live Latin music on the weekends.

SHOPPING

Paseo Atocha is a pedestrian part of Calle Atocha between Calle Isabel at Plaza de Las Delicias and Calle Vives. The sidewalk is lined by a variety of shops selling shoes, clothing, jewelry, electronics, discount housewares, sewing notions, and tourist trinkets. On weekends, Friday–Sunday, the sidewalk fills with street vendors selling flowers, lottery tickets, gift wrap and cards, sewing notions, tourist trinkets, and more.

Pick up a bag of locally grown coffee roasted on the premises of **Café Mayor** (2638 Calle Mayor at Calle Aurora, 787/812-1941, Mon.–Fri. 8 A.M.–5 P.M. Three roasts are available, but the French roast is the best.

Mi Coqui (9227 Calle Marina, facing Plaza de Las Delicias, 787/841-0216,

© SUZANNE VAN ATTEN

Paseo Atocha is a great place for shopping and people watching.

daily 9 A.M.–7 P.M.) is a two-level wonder. Downstairs is a large, densely packed trinket shop where you can find some low-end, locally made crafts, as well as bottles of rum and bags of coffee. But request access to go upstairs and you'll find a large gallery filled with original artwork, both traditional and contemporary, including oil paintings; *vejigante* masks; and the highly collectible Santos, small hand carved saints.

Utopia (14 Calle Isabel, 787/848-5441, fax 787/813-9899, daily 7 A.M.–6 P.M.) is a huge souvenir and import gift shop selling T-shirts, jewelry, and beachwear. There's also a small lunch counter serving coffee and sandwiches.

ACCOMMODATIONS

Several new hotels were under development as this book went to press. A historic building right on Las Delicias Plaza is being transformed into the 70-unit Ponce Plaza Hotel. It was slated to open in summer 2008 but is behind schedule. Meanwhile, the former Intercontinental Ponce, which closed in 1985, is being developed as the Magna Vista Resort.

In addition to 120 rooms, two restaurants, tennis courts, and a pool, plans include a casino and convention center. It will reportedly open in 2009, but construction projects in Puerto Rico often lag behind projections.

If you're looking for cheap accommodations in Puerto Rico, Ponce is the place to go. There are several in historic buildings around Plaza de Las Delicias, although attempts to modernize them on a budget have rendered them all into hodgepodges of old and new.

Hotel Melia (75 Calle Cristina at Plaza de Las Delicias, 787/842-0260 or 800/44-UTELL—800/448-8355, fax 787/841 3602, melia@coqui.net, home.coqui.net/melia, $95 s, $115 d, $130 for rooms with balconies and refrigerators, plus 9 percent tax, includes a modest continental breakfast) was established in 1900 as a world-class European-style hotel. Thankfully, the outdated circa-1970s rehab of the lobby has been banished, replaced with tasteful dark wood paneling, attractive ceiling detail, and all-new furnishings. The renovated rooms have the budget-corporate look of a business traveler's motel, but this hotel still retains a hint of the elegance that distinguished it in its glory days. Rooms come with air-conditioning, phones, satellite TV, Wi-Fi, and bathtubs (a rarity!). There are also a pool, a business center with two computers and free Internet access, laundry service, and room service. Hotel Melia is home to Mark's, one of Ponce's finest restaurants.

Hotel Fox Delicias (6963 Calle Isabel on Plaza de Las Delicias, 787/290-5050, fax 787/259-6413, www.hotelfoxdelicias.com, $75–86 s, $114 d, $125–135 suite, plus tax) is a bit of an oddity, but it offers the best bang for the buck if you don't mind the sterility of the place. The hotel is in what was once a lovely art deco theater. Although the exterior has been carefully restored and maintained, the interior has undergone a total redo. Before it was a hotel it was a shopping mall, and the first level retains that look—complete with escalators that carry guests to their rooms on the second floor. Upstairs are 30 clean, windowless, corporate-style rooms with air-conditioning, cable TV, telephones, room service, and excellent mattresses. There are a couple of two-bedroom units available.

Hotel Belgica (122 Calle Villa, 1 block off Plaza de Las Delicias, 787/844-3255, hotelbelgica@yahoo.com, www.hotelbelgica.com, $65 s, $85 d) has been a continuously operating hotel since its construction in 1872. The 20 very clean, simple rooms all have air-conditioning, satellite TV, and no telephones. Some rooms have shared balconies for no additional cost. Rooms have been recently furnished with pleasant Pier 1–style furnishings featuring brown basket weave and wrought-iron furniture. Rooms without windows have large mirrors tricked up with shutters and flower boxes to create a window effect, and all the bathrooms are modern. The hallways feature lovely patterned stone tile floors, while linoleum covers the floors in the rooms. There is no restaurant or bar on-site. If they're available, ask for rooms 9 or 10—they're the nicest of the bunch.

FOOD

◖ Mark's at the Melia (Hotel Melia, 75 Calle Cristina at Plaza de Las Delicias, 787/284-6275,

daily noon–3 P.M. and 6–10 P.M., $14–28) is not your typical hotel restaurant. The decor is fairly nondescript, but the low lighting and Rat Pack–era music helps create a classy, sophisticated vibe. The attentive Old World–style service makes every guest feel like a VIP, of which this restaurant has no doubt seen many. The menu features seafood and continental cuisine, as well as a few fancified renditions of traditional Puerto Rican dishes. Specialties include lobster saffron risotto, pan-roasted duck breast, rack of lamb, and an impressive cheese course. The huge old-fashioned wilted spinach salad with hot bacon dressing is highly welcomed, considering the scarcity of veggies served at most Puerto Rican restaurants. The excellent warm crusty bread is a treat too. There are also a full bar and an excellent wine list.

The waterfront development known as La Guancha is lined with a variety of dining spots, including **El Paladar Bar and Grill** (Paseo Tablado de La Guancha, 787/267-4491 or 787/842-1401, daily 11 A.M.–11 P.M., $11.50–19.95). The casual eatery serves traditional Puerto Rican cuisine with an emphasis on fish, such as fried *chillo* (snapper) and *dorado* (mahimahi), *asopao* stews, and rice dishes. The restaurant is in a large pavilion with enclosed dining downstairs and an open-air bar upstairs overlooking the boardwalk and marina.

Pito's Seafood Café and Restaurant (Carr. 2, Sector Las Cucharas, 787/841-4977, fax 787/259-8328, Sun.–Thurs. 11 A.M.–11 P.M., Fri.–Sat. 11 A.M.–midnight) is a popular stop for tourists, perhaps because it serves something for everyone. Although it specializes in every Puerto Rican seafood dish imaginable, it also offers several beef, pork, and chicken dishes. Trunkfish, a local delicacy, is served here when it's available. The three-level waterside restaurant has open-air dining, an enclosed fine-dining room, and private dining in the wine cellar. The wine list features 25 varieties by the glass from regions around the world. There is live music Fridays and Saturdays.

◖ La Gladiola Café (119 Calle Villa, 787/259-8021, Mon.–Sat. 6 A.M.–4 P.M., Sun. 7 P.M.–1 A.M., $3.50–9) is an authentically vintage café with a European ambiance. The cozy, bustling space features sky-high ceilings and pale yellow walls hung with old black-and-white photos of the island. There's a small bar and table seating where patrons dine on eggs, French toast, pancakes, and breakfast burritos in the morning, and sandwiches, salads, tacos, quesadillas, and burritos stuffed with choice of *churrasco* or chicken for lunch. Dinner specials include traditional Puerto Rican dishes, steak, and the popular chicken cordon bleu. There is a full bar and coffee drinks too.

Restaurante Rincon Argentino (69 Calle Salud at Calle Isabel, 787/284-1762, rinconargentinoponce@hotmail.com, daily 11:30 A.M.–10 P.M., $10–32) is in a lovely Spanish-style hacienda with patio dining enclosed by wrought-ironwork overlooking Calle Salud. The Italian-Argentine menu features grilled meats, fish, and pastas. To get a little taste of everything, order the mixed appetizer platter with croquettes, sausages, empanadas, prosciutto, and Manchego cheese.

((Classic Delights Bakery & Café (3 Calle Marina at Calle Comercio, 787/259-0558, daily 6 A.M.–7 P.M., $1.60–4.99) is a large, cheerful, all-purpose eatery serving everything from breakfast, soup, salads, and sandwiches to smoothies, pizza, lasagna, and a couple of daily Puerto Rican specialties with rice and beans. Three large glass cases contain a wide assortment of cakes, flan, cheesecake, doughnuts, and the traditional Mallorca pastry. On the brightly colored walls are original paintings of Puerto Rican courtyards and seascapes for sale by local artists.

Café Paris (Calle Isabel on Plaza de Degetau, 787/840-1010, Mon.–Sat. 7 A.M.–6 P.M., $4.95 or less) is a modest modern bakery decked out like a Parisian brasserie serving sandwiches and coffee drinks.

Kings Cream (9223 Calle Marina, 787/843-8520, daily noon–midnight, cup $1.25–1.60, pint $2.75, gallon $11.50) is a no-frills operation serving soft ice cream in a variety of flavors for those on the go, as there's no seating on the premises. The fresh fruit flavors are the best.

INFORMATION AND SERVICES

There are two hospitals in Ponce: **Hospital San Lucas I** (184 Calle Guadalupe, 787/840-4545) and **Hospital San Lucas II** (917 Ave. Tito Castro, 787/844-2080). There's a 24-hour pharmacy at **Walgreens** (Ave. Fagot, 787/841-2135). The U.S. **post office** has branches at 93 Atocha (787/842-2997, 787/842-8303, or 787/284-2186) and Carretera 100, km 123.3 (787/812-0206, 787/812-0207, or 787/812-0208).

GETTING THERE AND GETTING AROUND

Plans are underway to expand and renovate **Aeropuerto Internacional Mercedita** (PCE, 787/842-6292, fax 787/848-4715) to better accommodate bigger commercial jets. Currently there are two passenger terminals and one cargo terminal. Jet Blue offers direct flights to Ponce from JFK airport in New York City and from Orlando, Florida. All other U.S. airline companies go through San Juan's Aeropuerto Internacional Luis Muñoz Marín, where you can catch a plane to Ponce on one of several daily flights by Cape Air.

There is no public transportation service available from the airport, but you can catch a taxi waiting at the airport. There are several car-rental agencies at the airport, including Avis, Hertz, L&M, and Budget.

In central Ponce, it's fairly easy to wave down a taxi. You can also call **Abolition Taxi Cab** (787/843-0187), **Best Union Taxi Cab** (787/840-9126 or 787/840-9127), **Borinquen Taxi Cab** (787/843-6000 or 787/843-6100), and **Ponce Taxi Méndez** (787/842-3370 or 787/840-0088).

Ponce is a great place to spend a few days, but because this beautiful, culturally rich city is pocketed with economically depressed areas that can sometimes be unsafe, a car is recommended. Just be aware that Ponce drivers represent an old-school Caribbean style of driving that's less apparent in the rest of the island. Stop signs and traffic lights are more suggestion than law. Intersections can be a free-for-all, and horns are constantly blaring—often nanoseconds after a traffic light has turned from red to green.

SOUTH COAST

Coamo and Salinas

COAMO

The town of Coamo is a modest little village in the hilly terrain just south of the island's majestic Cordillera Central mountain range. The compelling reason to venture here is not for the town but for its nearby claim to fame, the Coamo Baños, a natural hot springs reputed to have restorative powers.

Sights

Baños de Coamo (end of Carr. 546, daily 8 A.M.–6 P.M., free) may well be Puerto Rico's very first tourist attraction. The hot springs, which retain a constant 110°F temperature and which are rich in minerals, were first discovered by the Taíno Indians, who shared their find with the Spanish colonists. By the mid-16th century, a steady stream of visitors was making its way here, and in the 17th century a resort was built that operated until the 1950s. Wealthy visitors from all over the world visited

Coamo, including the most illustrious U.S. proponent of hot springs himself, President Franklin D. Roosevelt.

The springs look very different today than they did then. The water has actually been contained in two places. One, which looks like a small standard swimming pool, is on the private property of the Hotel Baños de Coamo and is reserved for its guests. The public bath is an easy half-mile hike down a dirt road behind the hotel. Unfortunately, despite the size of the hotel parking lot, visitors to the public bath are forbidden to use it, so it's necessary to park alongside the dead-end road, where local farmers sometimes sell produce from the backs of their trucks.

Until recently the bath was contained in a stone pool, but that structure has since been replaced by a square ceramic-tile enclosure that looks a lot like a giant bathtub set down in the great outdoors. Families with small children and

The natural hot springs of Baños de Coamo have attracted visitors since the mid-16th century.

SOUTH COAST

many elderly folks gather here to relax for hours, bringing with them picnics (no alcohol allowed) and folding tables on which to play dominoes and cards. Whether the springs are truly healing can be debated, but that doesn't stop the clearly infirm who are drawn to the waters.

Dips are limited to 15 minutes at a time, and there is a small rustic changing room on-site.

Sports and Recreation

Coamo Springs Golf Club and Tennis Club (Carr. 153, km 1.5, 787/825-1370, www.coamo springs.com, daily 7 A.M.–7 P.M.) is an 18-hole course designed by Ferdinand Garbin in a residential community that will challenge your ability to golf in the wind.

Maratón de San Blás de Illesca (787/825-1370) is an internationally renowned half marathon held in early February.

Accommodations and Food

Parador Baños de Coamo (end of Carr. 546, 787/825-2186, fax 787/825-4739, hbcoamo@coqui.net, $87 s, $93 d, plus tax) has 46 very basic motel-style rooms on two levels, each with a private balcony. Rooms come with air-conditioning and cable TV and feature stone tile floors, worn furnishings, and institutional-looking bathrooms. But the thick, wild vegetation growing around the property creates a pleasant natural environment. At the center of the complex is a massive, reputedly 500-year-old *saman* tree covered in vines and cactus that shades the entire property. There are two pools, one for swimming adjoined by a bar, and the other containing water from the hot springs.

Aguas Termales (Hotel Banos de Coamo, end of Carr. 546, 787/825-2186 or 787/825-2239, daily 7–10 A.M., noon–3 P.M., and 5:30–9:30 P.M., $7.50–19) serves Puerto Rican cuisine, seafood, and steak.

At the Coamo Springs Golf Club & Resort is the **Coamo Springs Restaurant** (Carr. 153, km 1.5, 787/825-1370, www.coamosprings.com, Thurs. and Sun. noon–9 P.M., Fri.–Sat. 11:30 A.M.–10 P.M., $11–28) is the nicest restaurant in town, serving Puerto Rican cuisine, paella, and *churrasco*.

SALINAS

Despite its new, modernistic plaza featuring metal sculptures fashioned to look like a ship's smokestacks, Salinas is an economically depressed and depressing fishing village with poorly maintained roads, a small marina, and a hotel, which is best avoided. There's really only one reason to visit: to dine at one of the modest seafood restaurants that line the waterfront along Calle Principal.

Sights

Bahía de Jobos Reserva Nacional de Investigación Estuarina (Carr. 705, km 2.3, 787/853-4617 or 787/864-0105, Mon.–Fri. 8 A.M.–noon and 1–4 P.M., Sat. 9 A.M.–noon and 1–3 P.M., alternate Sun.) is a 2,800-acre reserve of mangrove forests and freshwater wetlands, pocketed with lagoons, salt flats, and mud beds. This is a great spot for kayaking, although rentals are not available on-site. Guided tours can be arranged in advance.

Albergue Olímpico (Carr. 712, km 0.3, 787/824-2607 or 800/981-2210, daily 8 A.M.–10 P.M., Sat.–Sun. 10 A.M.–5 P.M.) is the home of Puerto Rico's Olympic training center, with a variety of attractions that include the Puerto Rican Museum of Sports, a botanical garden, and a water park.

Sports and Recreation

Polita's Beach (Carr. 701, Marina de Salinas, $3 to park) is a small scrubby beach where you can rent personal watercraft for $5. There are a snack bar and portable toilets.

Marina de Salinas (end of Carr. 701, 787/752-8484 or 787/824-3185, fax 787/768-7676, jarce@coqui.net) accommodates 103 vessels and provides guests with water, electricity, ice, gas and diesel, private showers, laundry facilities, and a convenience store.

Accommodations

Marina de Salinas Waterfront Inn and Marina (end of Carr. 701, Playa Ward, 787/824-3185 or 787/824-5973, fax 787/768-7676, jarce@coqui.net, www.marinadesalinas.com, $95 s, $115–125 d, $135–175 suite,

© SUZANNE VAN ATTEN

Marina de Salinas

plus 9 percent tax) is a poorly maintained two-level motel-style hotel with thin walls and thinner towels. But you get a modern bath with a shower, air-conditioning, TV, telephone, and coin-operated laundry facilities. Suites come with a microwave and a refrigerator. There is a small pool, a snack bar, and a compact playground for toddlers on-site.

Food

Restaurante Costa Marina (Marina de Salinas, end of Carr. 701, Playa Ward, 787/824-3185, Sun.–Thurs. noon–9 P.M., Fri.–Sat. noon–11 P.M., $10–31.95) is a tastefully decorated, nautical-themed restaurant with round porthole windows overlooking the marina. The extensive menu serves mostly seafood, including whole snapper and lobster. It also serves steaks and traditional Puerto Rican cuisine.

Ladi's (A-86 Calle Principal, Carr. 701, 787/824-2035, Tues.–Fri. 11 A.M.–9 P.M., Sat.–Sun. 11 A.M.–10 P.M., $8–29), an institution for 54 years, is a huge, elegantly casual open-air restaurant just feet from the water. The menu features traditional Puerto Rican cuisine specializing in seafood, including paella, whole snapper, and *mofongo*. The *tostones* are some of the best on the island. Ask for the accompanying sauce, a thin, spicy garlic tomato sauce. It's a much better and more traditional option than the Thousand Island dressing most restaurants serve nowadays. Ladi's offers excellent service and a full bar.

El Balcon del Capitan (A-54 Calle Principal, Carr. 701, 787/824-6210, daily 11 A.M.–10 P.M., $9–27) is a small casual waterfront restaurant. Seated on plastic patio furniture, dine on the large selection of *empanadillas,* stuffed with everything from lobster and beef to octopus and shrimp. Other specialties include lobster and paella. It's very popular among families with young children.

Guayama and Arroyo

GUAYAMA

Guayama features a lovely central plaza, Plaza de Recreo Cristóbal Colón, distinguished by rows of unique umbrella-shaped trees and Iglesia San Antonio de Padúa, a neo-Roman-style church with twin towers. The church's construction was begun in 1827 but wasn't completed until 40 years later. Guayama is home to several significant natural attractions, including two forests and a butterfly reserve, as well as a couple of interesting museums.

Sights

Centro de Bellas Artes de Guayama (Calle McArthur, 787/864-7765 or 787/864-0600, ext. 2306, Tues.–Sat. 9 A.M.–4 P.M., Sun. 10 A.M.–4:30 P.M.) is a new art center in a restored 19th-century building. It contains 11 exhibition galleries devoted to art and history.

Museo Casa Cautiño (1 Calle Palmer, 787/864-9083, Tues.–Sat. 9 A.M.–4:30 P.M., Sun. 10 A.M.–4 P.M.) is on the main plaza in Guayama in a lovely 19th-century neoclassic *criolla*-style home distinguished by an ornately decorated exterior and lacy ironwork. The one-story U-shaped house was built in 1887 and belonged to wealthy landowner General Cautiño Vázquez. During the Spanish-American War, the home served as headquarters for American forces. The home contains the family's original, locally made furnishings and artwork.

Bosque Estatal de Aguirre (Carr. 7710, south of Carr. 3, 787/864-0105 or 787/724-3724, fax 787/853-4617, daily 7 A.M.–3:30 P.M.) is a pristine piece of undeveloped paradise containing mangrove forest, tidal flats, and large populations of birds and manatees. A wooden boardwalk provides easy access. Camping is not allowed.

Reserva Natural Mariposario Las Limas (Carr. 747, km 0.7, 787/864-6037, Thurs.–Sun. 10 A.M.–1 P.M., reservations required) is a wildlife reserve with gardens, walking trails, and butterflies galore.

Recreation and Entertainment

El Legado Golf Resort (Hwy. 52, 787/866-8894, www.ellegadogolfresort.com) is an 18-hole course designed by local legend Chi Chi Rodriguez in a residential condominium community. It includes several lakes, a waterfall, and a putting green shaped like the island.

Club Náutico de Guayama (end of Carr. 7701, 787/866-3162, fax 787/866-3162) is a private marina that accepts visitors.

Feria Dulces Sueños (787/864-7765, fax 787/864-5070) is a Paso Fino horse competition held at the fairgrounds in early March. Other festivities include food kiosks and music.

Fiesta de Reyes (787/864-7765, fax 787/864-5070) is held every year on January 6 to celebrate the traditional Puerto Rican holiday Three Kings Day. The royal pilgrims visit each barrio in the municipality before proceeding to Plaza de Recreo Cristóbal Colón for music, games, and more.

The **tourism office** (787/864-7765, fax 787/864-5070) is on Plaza de Recreo Cristóbal Colón. It operates a free trolley tour from Casa Cautiño or Centro de Bellas Artes to points of interest in the area.

ARROYO

Arroyo is a quiet agricultural community far off the tourist's beaten path, which makes it a pleasant place to visit if you want a peaceful getaway in a low-key, pastoral part of Puerto Rico.

Closed for renovation at press time, **Tren del Sur de Arroyo** (Carr. 3, km 130.9, Arroyo, 787/271-1574, Sat.–Sun. 9 A.M.–4 P.M.) is a nostalgic reminder of the height of Puerto Rico's sugarcane production, when the product was shipped to mills in Arroyo for processing. A section of the railway remains here where visitors can take a 25-minute ride each way through an old sugarcane plantation in historic train cars pulled by a diesel engine.

Also closed for renovation, **Museo Antigua Aduana** (Calle Morse, Arroyo, 787/839-8096, Tues.–Sun.) contains memorabilia from when Samuel Morse himself first brought the telegraph to the island.

Balneario Punta Guilarte (Carr. 3, km 126, Arroyo, 787/839-3565, daily 8 A.M.–4:30 P.M., $2) is a publicly maintained beach with facilities east of Arroyo on the west side of Puerto Patillas Bay. At the entrance is **Faro de Punta Figuras,** a recently renovated lighthouse built in 1893.

SOUTH COAST

WEST COAST

For many decades, the west coast of Puerto Rico has been a mecca for surfers and divers. The rocky coast—with its craggy points, protected lagoons, big swells, and underwater walls—is a nature-lover's wonderland. During surf season, from December to April, the population explodes, and a solid seasonal infrastructure of low-budget crash pads and burger bars has built up through the years to serve the seasonal visitors.

Recently nicknamed Porto del Sol by the tourism authority, the west coast is beginning to be promoted as a destination apart from San Juan. Thanks to the former Ramey Air Force Base that once occupied much of Aguadilla, the infrastructure existed for the birth of Rafael Hernandez International Airport, which now services flights from New York City, New Jersey, and Orlando, Florida. As a result, tourism has flourished, and more upscale resorts and restaurants are beginning to crop up in idyllic little spots along the coast to serve the leisure traveler.

The west coast has so much going on that it's worthy of an extended stay. It encompasses a huge range of environments within just a 50-mile range. Aside from the party-hardy surf towns of Isabela, Rincón, and Aguadilla, it includes the colonial city of Mayagüez, the fishing village of Boquerón, the phosphorescent bay in La Parguera, and the salt flats of Cabo Rojo.

Most important to some, the west coast is about as far away as you can get—both literally and figuratively—from San Juan. The fast-paced, high-stress urban environment in the

© SUZANNE VAN ATTEN

HIGHLIGHTS

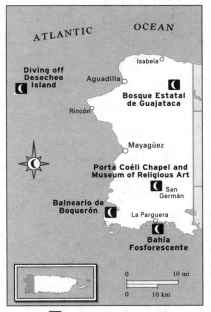

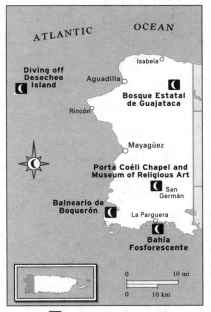 **Bosque Estatal de Guajataca:** This 2,357-acre forest reserve in the southern tip of Isabela is not only rich in flora and fauna, but the temperature hovers in the high 70s, making it a great escape from the summer heat (page 120).

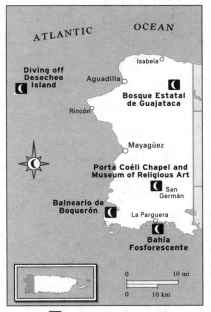 **Diving off Desecheo Island:** The west coast boasts an underwater wonderland, but the only way to see it is to don a mask and go deep. The waters around the uninhabited island of Desecheo provide spectacular spots to dive and snorkel. You can see all kinds of colorful marine life, including rays, parrot fish, grunts, porkpie fish, sharks, coral formations, and more (page 132).

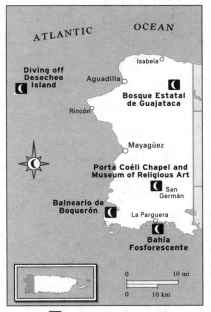 **Balneario de Boquerón:** One of the island's mostly lovely public beaches features a long wide crescent beach and modern new facilities, including bathrooms, showers, picnic shelters, and snack bars (page 143).

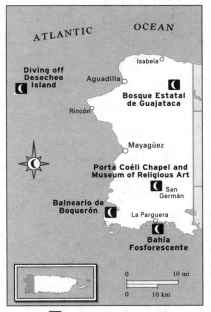 **Bahía Fosforescente:** Take a nighttime boat ride into this bioluminescent bay and marvel at the glittery microorganisms that sparkle in the water (page 148).

 Porta Coéli Chapel and Museum of Religious Art: The tiny primitive chapel established in 1606 in San Germán is a rare example of Gothic architecture in the New World. It contains a collection of 18th- and 19th-century religious paintings and sculpture (page 151).

LOOK FOR TO FIND RECOMMENDED SIGHTS, ACTIVITIES, DINING, AND LODGING.

island's capital is replaced by a slow-paced, nature-loving vibe that west coasters embrace.

PLANNING YOUR TIME

The entire west coast could be driven from tip to tail in less than two hours, but who would want to? There's so much to do and see, you could easily bypass San Juan and the eastern side altogether and spend an entire month on the west coast. In a pinch, though, a long weekend will suffice.

There are two main reasons you want to plan on spending as much time as possible on the west coast. For one, most of the charms are to be found by taking up some form of water sport, and that takes time. Whether it is mastering the art of surfing on the beaches in Isabela, Rincón, or Aguadilla; taking a scuba-diving expedition to Desecheo Island or Mona Island; or paddling a kayak through the mangrove channels or the Bahía Fosforescente in La Parguera, you've got to get in the water to appreciate all the west coast has to offer.

The other reason you'll want to linger here is that there is a laid-back, easygoing rhythm to life on the west coast that compels you to slow

WEST COAST

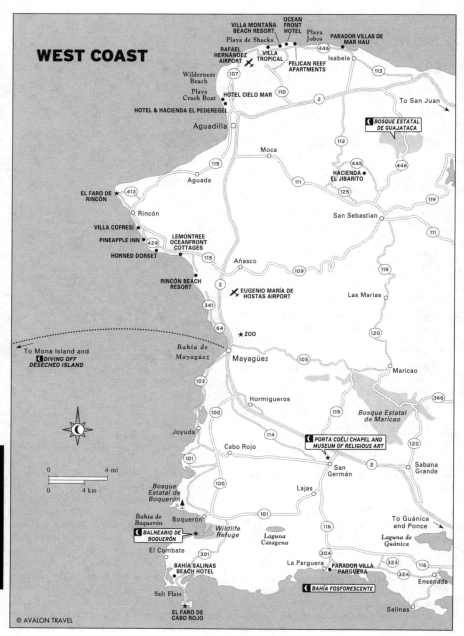

down, take your time, have another beer, and watch the sunset. And if you don't let yourself be a part of that magic, you'll miss the whole reason for coming here.

To fully explore the west coast, a car is essential. If you're arriving via San Juan, it's about a 100-mile drive and takes about 2.25 hours. It's also possible to fly into Aguadilla from San Juan, Newark, Orlando, or New York City's JFK airport and rent a car.

Isabela

The area known today as Isabela was once ruled by Cacique Mabodamaca, one of the island's most powerful Taíno chiefs. Legend has it that when faced with capture by the Spanish colonists, he leapt to his death off the cliffs of Isabela. When his body was recovered, the medallion that signified his lofty place in the hierarchy of Taíno culture was missing from around his neck and is still sought among the cliffs today. A striking monument to Cacique Mabodamaca exists at the intersection of Carretera 2 and Carretera 113. A large bust of the great Indian chief has been carved into the side of the mountain, his medallion respectfully replaced around his neck. The monument serves not only as a reminder of the Taíno culture that once prevailed in the area, but it marks the northern entrance to Puerto Rico's west coast.

The first Spanish settlement in this area was called San Antonio de la Tuna. The date of its origin is unknown, but it was situated on the banks of the Río Guajataca, which separates Isabela from Quebradillas. In the early 1800s the residents of the town made a formal request to the island's governor asking that the town be relocated closer to the coast, and in 1819 a new town was established and called Isabela after Queen Isabel of Spain.

The town of Isabela features a charming little plaza anchored by a church, as are all town plazas. But most visitors head to the municipality's gorgeous beaches along coastal road Carretera 466. This is where you'll find lots of opportunities for swimming, surfing, diving, and horseback riding, as well as a variety of hotels, restaurants, and bars.

The westward drive along Carretera 466 is pretty remarkable. The long stretch of road passes through undeveloped land lined by palm groves and the sea on one side and flat grassy plains grazed upon by herds of cattle on the other. Beyond the plains is a huge ridge that runs parallel to the beach, creating a dramatic backdrop to the pastoral scene.

Those seeking an idyllic patch of wilderness beach must hurry if they hope to find it in Isabela, though: Condo construction has exploded, and it won't be long before everyone discovers this pristine parcel of paradise.

BEACHES

Surfing and diving are two great reasons to stay in Isabela. There are two excellent beaches perfect for doing both, just a couple of miles apart.

Playa de Jobos

Playa de Jobos (Carr. 466 just east of Carr. 4466) has no public facilities, but it has sufficient parking to support the serious surfers who flock to the break point off Puntas Jacinto. It's renowned for its right-breaking tube just off the point. Carefully walk eastward on the point's rocky coral reef to find a big blowhole—where the ocean waves rush underneath and spray water into the air through a hole in the reef. It's a fantastic sight and a great place for photos.

Playa de Shacks

Playa de Shacks (Carr. 4466 in front of Villa Tropical) not only has good surfing and kite-surfing, it also has excellent snorkeling and diving. Blue Hole is touted as one of the north coast's best snorkeling spots. It's located in the surf just outside the office at Villa Tropical and about 500 meters east of Villa Montaña.

There are also underwater caverns accessible from the reef. Several dive shops offer excursions in the area, and horseback riding can be arranged at the resort. The only drawback to Shacks is the lack of parking, which is limited to the shoulders of the road or the occasional house where you're permitted to park for a small fee.

Punta Sardinera

Located on Punta Sardinera is Centro Empresarial Playero, a rustic complex containing patches of sandy beaches between coral outcroppings, a natural pool, basketball courts, and a cluster of kiosks selling fritters and booze tucked away in a thickly vegetated area overgrown with sea grape, devil's tongue, cedar trees, and palms. To get there, drive north on Carretera 112 through the central town of Isabela toward the beach. After you pass Carretera 446 on the left, continue straight past a condominium complex and turn right. If you turn left, you proceed along a short stretch of wilderness beach. There's no parking, but there are sandy pull-ins where you can park your car and walk down to the sea.

SIGHTS
Monumento al Indio

Monumento al Indio (intersection of Carr. 2 and Carr. 113 on the westbound side) is an astonishing artistic achievement made in memorial to the area's Taíno Indians and their leader, Cacique Mabodamaca. A large bust of the chief has been carved into the side of a mountain, marking the road to Isabela and the west coast.

San Antonio de la Tuna Ruins

San Antonio de la Tuna ruins (from Carr. 2, turn south just west of Carr. 113) is the site of the area's first town, which was relocated and renamed Isabela in 1819. The original town was situated on Río Guajataca and was believed to have been established

around 1725. The site is marked by the ruins of the town's church. Arrange a tour by trolley by contacting the tourism office (787/872-6400) in the *alcadia* (city hall) on Plaza Recreo de Isabela.

◖ Bosque Estatal de Guajataca

Bosque Estatal de Guajataca (Carr. 446 south of Carr. 2, 787/724-3724) is a 2,357-acre forest reserve in a mountainous region south of Isabela. Be advised, though: The drive here is not for the fainthearted. The closer you get to the forest, the narrower the road becomes until it's just one car wide, despite the fact it's a two-way road. Adding to the thrill, the road climbs steadily upward and takes many sharp twists and turns around mountains with steep, unprotected drop-offs just inches from the road's pavement. You know you're close—and none too soon—when you encounter a sign warning drivers to roll down their windows, turn off their radios, and honk their horns as they travel around the blind curves.

The forest is well worth the hairy drive to get there, though. A subtropical moist forest that receives 75 inches of rain a year, it's distinguished by its unique karst topography featuring underground limestone caves and dramatic haystack hills called *mogotes*. Because its temperature wavers between 75°F and 79°F, it's a great place to escape the heat during the hot summer.

Bosque Estatal de Guajataca is rich in indigenous flora and fauna. It is home to 186 species of trees, including Honduras mahogany and teak hibiscus, and is home to 45 species of birds, including the Puerto Rican woodpecker, screech owl, and bullfinch. It's also where you can find the rare, endangered Puerto Rican boa constrictor.

There are 27 miles of trails in the forest that lead to such sites as a lookout tower and El Viento Cave, a natural limestone cave formation with stalactites, stalagmites, and columns. There is also a 1.5-mile interpretive trail. Primitive camping is allowed, but a permit is required.

SPORTS AND RECREATION

There are lots of hot surfing spots in Isabela. In addition to Playas Shacks and Jobos, you can find more great breaks by traveling eastward from Jobos on the dirt road that follows the coast to reach sites called Golondrinas, Secret Spot, and Middles, in that order. For expert advice on when and where the best spots are, visit **Hang Loose Surf Shop** (Carr. 4466, km 1.1, Playa Jobos, 787/872-2490, Tues.–Sat. 10 A.M.–5 P.M., Sun. 11 A.M.–3 P.M.). This is the place to buy or rent boards, get your board replaced, or get private surfing lessons. Lessons must be scheduled and prepaid. No lessons are held on Sunday. The shop also sells beachwear and accessories, including towels, sunblock, sunglasses, sandals, bathing suits, beach chairs, snorkeling equipment, and souvenirs.

La Cueva Submarina (Carr. 466, km 6.3, 787/872-1390 or 787/872-1094 after 5:30 P.M., Mon.–Sat. 9:30 A.M.–5:30 P.M., Sun. 9 A.M.–4 P.M., dive trips Thurs.–Mon. 9:30 A.M. and 1:30 P.M. depending on weather, book at least 24 hours in advance) offers several tours, including snorkeling for $25; scuba for first-timers, $65; scuba for certified divers, $55; and a cavern dive, $55. It also offers diving certification instruction.

Isabela has great beaches for horseback riding, and **Tropical Trail Rides** (Carr. 4466, km 1.8, 787/872-9256, info@tropicaltrailrides .com, www.tropicaltrailrides.com, daily rides 9 A.M. and 4 P.M., $45 per person for 2 hours) offers two-hour guided tours along tropical trails on Paso Fino horses through an almond

PASO FINO HORSES

Although not indigenous to Puerto Rico, the Paso Fino horse is closely associated with the island because it was here and in the Dominican Republic where the Spanish conquistadors first introduced the mixed-breed horse. Sharing a family tree with the Moorish Berber, Spanish jennet, and Andalusian breeds, the Paso Fino is a superb saddle horse thanks to its unusual gait. Unlike other horses, its feet fall in a natural lateral pattern instead of a diagonal pattern, which creates a smoother ride for its passenger.

Puerto Rico's Paso Fino horse is typically smaller than horses in the United States, coming in somewhere between 13 and 16 hands high. Their body shape varies from stocky to lithe, and they can be found in every equine color except the Appaloosa pattern. Besides their unusual gait, Paso Finos are characterized by a high level of endurance, great agility, and remarkable obedience.

Juan Ponce de Léon reportedly first introduced the horse to the island in 1521, bringing with him 50 specimens of the mixed breed from Spain. They were quickly put into service working farms, providing transportation, and participating in military maneuvers.

In 1610 the San Juan Races were established as part of the city's patron saint festivities. As a testament to their smooth gait and obedience, the horses were raced without the use of reins. In fact, riders reportedly crossed their arms over their chests and smoked tobacco while their steeds raced to the finish line.

Through the careful selection of mares and stallions that best embodied the horses' unique traits, a specific breed began to develop by the 1700s, although it wasn't until the mid-1800s that the Spanish government officially recognized the breed.

Today, there are about 8,000 registered pure-bred Puerto Rican Paso Fino horses. Although replaced by automation long ago, they're still used for transportation in rural parts of the island – most notably in Vieques and Culebra, where they also roam and graze freely throughout the islands.

Guided trail rides on Paso Finos are available along beaches and through tropical forests by **Tropical Trail Rides** (787/872-9256, www.tropicaltrailrides.com) in Isabela on the west coast and **Hacienda Carabalí Riding** (787/889-5820, www.haciendacarabali puertorico.com) in Luquillo on the east coast.

forest, along secluded beaches, and to cliff-side caves. It includes a stop for a swim or exploring the caves. There's also a sunset tour available. Private rides can be arranged.

Triology Healing Body Studio (Carr. 466, km 6.3, 787/400-0675, Mon.–Thurs. 7:30 A.M.–8 P.M., Fri.–Sat. 8 A.M.–5 P.M.) is a full-service center offering yoga and Pilates instruction; spa services that include massages, body scrubs, and facials; a fitness center; and oxygen therapy.

ENTERTAINMENT AND EVENTS
Festivals
Isabela celebrates **Festival del Tejido** (787/872-1045) in late April or early May, featuring needlecraft exhibits, live music, and vendors selling local food and drinks in Plaza de Los Festivales.

Nightlife
Isabela's nightlife can be found along Carretera 466 at several very casual beachside bars that keep things hopping late into the night. One popular spot is **Happy Belly's Sports Bar and Grill** (Carr. 4466, Playa Jobos, 787/872-6566, daily 11 A.M.–2 A.M.). Skip the tiny rustic bar inside and find a picnic table on the huge open-air deck on the beach. This is a hot party spot, especially on the weekends. It has the potential to be rowdy. It also serves a huge menu of American bar fare and Puerto Rican cuisine.

A similar ambience can be found at **Ocean Deck Park and Grill** (Ocean Front Hotel, Carr. 4466, km 0.1, 787/872-3339, www.oceanfrontpr.com, Sun. and Wed. 11 A.M.–10 P.M., Thurs. 10 A.M.–11 P.M., Fri.–Sat. 11 A.M.–2 A.M.). It's a traditional Puerto Rican beach bar: a wooden pavilion-style structure with deck flooring, no walls, and a pitched umbrella roof supported by a central post, around which the bar wraps. It's a terrific place to sip a rum punch and gaze at the water. It serves seafood for lunch and dinner, and there's live music on Fridays and Saturdays.

ACCOMMODATIONS
$100-150
Ocean Front Hotel (Carr. 4466, km 0.1, 787/872-0444, www.oceanfrontpr.com, $85 d Sun.–Thurs., $100 d Fri.–Sat., $125 d holidays, plus 9 percent tax) has undergone a dramatic transformation. The former crash pad for surfers and divers has been expanded and refurbished. The rooms have a new, light airy feel thanks to freshly painted walls, bleached wood furnishings, quality bedding, and new fixtures in the bathrooms. There's also a new sundeck. The small hotel is on the water and within walking distance to Playa de Jobos. Amenities include air-conditioning and cable TV. There is an upscale restaurant and bar downstairs and an open-air bar right on the water.

Villa Tropical (Shacks Beach, 326 Barrio Bajuras, Isabela, 787/872-7172 or 787/354-7685, villatropical@aol.com, www.villatropical.com, $70 studio, $150 one-bedroom, $170 two-bedroom, $320 three-bedroom, plus 9 percent tax) manages 27 oceanfront, fully equipped apartment units in several buildings along Shacks Beach. Each apartment is different, but they all come with full kitchens, satellite TV, air-conditioning, and free parking. Wireless Internet is available outside the main office and in some apartments. A coin-operated laundry is on-site. Weekly cleaning service is available. To get there from Carretera 4466, turn right just before you get to Carretera 110 at the Villa Montana and Villa Tropical signs.

◖ **Parador Villas del Mar Hau** (Carr. 466, km 8.3, Playa Montones, Isabela, 787/872-2021, fax 787/872-2045, www.hauhotevillas.com, $110 s, $150–160 d, $185 two-bedroom cottage, $260 three-bedroom, plus tax) is a quaint, casual paradise. Tucked away from civilization on a gorgeous stretch of beach and grassy plains, the property runs wild with bougainvillea, hibiscuses, begonias, and sea grapes. A herd of horses grazes in a fenced field. At the center are two beaches, one a protected lagoon. Along the water's edge, shaded by palms, are individual cabanas, some with porches, and small clusters of studio apartments. Although authentically rustic, the interiors are plush, decorated in cool jewel tones that contrast smartly with the bright pastel exteriors. Rooms come with air-conditioning and cable TV. Other amenities include barbecue grills, a pool, a basketball court, laundry facilities, snorkel-equipment rental, and horseback riding. The restaurant Olenas y Arenas offers lovely fine dining by the water.

Ocean Blue Villa (Carr. 4466, km 5.2, 787/546-8038, www.oceanbluevilla.com, from $99) is a new property from the same folks who own and operate Ocean Front Hotel. This upscale, newly constructed self-serve property features six stunning townhouse-style units tastefully filled with contemporary dark wood furnishings, art glass lighting fixtures, lovely artwork, tile floors, plush rugs, and tons more terrific little touches. Rooms come with plasma TVs, DVD/CD players, and satellite TV. There's a small pool and covered whirlpool. And it's just a block to the beach.

Pelican Reef Apartments (Carr. 4466, km 0, Jobos Beach, 787/872-6518 or 866/444-9818, www.pelicanreefapartments.com, $95–110 studio, $125 apartment with a king bed and full-size futon) is a salmon-colored condo on the beach that rents studio and one-bedroom apartments by the day, week, or month. Accommodations are simple, clean, and modern. Rooms come with air-conditioning, cable TV, microwaves, refrigerators, and stovetops. All are oceanfront, although there's no beach, and have balconies. The building is purely self-serve, and part of it appears to be under renovation. There are laundry facilities on-site.

Over $250

C Villa Montaña Beach Resort (Carr. 4466, km 1.9, 787/872-9554, 877/882-8082, or 888/780-9195, fax 787/872-9553, www.villamontana.com, $230 standard room, $325 suite, $380 one-bedroom, $485 two-bedroom, $765 three-bedroom, plus 9 percent tax and 6 percent resort tax) is a super-exclusive gated resort with meticulously landscaped grounds and posh accommodations decorated in an antique Caribbean style. The 26-acre property has 35 villas and 52 rooms with air-conditioning, phones, cable TV, kitchens or kitchenettes, and terraces. Some have whirlpool baths, roofless showers, and laundry facilities. There are two swimming pools, a fitness room, a rock-climbing wall, and spa services. Mountain-bike and sea-kayak rentals are available on-site. Eclipse Restaurant and Bar serves Caribbean-Asian fusion cuisine with an emphasis on seafood.

FOOD
Puerto Rican

Ocean Front Restaurant (Ocean Front Hotel, Carr. 4466, km 0.1, 787/872-0444 or 787/872-3339, www.oceanfrontpr.com, Sun. and Wed. 11 A.M.–9 P.M., Thurs. 10 A.M.–10 P.M., Fri.–Sat. 11 A.M.–11 P.M., $16–22) serves creative Puerto Rican cuisine including mahimahi seviche with coconut milk, tamarind *churrasco*, guava-glazed shrimp, and lobster ravioli in pesto sauce. Dress up and eat in the upscale dining room or dress down and eat the same fare at the bar or at the open-air seaside bar next door.

Olas y Arenas (Villas del Mar Hau, Carr. 466, km 8.3, Isabela, 787/830-8315, breakfast, lunch, and dinner on weekends; dinner only weekdays 5–9 P.M., $11.95–33.95) is a lovely, elegantly casual restaurant under a beachside pavilion. Specialties include *mofongo* paella, a creative combination of classic Puerto Rican and Spanish dishes, and a refreshing citrus *dorado* salad. Other menu items include the daily catch, steak, veal, and lamb chops. There's also a children's menu.

Trebol Bakery (272 Ave. Noel, Estrada, just east of town on Carr. 113, 787/872-8067, daily 6 A.M.–11 P.M.) is a great place to pick up pastries, soft drinks, coffee, and sandwiches, or to get a hot meal from the steam table of Puerto Rican fare—various combinations of plantains, beans, rice, pork, and chicken. It also carries emergency provisions such as water and toilet paper from a small selection of dry goods. It's an excellent place for breakfast.

American

Happy Belly's Sports Bar and Grill (Carr. 4466, Playa Jobos, 787/872-6566, daily 4:30 P.M.–late, $6.95–18.95) is a huge open-air beachside deck with an enormous menu. Happy Belly's specializes in typical pub fare—Buffalo wings, fried cheese sticks, and burgers—but it also serves pasta dishes, fajitas, steak, and seafood, as well as some traditional Puerto Rican fare. It has a full bar and modest wine list.

INFORMATION AND SERVICES

The **Isabela tourism office** (787/872-6400, Plaza Recreo) offers a free trolley tour of its major points of interest by appointment only. To call a **taxi,** dial 787/918-5106. **Banco Popular** (73 Ave. Calero, 787/872-3100) has an ATM. For pharmacy needs, try **Isabela Farma Express** (1–350 G. Ave. Noel Estrada, 787/872-1930).

Aguadilla

When the Rafael Hernandez International Airport in Aguadilla expanded in 2005, it opened up more passenger service to Puerto Rico's west coast, and as a result the town of Aguadilla has undergone a transformation. What was once a bit of a rough-and-tumble town is fast becoming a destination for vacationing families, thanks to the addition of a new water park and the island's only ice skating rink. And the downtown area is being rapidly spruced up by multiple new-construction and renovation projects. There are still plenty of traditional wooden *criolla*-style houses remaining downtown, but sadly they are falling into disrepair.

Unlike most coastal towns in Puerto Rico, much of the downtown area stretches along the waterfront. At its center is Plaza de Recreo, a lovely old-fashioned square, except for a striking modern steel fountain sculpture, and flanked by the city hall and the San Carlos Barromeo Cathedral. Surrounding it is a bustling commercial district. A second, more modern plaza, Jardin de Atlantico, located right on the waterfront, is a popular gathering spot at night. Not only does its adobe-colored walls, balustrades, and wrought-ironwork provide an attractive setting for watching the sunset, a half dozen Spanish-tiled kiosks serve Puerto Rican cuisine and all manner of beverages without putting much of a dent in the wallet. Plans are underway to build a boardwalk along the beach.

Of course, Aguadilla has long been a popular destination for water sports enthusiasts—particularly surfers—thanks to a number of excellent beaches.

BEACHES

Playa Crash Boat (Carr. 458 to Carr. 107, Mon.–Sun. 7 A.M.–6 P.M., $3) is a beach with two parts to it. The first area you encounter is a small but wide public beach popular with families and groups who flock to the *balneario*'s bright blue and yellow picnic tables and huge pavilion tucked into a shady spot on the shore. There are bathroom facilities and tons of parking. Marring the view, though, are a series of concrete pilings and a long concrete pier in the water.

A short distance farther down Carretera 458 is another beach area without facilities or entrance fees. You'll find more parking here and lots of food vendors selling drinks and fried treats. There is a mini underwater wall here that makes it a popular dive spot where you'll see lots of fish, sponges, and corals.

Wilderness Beach (from Carr. 107, turn west on a narrow unmarked road that passes through the Punta Borinquen golf course, Ramey) is also called El Natural. This remote beach is accessible by several small roads that branch off in different directions, but they all dead-end at the same place—a lovely patch of sand and sea. The beach is just past **Las Ruinas,** the ruins of the Punta

© SUZANNE VAN ATTEN

Wilderness Beach in Aguadilla

Borinquen lighthouse, which was destroyed by a tsunami in 1918. There are no facilities at Wilderness Beach and minimal space for parking. Continue down the bumpy rutted road past Wilderness Beach to reach the big waves at **Surfer's Beach.** This is where you'll find the popular surfing spots Table Top and Survivor. Women traveling solo are ill-advised to hang around here. It's quite remote and attracts Peeping Toms.

Parque Recreativo Cristóbal Colón (end of Carr. 440/442 dead-end, free) is a terrific little waterfront park featuring a boardwalk, playground, picnic pavilion, and basketball court. The highlight, though, is **Casa de Arbol,** a huge tree house built around a shady banyan tree. There are often vendors on the park grounds selling fritters, beverages, and produce. For more substantial sustenance, El Pabellon restaurant offers indoor and outdoor dining overlooking the ocean.

SPORTS AND RECREATION
Water Sports

Aguadilla has several fantastic surfing spots, especially along the former Ramey Air Force Base. As you travel north from Playa Crash Boat to Punta Agujereada, the island's farthest north-western point, surf sites include (in order) Gas Chamber, Wishing Well, Wilderness, Ponderosa Ruins, Surfer's Beach, and Table Tops. There are two surf shops in the area, which are great sources for surfing tips and advice on when and where to hit the best swells. Both can provide you with maps to all the great sites.

El Rincón Surf Shop (703 Belt Rd., Ramey Shopping Center, Ramey, Aguadilla, 787/890-3108, info@elrinconsurfshop.com, http://elrinconsurfshop.com, Mon.–Sat. 9 A.M.–6 P.M., Sun. 11 A.M.–5 P.M.) rents and sells surfing, sail-boarding, and snorkeling equipment. It has an excellent selection of quality bathing suits, sandals, sunglasses, and other beach accessories.

Aquatica Dive and Surf (Carr. 110, km 10, Gate 5, Ramey, Aguadilla, 787/890-6071, Mon.–Sat. 10 A.M.–5:30 P.M., Sun. 9 A.M.–3 P.M., aquatica@caribe.net, http://premium.caribe.net/~aquatica) has mountain-bike tours of the west coast, as well as dive and snorkeling trips and surf instruction.

WEST COAST

Golf

Punta Borinquen Golf and Country Club
(Ramey Base, Aguadilla, 787/890-2987 or
787/890-1196) is one of only a handful of
courses in Puerto Rico that are not associated with a resort. Designed by Fred Garbin,
it opened in 1940 to serve the military base.
When the base closed, the course was opened
to the public. It features 18 holes with straight
and open fairways overlooking the ocean.
Walking is permitted on certain days.

ENTERTAINMENT
AND EVENTS

Las Cascadas de Aguadilla (Carr. 2, km
126.5, 787/819-1030, fax 787/819-0730,
www.parqueacuaticolascascades.com, daily
10 A.M.–5 P.M. late May–early Aug., Sat.–Sun.
10 A.M.–5 P.M. late Feb.–late May and most of
Aug., closed Jan.) is a new water park with tons
of slides, tubes, and pools.

Aguadilla Ice Skating Arena (Calle
Marina, Carr. 442, 787/819-5555) is a large
new municipal facility that also features a
sport shop, boxing rink, and two fast-food
restaurants.

Crash Boat Summer Festival (787/891-
1005) kicks off the high season in late May
with a celebration of sun, surf, and water.
Festivities include live music, beach games,
and food vendors. It's held at Playa Crash Boat
off Carretera 107.

SHOPPING

Pequeño Angelito (200 Calle Blanca E. Chico,
Moca, 787/877-4092, daily 9 A.M.–5 P.M.) is
technically in the municipality of Moca, just
10 minutes east of Aguadilla. It is a children's
clothing and furniture store, but a tiny corner
of it is devoted to the sale of *mundillo,* a delicate Spanish-style bobbin lace made by hand
and a dying art form. The store is operated
by three generations of lace-makers: matriarch
Leonides López, her daughter Celia Vale, and
her daughter Somorie Domenech. The stock
has been reduced to primarily baby booties
and christening gowns, but you can still buy
the handmade lace by the yard. To get there
from Aguadilla, take Carretera 2 to Carretera
111 east. As you approach the town of Moca,
take Ramal 110 to the main plaza and park the
car. Continue walking south down Ramal 110,

fishermen's boats gathered on Playa Crash Boat

now called Calle Blanca E. Chico, and it's on the left just past the plaza.

ACCOMMODATIONS

Hotel Cielo Mar (84 Ave. Montemar, Carr. 111, km 1.3, 787/882-5959 or 787/882-5960, fax 787/882-5577, www.cielomar.com, $90–101 s, $106–117 d, plus 9 percent tax) is a large corporate-style hotel that's a bit past its prime. High on a hill overlooking the ocean and the town of Aguadilla, the hotel has a flashy 1970s-style lobby with lots of elaborate chandeliers and a mirrored ceiling, and the rooms are pretty basic. Rooms have air-conditioning, DSL Internet, and satellite TV. The pool has recently been renovated and features a giant whale slide for the kids, a grotto, and a whirlpool. A large open-air restaurant and bar overlooks the Bay of Aguadilla. Unfortunately, that view is marred by an enormous abandoned sugarcane shipping operation below.

Hotel and Hacienda El Pedregal (Carr. 111, km 1.1, 787/891-6068 or 888/568-6068, fax 787/882-2885, info@hotelelpedregal.com, www.hotelelpedregal.com, $81 s, $92–85 d/t, $263 two-bedroom villa, $316 three-bedroom, $329 four-bedroom, plus 9 percent tax) is a popular spot for families with young children. The 27 modern, basic rooms come with air-conditioning, satellite TV, telephones, and Wi-Fi. There's a small pool with a kiddie pool, a game room with pool tables and arcade games, and a small modest restaurant with a limited bar. Maintenance and upkeep is pretty slack, but the staff is friendly and there's a homespun charm about the place.

FOOD

Restaurante Terramar at Hotel Ceilo Mar (84 Ave. Montemar, Carr. 111, km 1.3, 787/882-5959 or 787/882-5960, fax 787/882-5577, www.cielomar.com, $9.95–24.95) should be a great spot for outdoor ocean-view dining from a perch up on a mountain overlooking the sea, but the Puerto Rican food is only adequate and the service is consistently curt. Primarily recommended for cocktails and snacks.

El Pabellon (800 Ave. Cristóbal Colón, inside Parque Recreativo Cristóbal Colón,

787/997-2626, Mon. noon–6 P.M., Wed.–Thurs. and Sun. noon–9 P.M., Fri–Sat. noon–10 P.M., lunch specials Mon.–Fri. $8.95, dinner $8.95–19.95) serves Puerto Rican cuisine and a full bar in a fine-dining atmosphere downstairs and a casual open-air rooftop terrace overlooking the ocean upstairs.

Panadería Borinqueña (Carr. 107, Ramey, 787/882-4141, daily 6 A.M.–9:45 P.M.) and **El Ramey Bakery** (Belt Rd., Ramey Shopping Center, Ramey, 787/890-2768, daily 6 A.M.–9 P.M.) serve pastries, sandwiches, and hot Puerto Rican fare from a steam table. You can also pick up essentials such as ice, toilet paper, and water.

INFORMATION AND SERVICES

The **tourism office** (787/890-3315, daily 8 A.M.–4:30 P.M.) is in Rafael Hernández International Airport. There are several banks, including **Banco Popular** (Carr. 2, km 129.2, 787/891-9500) and **Banco Santander** (Ave. Kennedy, 787/891-8282). **Walgreens** (Carr. 2, km 129.7, 787/882-8005) operates a 24-hour pharmacy. Medical services are available at **Hospital Buen Samaritano** (Carr. 2, km 141.7, 787/658-0000).

GETTING THERE AND GETTING AROUND

Rafael Hernández International Airport (north of Carr. 2 on Carr. 110, between Isabela and Aguadilla, 787/891-2286) boasts the longest runway in the Caribbean. Several airlines have begun offering direct flights here from the United States.

Direct flights to Aguadilla are operated by Jet Blue (from Orlando and from JFK airport in New York City); Spirit Airlines (from Fort Lauderdale); Delta (from Newark); and Continental (from Newark).

Several national **car-rental** agencies operate out of the airport, including Avis (787/890-3311), Budget (787/890-1110), Hertz (787/890-5650), and L&M (787/890-3010). Taxi service is available by calling **Mega Taxi** at 787/819-1235.

WEST COAST

San Sebastián

Located inland in karst country, where limestone cave systems create dramatic sinkholes and exposed hilly outcroppings called *mogotes,* San Sebastían is a sleepy little agricultural town of dairy and coffee farms. But in July it explodes in a riot of color, music, and festivities for the annual Festival Nacional de la Hamaca, which celebrates the colorful hand woven hammocks that are made here and can be bought from roadside vendors and shops throughout the island.

San Sebastían is also home to a unique luxurious agritourism complex called Hacienda El Jibarito.

ENTERTAINMENT AND EVENTS

Festival Nacional de la Hamaca (Plaza Publica Roman Baldorioty de Castro, 787/896-1550 or 787/896-2610) is a major annual festival that celebrates traditional Puerto Rican artisans and their crafts. Held for three days in early July, it specifically recognizes the handmade hammocks that are crafted here. But it's oh-so-much more than hammocks: More than 200 artisans participate, selling everything from seed jewelry and cigars to wood carvings and masks. There's also plenty of food, music, and children's activities.

ACCOMMODATIONS

◖ **Hacienda El Jibarito** (Carr. 445, km 6.5, Barrio Saltos, 787/280-4040 or 787/896-5010, info@haciendaeljibarito.com, www.haciendajibarito.com, $148–171 s, $194 d, $205 one-bedroom, $263–320 two-bedroom, tax included) is a newly developed property that combines tourism and agriculture to provide an educational stay in the lap of luxury. Originally a sugarcane farm that ceased operations in 1980, it has been transformed into a family-friendly resort where guests can commune with farm animals, witness farm technique demonstrations, and dine on the fruits and vegetables grown on-site. The lobby and fine-dining restaurant, Restaurante Laurnaga, are located in a striking Spanish-colonial plantation house with soaring ceilings and mission-style furniture. The 11 rooms and six villas are well furnished and come with all the amenities one would expect from an upscale resort, including air-conditioning, satellite TV, and wireless Internet. The grounds include a kidney-shaped pool with an octagonal bar that offers 360-degree views of the surrounding mountains, an indoor pool and whirlpool, a pond with a gazebo, greenhouses, and stables. A spa offers a menu of massages, body wraps, and nail services. In addition to the restaurant, Casa Café coffee shop and bakery serves delicious locally grown coffee in a variety of cold and hot beverages, plus fantastic pastries. Try the sticky, flaky *quesitos,* stuffed with cream cheese.

For a more economical option, **Hotel El Castillo** (Carr. 111, km 28.3, Barrio Eneas, 787/517-6233 or 787/896-2365, $65 s, $70 d) is a bright modern faux hacienda-style hotel with 18 rooms that have air-conditioning, satellite TV, and wireless Internet. Other amenities include a large pool with a waterfall, a kiddie pool, a barbecue pit, and a couple of arcade games in the large tiled lobby.

FOOD

Restaurante Laurnaga (at Hacienda El Jibarito, Carr. 445, km 6.5, Barrio Saltos, 787/280-4040 or 787/896-5010, info@haciendaeljibarito .com, www.haciendajibarito.com, Mon.–Thurs. 11:30 A.M.–8:30 P.M., Fri.–Sun. 11:30 A.M.–9:30 P.M., $12.95–20) is a lovely fine-dining restaurant in a cavernous two-level building made from dark rough-hewn wood that imparts a rustic lodge vibe. A self-serve buffet of Puerto Rican cuisine is served during lunch for $12.95. The dinner menu specializes in seafood and pasta dishes. The fried shrimp are huge and crispy.

INFORMATION

The **Tourism Information Office** (787/896-2300, 787/896-1550, or 787/896-2610, www .sansebastianpr.com) is at 3 Padre Feliciano, on the main Square at Ramon Baldorioty de Castro.

Rincón

Rincón is a fun-loving bohemian surf town, and the kind of place where people come to visit and never leave. Local lore says 80 percent of the beachfront property is owned by people from the States, and there are so many expatriates here that it's often referred to as "Little America."

For many decades, tourism in Rincón catered primarily to surfers with cheap barebones accommodations, casual restaurants, and beachfront bars. But the world is quickly discovering this little burg's unparalleled charms. More upscale accommodations have set up shop, and restaurants that combine fine dining with a casual atmosphere are following

suit. Rincón is also on the verge of a condo explosion that residents are trying to stem.

Officially, Rincón is one town, but it has three distinct parts to it—north Rincón, south Rincón, and downtown Rincón. Other than a stretch of public beach called Balneario Rincón, the main reason to go to the plaza area downtown is to find an ATM, mail a letter, or have a prescription filled. There are also a couple of boutiques for shopping. Most of the action takes place north of town along Carretera 413 in barrios Puntas and Ensenada. Hotels, restaurants, bars, and excellent surfing beaches cling to the coast here. The area south of town, barrios Barrera and Parcelas and the town of Añasco, is more laid-back, offering a variety of accommodations from full-service hotels to guesthouses located away from the party-hardy attitude that prevails north of town.

Because surfing is best from December through April, winter and spring is high season in Rincón. Some businesses close in the summer or limit their hours of operation.

SIGHTS

A terrific new park has been built around **El Faro** (El Faro Rd., Carr. 4413 off Carr. 413, 787/823-5024), a lighthouse built in 1922. You can't go inside, but the tower provides a lovely backdrop to the landscaped grounds complete with picnic tables, shelters, restrooms, and an observation deck offering gorgeous views of the coastline. There's plenty of parking on-site.

SPORTS AND RECREATION

Water-sports enthusiasts will think they've died and gone to heaven in Rincón. Not only is it world-renowned for its outstanding surfing, but the diving and fishing are stellar. The water along the west coast can be choppier than one is used to. If you plan to ride on a boat, take a motion-sickness pill the night before you go out, and then take another the next morning. Local pharmacies sell the pills for $0.10 apiece.

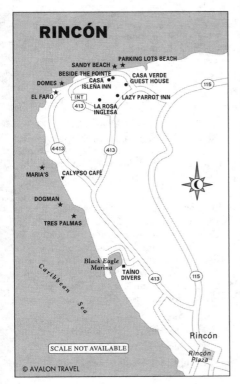

RINCÓN

SANDY BEACH
PARKING LOTS BEACH
BESIDE THE POINTE
DOMES
CASA VERDE GUEST HOUSE
CASA ISLEÑA INN
EL FARO
115
INT
LAZY PARROT INN
413
LA ROSA INGLESA
4413
413
MARIA'S
CALYPSO CAFÉ
DOGMAN
TRES PALMAS
Black Eagle Marina
Caribbean Sea
TAÍNO DIVERS
413
115
Rincón
Rincón Plaza
SCALE NOT AVAILABLE
© AVALON TRAVEL

WEST COAST

MONA ISLAND: RICH IN HISTORY AND WILDLIFE

Oh, the tales it could tell if Mona Island could speak. The 13,000-acre, virtually uninhabited island 47 miles southwest from Mayagüez and 37 miles east of the Dominican Republic has seen much drama through the years. At various times in its history, it was home to a thriving Taíno Indian village, a favorite stopover for marauding pirates, a secret hideaway for stolen treasure, the site of a lucrative mining operation, a vital breeding ground for migratory birds and sea turtles, and the final resting place for many a sailing ship sent careening into its unforgiving cliffs by rough waters and winds.

Today, Mona Island is a protected wildlife refuge, but unlike Desecheo Island, up to 100 visitors per day are allowed to hike its trails, explore its ruins, camp on its beaches, dive or snorkel its crystal-clear shoreline, and hunt its feral pigs and goats, as long as permission is obtained from the **Department of Natural Resources** (787/722-1726). The island is a six-hour boat ride from Rincón or Mayagüez across the rough waters of Mona Passage, an important shipping lane that reaches 3,000

feet in depth. Several outfitters along the west coast offer overnight camping tours to the island, including **Adventure Tourmarine** (Carr. 102, Joyuda, 787/375-2625 or 787/255-2525, tourmarinepr@yahoo.com, www.tourmarinepr. com) and **Mona Aquatics** (Calle José de Diego, next to Club Náutico, Boquerón, 787/851-2185, fax 787/254-0604, www.monaaquatics.com).

Commonly described as shaped like a lima bean, Mona is a semiarid subtropical island with 20 miles of coastline, most of it vertical cliffs rising from the sea to heights of more than 200 feet. The cliffs are penetrated by an intricate marine cave system that extends 150-800 feet under the island's surface in some places. There are also three sandy beaches on the south and southwest coast.

The surface of the island is mostly flat coastal plain with little vegetation, but it is home to a rich diversity of wildlife, most notably the world's only indigenous population of Mona iguana. This prehistoric-looking reptile grows up to four feet long and wields its massive tail like a billy club. It has an aggressive appearance, thanks to a horned snout and

Surfing

The beaches in Rincón are legion for surfing thanks to the water's great breaks and long tubes, especially around the lighthouse during high season, December to April. You can pick up maps to the surf sites at many businesses around town, and surf-shop operators can give you tips on the various sites.

Pick up a map of surf spots at any surf shop in town. The following is a list of hot surf spots in order of location if traveling north along Carretera 413 from Rincón:

- **Tres Palmas:** For pros only, this spot features long, powerful waves with occasional breaks over a rocky reef bottom. Waves can get up to 25 feet. Rarely crowded.

- **Dogman:** A superior winter spot. Not for inexperienced surfers.

- **María's:** Beside the Calypso Café, on El Faro Road, off Carretera 413, this spot features long, fast waves running right and left over a rocky reef bottom. A regional classic but for experienced surfers only. Very crowded on weekends.

- **Domes:** This spot is often referred to as BONUS, the acronym for the name of a retired nuclear power plant distinguished by two green domes that sit idle on the shore just north of the Lighthouse. This is one of the most popular surfing sites in Rincón, and it can get quite crowded. The right point break is for experienced surfers.

- **Sandy Beach:** A great sandy-bottomed spot, ideal for beginners. Located in Barrio Puntas just west of Casa Isleña guesthouse.

- **Parking Lots:** Beside Sandy Beach just east

jagged bony crest down its back, but it's a harmless vegetarian that can survive as long as 50 years. Mona is also an important habitat for the inch-long *geco oriundo* lizard, hawksbill and leatherback sea turtles, and the red-footed booby, among other sea birds.

The island was first visited by Christopher Columbus in 1493 or 1494. He was followed by Ponce de León, who arrived in 1508 and discovered a Taíno village of about 80 inhabitants, who fished the waters and cultivated yucca and sweet potatoes. During the early colonial years, Mona became an important source of agricultural products for the main island. Because of its location and lack of fortification, Mona became a pawn during Spain's defense of Puerto Rico and the Dominican Republic against the French, Dutch, and English. Enemy ships would often stop here to obtain freshwater, raid the Taíno of their food and goods, and sink their enemies' ships. In 1578 the 10–30 Taíno remaining on the island were transferred to Puerto Rico for protection from French raiders.

Mona remained virtually abandoned until the early 1800s, during which time its primary visitors were pirates, who stopped off to get water, repair their ships, or lie in wait to raid passing cargo ships. Infamous pirates, including Mateo Congo, Adrian Cornelis, William Kidd, and Roberto Cofresí all spent time on Mona. Around the mid-1800s, it was discovered that Mona was a rich source of guano, and several mining operations were established. Several significant shipwrecks along Mona's shore in the late 1800s contributed to the termination of operations. The last major operation on the island was the construction of a lighthouse by the United States in 1900.

Today Mona is home to a few rangers, employed by the Department of Natural Resources, who watch over conservation efforts and educate visitors on the unique environment. There are three trails on the island that connect its three beaches to the lighthouse on the eastern point. In addition to enjoying the island's great hiking, diving, and bird-watching, visitors can explore the faint remains of the Taíno civilization and mining operations. Petroglyphs, stone walls, cabins, and graves are enduring reminders of Mona's colorful past.

of Casa Isleña guesthouse, this is a great spot for six-foot swells and a good alternative when adjacent Sandy Beach gets crowded.

SURF SHOPS AND INSTRUCTION

Rincón Surf School (787/823-0610, info@rinconsurfschool.com, www.rinconsurfschool.com) conducts a surf school for beginners and experienced surfers looking to up their game. You can get a 2.5-hour private lesson, or between one and five full days of class instruction. It also offers a Surf & Yoga Retreat for women.

Mar Azul Surfboard Rental (Carr. 413, km 4.4, Bo. Puntas, 787/214-7224, www.puertoricosurfing.com) rents long boards, shorts boards, and stand-up paddle boards by the day and week.

Surf Town Surf Shop (40 Muñoz Rivera, 787/823-2515, www.surftownpr.com, Mon.–Sat. 9 A.M.–6 P.M., Sun. 10 A.M.–4 P.M.) sells surfboards, skateboards, shoes, clothes, and sunglasses.

West Coast Surf Shop and School (2E Muñoz Rivera, 787/823-3935, www.westcoastsurf.com, 10 A.M.–6 P.M.) sells surfboards, equipment, and clothes, and also offers surf instruction.

Surf 787 Summer Camp (Carr. 115, behind Angelo's Restaurant, 787/448-0968 or 949/547-6340, www.surf787.com) offers accommodations and surf instruction for adults only from December through April. From June through September, children ages 11–17 can attend the kid's day and overnight surf camp that features a full day of surf instruction, three meals a day, and evening activities.

Swimming

Much of Rincón's coastline is better suited to surfing than swimming, but there are several beaches ideal for sunbathing and swimming. **Balneario Rincón** (off Carr. 413, 0.5 mile south of downtown behind the junior high school and across from Costa Ensenada condominiums) offers a nice swimming beach with a small picnic shelter, restrooms, a playground, and a boardwalk. Wilderness beaches in Barrio Puntas include **Sandy Beach** (off Carr. 413 Int. just west of Casa Isleña guesthouse), which can get crowded and lively. If you want a quieter beach experience, walk a little ways out of Casa Isleña to reach the quieter **Antonio Beach.** On the southern end of Rincón, you'll find a small sandy beach at the end of Calle 11 in Barrio Parcelas. Amenities include a playground, baseball field, basketball court, covered picnic shelters, restrooms, and a small pizzeria.

Diving and Snorkeling
DIVING OFF DESECHEO ISLAND
Not only does the west coast have lots of great reef diving along its shore, but there is a small uninhabited island 12 miles offshore that offers exceptional diving spots in pristine waters.

From a distance, Desecheo looks like a gray mountain in the sea. Its tall peaks once served as a hideout for pirate ships that would lie in wait for unsuspecting cargo ships to pass by. Today the island is a protected wildlife refuge, and no one is allowed to enter it. But everyone's welcome to don a mask and explore its reefs. You can see all kinds of colorful marine life, including rays, parrot fish, grunts, porkpie fish, sharks, coral formations, and more.

There is no regularly scheduled transportation between Desecheo Island and Rincón, but all the tour operators in town offer snorkeling and scuba trips to its shores.

DIVE SHOPS
Taíno Divers (Black Eagle Marina, Carr. 413, Barrio Ensenada, 787/823-6429, www.taino divers.com, daily 9 A.M.–6 P.M.) offers daily snorkeling and dive trips on a 32-foot catamaran to various dive sites, including Desecheo Island. Snorkeling trips are $50–95, scuba trips are $65–129, and Discovery scuba dives

Underwater caves and reefs create excellent sites for deep-sea diving.

© JOHN W. THOMPSON

for first-timers are $119–170. Taíno also offers whale-watching cruises (late Jan.–mid-Mar.), as well as fishing charters and sunset cruises. Private excursions to Desecheo Island can be arranged. There is also equipment for rent or sale.

Desecheo Dive Shop (El Faro Road off Carr. 413, María's Beach, Barrio Puntas, 787/823-0390, www.divepr.net) rents dive, snorkeling, and surfing equipment and offers dive charters.

Fishing

Taíno Divers (Black Eagle Marina, Carr. 413, Barrio Ensenada, 787/823-6429, www.taino divers.com, daily 9 A.M.–6 P.M.) offers half-day offshore fishing charters including tackle, bait, lunch, and soft drinks for $1,200. It also offers snorkeling, dive, and whale-watching tours.

Moondog Charters (787/823-3059, moon dogcharters@yahoo.com) offers deep-sea fishing, dive, and whale-watching tours.

Makaira Fishing Charters (787/823-4391 or 787/299-7374, www.makairafishing charters.com, $575 half-day charter, $850 full-day charter) offers half-day and full-day charters aboard a 34-foot 2006 Contender. Rates include tackle and refreshments; six passenger maximum. Half-day charters are 7 A.M.–1 P.M. and 1–7 P.M. Full-day charters are 7 A.M.–4:30 P.M.

Whale-Watching

Migrating humpback whales can be spotted off the coast of Rincón during the winter, and several local operators offer boat tours to see them, including Taíno Divers and Moondog Charters.

Horseback Riding

Pintos R Us (Carr. 413 Int., Barrio Puntas, 787/361-3639, www.pintosrus.com) leads daily rides starting at 8:30 A.M. and 4 P.M. on Paso Fino horses for beginners and advanced riders. The trail takes you alongside lovely beaches, cliffs, and tropical trails. It also offers riding lessons, trail rides, and full moon rides.

Spa

Annette Weimmer Massage & Spa Treatments (787/823-2199 or 787/382-6299, by appointment only) offers certified and licensed therapeutic massage and bodywork. Services include stone massage, brown sugar and sea-salt passion fruit oil scrub, facials, pedicures, reflexology, waxing, and haircuts.

ENTERTAINMENT AND EVENTS
Nightlife

Rincón may be famous for its fabulous water sports, but it is equally renowned for its party-hardy atmosphere. Nothing complements a day spent surfing and diving like a pub crawl, and Rincón has no shortage of great bars and watering holes for partying into the wee hours.

A funky, casual open-air tiki bar and eatery, **◖ Shipwreck Bar & Grill** (beside Taíno Divers at Black Eagle Marina off Carr. 413, Barrio Ensenada, 787/823-6429, www.rinconshipwreck.com/AHOY/Home_Port.html, daily 11 A.M.–late high season, Thurs.–Mon. noon–late off-season, $10–24) looks like something Gilligan might have built. Don't be put off by the gravel floor and the tin roof or the bathrooms that look like outhouses. It serves excellent, freshly prepared food ranging from hot wings to poached halibut. But it's the laid-back beach-bum vibe that invites visitors to tarry longer than you'd planned, sipping cocktails, noshing on fried shrimp with coconut curry dipping sauce, and chatting up the colorful characters who hang out here—especially during happy hour 3–6 P.M.

Located below Smilin' Joe's restaurant, nautical-themed open-air **◖ Seaglass Bar** (Lazy Parrot Inn, Carr. 413, km 4.1, Barrio Puntas, 787/823-5654 or 800/294-1752, fax 787/823-0224, lzparrot@lazyparrot.com, www.lazyparrot.com, daily 5:30–10 P.M., $18–27) is heavy on atmosphere, especially at night when the lushly landscaped grounds are lit with torches. You can dine on the same great fare (jerked mahimahi, fried whole snapper, pad thai) served upstairs but in a much more casual atmosphere. Check out the cocktail menu for

© SUZANNE VAN ATTEN

Calypso Cafe at María's Beach

fruity, frosty concoctions such as the Bailey's Banana Daiquiri, featuring rum, Bailey's Irish Cream, fresh banana, and chocolate syrup.

At **Calypso Cafe** (on El Faro Rd., off Carr. 413, María's Beach, 787/823-1626, daily 11 A.M.–9:30 P.M. off-season, open later Dec.–Apr.), a funky laid-back spot on the water at María's Beach, happy hour (5–7 P.M.) happily coincides with sunset every day. Everyone in town seems to start the evening here, sipping rum punch and watching the glorious pink and orange light show courtesy of Mother Nature. The menu has expanded to include fish seviche, grilled *dorado* burritos, and *churrasco*. And there's free Wi-Fi.

◖ Villa Cofresí Patio Bar (Villa Cofresí Hotel, Carr. 115, km 12, Barrio Parcelas, 787/823-2450, fax 787/823-1770, www.villa cofresi.com) is named after Puerto Rico's claim to piracy fame—Roberto Cofresí, a seafaring Robin Hood who terrorized passing ships and stole their goods until he was captured and executed in 1825. This beachside bar is off the lobby of Villa Cofresí Hotel, and it's a popular spot for vacationing Puerto Ricans, who come to play pool, dance to live music or the jukebox, and break away for romantic walks on the beach. The patio bar is a great place to wrap up the night with the bar's drink special, called Pirata (pirate). The sweet, potent concoction features three kinds of rum, coconut juice, crème de cacao, and cinnamon, and it's served in a freshly cracked coconut.

Rock Bottom (at Casa Verde Guest House, Carr. 413, Sandy Beach, Barrio Puntas, 787/605-5351, www.enrincon.com/restaurant_bar.html, restaurant daily 11 A.M.–10 P.M. high season, 5–10 P.M. low season, bar until 2 A.M. high season, $6.95–8.95) is a small, funky treetop bar and restaurant with a tin roof and palm-frond decor punctuated with surfing memorabilia. A sign proclaims: "Free beer for broken boards." True to its word, this nightspot is decorated with broken and (faux) shark-bitten surfboards that earned their owners a free beer each for the loss. A small menu offers pub food such as burgers, wings, and quesadillas. The inn has a few bare-bones rooms to rent, which are frequented by surfers. Rates are $60 for a studio, $120 for a two-bedroom apartment.

Festival

Rincón honors Santa Rosa de Lima with its **Patron Saint Festival** (787/823-5024) on the beach in late August or early September with music, games, and food.

SHOPPING

Playa Oeste Tropical Surf Art Gallery & Gift Shop (Carr. 413, km.0.5, off Carr. 115 before El Faro Rd., Tres Palmas Beach, 787/823-2287, playaoeste@aol.com, www.playaoeste .com, Tues.–Sun. 11 A.M.–5 P.M. high season, Thurs.–Sun. 11 A.M.–5 P.M. low season) sells original artwork by artists both local and global, plus great gift items: ceramics, hammocks, hot sauces, coffee, and casual wear.

Nahyhatz Art Designs and Gallery (176 Calle Sol, Esquina Progreso, downtown Rincón, 787/502-8138, Mon.–Sat. 9 A.M.–6 P.M., Sun. 11 A.M.–5 P.M., cash only) is where owner and artist Celines Irizarry sells her uniquely handcrafted jewelry, clothing, purses, and more. Check out her lovely silver-and-sea-glass earrings and hip party purses made from recycled inner tubes.

Caribbean Casuals (El Faro Rd., off Carr. 413, Marías Beach, 787/823-3942, daily 11 A.M.–6 P.M. high season, call for hours off-season) sells casual beachwear, bathing suits, T-shirts, jewelry, and flip-flops.

Artistic Invisions Art & Artisan Gallery (Carr. 414, km 0.2, Barrio Rio Grande, 787/431-2439, www.artisticinvisions.com, Wed.–Sat. noon–5 P.M., Sun. noon–4 P.M.) sells locally crafted items that include paintings, wood sculpture, sea-glass jewelry, mosaics, stained glass, and more.

ACCOMMODATIONS

Accommodations run the gamut in Rincón, from cheap basic crash pads for surfers and mid-range B&B's to upscale resorts and an exclusive enclave for the rich and famous.

$50-100

Casa Verde Guest House (Carr. 413, Barrio Puntas, Sandy Beach, 787/823-3756, www.en rincon.com, $70 suite, $90–140 one-bedroom, $160 two-bedroom) has been completely renovated and redecorated, making it a pleasant, convenient place to stay if you want to be close to popular bars, restaurants, and surfing spots. Rooms come with kitchenettes and air-conditioning. Rock Bottom bar and grill is right next door, and you can walk to Sandy Beach.

$100-200

⬟ La Rosa Inglesa/The English Rose (Carr. Int. 413, km 2.0, Barrio Ensenada, 787/823-4032 or 787/207-4615, jethrowr@coqui.net, www.larosainglesa.com, $115–200, including full breakfast), newly constructed atop a high ridge overlooking the ocean, is an idyllic three-unit guesthouse offering everything you could want: peace and quiet; gorgeous views; a natural setting; proximity to restaurants, bars, and the ocean; comfortable contemporary accommodations; a small pool; and what's considered by many to be the best breakfast in Rincón. The place is operated by a friendly young couple who live on the top floor of the property: Ruth, who's British, and Jethro, who's Puerto Rican. Don't be intimidated by the steep drive up the hill to reach the inn. Once you do it a time or two, you won't even notice its dizzying heights. Even nonguests make the trek to dine on Ruth's amazing, freshly prepared dishes. Rooms come with air-conditioning, mini-kitchens, refrigerators, satellite TV, and free Wi-Fi.

Lazy Parrot Inn (Carr. 413, km 4.1, Barrio Puntas, 787/823-5654 or 800/294-1752, fax 787/823-0224, lzparrot@lazyparrot.com, www.lazyparrot.com, $125–165 s/d, plus 9 percent tax and 5 percent energy surcharge) is a 23-unit fun-loving hotel that has recently expanded. Stay in the original part of the hotel and you get a simple, modestly furnished no-frills room. Or stay in the recently built poolside suites, which are roomier and more nicely furnished. Either way, you get air-conditioning, a mini-refrigerator, a microwave, free continental breakfast buffet, and free Wi-Fi by the pool. The pool and its recently renovated, grotto-style grounds are the best part. And you've got three restaurants on-site: Smilin' Joe's, Seaglass Bar, and the poolside Rum Shack.

Surf 787 Resort (Carr. 115, behind Angelo's Restaurant, 787/448-0968 or 949/547-6340, www.surf787.com, $150 private bath and ocean view, $100–120 shared bath) is a small, newly constructed year-round guest villa that also offers surf instruction for adults and children. Rooms come with air-conditioning, mini-refrigerators, TVs, and DVD players; there's a small pool on-site. No children are allowed from December through April, when it offers all-inclusive surf and board packages for adults only. From June through September, children ages 11–17 can attend the kid's day or overnight surf camp.

Pineapple Inn (2911 Calle 11, off Carr. 115, Barrio Parcelas, 787/823-1430 or 787/245-9067, fax 787/823-3963, info@thepineappleinn.net, www.thepineappleinn.net, $95–145 s/d) is run by the eco-conscious Nelson Santos and Mark Kelly, who have won multiple hospitality awards for its conservation efforts. Solar energy is used to heat water, the grounds' lush flora is fed recycled water, and guests' sheets and towels are only laundered every three days. The compact property in a residential neighborhood just a half-block away from a small public beach and offers small rooms with air-conditioning, mini-refrigerators, microwaves, coffeemakers, satellite TV, and Wi-Fi. There's a small pool, and continental breakfast is delivered daily in a wicker basket. Beach chairs, boogie boards, noodles, and coolers are available for use. Honeymoon packages are available, as well as in-room massages and handicap accessibility.

(Lemontree Oceanfront Cottages (Carr. 429, km 4.1, Barrio Barrera, 787/823-6452 or 888/418-3733, bellajane.lemontree@gmail.com, www.lemontreepr.com, $165 studio, $195 one-bedroom, $295 three-bedroom; as low at $80 off-season) is operated by Bella Jane and Ted Davis. The six darling, recently renovated, connected units are named after fruits, and all are oceanfront with terraces, mini-kitchens, and small libraries. The rooms are tastefully furnished with contemporary dark wood and rattan furniture and whimsical art glass. Amenities include satellite TV, DVD players, Wi-Fi, and flat-screen TVs. Some rooms come

with big-screen TVs; the three-bedroom unit has a bar, and the Banana cottage has a two-person hot tub. The property is located on a swimmable beach, and beach chairs, a grill, floats, and tubes are available for use.

(Casa Isleña Inn (Carr. 413 Int., km 4.8, Parking Lot Beach, Barrio Puntas, 787/823-1525 or 888/289-7750, fax 787/823-1530, reservations@casa-islena.com, www.casa-islena.com, $145–205 s, $185 d) is a new, well-maintained luxury property designed to resemble a Spanish hacienda, complete with imported tile and mission-style furniture. There are only nine units, and each one comes with air-conditioning, cable TV, and a mini-refrigerator. Some have whirlpool baths and balconies. Other amenities include a pool and beachfront. There's an exceptional tapas restaurant on-site.

Beside the Pointe on the Beach (Carr. 413 Int., km 4.4, Punta Higüero Beach, 787/823-8550 or 888/823-8550, btpe@besidethepointe.com, www.besidethepointe.com, $105–210 for rooms that sleep 2–6, plus 9 percent tax) is a funky bare-bones beachside property with eight units with air-conditioning, cable TV, refrigerators, and coffeepots. Some rooms have full kitchens and balconies. The decor appears to be secondhand and mismatched, and the walls feature palm-tree murals. The Tamboo Tavern and SeaSide Grill is open daily noon–10 P.M. high season, Thursday–Sunday low season. The bar is open daily noon–midnight year-round.

Villa Cofresí Hotel and Restaurant (Carr. 115, km 12, 787/823-2450, fax 787/823-1770, villacofresi.com, $145 d, $155 d with kitchenette, $170 two-bedroom apartment, plus 9 percent tax) has 80 modern ocean-side units with air-conditioning, mini-refrigerators, coffeepots, telephones, and cable TV. Some rooms have balconies, whirlpool baths, kitchens, and bathtubs. The large lobby is a tad shabby, but it contains an enormous and very popular bar. The rooms are recently renovated and very comfortable. Amenities include a pool, a game room, a gift shop, and a restaurant. Personal-watercraft and kayak rentals are available on-site.

Over $250

Rincón Beach Resort (Carr. 115, km 5.8, Añasco, 787/589-9000 or 866/589-0009, fax 787/589-9020 or 787/589-9040, info@rincon beach.com, reservations@rinconbeach.com, www.rinconbeach.com, $240–285 s/d, $459 one-bedroom suite, $660 two-bedroom, plus 5 percent resort fee and 9 percent tax; inclusive packages available) is a 118-unit upscale oceanfront resort in Añasco, south of Rincón. The huge open-air lobby has high ceilings, a wrought iron chandelier, and pink and adobe tile floors. On one end is a full bar; on the other is the reception desk. Outside the lobby is an open courtyard with patio umbrellas, tables, and chairs surrounded by *flamboyan* trees overlooking a long scalloped-edge pool with a swim-up bar and a hot tub. Other amenities include a boardwalk along a sandy beach, a playground, an exercise room, meeting rooms, and a gift shop, plus fine dining at Brasas Restaurant and casual dining at Pelican Grill.

◖ **Horned Dorset Primavera** (from Carr. 115, turn west on Carr. 429, bear right at the fork, discreet entrance on the right, $596–1,070 d, $1,695 two-bedroom, including all meals, plus 9 percent tax and 9 percent service fee) is where pop stars and Academy Award–winners stay for the most lavish and luxurious experience available in Puerto Rico. This Relais and Chateau property has 37 spacious, tastefully appointed suites and villas decked out with Italian lighting fixtures, custom-made mahogany furniture, Moroccan rugs, and Spanish tiles. Each unit has a private plunge pool, wet bar with mini-refrigerator, canopy beds, balconies, and oversized pedestal tubs. There are in-room massages, manicures and pedicures, and hair-care services. The white stucco main building, constructed in 1987 in a Spanish colonial style, contains a fabulous library with an ornate antique bar and a restaurant. The lushly landscaped grounds feature gardenias, hibiscuses, bougainvillea, and palm trees. It's the perfect backdrop for the property's long, gorgeous stretch of tranquil wilderness beach. Snorkeling equipment and kayaks are available at no charge. In-room massages are available.

FOOD

The dining options keep getting better and better in Rincón, but be prepared to pay top dollar even at the most casual places. And if you're traveling off-season, expect your options to be fewer. Many restaurants are open December–April only.

Puerto Rican

◖ **El Nuevo Flamboyan** (Carr. 413, km 0.3, Camino Martillo, Barrio Puntas, 787/307-0703, kitchen Mon.–Sat. 5–9 P.M. Dec.–Apr., $9.95–17.95) is a casual low-tech operation serving the best Puerto Rican food in town. The menu features excellent seafood, steak, *empanadillas, mofongo,* and soups, plus there's a full bar. There are two tables outside that have a great ocean view if you want to dine alfresco.

Restaurante El Coche (Carr. 115, km 6.6, Añasco, daily 11 A.M.–11 P.M., $10.95–29.95) serves *criolla* cuisine in your choice of old-fashioned formal dining inside or a casual open-air terrace on the back overlooking the ocean. Dishes include *asopao*, shrimp, lobster, and snapper served broiled, fried, stewed, and scampi.

Kaplash (Carr. 115, km 6.7, Curvas de Rincón, Añaso, 787/826-4582, Sun.–Wed. 11 A.M.–10 P.M., Thurs. 11 A.M.–11 P.M., Fri.–Sat. 11 A.M.–midnight, $1–2.50) serves a simple menu featuring nothing but beer and *empanadillas*—lobster, conch, crab, shark, grouper, shrimp, seafood combo, pizza, lasagna, and meat. The bright orange exterior welcomes visitors into a small bar inside decorated with Pedro Albizu Campos posters and kitschy beach tchotchkes. Upstairs are two levels of outside seating that overlooks the ocean. The rooftop floor has its own bar.

Puntas Bakery, Reposteria, and Panadería (Carr. 413, km 3.4, Barrio Puntas, 787/823-2402, daily 6 A.M.–9 P.M.) is a great place to pick up breakfast, coffee, pastries, or sandwiches. There's also a small selection of groceries.

Seafood

◖ **Casa Isleña Tapas** (At Casa Isleña, Carr.

413 Int., km 4.8, Parking Lot Beach, Barrio Puntas, 787/823-1525 or 888/289-7750, fax 787/823-1530, reservations@casa-islena.com, www.casa-islena.com, daily 11 A.M.–3 P.M. and 5–9 P.M. high season; Fri.–Sun. 11 A.M.–3 P.M. and 5–9 P.M. off-season, no lunch served in May, $3–10) is a lovely fine-dining restaurant situated in the breezeway between the patio bar and the pool of this small guesthouse. The expertly prepared, creatively conceived small plates include grilled *dorado* topped with apple slices and chili-lime butter, and marinated grilled swordfish in coconut butter. Or try a cold plate of sardines, apple slices, Manchego cheese, olives, and roasted red pepper served with a toasted baguette.

℃ The Spot (Black Eagle Marina, Carr. 413, 787/823-3510, www.rincononline.com/spot/home.htm, Wed.–Mon. 4:30 P.M.–late high season, closed late Apr.–Thanksgiving, $21–32) serves outstanding cuisine in a funky, casual setting right on the water. Sit inside, at the bar, or on the seaside patio lit by tiki torches. The menu runs the gamut from a mushroom and lobster risotto appetizer to the grilled mahimahi in papaya teriyaki sauce.

Shipwreck Bar & Grill (Black Eagle Marina, Carr. 413, beside Taíno Divers, Barrio Ensenada, daily 11 A.M.–late high season, Thurs.–Mon. noon–late off-season, 787/823-6429, $10–24) is a funky, casual open-air tiki bar and eatery that serves excellent freshly prepared food that includes hot wings, mussels, burgers, veggie wraps, ravioli Florentine, and poached halibut.

Smilin' Joe's (Lazy Parrot Inn, Carr. 413, km 4.1, Barrio Puntas, 787/823-5654 or 800/294-1752, fax 787/823-0224, lzparrot@lazyparrot.com, www.lazyparrot.com, daily 5:30–10 P.M., $18–27) is a pleasant, slightly formal restaurant serving jerked mahimahi, grilled shrimp and pad thai, fried whole snapper, and coconut seviche.

New American

Brasas Restaurant (Rincón Beach Resort, Carr. 115, km 5.8, Añasco, 787/589-9000 or 866/589-0009, reservations@rinconbeach.com, www.rinconbeach.com, breakfast Mon.–Fri.

7–10:30 A.M., Sat.–Sun. 7–11 A.M., brunch Sat.–Sun. 12:30–4:30 P.M., dinner daily 5–11 P.M., $18–27) offers fine dining in a dramatic setting featuring dark woods, adobe accents, a massive wrought iron chandelier, and an open kitchen. Outside dining is available on the terrace. Entrées include tuna tartare, rack of lamb, and duck breast glazed with honey and Grand Marnier.

Vegetarian

℃ Natural High Juice Bar & Café (99 Calle Sol, Carr. 115, km 14.3, downtown Rincón, 787/823-1772, www.naturalhighcafe.com, daily 8 A.M.–8 P.M., $5–16) is a vegetarian restaurant, bakery, and organic market, as well as clearinghouse and gathering place for the local organic community. It serves pancakes, breakfast burritos, and smoothies in the morning, soups and sandwiches for lunch, and salads and entrées that include Thai red curry and maple glazed veggie "salmon" for dinner. Be sure to save room for a decadent treat from the bakery, such as the pumpkin chocolate chip muffin.

Breakfast

℃ La Rosa Inglesa/The English Rose (Carr. 413 Int., km 2.0, Barrio Ensenada, 787/823-4032 or 787/207-4615, jethrowr@coqui.net, www.larosainglesa.com, Wed.–Sun. 8 A.M.–noon for nonguests of the bed & breakfast, daily for guests, hours may change off-season, $6–9) is considered by many to serve the best breakfast in Rincón. Freshly prepared dishes made to order include eggs Benedict, juevos rancheros, omelets, breakfast burritos, and French toast served with caramelized bananas.

Mexican

Pancho Villa Mexican Grill (115 Calle Progreso, Rincón plaza, 787/823-8226, www.panchovillapr.com, Tues.–Sun. noon–10 P.M., $7.95–12) is a newly opened restaurant with a lovely Southwestern ambience, serving Mexican fare such as burritos and fish tacos.

Ice Cream

Sugar Chef (in Sunset Village, Carr. 115, km

13.2, beside Balneario Rincón, Mon.–Thurs. 1–9:30 P.M., Fri.–Sat. 1–10 P.M., 787/951-5722, $1.60–3.50) is an ice cream shop and bakery serving German apple pie, chocolate mousse, and brownie cheesecake. Get a cone and walk outside to the parklike oceanfront grounds of this shopping center to enjoy your treat.

INFORMATION AND SERVICES

Taxi service is provided by **AA Taxi Service** (Carr. 413, km 3.4, Barrio Punta, Rincón, 787/823-0906). Banking services can be found at **Banco Popular** (787/823-2055), on the main plaza in town. It has an ATM.

Mayagüez

Mayagüez is a lovely colonial city and a bustling mini-metropolis that has resisted the siren's call of tourism and mainland influence. It's as sophisticated as it is traditional. Not only is it home to a branch of the University of Puerto Rico and other colleges, but the heart of the city—Plaza de Colón—features a pleasantly large and thriving central town square.

Mayagüez has endured more than its share of hard times. Established in 1760, the city was destroyed in 1841 by a great fire. The town reportedly had 700 homes at the time, and only 10 percent survived the devastation. Much of the city was leveled again in 1918, this time by an earthquake estimated to have registered 7.5 on the Richter scale. That was followed by a tsunami that reached 19 feet in height.

The city has also struggled through economic ups and downs. Under the Spanish crown, Mayagüez was a major shipping port for coffee production, but after the United States arrived, trade restrictions sent the island's coffee industry into decline. The void was filled by a massive tuna-canning industry, which reportedly produced more than half the canned tuna consumed by the United States, but that too has declined. Once the third-largest city in Puerto Rico, Mayagüez now ranks fifth, with 100,000 residents.

Despite its hard times, Mayagüez is a pleasant place to spend an afternoon walking around the plaza or visiting its zoo.

SIGHTS

Plaza de Colón (Calle McKinley) is a lovely, large, shady Spanish-style plaza with a huge statue of Christopher Columbus surrounded by 16 other statues, all from Barcelona, Spain. Around the plaza are several shops—mostly budget American chain stores. At night, the plaza is a gathering place for cross-dressing prostitutes.

The plaza is anchored by **Santa Iglesia Catedral Nuestra Señora de La Candelaria** (220 Apartado, 787/831-2444), a beautiful cathedral featuring marble floors and a wood-beamed ceiling. Built between 1833 and 1847, it underwent a major renovation that was completed in 2003. The religious statuary is incredible, particularly the crying Mary with a pierced heart on her chest, where female worshippers gather to kiss the hem of her gown.

Zoológico de Puerto Rico (Carr. 108, just north of Carr. 65, 787/834-8110, Wed.–Sun. and holidays 8:30 A.M.–4 P.M., $6) is Puerto Rico's only zoo. It's a nicely landscaped, modern facility divided into African Forest and African Savannah viewing compounds. Among its inhabitants are monkeys, zebras, lions, tigers, caimans, and hippos. There are also a small lake and a children's playground.

Grande Casa Museo y Centro Cultural (104 Calle Méndez Vigo, 787/832-7435, Mon.–Fri. 8 A.M.–4 P.M., free) was once the private home of Don Guillermo Santos de la Mano and his family, built in 1890—"before the Americans came," reminds the manager. Today it houses a collection of amateur artworks—oil paintings of important men in suits and a dreadful reproduction of *The Last Supper*. Although the house has been poorly maintained, it's a great example of the city's

WEST COAST

turn-of-the-20th-century architecture, with its wide terrace, wrought-iron metalwork, and dramatic French doors. And don't miss the traditional red-tile kitchen, complete with an enormous woodstove and original cabinets.

ENTERTAINMENT

Mayagüez is home to the west coast's only casinos. **Holiday Inn Tropical Casino Mayagüez** (Carr. 2, km 149.9, 787/265-4200 or 787/833-1100, fax 787/833-1300, www.hidpr.com/him_main.asp) has more than 400 slot machines and 13 gaming tables, including blackjack, Caribbean stud poker, craps, let it ride, mini-baccarat, poker, and roulette. **Mayagüez Resort and Casino** (Carr. 104, km 0.3, 787/832-3030, fax 787/265-3020, www.mayaguezresort.com) has slot machines, blackjack, craps, roulette, baccarat, and video poker.

SHOPPING

Shopping in Mayagüez is limited to budget American chain stores, but at **Libreria Catolica Anawim** (16 Calle Méndez Vigo, 787/878-8844, www.libreriaanawimpr.com, Mon.–Fri. 8:30 A.M.–5:30 P.M.) you can buy Catholic totems, such as prayer cards, ceramic saints, statuary, rosaries, religious books, holy-water vessels, key chains, and more.

ACCOMMODATIONS
$50-100

◖ **Howard Johnson Downtown Mayagüez** (70 Calle Méndez Vigo, 787/832-9191, fax 787/832-9122, 15370@hotel.cendant.com, www.hojo.com, $85 s, $95–125 d, $140 suite) is not your typical chain hotel. Once the home for priests serving at the city's cathedral, it was recently acquired by Howard Johnson, which renovated it and added lots of 21st-century amenities. Rooms have air-conditioning, cable TV, coffeemakers, and hair dryers. The suite has a kitchenette and high-speed Internet access. There's a restaurant on-site.

Hotel Colonial (14 Iglesia Sur, 787/833-2150, colonial@hotelcolonial.com, www.hotelcolonial.com, $39–99, plus tax) is in a former convent built in 1920 that housed the nuns of Santa Iglesia Catedral Nuestra Señora de La Candelaria. The property is a bit shabby but functional, offering very basic accommodations for very little money. There's no restaurant or bar, but a continental breakfast is included. Ask for room 23—it's in what was once the top of the chapel and features a fantastic dome ceiling and amazing woodwork.

$150-250

Mayagüez Resort and Casino (Carr. 104, km 0.3, 787/832-3030, fax 787/265-3020, www.mayaguezresort.com, $169–229 s, $189–259 d, $335 suite, plus 11 percent tax, $5 per room resort fee) is an independently owned, modern hotel with a pool, casino, and restaurant on-site.

FOOD

◖ **Ricomini Bakery** (131 Calle Méndez Vigo, 787/832-0565, daily 5 A.M.–midnight, $3.50–5) is much more than a bakery. This large modern restaurant serves eggs, ham, and Spanish tortilla for breakfast, as well as over-stuffed hot sandwiches, barbecued chicken, stews, salads, and more. Plus there are several cases offering a huge selection of pastries. Buy a couple of gift boxes of jelly rolls, a local favorite, stuffed with guava and cream cheese or pineapple to bring home.

INFORMATION AND SERVICES

There are several banks in town, including **Banco Popular** (locations at 1 Suau, Mayagüez, 787/831-6845; and 975 Ave. Hostos, Mayagüez, 787/834-4790). Medical services are available at **Hospital San Antonio** (Calle Post 18 N, 787/834-0050) and **Hostos Medical Services** (28 José De Diego, 787/833-0720 or 787/265-2929). **Walgreens** (Mayagüez Mall, Ave. Hostos, 787/831-9251) operates a 24-hour pharmacy.

GETTING THERE AND GETTING AROUND

Mayagüez is served by **Eugenio María de Hostos Airport** (north of town, Carr. 341, km 148.7, 787/265-7065). It is serviced primarily by **Cape Air** (800/352-0714, www.flycapeair.com), which provides several daily flights from San Juan. There are no direct flights from the United States to Mayagüez. Several car-rental agencies service Eugenio María de Hostos Airport, including **Avis** (787/833-7070), **Budget** (787/832-4570), **Hertz** (787/832-3314), and **Thrifty** (787/834-1590), among others.

Ferries del Caribe (787/832-4800, www.ferriesdelcaribe.com), which provides transportation between Mayagüez and Santo Domingo in the Dominican Republic on a 12-hour overnight voyage, is primarily a car ferry, but sometimes it's like a cruise ship. On select dates, you can book a cabin and make it a mini-vacation by enjoying the restaurant, lounge, game room, and disco. Catch it from the Mayagüez ferry terminal (787/831-3368, fax 787/831-3345, Mon.–Fri. 8 A.M.–9 P.M.) at 31 Avenida Gonzalez Clemente.

There are several taxi services in Mayagüez. They include **City Taxi** (787/265-1992), **Taxi Western Bank** (787/832-0563), and **White Taxi** (787/832-1154).

Cabo Rojo

Because of its remote location and unusual topography, the municipality of Cabo Rojo is quite unlike anywhere else on the island. For one thing, it is hotter and more arid than the rest of the island, and the foliage gets scrubbier and browner the farther south you travel. Its geography is distinguished by two unique environments: more than 1,000 acres of natural salt flats along Bahía Salinas, and the red limestone cliffs along its southernmost tip that inspired the municipality's name, which means "red end."

Most international travelers don't make the trek this far southwest, but Puerto Ricans are well familiar with Cabo Rojo's charms thanks to three major points of interest: Joyuda, a fishing village with scores of terrific seafood restaurants; Boquerón, another fishing village turned party beach town popular with local vacationers; and Cabo Rojo peninsula, site of the island's most picturesque lighthouse.

JOYUDA

The main reason to visit Joyuda is to indulge in some of the freshest seafood on the island. The town is basically one seafood restaurant after the other. And while there are a number of hotels and guesthouses in Joyuda, they're nothing special, and it's pricey for what you get. Joyuda caters mostly to Puerto Rican vacationers, who tend to travel in large groups of extended family members, so a big selling point is how many people a unit can sleep. Kitchenettes are also popular. High season is from Mother's Day to Labor Day.

Sights and Recreation

Isla Ratones is a tiny (like a mouse, hence its name) island half a mile off the coast of Joyuda managed by the Department of Natural and Environmental Resources. Its sandy beach and clear waters make it an excellent place to swim and snorkel. To get here, catch the ferry from the dock (Carr. 102, km 13.7) beside Island View Restaurant. It runs Tuesday–Sunday 9 A.M.–5 P.M. and costs $3 round-trip. For information call 787/851-7708.

Adventure Tourmarine (Carr. 102, Joyuda, 787/375-2625 or 787/255-2525, tourmarinepr@yahoo.com, www.tourmarinepr.com) is operated by Captain Elick Hernández García, who pilots two-hour snorkeling trips for $35 per person, plus $10 for equipment rental. Trips to Desecheo Island are $75, including equipment, and Mona Island is $115 with equipment. Deep-sea fishing charters run 6:30–11:30 A.M. for $375 or 6:30 A.M.–2:30 P.M. for $500, including tackle. Camping equipment is available for rent.

WEST COAST

Club Deportivo del Oeste (Carr. 102, km 15.4, Joyuda, 787/254-3748 or 787/851-8880, cdo@coqui.net, www.clubdeportivodeloeste.com) is a hilly nine-hole golf course with a practice putting green, a driving range, and club rentals. A PGA pro is available for lessons. It also has a golf shop and full-service restaurant.

Accommodations

Hotel Costa de Oro Inn (Carr. 102, km 14.7, 787/851-5010, $39 and up) is a small homespun guesthouse with a tiny pool and lobby and super-clean little rooms to match.

Parador Joyuda Beach (Carr. 102, km 11.7, 787/851-5650 or 800/981-5464, fax 787/255-3750, mail@joyudabeach.com, www.joyudabeach.com, $80 s/d Sun.–Thurs., $96 s/d Fri.–Sat., $159 waterfront room with refrigerator, tax included) has 41 no-frills units with air-conditioning, cable TV, telephones, Internet, and tubs or showers. There are a small triangular pool, a waterside bar and restaurant, and a small beach area. The kitsch-crazy lobby with big gold statues of angels, fake flowers, and floral brocade upholstery on rattan furniture is quite a sight.

Parador Perichi's (Carr. 102, km 14.3, 787/851-3131 or 800/435-7197, fax 787/851-0560, perichi@prtc.net, $64–115 s, $69–125 d, tax included) has a bright perky exterior, but the rooms in the main building are pretty drab. Some overlook the pool; others overlook the parking lot. All rooms have air-conditioning, cable TV, bathtubs or showers, and hair dryers. A better option is the higher-priced "hacienda" rooms, in a separate building on the back of the property. They have spiffier decor, refrigerators, and wireless Internet. Other amenities include a large pool with umbrella tables, wheelchair-accessible rooms, a restaurant, and a cocktail lounge.

Food

Parada Los Flamboyanes (Carr. 102, km 15.9, 787/255-3765, fax 787/255-6177, matls9@aol.com, www.paradalosflamboyanes.com, daily 11 A.M.–10 P.M., $6–16) is a casual, cheerful operation in an attractive salmon-colored structure with dining tables on a wraparound porch. Young families flock here to feast on affordable Puerto Rican seafood specialties, including *empanadillas, mofongo,* conch and octopus salad, and seafood soup.

◀ **Tino's Restaurant** (Carr. 102, km 13.6, 787/851-2976, Sun.–Mon. and Wed.–Thurs. 11 A.M.–10 P.M., Fri.–Sat. 11 A.M.–11 P.M., $13–32) is a slightly upscale eatery serving Puerto Rican seafood dishes and specializing in *mofongo.* The decor is simple, punctuated with stuffed fish hanging on the wall. It also offers monthly wine specials.

Vista Bahía Restaurant (Carr. 102, km 14.1, 787/851-4140, Mon.–Thurs. 11:30 A.M.–10 P.M., Fri.–Sat. 11:30 A.M.–11 P.M., Sun. 11 A.M.–10 P.M., $12.95–25.95) has a cool chrome-and-glass-block exterior with patio dining overlooking the water. It specializes in seafood *mofongo* and has a full bar.

Information and Services

In the municipality of Cabo Rojo, your best bet for tourist information, banking, or health-care needs is the town of Cabo Rojo, on Carretera 101, east of Carretera 100. Just outside of town is the **tourism office** (Carr. 100, km 13.7, 787/851-7015, daily 8 A.M.–4:30 P.M.), which has tons of brochures and a helpful staff. In town you can find a hospital, **Hospital Metropolitano Cabo Rojo** (108 Muñoz Rivera, 787/851-2816 or 787/851-0888) and a pharmacy, **Farmacia Encarnacion** (45 Muñoz Rivera, 787/891-4723). For banking services, **Western Bank** with an ATM is on the corner of Carretera 100 and Carretera 102, on the way to Joyuda.

BOQUERÓN

Traveling south from Joyuda to Boquerón along Carretera 100 is a beautiful drive through lush green hills and medians filled with flowering plants. To the east is a lovely pastoral valley with mountains visible in the distance, and to the west is the sea. The scenery is a perfect prelude to a journey into Boquerón and one of the last sights of greenery you'll see as you continue south to El Combate, where the topography turns desertlike.

Boquerón is a sleepy little fishing village that explodes during weekends and the summer into a popular family beach destination. Puerto Rican vacationers flock here to swim, fish, dine on seafood, browse souvenir shops, and barhop late into the night. Book early if you plan to come during a holiday. Boquerón gets really packed then, and the traffic getting into and out of town can be fierce.

Reminiscent of popular beach towns such as Myrtle Beach, South Carolina, or the Jersey Shore, Boquerón's streets are lined with vendors selling T-shirts, hammocks, shell crafts, fresh oysters, and more. The main thoroughfare, Calle Muñoz Rivera/Carretera 101 Interior, is closed to automobile traffic Friday–Sunday, turning the town into a pedestrian mall.

Because Boquerón primarily serves Puerto Rican tourists, hotels and guesthouses cater to families who bunk together in single units. Many rooms sleep up to 6–8 people and are priced accordingly.

Sights

Bosque Estatal de Boquerón (Carr. 307, km 8.8, 787/851-7260, open 24-7) has a short, well-maintained boardwalk through a mangrove swamp that is great for bird-watching. It's also home to a million baby land crabs. **The Caribbean Ecological Field Services Office** (787/851-7297, Edwin_muniz@fws .gov, http://caribbean-ecoteam.fws.gov, daily 7 A.M.–noon and 1–3:30 P.M.), which oversees conservation efforts to protect the island's endangered species, is here.

Refugio de Vida Silvestre (Camino Mediano Rodríguez, off Carr. 301 at km 5.1, south of Boquerón, 787/851-4795, Mon.–Fri. 8 A.M.–4 P.M., http://caribbean-ecoteam.fws. gov) is a wildlife refuge encompassing more than 400 acres of mangrove wetlands, an important breeding ground for birds, sea mammals, and fish. More than 60 species of birds have been identified here. The center has a few small nature exhibits featuring stuffed birds and a freshwater aquarium. Signage is in Spanish only, as are most of the printed educational materials. There are several hiking trails that start here.

a wooden boardwalk through a mangrove forest in Bosque Estatal de Boquerón

© SUZANNE VAN ATTEN

(Balneario de Boquerón

Balneario de Boquerón (Carr. 101, km 18.1, 787/851-1900, daily 8 A.M.–4:30 P.M., $2) is one of Puerto Rico's most beautiful public beaches. The beach is a very long white crescent gently lapped by calm waters. Dozens of sailboats moored in the distance provide a picturesque sight. The property is very shady, thanks to all the palm trees and sea grapes that grow in the area, and the new facilities are very clean and modern. There's an enormous activities pavilion on the grounds, as well as picnic tables with umbrellas, a baseball field, and a cafeteria. The three huge parking lots are indicative of the crowds that descend here on weekends and during the summer.

Sports and Recreation

Boquerón is an excellent launching point for dive and snorkeling trips to Desecheo Island and Mona Island, two uninhabited wildlife refuges.

Mona Aquatics (Calle José de Diego, next to Club Náutico, 787/851-2185, fax

WEST COAST

EL PIRATA COFRESÍ: PUERTO RICO'S PIRATE MARAUDER

The west coast of Puerto Rico abuts the 3,000-foot-deep Mona Passage, an important shipping lane since the early days of colonialism. The area was a popular hideout for pirates lying in wait for passing ships filled with goods traveling between Europe and the New World.

Among historical records are reports of pirate activity in Mona Passage that include the capture of a frigate in 1625 by the African pirate Mateo Congo. And in 1637, Dutch pirate Adrian Cornelis led 14 ships in the capture of an African ship carrying a load of cedar. It is believed that English pirate William Kidd hid out on Mona Island after capturing an Armenian vessel carrying goods worth 100,000 sterling pounds – some believe that treasure may still be found within Mona's intricate cave system.

Born more than 100 years later but likely inspired by tales of those notorious pirates, Roberto Cofresí took up the piracy game as a young man and gained hero status among many Puerto Ricans along the way.

Roberto Cofresí was born in Cabo Rojo in 1791, and as a young boy he had a small boat called *El Mosquito* that he used to putter around the shore of his hometown. For a brief time he was employed as a corsair, licensed to bring in foreign ships seeking authorization to dock. But he soon turned his attentions to raiding passing ships of their riches.

Acquiring a schooner he dubbed *Ana*, Cofresí and his men raided eight ships, including one from the United States, and crew members were killed in the process. Because he often shared his ill-gotten goods with fellow townspeople, he quickly gained a reputation as a Puerto Rican Robin Hood who robbed the exploiters and gave back to their victims. Although it had previously turned a blind eye toward pirates who attacked its enemy's ships, Spain's empire was beginning to crumble and it had begun to initiate trade with other countries to bolster its pocketbook. In collaboration with the United States, Spain set a trap for Cofresí and his men. Using as bait a U.S. Navy ship disguised as a commercial vessel, they captured Cofresí and his men, who were incarcerated at El Castillo del Morro in San Juan. Cofresí was tried by the Spanish Council of War and found guilty. He was executed at El Morro on March 29, 1825, and buried just outside the confines of the historic Old San Juan Cemetery.

Cofresí's legend has grown with time, and his memory is still celebrated in songs, books, and dance. A statue by artist José Cuscaglia Guillermety in Cabo Rojo's Boquerón Bay stands in monument to the notorious and beloved "El Pirata Cofresí."

787/254-0604, www.monaaquatics.com) has been operating scuba-diving trips to Mona and Desecheo islands for 20 years. The boat leaves Tuesday–Thursday at 8 A.M. Mona Aquatics also offers night dives Wednesday at 7 P.M., sunset cruises Saturday–Sunday at 6 P.M., night trips to the bioluminescent bay in La Parguera Friday–Sunday at 8 and 9:30 P.M., and transportation for overnight camping stays on Mona Island (permit required). Rental equipment is available.

Light Tackle Adventure (Boquerón pier, 787/849-1430 or 787/547-7380, www.lighttackleadventure.8k.com) specializes in light tackle and fly-fishing excursions.

Excursions are four hours ($300), six hours ($375), or eight hours ($475) for two people, and $50 for an additional person. No more than three guests are permitted. This company also provides kayak trips to the Cabo Rojo salt flats, Boquerón Bay, Joyuda, and La Parguera. Bird-watching tours in Cabo Rojo salt flats are also available.

Entertainment and Events

There is no shortage of bars in Boquerón. During the weekends, when the main street is closed to car traffic, partiers freely stroll from bar to bar, drink in hand.

Galloway's (Calle José de Diego, 787/254-

3302, Sun.–Thurs. noon–midnight, Fri.–Sat. noon–1 A.M., kitchen until 10 P.M.) is a friendly, casual, open-air waterfront bar serving an excellent rum punch and good Puerto Rican cuisine.

Shamar (Calle José de Diego, beside Boquerón pier, 787/851-0542, Mon.–Thurs. 11 A.M.–midnight, Fri.–Sat. noon–1 A.M.) is a big popular beer hall with a full bar, pool tables, and a jukebox. This is the place to go for long happy hours and karaoke on Friday and Saturday nights. A small counter outside serves breakfast items, sandwiches, tacos, pizza, and fried treats ($5–10). Grab a cold Medalla beer from the bar, an *empanadilla* from the food counter, and walk out back to sit by the water.

Accommodations

Wildflowers Guest House (13 Calle Muñoz Rivera, 787/851-1793, www.wildflowersguesthouse.com, $115 s/d, $135 s/d with balcony, plus 9 percent tax) is a small property with eight clean, compact rooms. Amenities include air-conditioning, cable TV, and mini-refrigerators.

Boquerón Beach Hotel (Carr. 101, by the entrance to Balneario de Boquerón, 787/851-7110, fax 787/851-7135, www.westernbayhotels.com, $109 s/d) is a modern bright blue-and-yellow high-rise hotel offering clean comfy accommodations. Rooms have air-conditioning, cable TV, and private balconies. Other amenities include a pool, uninvitingly located in the parking lot, and a restaurant.

Cofresí Beach House (57 Calle Muñoz Rivera, 787/254-3000, fax 787/254-1048, vacations@cofresibeach.com, www.cofresibeach.com, $129 sleeps 4, $165 sleeps 6, $219 sleeps 8, plus 9 percent tax) has a modernistic, art deco exterior with clean, simply furnished rooms. It offers 16 one-, two-, and three-bedroom apartments with air-conditioning, cable TV, VCRs, telephones, and fully equipped kitchens. Some rooms have balconies, and there's a pool on the fourth floor.

Food

Galloway's (Calle José de Diego, 787/254-3302, daily noon–10 P.M., $7.95–12.95) is a casual, open-air waterfront bar and restaurant serving a huge menu heavy on seafood and Puerto Rican cuisine. Shrimp, lobster, snapper, and *dorado* are served in your choice of sauce, including garlic butter, creole, spicy creole, and *fra diabla*. Other items include *mofongo,* fried chicken, pork chops, and steak. The coconut shrimp with tamarind sauce is highly recommended. Daily lunch specials are served for $4.95. Diners can eat in the bar or cross a little bridge over the water into a separate dining room.

Roberto's Fish Net (Calle José de Diego, 787/851-6009, Wed.–Sun. 11 A.M.–9 P.M., $5–20) is so popular it operates two restaurants across the street from one another. They both reputedly serve the best, freshest seafood in town.

Other options in Boquerón include **Kokomo Bar and Restaurant** (Calle José de Diego, 787/255-2370, Wed.–Mon. 3 P.M.–midnight, $7.95–29.95), serving seafood, Puerto Rican cuisine, and paella, and **Brasas Steakhouse** (Calle José de Diego, 787/255-1470, $8.95–29.95), serving steak and baby back ribs for those who've had their fill of seafood.

Information and Services

For taxi service in Boquerón, give **Mini Taxi** (787/851-0941) a call. There's an ATM in **Boquerón Liquor Store and Grocery** (Calle Muñoz Rivera, 787/851-6820, daily 8 A.M.–10 P.M.).

CABO ROJO PENINSULA

Cabo Rojo peninsula has such a dramatically different topography from the rest of Puerto Rico that you might think you've left the island altogether. It's incredibly flat, dry, and desolate, with little vegetation. Be sure to gas up before you leave Boquerón because there are few gas stations—or any other businesses, for that matter—in the area.

There are several interesting things to do and see, though. El Combate is a quiet little fishing village with a nice beach for swimming. Farther south are more than 1,000 acres of salt flats, which have been mined for centuries and which are a great place for bird-watching. At the farthest tip of the island's southwest corner

WEST COAST

WEST COAST

© SUZANNE VAN ATTEN

the fishing pier in El Combate, on Cabo Rojo peninsula

is the Cabo Rojo lighthouse, which sits atop dramatic red limestone cliffs that contain an intricate system of caves once frequented by the pirate Roberto Cofresí.

Sights

El Combate (end of Carr. 3301, off Carr. 301) is a small village that turns into something of a hotspot on weekends and holidays, thanks to a nice wilderness beach area and great fishing. It's also the peninsula's sole concentration—albeit a small one—of businesses such as gas stations, restaurants, and hotels that cater to visitors. The community has a small cluster of modest and luxury homes, with a couple of new condominium complexes cropping up.

There are two places to access the water in El Combate. Traveling toward Combate on Carretera 3301, turn left at the Combate Beach Hotel sign to reach a narrow sandy beach with calm, crystal-clear water. There's plenty of parking, little shade, and no facilities. To reach the fishing and small boat-launch area, continue along Carretera 3301 past the Combate Beach Hotel sign, past Annie's Place, to a small

sandy parking lot on the left. Here you'll find small fishing boats moored in the water and a long wooden pier where fishermen gather to drown worms. There are no facilities.

In 1999, the U.S. Fish and Wildlife Service bought 1,249 acres of the **Cabo Rojo salt flats** (Carr. 301, south of Combate), tripling the size of the Cabo Rojo National Wildlife Refuge. The salt flats have also been an important place for humans, who have mined the mineral since pre-Taíno times. The area encompasses coastline, mangroves, sea grass beds, and offshore reefs that are vital to migratory shorebirds and an important feeding ground for sea turtles and manatees. Local outfitters offer bird-watching tours of the area.

For a roadside view of the salt flats, there is an observation tower along Carretera 301 south of El Combate. Unfortunately, it's open sporadically, despite posted hours that claim it's open daily 8 A.M.–4 P.M.

El Faro de Cabo Rojo (end of Carr. 301, km 11.5), also called Los Morillos, built in 1882, is one of Puerto Rico's most picturesque lighthouses, although it's best viewed from the water. That's the only way to appreciate its dramatic location 200 feet above the sea on top of enormous red limestone cliffs that line the coast in this remote corner of the island. To reach the lighthouse on foot, follow Carretera 301 to the end and continue along a bumpy dirt road through the dry scrubby wilderness area to a crude parking area. From here you can hike in along a rocky road closed to traffic. Another option is to turn left to another small parking area and the head of a narrow wilderness trail that will also take you there. Visitors are advised to go early in the day, apply lots of sunscreen, wear a hat, and bring water. It's scorching here, and there's no shade whatsoever.

Sports and Recreation

Light Tackle Adventure (Boquerón pier, 787/849-1430 or 787/547-7380, www.lighttackleadventure.8k.com) specializes in light tackle and fly-fishing excursions. One or two people can go out for four hours ($275), six hours ($325), or eight hours ($400). This company also provides kayak trips to the Cabo Rojo salt flats, Boquerón Bay, Joyuda, and La Parguera. Bird-watching tours in Cabo Rojo salt flats are also available.

Accommodations and Food

⬤ Bahía Salinas Beach Hotel (Carr. 301, km 11.5, 787/254-1212, fax 787/254-1215, bahiasl@centennialpr.net, www.bahiasalinas

.com, $172 for 2 people, $194 for 3, $215 for 4, inclusive breakfast and lunch package available, limited dinner menu, plus tax and resort fees) is by far the best accommodation in all of Cabo Rojo. Across the street from the salt flats, this waterside paradise features lush, naturally landscaped grounds, a lovely open-air restaurant, covered terraces, verandas, porches, hammocks, an adult pool, a children's pool, a whirlpool bath, a mineral bath, and a small pier. The rooms are small, but they come with superior four-poster beds with thick, plush mattresses, air-conditioning, cable TV, and coffeepots. Suites have mini-refrigerators.

Combate Beach Hotel and Restaurant (Carr. 3301, km 2.7, 787/254-2358 or 787/254-7053, $98, including tax) is a modern motel-style property on the beach. Rooms are simple and clean and come with air-conditioning and cable TV. There are a small pool and restaurant on-site.

The restaurants in El Combate are all casual open-air affairs serving cheap Puerto Rican cuisine with an emphasis on seafood and *mofongo*. They also tend to do double duty as popular watering holes late into the night on weekends and holidays. Options include **Annie's Place** (Carr. 3301, km 2.9, 787/254-2553, $2–6), **Luichy's Seafood Restaurant and Guest House** (Carr. 3301, km 2.9, 787/254-7053 or 787/254-2358), and **Colmado Chiquitin** (Carr. 3301, km 3, 787/254-7070).

La Parguera

In the municipality of Lajas, La Parguera is a popular and picturesque vacation destination for Puerto Ricans. If you don't get on the water while you're here, though, you won't experience the real La Parguera. Its biggest draw is the Bahía Fosforescente, a bioluminescent bay, home to millions of dinoflagellates, microscopic organisms that glow in the water on moonless nights. Some claim the number of organisms has diminished through the years, so the bay

is less spectacular than it used to be. But that doesn't stop visitors from flocking to the town's docks to catch boat rides to the bay after dark.

La Parguera is also the site of the famous La Pared, an underwater wall that is one of the most popular diving spots on the island. Deep-sea fishing and boat rides through mangrove channels, where enormous starfish, sea anemones, blowfish, and manatees live, are also popular activities.

a mangrove channel near La Parguera

© SUZANNE VAN ATTEN

The town of La Parguera is basically a small group of seafood restaurants, bars, and boating outfitters clustered around the waterfront docks. Radiating from that are lovely private homes—some situated on pilings over the water, where instead of cars there are boats floating in the garages. On the hills overlooking the town are expensive, architecturally daring homes.

SIGHTS
La Pared

La Pared is an underwater coral reef wall that runs parallel to the coast from Guánica to Cabo Rojo and is a world-class dive site. The wall drops from 55 feet to more than 1,500 feet in depth, and the water visibility ranges 60–150 feet. There are plenty of other outstanding dive sites in the area, where you can see rays, moray eels, parrot fish, grunts, sharks, rare black corals, and more.

Los Canales Manglares

Los Canales Manglares (787/899-1660 or 787/899-1335) is a cluster of more than 30 mangrove cays (islands) around the coast of La Parguera that form an intricate system of channels that are prime for wildlife exploration. On weekends and holidays, locals motor to their favorite cays and anchor for the day to swim and fish in shallow crystal-clear waters. Go to the boat docks in the heart of town to arrange a trip with one of several boating outfitters. The cost is $25 per person, or less for groups. Be sure to ask your captain to take you to see the enormous Mona iguanas that live on one of the cays. And watch the water for starfish, sea anemones, blowfish, manatees, and more.

◖ Bahía Fosforescente

Puerto Rico is blessed with several bioluminescent bays and lagoons. These are small warm bodies of water surrounded by mangrove forests that contain millions of dinoflagellates, unique microorganisms that emit a phosphorescent glow when they sense motion. The only way to see them is to enter the bay at night, preferably where the moon is not visible.

Arguably Puerto Rico's most spectacular bioluminescent bay is in Vieques, where there's little pollution or ambient light. But La Parguera's Bahía Fosforescente is probably the best-known and most popular one because of its easy access and long history as a tourist attraction.

Unlike in Vieques, gas-operated boats are permitted into La Parguera's Bahía Fosforescente, which some believe has contributed to a diminishing number of dinoflagellates in the water. Those who remember it from years ago claim it was much brighter then than it is now.

Nevertheless, if you've never experienced the thrill of a nighttime boat ride into the sparkling waters of a bioluminescent bay, a trip into Bahía Fosforescente is in order. Several tour operators offer nightly rides into the bay on kayaks, fishing boats, and double-decker catamarans beginning at 7:30 P.M. from the docks in La Parguera.

SPORTS AND RECREATION

Paradise Scuba Snorkeling and Kayaks (Carr. 304, km 3.2, 787/899-7611, paradise scubapr@yahoo.com, www.puertoricofishing charters.com) offers scuba-dive tours ($70–80),

night dives ($60), snorkeling tours ($50), sunset snorkeling tours ($50–65), phosphorescent bay tours ($25), gear rental, and dive instruction. Dive sites include El Pared, Enrique, El Mario, Chimney, and Old Buoy.

Parguera Fishing Charters (Carr. 304, 787/382-4698, mareja@aol.com, http://home town.aol.com/mareja) offers full- and half-day charters to fish for *dorado*, tuna, blue marlin, and wahoo on a 31-foot, twin diesel Bertram Sportfisherman. Trips include bait, tackle, beverages, snacks, and lunch. It also offers light-tackle reef fishing, half-day snorkeling trips, and customized charters.

Along the docks in the heart of La Parguera are several boating operators, including **Cancel Boats** (787/899-5891 or 787/899-2972, call in advance for reservations) and **Johnny Boats** (787/299-2212, call in advance for reservations), which offer on-demand tours of the mangrove canals for $25 per person (less if you have a group) and nighttime tours of the phosphorescent bay for about $6.

Aleli Tours (Carr. 304, km 3.2, 787/899-6086 or 787/390-6086, alelitours@aol .com, http://alelitours.com) provides sailing,

DRUG BLIMP

At first glance, the plump white dirigible floating above La Parguera looks like an albino version of the Goodyear blimp drifting overhead. That is, until you notice that it is tethered to a spot on the coast just west of town, surrounded by a high cyclone fence posted with No Trespassing signs. It is, in fact, a weapon in the U.S. war on drugs. Its proper name is aerostat unmanned radar system, and it is used to detect low-flying aircraft bringing in cocaine, heroin, and marijuana from Venezuela and the Dominican Republic.

One of 12 such radar systems operating in the southern United States and the Caribbean, the aerostat has a detection range of 200 miles. It's constructed of a lightweight polyurethane-coated fabric filled with helium, and it typically operates at 12,000 feet in the air.

But keeping it in the air during high winds and rain is no small feat. The Las Lajas aerostat is grounded more often than it is airborne, and some believe it is a financial folly.

Some people think the blimp's true purpose is to detect intelligent life elsewhere in the universe, because many believe this part of the island has experienced extraterrestrial activity. Threatening to turn Lajas into the Roswell, New Mexico, of Puerto Rico, a local schoolteacher and a farmer recently announced plans to build a UFO landing strip near La Parguera, where some claim to have seen an alien craft crash in 1997. Despite some residents' ridicule of the proposed project, city leaders support the privately funded effort and reportedly have designs on making it a tourist attraction.

snorkeling, and mangrove channel tours around La Parguera and Guánica on a catamaran. It also has kayaks for rent.

Fondo de Cristal III (end of Carr. 304, La Parguera, 787/899-5891 or 787/344-0593) offers daytime trips to nearby cays and nighttime tours of Bahía Fosforescente on a 72-foot bi-level glass-bottomed catamaran that is wheelchair accessible.

ACCOMMODATIONS
$50-100
Andy's Guest House (133 Calle 8, 787/899-0000, $75 weekends, $55 weeknights, tax included) is possibly the best deal in La Parguera. The basic, three-story, well-maintained concrete structure is in a pleasant residential area. To get there from Carretera 304, turn onto Calle 7 and then right on Calle 8. It's also called Andino's.

La Parguera Guest House (Carr. 304, km 3.3, 787/899-3993, www.pargueraguesthouse.com, $65 s, $76 d) is a modest little blue and yellow guesthouse with simple basic rooms that have air-conditioning, cable TV, and mini-refrigerators. There's no pool, restaurant, or bar, but there are barbecue grills on the grounds for guests' use.

$100-150
C **Parador Villa Parguera** (Carr. 304, 787/899-7777, fax 787/899-6040, pvparguera@prtc.net, www.villaparguera.net, $107–155 s/d sea view, $96–144 s/d garden view, including breakfast) is one of the most romantically old-fashioned paradors in Puerto Rico. Time seems to have stopped still at this sprawling property. The low-profile, white clapboard hotel sits right on the bay in La Parguera. Although the lobby is fairly dated and underwhelming, the rooms are immaculate, comfortable, and overlook beautifully landscaped gardens and the water. Rooms come with air-conditioning, cable TV, telephones, showers and tubs, and balconies. There are also a large pool, a good restaurant, and a small bar that serves a tasty piña colada made from scratch. There's also a cabaret show in Spanish on the weekends.

FOOD
Puerto Rican
El Karokal (in front of the boat dock, 787/899-5582, daily 11 A.M.–midnight or later) is a casual fast food–style establishment serving Puerto Rican cuisine and seafood. Thanks to the signs all over town hyping it, it's famous for its coconut sangria.

Seafood
La Casita Seafood (Carr. 304, km 3.3, 787/899-1681, Tues.–Thurs. 4–10 P.M., Fri.–Sat. 11 A.M.–10 P.M., $7.95–25) is a large casual family-oriented restaurant serving Puerto Rican cuisine and seafood. Its specialties include whole fish and *asopao,* a seafood stew featuring octopus, lobster, or shrimp. There's no bar, but it does serve wine and beer.

La Pared (Posada Porlamar guesthouse, Carr. 304, km 3.3, 787/899-4343, Mon.–Sat. 6–11 P.M., Sun. 1–11 P.M., $14.95–28.95) is a romantic, upscale fine-dining establishment overlooking the water. The restaurant specializes in creative seafood dishes with a Caribbean flair, including shrimp in papaya sauce and crab cakes in black bean and coconut sauce. Meat dishes include rack of lamb with goat cheese and pistachios in a wine-reduction sauce and pork with mango chutney and parmesan cheese.

SAN GERMÁN
San Germán is the second-oldest colonial city in Puerto Rico. It was established in 1573 after the original village, built in 1511, was sacked by the French 17 years later. It's a lovely town with two plazas and lots of hilly streets lined with grand 18th- and 19th-century homes decked out in intricate wrought-iron balconies, massive columns, and shades of pastel blues, pinks, and greens. Unfortunately many are vacant and falling into disrepair, though many have been restored along Calle Luna.

The town's big attraction is Porta Coéli, a small Gothic chapel built in the early 1600s. Accommodations and restaurants are limited in San Germán, but it's a great day trip. Getting there is a pleasant shady drive through winding mountain roads, and it's a wonderful opportunity to experience a colonial town that's fairly untouched by mainland influence.

☀ Porta Coéli Chapel and Museum of Religious Art

Porta Coéli Chapel and Museum of Religious Art (at Calle Ramos and Calle Dr. Santiago Veve, on the south end of Plazuela Santo Domingo, 787/892-5845, Wed.–Sun. 8:30 A.M.–noon and 1–4:20 P.M., $1), is one of the few examples of Gothic architecture built in the New World, and it's the oldest chapel in Puerto Rico, having been established in 1606. Its primitive, dark sanctuary contains a fantastic collection of 18th- and 19th-century religious paintings and sculpture, including striking primitive-style wood carvings of the 12 stations of the cross. Beside the chapel are the brick ruins of a building that once housed the parish priests. Information is in Spanish only. Limited information in English is available at www.icp.gobierno.pr/icp/ingles/aboutus.htm. A couple of blocks away is **Iglesia San Germán de Auxerre,** a larger, more elaborate church on Plazuela San Germán.

Shopping

Botánica San Miguel (23 Calle Dr. Santiago Veve, 787/892-1039, Mon.–Sat. 8 A.M.–11:45 A.M. and 1–5 P.M.) is a tiny shop packed to the rafters with scents, oils, candles, soaps, herbs, holy water, and more. Want to attract a paramour, make more money, or remove evil spirits from your home? The friendly proprietor is sure to have something to help you out.

Food

There aren't any real standouts among the restaurants in San Germán, but there are a few small modest places that will keep you from going hungry. Options include **Chaparritas Bar and Restaurant** (Calle Luna, 787/892-1078, Wed.–Thurs. 11:30 A.M.–3 P.M. and 6–9 P.M., Fri. 11:30 A.M.–3 P.M. and 6–10 P.M., Sat. 6–10 P.M., $11–15), a casual, brightly painted restaurant serving Mexican cuisine; and **Tapas Café** (Calle Dr. Santiago Veve, Wed.–Thurs. 4:30–10 P.M., Fri. 4:30–11 P.M., Sat. 11 A.M.–11 P.M., Sun. 11 A.M.–9 P.M.).

Information and Services

Hospital Metropolitano de San Germán (Javilla CDT, 787/892-5300) supplies medical services to San Germán, and **Walgreens** (at Calle Luna y Carra, 787/892-1170) operates a pharmacy.

WEST COAST

NORTH COAST

The north coast of Puerto Rico is a wild expanse of rocky coastline and gorgeous ocean views, hilly karst country, and green farmland. It's also thick with industrial plants, shopping centers, fast-food restaurants, road construction, and traffic. Despite the urban sprawl, though, the north coast has a lot going for it.

Although craggy, rocky shores and rough waters can make finding the ideal swimming spot a challenge, there are several spectacular ocean-side jewels worth seeking out—at the resorts in Dorado, Punta Cerro Gordo in Vega Alta, and Playa Mar Chiquita in Manatí. Meanwhile, the powerful waves along the north coast make for excellent surfing, especially around Manatí and Arecibo. The major sport on the north coast, though, is golf. Dorado is home to five classic courses.

The two biggest attractions on the north coast, and the main reason most visitors venture there, are the Observatorio de Arecibo, the world's largest radio telescope, and Las Cavernas del Río Camuy, a major cave system with hiking trails and a nature park. Both places are about a 30-minute drive south of Arecibo into the island's mountainous karst country. The unusual topography alone is worth the drive. An intricate system of underground limestone caves creates enormous sinkholes and haystack hills—called *mogotes*—on the earth's surface. It's a stunning sight completely unlike anywhere else on the island—and nearly the world.

© SUZANNE VAN ATTEN

HIGHLIGHTS

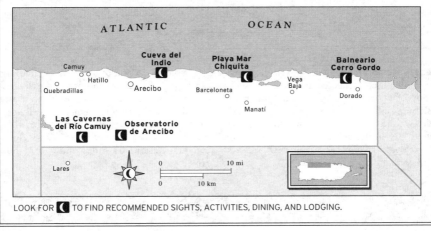 **Balneario Cerro Gordo:** Brand-new facilities and a superb campground just add to the idyllic setting of this publicly maintained beach on Punta Cerro Gordo in Vega Alta, making it a great spot to sun, swim, and surf (page 159).

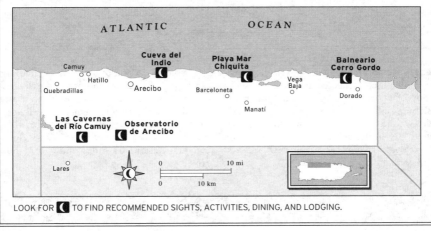 **Playa Mar Chiquita:** Tucked down at the bottom of a cliff, this small protected cove in Manatí offers calm waters for swimming and an intricate system of limestone caves where you can find Taíno petroglyphs (page 161).

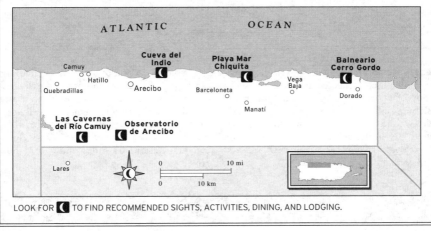 **Observatorio de Arecibo:** Check out the largest and most sensitive radio telescope in the world. The 18-acre dish is in a natural sinkhole created by the hilly karst landscape (page 162).

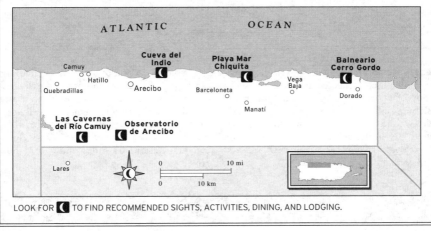 **Cueva del Indio:** Explore the petrified sand dunes, natural arches, blow holes, and ancient Taíno petroglyphs found at this off-the-beaten-path site on the coast just east of Arecibo (page 163).

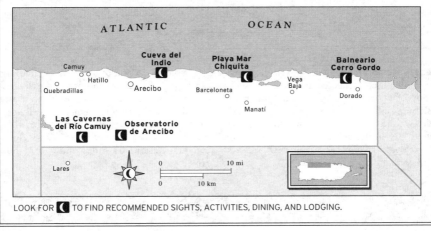 **Las Cavernas del Río Camuy:** The third-largest river cave system in the world, the Camuy caves are located in a well-maintained park providing easy access to Puerto Rico's underground natural wonders (page 166).

LOOK FOR 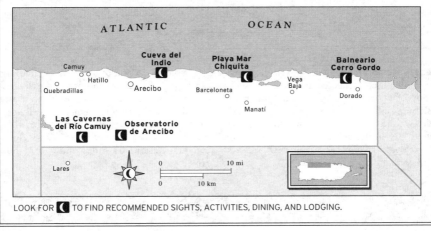 TO FIND RECOMMENDED SIGHTS, ACTIVITIES, DINING, AND LODGING.

PLANNING YOUR TIME

Puerto Rico's north coast is a great place for a day trip, an overnight stay, or a long weekend. Thanks to two major roadways it's easily accessible whether you're approaching it from San Juan or from the west coast.

Despite what you might think, Highway 22, a multilane divided toll road with six toll booths between San Juan and Arecibo, is the best route along the north coast. Although construction projects and commuter rush hours can sometimes slow your progress, it is the most expeditious route. The alternative is Carretera 2, a congested multilane commercial route that bisects the island's longest, most unsightly stretch of urban sprawl. It should be avoided when possible.

Dorado is the farthest eastern municipality, about 17 miles and 30 minutes from San Juan. A popular resort area, it has lovely beaches and world-class golf courses. Farther westward are the municipalities of Vega Alta and Manatí, which have some spectacular beaches—**Balneario Cerro Gordo** and **Playa Mar Chiquita,** respectively—that are ideal for swimming.

But the most popular sights along the north coast are **Las Cavernas del Río Camuy** and

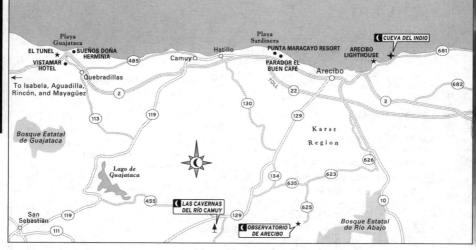

Observatorio de Arecibo, both in the southern tips of their respective municipalities and about 1.5 hours from San Juan. It's possible to visit both sights on a day trip if you get an early start. While in Arecibo, be sure to check out **Cueva del Indio,** an amazing geological and archaeological wonder featuring petrified sand dunes and Taíno petroglyphs.

The best selection of hotels and restaurants can be found at either end of the north coast. In Dorado, the accommodations are mostly upscale. There are more budget-minded hotels and restaurants in Hatillo and Quebradillas, the north coast's farthest municipality from San Juan, about 65 miles and a 1.75-hour drive away.

Toa Baja and Toa Alta

Toa Baja and Toa Alta were once home to one of the largest Taíno Indian populations on the island, probably for the same reasons the Spanish colonists were drawn here—the excellent fishing and fertile soil. The land was taken and the Taíno enslaved in 1511 when Juan Ponce de León established the King's Farm on the rich shores of Río de la Plata, one of several rivers that converge in the area. The farm played an important role in the Spanish colony. Not only did farmers use it to figure out how to cultivate European vegetables in the tropics, but it produced much of the produce consumed by the colonists.

Eventually settlers began to flock here to farm the fertile soil and fish the rich rivers. In 1776, just as the United States was gaining independence from England, the Spanish were establishing cattle ranches and sugarcane plantations throughout Toa Baja and Toa Alta.

To many travelers, Toa Baja and Toa Alta are just municipalities you have to blow through to get to points farther west. But these communities have their charms. There are some good swimming and fishing spots to be found. And the town of Toa Alta boasts the Parroquia San Fernando Rey, a church built in 1752, and the beloved Bala de Cañon tree,

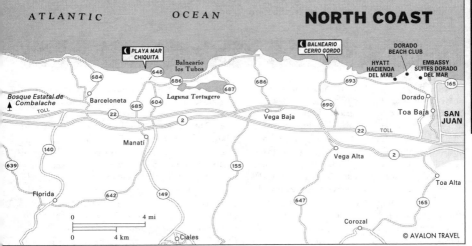

which bears fruit that looks like cannonballs. The best reason to stop, though, is to dine at Millie's Place.

SIGHTS AND RECREATION

The lovely drive along Carretera 165 east from Dorado toward **Balneario Punta Salinas** (daily 8:30 A.M.–6 P.M.) is reason alone to visit the publicly maintained beach. The highway runs between a picturesque stretch of roadway that divides an undeveloped palm grove from the rocky coastline. The beach lies on both sides of an isthmus that juts into the Atlantic and offers a great view of Old San Juan. The facilities include picnic shelters, bathrooms, and a snack bar. There's a space-age–style geodesic dome that sits on a hill overlooking the beach that houses the 140th Air Defense Squadron.

Area Recreativa de Lago La Plata (Carr. 824, km 4.9, Toa Alta, 787/723-6435, Tues.–Sun. 6 A.M.–6 P.M.) is a new recreation area popular with freshwater anglers. It features bathroom facilities, picnic shelters, and barbecue grills. The lake is stocked with fish, including largemouth bass, by the Maricao Fish Hatchery.

FOOD

It's well off the beaten path, but **C Millie's Place** (377 Calle Parque at Acueducto, Barrio Sabana Seca, Toa Baja, 787/784-3488, Wed.–Thurs. 11 A.M.–4 P.M., Fri. 11 A.M.–8 P.M., Sat.–Sun. 11 A.M.–6 P.M., $16–45) is well worth the trip. People travel from far and wide to dine on Millie's magnificent land crabs. The big blue crustaceans are captured and corralled in pens behind the restaurant. The trick is how to find this modest blue concrete structure, across the street from a neighborhood ball park. From San Juan, travel west on Highway 22, and then go north on Carretera 866, which takes several turns. The road dead-ends at a T intersection in front of a pharmacy. To the left is Carretera 187, but you'll want to turn right. Go about a quarter mile and turn left onto Acueducto beside the El Semaforo auto parts store. Millie's Place is on the left across from the baseball field. The good thing is, if you get lost, just call. The English-speaking staff gives great directions.

At a sharp bend in the road between Dorado and Punta Salinas is **El Caracol** (Carr. 165, Toa Baja), a large, very casual open-air restaurant and pool hall right on the beach. In addition to selling bottles of beer for $1 during its "permanent happy hour," it has a great selection of fried fare, including empanadas, *pastelillos*, and *taquitas*.

Dorado

Dorado means "golden" in Spanish, but the only thing that glitters here are the beaches. Dorado is home to the grand dame of resorts, the Dorado Beach Club, developed in the late 1950s on what was once a plantation of grapefruit and pineapples. Its claim to fame, aside from its beautifully maintained natural grounds and perfect beaches, is its world-famous golf courses. For the well-heeled traveler who likes golf and gorgeous beaches, it's a great spot to spend a long weekend.

Just because there's no gold in Dorado doesn't mean fortunes aren't made here. The community has experienced a mini–housing boom in the last few years, and developers are doing quite well. Everywhere you look are gated subdivisions filled cheek by jowl with homes and condos for sale in the $400,000 range.

The town is small and, like so many town centers throughout Puerto Rico, undergoing a major renovation of its plaza and surrounding streets. But there are a couple of tiny museums worth a look if you need a culture fix. The best restaurants are at the town's resorts, although there are a couple of interesting standouts in town. Once those new neighborhoods fill up, the trendy dining options should follow suit.

SIGHTS

There are two small museums in Dorado. **Museo y Centro Cultural Casa del Rey** (Méndez Vigo, Dorado, 787/796-5740, call for hours) is based in a lovely 19th-century Spanish garrison built in 1823. Restored by the Puerto Rican Institute of Culture in 1978, it contains 19th-century furnishings and fixtures. **Museo de Arte y Historia de Dorado** (Méndez Vigo at Juan Francisco, Dorado, 787/796-5740, Mon.–Fri. 8 A.M.–3:30 P.M., Sat. 9 A.M.–3:30 P.M.) has three exhibition halls featuring displays of art, archaeological artifacts, and illustrations depicting the city's history.

El Ojo del Buey (end of Carr. 698, Barrio Mameyal, Dorado, 787/796-5740 or 787/796-6001) is a fantastic recreational area along the rocky coast with terrific views of the water. It's great for hiking, but be sure to wear sturdy shoes such as sneakers or hiking boots to help you navigate the hills and craters. And be sure to follow the path through the thick sea-grape bushes to the site's namesake—El Ojo del Buey (The Ox's Eye)—an impressive rock formation that resembles the head of an ox. Legend has it that the Puerto Rican pirate Roberto Cofresí buried his treasure here.

Much of the coastline along Dorado is rocky, except for that occupied by the resorts, but you can find a nice little patch of sandy beach at **Playa de Dorado** (end of Carr. 697, Dorado, 8:30 A.M.–5 P.M.) in town.

SPORTS AND RECREATION

When it comes to sports in Dorado, golf reigns supreme. **Dorado Beach Club** (Carr. 693, Dorado, 787/796-1234 or 800/981-9066, ext. 3710, www.doradobeachclub.com) has two 18-hole courses designed by Robert Trent Jones Sr. It has hosted the Senior PGA Tour Championship, the Chi Chi Rodriguez Pro Am Golf Classic, the Johnnie Walker International Pro Am, and the World Cup golf tournaments. The 72-par East Course (7 A.M.–5:30 P.M.) was built in 1958 and modified by Raymond Floyd in 1999. Its highlight is the fourth hole, a double dogleg over two lakes that was named one of the 10 best-designed holes in the world by Jack Nicklaus. The 72-par West Course (7 A.M.–5:30 P.M.) was built in 1960 and modified by Raymond Floyd in 2003.

The Plantation at Dorado club (787/796-8915, www.doradobeach.hyatt.com) has two 18-hole courses designed by Robert Trent Jones Sr. and renovated by Raymond Floyd. The North Course (6:45 A.M.–5:30 P.M.) features challenging sand traps and sweeping mountain views. The South Course (7 A.M.–5:30 P.M.) has great water hazards and views.

The Hyatt also has five hard-surface **tennis** courts and a tennis pro who offers private instruction and daily tennis clinics (Carr. 693, Dorado, 800/981-9066, pro shop 787/796-1234, ext. 3724, www.doradobeach .hyatt.com).

Dorado del Mar Golf Club (Embassy Suites Dorado del Mar Beach and Golf Resort, 201 Dorado Del Mar Blvd., Dorado, 787/796-3070, 6 A.M.–9 P.M., campgolf@coqui.com) is an 18-hole course designed by Chi Chi Rodriguez. Twelve holes are on the water.

ENTERTAINMENT AND EVENTS

In its effort to encourage tourism, Dorado hosts quite a few festivals, including **Carnaval de la Plata** in February, **Fiestas de la Cruz** in May, **Festival de la Cocolía** in August, **Discovery of Puerto Rico** in November, and a **Christmas Festival** in December. For details, call the tourism office at 787/796-5740.

ACCOMMODATIONS

The impetus that transformed Dorado from a grapefruit and pineapple plantation into a world-class vacation destination is ◖ **Dorado Beach Club** (Carr. 693, Dorado, 787/796-1234, fax 787/798-2022). Built in 1958, the resort was the brainchild of Laurance Rockefeller, who envisioned a quiet low-key resort that catered to its guests' every desire and complemented the property's natural beauty. Rockefeller's proclamation that no structure could be higher than the tallest palm tree set the ideal stage for this elegant, sprawling, low-profile resort that blended beautifully into the thick, mature vegetation and pristine beaches.

Dorado Beach Club has undergone significant changes over the years. The property evolved over time, eventually encompassing 262 units and four restaurants. The Hyatt was operating the property when it closed in 2006. It has since been bought by Kemper Sports, a golf management company, and scaled down to 36 casita units and two restaurants. But it still boasts gorgeous oceanfront views and four championship 18-hole golf courses designed by Robert Trent Jones Sr.

Nearby is **Hyatt Hacienda del Mar** (301 Highway 693, 787/796-3000, fax 787/796-3610, www.hyatthaciendadelmar.hyatt.com/ hyatt/hotels, $99 studio, $139 one-bedroom unit, $199 two-bedroom, plus taxes), a privately owned vacation rental property located at what used to be the Hyatt Cerromar Beach Resort. Rooms come with air-conditioning, TV, wireless Internet, and full kitchens and kitchenettes. On-site dining is provided by the casual Bohio bar and grill. The casino, swimming pool, and grounds were undergoing renovation at press time.

You can't miss **Embassy Suites Dorado del Mar Beach and Golf Resort** (201 Dorado Del Mar Blvd., Dorado, 787/796-6125, 800/ EMBASSY—800/362-2779, www.embassy suitesdorado.com, $179–219, plus 9 percent tax and 12 percent resort fee). It's the tallest and flashiest building in the area. Three buildings contain 174 suites with balconies and 38 two-bedroom villas, decked out with microwaves, refrigerators, coffeepots, hair dryers, cable TV, and dual-line telephones. Amenities include the Dorado del Mar Gold Club, an 18-hole, 72-par golf course designed by Chi Chi Rodriguez, a lagoon pool overlooking the beach, a whirlpool bath, tennis courts, a fitness room, and two restaurants.

FOOD

◖ **El Ladrillo** (334 Méndez Vigo, Dorado, 787/796-2120, www.restauranteelladrillo.com, dinner daily, lunch Tues.–Fri. and Sun.) is a lovely Old World fine-dining restaurant that has been serving expertly prepared steaks, seafood, and Puerto Rican cuisine to locals and visitors alike for 30 years. Red brick arches and colorful paintings by local artists contribute to the warm atmosphere. Specialties include plantain soup, rice dishes, and a variety of lobster dishes and steaks. It has a full bar and a well-stocked wine cellar.

La Terraza (Calle Marginal C-1, Costa de Oro, Dorado, 787/796-1242, daily noon–midnight, $15–45) is a pricey tourist-friendly restaurant on an open-air terrace decked out in a cheery nautical theme. The menu features mostly traditional Puerto Rican cuisine, and its specialty is *mofongo* stuffed with everything from octopus to lobster to chicken. Other dishes include veal chops, scallops in champagne sauce, and stuffed plantains. Up top is a sports bar.

INFORMATION AND SERVICES

The **police department** is at Calle Méndez Vigo and Avenida Albizu Campos. **The Dorado Medical Hospital** (Carr. 698 just off Calle Méndez Vigo, 787/796-6050) has a 24-hour emergency room. **Walgreens** (Carr. 693, 787/278-5800) is open 24 hours. **Banco Popular** (787/278-1171) has an ATM in the **Grande supermarket** (787/278-2400) on Calle Méndez Vigo.

Vega Alta and Vega Baja

Vega Alta and Vega Baja are on fertile low-lying land divided by Río Cibuca, and it was here—not Dorado—where gold was found on the north coast. And naturally, where there was gold there were conquistadors. During colonization, the river's shores were populated by the Spanish, who used Taíno labor to mine the valuable mineral, which was washed into the river's channels by the strong ocean current. After the gold rush depleted the deposit, then came the sugar rush: The rich, level soil made the area perfect for growing sugarcane, and many slaves were brought in to work the land. In 1848 there was an attempted revolt among the slaves in Vega Baja, which was squelched when one of the main agitators was killed.

The highlight of the Vegas is definitely Punta Cerro Gordo, a gorgeous piece of coastline that boasts one of the island's best publicly maintained beaches and a great camping area.

SIGHTS
Museo de Arte Casa Alonso

Believed to have been built around the time Vega Baja was established, around 1776, Museo de Arte Casa Alonso (34 Calle Betances, Vega Baja, 787/855-1364, fax 787/855-1931, Tues.–Sat. 9 A.M.–noon and 1–4 P.M., free) is a two-story, 2,000-square-foot neoclassic creole-style home constructed of wood, bricks, and stone. The interior has been restored and now serves as an art and history museum, displaying, among other objects, many of the artifacts recovered from the home, including ceramics, tiles, stoneware, and coins. In the first-floor courtyard is a 40-foot well, which provided water to the home's residents, the first of whom was Vega Baja Mayor Pablo Soliveras from Catalan. In addition to a collection of 19th-century furnishings, the house contains a room devoted to Puerto Rican popular music that includes photographs, phonographs, records, and radios.

Puerto Nuevo

Puerto Nuevo (Carr. 686, km 12, at Carr. 692, Vega Baja, 787/858-6447) has two parts to it. One part is a *balneario,* a free city-maintained recreation area with a lovely natural lagoon at its disposal. Facilities include lots of covered picnic shelters, outdoor showers, a playground, and a variety of food vendors selling fried snacks. Directly east of the *balneario* is a narrow road that takes you to a spot of wilderness coast where rocky outcroppings and soft patches of beach compete for space. Sandy pull-offs into the low-lying shrubs and trees that line the beach in some places suggest the area is something of a lover's lane at night. But on weekend days and holidays, it's a popular party beach for teenagers and young adults. There are no facilities, and the property is not well-maintained, as evidenced by the amount of litter. Women should avoid going here alone, as it's very remote. And don't leave any valuables in the car.

El Trece Recreational Area

El Trece Recreational Area (Carr. 160, km 13, Vega Baja) is a 13-acre city-maintained sports and recreation park on the Indio River where visitors can swim in natural pools of fresh river water. There are also hiking trails, picnic shelters, bathroom facilities, a handball court, and a grass volleyball court.

◖ Balneario Cerro Gordo

Even if there weren't a shortage of beaches suitable for swimming on the north coast,

Balneario Cerro Gordo (end of Carr. 6690, off Carr. 693, Vega Alta, 787/883-2730, daily 8:30 A.M.–6 P.M., parking $2 cars, $3 vans) would still be a wildly popular place to plunk down in the sun or frolic in the surf. It is a large, drop-dead gorgeous spot of forested coastline with dramatic cliffs, a rocky peninsula, and a palm-lined beach. There's a large protected cove that's perfect for swimming, and on the other side of the point are rougher waters ideal for surfing.

Thanks to a recently completed, multimillion-dollar investment by the government, this public beach has spanking new facilities, including bathrooms, showers, food vendors, lifeguards, and picnic tables. On the eastern end, on a shady mountaintop, are some great campsites ($13 per person) with ocean views. Expect a crowd on weekends and holidays.

SPORTS AND RECREATION

Reserva Natural Laguna Tortuguero (Carr. 687, km 1.2, Vega Baja, 787/858-6617, reserve open Wed.–Sun. 6 A.M.–5 P.M., office open

the view from the campgrounds at Balneario Cerro Gordo in Vega Alta

© SUZANNE VAN ATTEN

Mon.–Fri. 8 A.M.–4 P.M.) is a two-mile-long lagoon surrounded by swamps, marshlands, and karst mountains. A fishing dock provides a great place to angle for tilapia. In addition to fish, the lagoon is home to an estimated 1,000 caimans, a species of crocodile, believed to have originated from baby caimans that were imported from South America in the 1970s as pets and eventually released. They grow to six feet and can be vicious, but they're typically encountered only at night when the lagoon is closed.

The **Vega Baja Eco-Tourism Office** (Laguna Tortuguero, Carr. 687, km 1, 787/807-1822, Mon.–Fri. 8 A.M.–3 P.M., reservations required) offers guided nature tours through the lagoon. It also operates tours at El Trece recreation area and other areas.

ENTERTAINMENT AND EVENTS

It's all about the celebration of food in the Vegas. In mid-July, Vega Alta heralds the versatility of breadfruit with the **Festival de Panapén** (787/883-5900). In addition to performances by musicians and dancers, there are arts and crafts booths, food kiosks, and a breadfruit-cooking contest.

In Vega Baja, it's all about syrup at the **Festival del Melao Melao** (787/858-6617) held in early October. Artisans and food vendors line the Plaza de Recreo, where wood-carving competitions are held.

PRACTICALITIES

Costa Norte Restaurante (Carr. 686, km 12 at Calle Joaquin Rosa Gomez, Vega Baja, 787/858-4247, daily 9 A.M.–9 P.M., $2–6) is easy to spot, thanks to the bright green metal fencing that encloses the patio at this glorified fry shack across from Balneario Puerto Nuevo, Vega Baja's public beach. It's an excellent place to pick up fried chunks of *dorado, mofongo,* and "tacos" filled with fish, meat, shrimp, or chicken.

Vega Baja Casa de Cultura y Turismo (Calle Betances at Tulio Otero, Vega Baja, 787/858-6447, Mon.–Fri. 8 A.M.–4:30 P.M.) offers information on the history and culture of the area and provides tours upon request.

Manatí and Barceloneta

The town of Manatí proper, south of Highway 22, isn't much of a draw for visitors, but north of town along its coast is a lovely wonderland of rolling green hills and delightful beaches ideal for swimming and surfing. The thick vegetation and elevation make it a cool enclave for the fabulous new homes and condos that have cropped up here. Once known for their grand sugar plantations and haciendas, Manatí and Barceloneta's economies now revolve around pharmaceutical manufacturing and growing pineapples. Barceloneta is notable as the starting point for a spectacular scenic drive to Arecibo and as home to the Bosque Estatal de Combalache, a small forest popular for its wooded mountain-bike trails.

SIGHTS
Balneario Playa Los Tubos

Balneario Playa Los Tubos (Carr. 686, Manatí, 787/884-3428, Wed.–Fri. 8 A.M.–4 P.M., Sat.–Sun. 9 A.M.–5 P.M.) has to hold the distinction of being the most fanciful public beach in all of Puerto Rico. Set high on a hill and ensconced behind impressive steel gates are the standard facilities—bathrooms, showers, picnic shelters, food vendors, and so on—but they're tricked out like something from a Dr. Seuss book. Enormous animal statues in bright shades of yellow, green, and pink stand sentry over the elaborate columned picnic shelters with stacked pyramid rooftops and a magnificent view of the Atlantic. Beside the *balneario* is a stretch of wilderness beach that's renowned for its surfing.

© SUZANNE VAN ATTEN

Playa Mar Chiquita in Manatí

Hacienda La Esperanza

Today, Hacienda La Esperanza (Carr. 616, Manatí, 787/854-2679, Fri., Sun., and holidays 8 A.M.–4 P.M., free) is a lovely, quiet natural preserve, but in the late 19th century it was one of the biggest, richest sugar plantations in Puerto Rico. In addition to the manor house, the sugar mill, and an ornate 1861 steam engine, the property encompasses more than 2,000 acres of karst formations. In addition, recent excavations have revealed that it was once occupied by indigenous people. A *batey* (a pre-Columbian ceremonial ball park), four plazas, a burial ground, and petroglyphs have been discovered. Although visitors are welcome to enjoy the grounds, the structures and archaeological sites are closed to the public while the Historic Conservation of Puerto Rico works to preserve the area.

◖ Playa Mar Chiquita

If you're anywhere near Manatí, don't pass by without stopping at Playa Mar Chiquita (end of Carr. 648, off of Carr. 685, Manatí),

an enchanting wonderland of natural beauty. Tucked down in the base of a wooded cliff is a perfectly formed natural pool almost completely enclosed by two long reaches of rocky coral that embrace a pristine crescent of sandy beach and crystal-clear water ideal for taking a dip.

The formation of Playa Mar Chiquita is so picture-perfect that a legend has grown up around it to explain its creation. As the story goes, a beautiful woman went to Mar Chiquita and fell into the ocean. She began to drown, but then the sea opened up and the waves washed her ashore. A few days later she returned to Mar Chiquita and was surprised to discover that the lovely fan-shaped pool had formed.

There's more to Playa Mar Chiquita than its baby-safe beach, though. The mountain base contains an intricate system of caves, where the adventurous can discover stalagmites and stalactites, as well as petroglyphs left behind by indigenous people. Mangrove trees and sea grapes grow thick and low throughout the area, creating their own cave-like nooks where lovers park for rendezvous. Crumbling ruins of small buildings and walls add a bewitching quality. And set high into a cliff wall is a tiny shrine containing a likeness of the Virgin Mary, who looks down on all the mysterious beauty below.

Scenic Drive

A scenic drive from Barceloneta to Arecibo is one excellent reason to venture off Highway 22. This 10-mile stretch along Carretera 684 north and Carretera 681 is like Puerto Rico's own little version of California's Pacific Coast Highway, rich in gorgeous views of the ocean with lots of spots to pull over and go for a swim. There's also a great surfing point break at Machuca's Garden at La Boca off Carretera 684.

SPORTS AND RECREATION

Thanks to powerful waves and easy access, some of the best surfing in Puerto Rico can be found at **Los Tubos** (Carr. 686, Manatí), beside Balneario Playa Los Tubos. The best time to go is November–March, when the hollow swells can get up to 16 feet or more. It's rarely very crowded, and you can drive right down to the water. Just watch out for the sharp rocky bottom and sea urchins. Los Tubos is not for the inexperienced surfer.

Mountain-bike enthusiasts will want to check out **Bosque Estatal de Cambalache** (Carr. 682, km 6.3, beside the Job Corps facility, Barceloneta, 787/791-1004 or 787/878-7279, office Mon.–Fri. 8 A.M.–4:30 P.M.), a small wooded recreation area open Saturday–Sunday 9 A.M.–5 P.M.), where trails meander through this 1,000-acre subtropical forest reserve distinguished by its dramatic hilly karst formations. There are also four miles of hiking trails, a wheelchair-accessible trail, and camping for up to 40 people. To obtain permits to camp ($4) or cycle ($1), call 787/724-3724. Unfortunately, there's no bike-rental outfitter, so bring your own gear.

Arecibo

Before the Spanish arrived, Arecibo was home to a peaceful group of about 200 Taíno natives led by Cacique Arasibo, reputed to be a fair ruler over his village of fishermen. In 1515, Spain claimed the Arecibo area and enslaved the Taíno, most of whom died shortly thereafter. Today Arecibo is the most populated municipality on the north coast, with more than 100,000 residents who call it home. It is also a major industrial hub, producing textiles, chemicals, electronics, and medical instruments. As a result, Arecibo has been blighted by massive urban sprawl distinguished by traffic-clogged thoroughfares and unfettered commercial development.

Nevertheless, there are several good reasons to visit the municipality of Arecibo. In the mountainous karst country south of town is the world-famous Observatorio de Arecibo. On the coast is Cueva del Indio, a geographic wonder that illustrates what happens when crashing waves meet massive petrified sand dunes—it's also a natural repository for petroglyphs. And for children, there's the Faro de Arecibo Lighthouse and Historical Park with its themed playgrounds and welcoming patch of beach.

SIGHTS
◖ Observatorio de Arecibo

You know you're headed someplace unique as you travel south from the town of Arecibo toward the Observatorio de Arecibo (end of Carr. 625, Arecibo, 787/817-1936 or 787/880-7420, www.naic.edu, Wed.–Fri. noon–4 P.M., Sat.–Sun. and holidays 9 A.M.–4 P.M., $4 adults, $2 children and seniors), the world's largest and most sensitive radio telescope. The bustle of commerce, industry, expressways, and road-construction projects eventually gives way to a bright green grassy landscape dotted with dramatic haystack-shaped hills called *mogotes*.

COURTESY OF NATIONAL ASTRONOMY & IONOSPHERE CENTER

the telescope at Observatorio de Arecibo

Passing cars become few as the curvy road winds around the hills and ever upward, past sprawling cattle farms and errant chickens.

Be sure to bring sturdy walking shoes and an umbrella. Entry to the observatory requires a half-mile hike—mostly up stairs—from the parking lot to the entrance, and there's little shelter along the way. As you climb ever higher toward the observatory, the first glimpse between treetops of the telescope's suspension apparatus is a startling sight. Its cold, clinical, metal construction is in sharp contrast to the wilderness that surrounds it. The road ends at a guardhouse, where you park your car and begin the long uphill trek on a concrete surface to the top of the massive sinkhole that contains the telescope's dish. There are 500 steps, according to one source, and the hike can be so steep and arduous that there are little covered resting stations along the way for those who need to catch their breath. Visitors unable to make the journey by foot can get permission from the guard to drive up to the entrance.

Because there's not really much to do on a tour of the observatory, other than gawk at the sheer size of the telescope dish, a newly constructed educational center has been added. Inside are two levels of informative displays and interactive exhibits that educate visitors on the finer points of the study of space and the atmosphere. A short film on the telescope is screened throughout the day in both English and Spanish. But the highlight of the center is its observation deck, from which visitors can peer over the side of the massive dish. There's also a great gift shop that sells all kinds of great educational books, models, and toys. It's a good source for maps of the island too.

◖ Cueva del Indio

Because it's not technically an official tourist site—no government-sanctioned bathrooms, marked trails, information center, and so on—the Cueva del Indio (Carr. 681, km 7, $1) is Arecibo's lesser-known attraction, but it's well worth investigating. In fact, its down-home operation is part of its charm. A hand-painted sign marks the turn that takes visitors to the home of the caves' kindly overseer, Richard.

IS ANYBODY OUT THERE?

Built in 1963, the Observatorio de Arecibo is a curved dish telescope set into the earth on what was once a coffee plantation in the upper regions of Puerto Rico's karst country. The landscape is distinguished by an underground system of limestone caves that has transformed the topography into clusters of fertile green hills and sinkholes. It is because of the landscape's natural depressions, which were big enough to contain the telescope's dish, that the observatory was built here.

To convey a sense of its immensity, consider these statistics: The aluminum-lined dish is 1,000 feet wide from rim to rim and encompasses 18 acres. The receiver is on a 900-ton platform suspended 450 feet above the dish on a 304-foot moveable arm. Operated by Cornell University in association with the National Science Foundation, the observatory employs about 140 scientists and engineers from around the world.

Many significant astronomical discoveries have been made at the observatory in the last four decades. Joseph Taylor won the Nobel Prize in 1993 for discovering the first binary pulsar from Arecibo. Other discoveries made at Arecibo include the discovery of polar caps on Mercury and the existence of planets around a pulsar.

But Arecibo's most infamous contribution to science has been as the center of operations for the Search for Extraterrestrial Intelligence Institute's Phoenix Project, which monitored the telescope for signs of intelligent life in the universe. A respected organization of some of the world's foremost scientists, including three Nobel Prize winners, the SETI Institute and its Arecibo research project was funded through grants by NASA for many years before the organization became private in 1993. The project is not as "ET" as it sounds, though. The telescope doesn't so much "seek" intelligent life as listen for radio signals that might indicate its presence. Nevertheless, its otherworldly visage has made it a popular backdrop for filmmakers. In fact, much of the Jodie Foster movie *Contact* was filmed here.

There's one more thing about the Arecibo Observatory that is unique, and that is its longevity. Most major telescopes become obsolete after about 10 years as technological advancements are made, but not Arecibo. Multimillion dollar upgrades have been made through the years that have extended its viability. Most recently a new "eye" was installed in 2004 that enables it to take photographs of space.

Pay him $1, and he takes you for a personal tour of his amazing backyard.

The journey begins with a short trek through scrubby, prickly brush that soon gives way to what looks like a massive moonscape rising out of the sea. The coral surface was formed from enormous petrified sand dunes whose guts have been scooped out through time from the pounding sea beating against its base. To the west is a large hole in the surface that leads down into a cave, which bottoms out on the sea floor. On its interior walls are faint petroglyphs—a sun, an owl, human faces—believed to have been made by the Taíno more than 500 years ago. To the east are huge natural arches where the sea has cut through

the coral mass. During high tide, waves crash into it with such force that the water shoots 20–30 feet in the air.

Hiking shoes or sturdy sneakers are a must, as the coral surface is very rocky and covered with camouflaged tree roots in some places. Stay away from the precarious edges and keep your eyes peeled for holes in the surface. Perhaps the government chose not to make this an official tourist site because of the liability: Take one false step and it may be the last step you take. If you're nice, maybe Richard will show you where he collects big blue land crabs in an old tractor tire in his backyard, saving them up until he has enough to cook for dinner.

Faro de Arecibo Lighthouse and Historical Park

Families will enjoy Faro de Arecibo Lighthouse and Historical Park (Rte. 655, Barrio Islote, Arecibo, 787/880-7540 or 787/880-7560, fax 787/880-7520, www.arecibolighthouse .com, Mon.–Fri. 9 A.M.–6 P.M., Sat.–Sun. 10 A.M.–7 P.M., $9 age 13 and up, $7 children 2–12, parking $2.) Built in 1898, the neoclassical-style lighthouse was the last one built by colonial Spain. It's on top of Punta Morrillo, a rocky mountain overlooking the north coast, and offers spectacular views of the Atlantic Ocean and surrounding area. The lighthouse is still operational, and inside are historical displays and artifacts of curiosities found in the ocean, including a 1910 diving suit.

Road-tripping families will want to stop here to let their young children burn off some energy in the recently constructed historical park. Representing the island's historical eras are interactive, kid-friendly representations of an Arasibo Taíno Village; Columbus's ships the *Niña,* the *Pinta,* and the *Santa María;* African slave quarters; a replica of Blackbeard's pirate ship, the *Queen Anne's Revenge;* and a spooky Pirate's Cave containing tanks of sharks, turtles, and alligators. There are also a petting zoo and a standard playground with swings and so on.

The park also contains a small, well-maintained beach on the left as you approach the lighthouse. A smaller, scruffier patch of beach is outside the park just east of the lighthouse.

SPORTS AND RECREATION

Extreme-sports enthusiasts can enjoy caving, rappelling, and body-rafting expeditions along the Tanamá River with local outfitter

Expediciones Palenque (787/823-4354 or 787/306-4382, info@expedicionespalenque .com, www.expedicionespalenque.com, $90). The daylong adventure starts in the parking lot of Observatorio de Arecibo and takes thrill-seekers over waterfalls, into natural swimming holes, and on an optional 15–20-foot cliff dive.

PRACTICALITIES

On a former coffee plantation, **TJ Ranch** (El Valle, Río Arriba, Arecibo, 787/880-1217, reservations@tjranch.com, www.tjranch.com, $100, includes breakfast) is an oasis of quiet simplicity in a lovely spot of pristine nature between Arecibo and Utuado. The property has three little casitas, each with a bedroom, bathroom, and screened porch. There is also a pool, along with a restaurant specializing in seafood, local cuisine featuring goat and rabbit, and more continental dishes such as chicken marsala and lamb chops.

Restaurant El Observatorio (Carr. 625, km 1.1, Barrio Esperanza, Arecibo, 787/880-3813, Wed.–Sun. 11 A.M.–5 P.M., $6.95–16.95) is a bit pricey for the average quality of its food, but it's the only game around if a tour of the nearby Observatorio de Arecibo has left you hungry. The dining room is on an open-air patio overlooking the hilly karst country, and the menu features Puerto Rican cuisine, including *mofongo,* octopus salad, steak, and fried pork. There is a full bar.

The **police department** (787/878-2020) is on Avenida Hostos. The 24-hour **hospital** (787/878-7272) is at Carretera 129 and Avenida Rotario. **Banco Popular** (787/878-8500) has an ATM on the plaza at 65 Avenida Gonzalez Marín.

Camuy

Bypass the town of Camuy and go straight to Parque de Las Cavernas del Río Camuy, a fantastic nature park in the island's karst country where visitors can explore caves and hike nature trails to their hearts' content.

◖ LAS CAVERNAS DEL RÍO CAMUY

Puerto Rico is home to one of the largest underground river-cave systems in the world, and the easiest way to explore the island's subterranean world is at Las Cavernas del Río Camuy (Carr. 129, km 18.9, 787/898-3100 or 787/898-3136, Wed.–Sun. 8 A.M.–3:45 P.M., $10 adults, $7 children under 12, free for senior citizens over 75, parking $2). The park is a well-maintained, tightly run ship, and it's a good thing. This place draws major crowds, including busloads of schoolchildren. Buy a ticket, browse the gift shop, and watch a 10-minute film (English and Spanish) while waiting for the trolley, which runs every 30 minutes.

Once aboard, you zip down, down, down toward the mouth of Cueva Clara. Along the way you pass a mind-boggling display of virgin tropical forest. African tulips, mamey apples, passion fruit, red ginger, bananas, begonias, ferns, and the tiniest, most delicate orchids you've ever seen are everywhere. Before you know it, you're standing at the entrance to Clara.

The cavern's natural opening has been preserved. Visitors enter to the right of it through a larger, artificially constructed opening. The path steeply descends, bottoming out just below the natural opening, through which the sun shines brilliantly, creating the sort of mystical scene that could inspire visions of hobbits and fairies. But farther down are even more magnificent sights as the cavern opens into a 170-foot room thick with stalactites and stalagmites, most notably the Giant Stalagmite, measuring 17 feet tall and 30 feet in diameter. There's also a subterranean waterfall created by the Río Camuy, which runs through parts of the cave. In addition to bats, crickets, and

spiders, the cave is home to a creature that is so rare that this is the only place it lives. It's a microscopic crustacean called *Alloweckelia gurneii,* and it can't be seen by the naked eye.

Other natural sights in the park include Tres Pueblos sinkhole, seen from a viewing platform; Cathedral Cave; and Spiral Cave, accessible by a 200-step staircase to its mouth. There are also an interactive miniature gold mine where kids can pan for "nuggets," a snack bar, a gift shop, and trails. And although it's not publicized, there are a limited number of wooded campsites.

Of course, the part of the caves the general public sees is a tiny fraction of the wonders to be found. Lucky for experienced spelunkers, they can arrange tours to explore more remote parts of the caves. Sturdy, nonslip shoes are required; the cave paths get very slippery.

Expediciones Palenque (787/823-4354 or 787/306-4382, info@expedicionespalenque .com, www.expedicionespalenque.com, $90) offers a daylong adventure hiking, rappelling, caving, and body-rafting along the Río Camuy and into Resurgencia Cave.

Food

Just a short distance south of the entrance to the Camuy caves, **Restaurant El Taíno** (Carr. 129, km 21.1, Camuy, 787/645-4591, Wed.–Sat. 10:30 A.M.–7 P.M.) is the perfect place to grab a bite to eat after tromping through the nearby park's subterranean wonderland. The specialty of the house is rice with guinea hen, but the menu of traditional Puerto Rican fare also includes fried pork chops, rabbit in wine sauce, red snapper with scrambled eggplant, and *mofongo*. There's also a full bar and a recently constructed cocktail lounge made to resemble a Taíno hut.

HATILLO AND QUEBRADILLAS

Hatillo and Quebradillas are distinctly different municipalities, but they share one thing in common: Together they offer a pretty good selection of budget-minded hotels and restaurants, something that's lacking along much of the north coast.

Hatillo is best known for its dairy farms and its masked festival in December. People from all over the island flock to Hatillo for the annual Festival de la Máscaras, a three-day celebration that culminates on December 28, when hundreds of elaborately costumed and masked men and women dance through the streets, gathering at the town plaza at 3 P.M. for a parade.

Milk production drives the local economy, which reportedly produces one-third of the milk consumed on the island. A bronze statue of a farmer holding a calf in the split between Carretera 2 and Carretera 485 is a testament to the community's reverence for the industry.

Hatillo's commercial district along Carretera 2 is mostly a thick tangle of urban sprawl, but it soon gives way to an amazing view of the sea as you approach Quebradillas. A long, curved descent out of the mountains seems to hurtle you downward toward an enormous expanse of blue as far as the eye can see.

Sights

They're not necessarily worth going out of your way for, but if you're in the area and just need to get to a beach, there are a couple of options. **Paseo del Carmen** (on Carr. 119, Hatillo) is a small patch of beach by a shady pull-over in town. A bright blue balustrade lines a short sea walk that ends at a matching pavilion. The other option in Hatillo is **Playa Sardinera** (Carr. 2, km 84.6, turn beside entrance to Punta Maracayo Resort, Hatillo). This is also the site of the **Luis Muñoz Marín Vacation Center** (787/820-0274, fax 787/820-9116, Mon.–Fri. 8 A.M.–4:30 P.M., Sat.–Sun. 8 A.M.–5 P.M., $3), which features a protected lagoon and a well-maintained beach lined by a wooden boardwalk. Facilities include bathrooms, a pool, a playground, a basketball court, a volleyball court, and a cafeteria. There are also a campground and villa rentals. The main drawback is that there's not a lick of shade in sight.

In Quebradillas, **Playa Guajataca** (Carr. 2, km 103.8) is a scruffy patch of sand with no facilities tucked down between two escarpments. The tide is too rough for swimming, but it's a popular surf spot that's great for beginners. The western escarpment bears a reminder of the sugarcane train that once connected one side of the island to the other: **El Tunel** is an abandoned train tunnel that can be seen disappearing into the mountain.

Entertainment and Events

Hatillo hosts one of the island's most celebrated annual festivals. Originating in 1823 with the Spaniards who settled this part of the island, **Festival de la Máscaras** is a three-day costumed celebration held December 26–28. Originally it was meant to retell the story of King Herod's attempt to kill the infant Jesus by ordering the death of all male babies. Men would don elaborate costumes and masks and travel house-to-house on horseback. After playfully harassing the residents and demanding money, which was donated to the church or a civic organization, they would receive homemade treats and beverages. Today festivities revolve around street parades, music, dance, food, and crafts on the main plaza. The last day is reserved for **Día de Inocentes,** a festival specifically for children.

For some local nightlife, there's **El Tunel Nightclub** (Carr. 2, km 103.8, Quebradillas, 787/964-8489, Fri.–Sun.), a no-frills bar on Playa Guajataca beside the train tunnel. There's live music at night, plus the occasional reggaetón festival. It's probably not the best place for unaccompanied women.

Accommodations

If you're looking for an inexpensive and lively place to stay, little **Sueños Doña Herminia Guest House** (725 Calle Estacion off Carr. 2, Quebradillas, 787/379-8604, $65, cash or traveler's checks only) may be the answer. The bright orange contemporary concrete house contains eight guest rooms, three with ocean views and all with air-conditioning and cable TV. There's no access to the beach, but there's

Mike's Bar and Cocktail Lounge (Fri.–Sat. 11 A.M.–midnight, with live music starting at 9 P.M.).

If you're looking for **Vistamar Hotel Parador** (Carr. 113 south, off Carr. 2 at km 103.8, Quebradillas, 787/895-2065 or 888/391-0606, www.paradorvistamar.com, $71 s/d, $125 s/d with ocean-view balconies), don't mistake it for nearby Parador El Guajataca, which is comparably priced but significantly inferior. Vistamar Hotel Parador is on the south side of Carretera 2, high on a hill overlooking the ocean. It's a strictly self-serve operation without any frills, but it's clean and comfortable. Air-conditioning and cable TV come standard. But oddly, no food, beverages, or coolers are allowed in the rooms, and ice is $0.25 a bucket. There is a restaurant, but it doesn't appear to be either professionally run or particularly inviting. There is a pool on-site, though, which is nice since the hotel has an ocean view but does not have beach access.

◖ **Parador El Buen Café** (Carr. 2, km 84, 381 Carrizales, Hatillo, 787/898-1000, fax 787/820-3013, reservations@elbuencafe .com, www.elbuencafe.com, $90–105 s, $120 d, $195 suite, plus 7 percent tax) is short on charm but long on clean, comfortable, modern accommodations. The property has 33 rooms with air-conditioning, satellite TV, and mini-refrigerators. There's also a tiny pool, and El Buen Café across the street serves breakfast, lunch, and dinner.

The Puerto Rican government has recently gone into the hospitality industry. The island's first government-owned hotel, **Punta Maracayo Resort** (Carr. 2, km 85, Hatillo, 787/544-2000 or 877/887-0100, $99 d, $210 suite that sleeps 6, plus 9 percent tax), opened in August 2004. The bright yellow three-floor hotel sits in the middle of an enormous parking lot and has virtually no landscaping to speak of. But the rooms are clean and modern with air-conditioning, minibars, and cable TV, and there's a pool on-site. Gorgeous new Restaurant Chef Miguel serves upscale seafood dishes in a glamorous modernistic space decked out in dark blues and glass. There's also a tapas

restaurant on the second floor and a poolside snack bar. Although the hotel isn't right on the ocean, it is within walking distance to Playa Sardinera, and rooms on the second and third floors have ocean views.

Luis Muñoz Marín Vacation Center at Sardinera Beach (Carr. 2, km 84.6, Hatillo, 787/820-0274, fax 787/820-9116, $195–290, two-night minimum, Hatillo) is primarily a beachside vacation site for Puerto Rican families. Accommodations include rustic wooden villas and cabanas with air-conditioning, but not much else in the way of amenities. There's also tent and trailer camping. Facilities include a swimming pool, a playground, a basketball and volleyball court, and a cafeteria with pool tables.

Food

◖ **Restaurante La Llave del Mar** (Calle Estacion, off Carr. 2, directly across from Carr. 113 south, Quebradillas, 787/895-5843, $7.95–34) is an old-fashioned open-air restaurant dramatically perched on a cliff overlooking the pounding surf. As if the view weren't enough, it serves excellent Puerto Rican–style seafood dishes, including shrimp, enormous lobsters, *dorado,* snapper, and grouper with your choice of a selection of sauces, including garlic sauce, creole, thermidor, or *arrecife* (with shrimp, bacon, and cheese). It also serves a selection of Angus beef. The staff is very friendly.

For a good solid breakfast, you can't do much better than **El Buen Cafe** (Carr. 2, km 84, 381 Calle Carrizales, Hatillo, 787/898-3495, fax 787/820-3013, reservations@elbuencafe.com, www.elbuencafe.com, daily 5:30 A.M.–10 P.M., $3.95–20). The cafeteria serves great bacon and eggs, as well as sandwiches, soups, and heartier fare such as chicken and rice, *mofongo,* roast pork, and more. There's an upscale side next door with its own entrance, open noon–10 P.M., where you can buy a cocktail and dine on *mofongo,* roast pork, steak, and lobster. Other than breakfast and sandwiches, the food is only fair and it's a bit pricey for what it is, but the place really packs them in.

CORDILLERA CENTRAL

It's hard for some visitors to wrap their heads around the idea of spending time in Puerto Rico not on the beaches but in the mountains. That's what makes the Cordillera Central, Puerto Rico's central mountain region, one of the island's greatest hidden gems. Thousands of acres of undeveloped land thick with tropical jungle, high mountain peaks, waterfalls, rivers, intricate cave systems, and a canyon comprise the interior of the island, making it one of the most beautiful regions of Puerto Rico. But the natural beauty isn't the only reason to visit Cordillera Central. This is where adventurous travelers go to escape any semblance of mainland American influence and experience authentic traditional Puerto Rican culture and explore its Taíno Indian roots.

Although tourism is a fairly new concept in the Cordillera Central, efforts are being made to attract more visitors. To that end, a fantastic scenic route called La Ruta Panorámica has been established that runs the length of the region from east to west along several well-marked highways, starting on the southeast coast in Maunabo and ending on the west coast in Mayagüez. Along the way, travelers pass through the Toro Negro Forest and the highest peaks on the island. It's also centrally located, making it ideal for branching off the route to explore other nearby sights and towns.

PLANNING YOUR TIME

One of the great things about the Cordillera Central is that it's possible to get a taste of its charms on a day trip from just about anywhere on the island. On the east side, Carretera 52 vertically bisects the island from San Juan on

the north side through Cayey to Salinas on the south side. On the west side, Highway 10 runs south from Arecibo on the north coast to Utuado. Eventually the highway will continue farther south and connect with Adjuntas, but now travelers must take Carretera 123 to Adjuntas, where Highway 10 starts again, ending in Ponce on the south coast.

Ambitious travelers who want to travel the length of La Ruta Panorámica will want to reserve three or four days for the journey. Mountain roads can be narrow, twisty, and occasionally harrowing because of the steep ascents and descents, so travel proceeds at a fairly slow rate. Luckily traffic is typically light, and the roads are well maintained and fairly well marked. If you get lost, locals are usually eager to help you find your way, even to the point of jumping into their own cars and leading you where you want to go.

Starting from the eastern end of the mountain region, stop off in Cayey for a meal at one of the many *lechoneras* in the area, where whole pigs are roasted over an open fire, and then journey westward through the mountain towns of Aibonito and Barranquitas, between

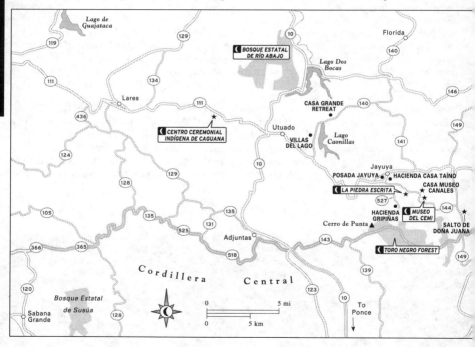

which is the lovely verdant San Cristóbal Cañon, where tour guides take thrill-seekers hiking and rappelling. But the most spectacular sights are on the western end. Jayuya is the site of **Toro Negro Forest,** home to the island's highest peaks; **La Piedra Escrita,** featuring a natural pool and large boulder covered in Taíno petroglyphs; and **Museo del Cemi,** a unique museum shaped like a Taíno amulet containing Indian artifacts found in the area. In Utuado is the 5,000-acre subtropical humid forest, **Bosque Estatal de Río Abajo,** and **Centro Ceremonial Indígena de Caguana,** a major Taíno archaeological site dating to A.D. 1100.

The municipalities with the best options for accommodations are Cayey, Jayuya, Utuado, and Adjuntas. Note that it rains quite often in the mountains and can be cool at night, so pack accordingly. And keep an eye on the weather. Heavy rains occasionally result in mudslides and flooding, which could close some roads. Also watch out for livestock. It's not unusual to see a cow or horse tied up to a house right smack beside the road, and chickens are forever crossing the asphalt.

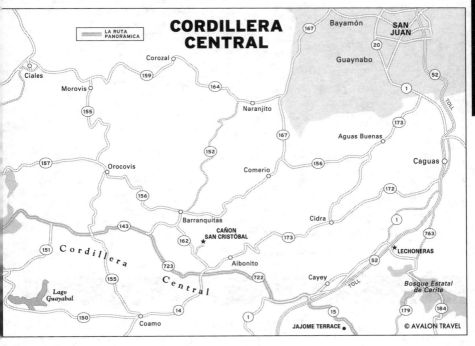

CORDILLERA CENTRAL

HIGHLIGHTS

(Toro Negro Forest: The forest preserve contains Puerto Rico's highest peak, Cerro de Punta, which is 4,390 feet above sea level, and one of the island's highest waterfalls, Salto de Doña Juana (page 177).

(Museo del Cemi: Shaped like a Taíno amulet, this unique museum in Jayuya contains artifacts of Puerto Rico's indigenous culture (page 178).

(La Piedra Escrita: A boulder covered with Taíno petroglyphs is in a river by a large natural pool ideal for swimming (page 179).

(Centro Ceremonial Indígena de Caguana: The public can tour this significant Taíno Indian archaeological site, which dates to A.D. 1100. Many artifacts, petroglyphs, and ceremonial ball fields have been excavated here (page 183).

(Bosque Estatal de Río Abajo: The 5,000-acre subtropical humid forest spanning Utuado and Arecibo encompasses the heart of Puerto Rico's karst country and contains a private aviary where attempts are being made to raise and release the endangered Puerto Rican parrot (page 184).

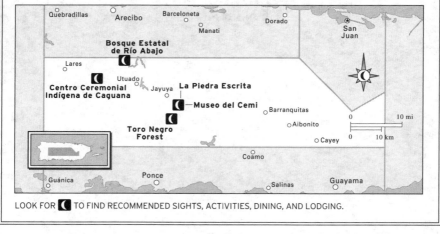

LOOK FOR (TO FIND RECOMMENDED SIGHTS, ACTIVITIES, DINING, AND LODGING.

Cayey

Both geographically and culturally speaking, Cayey is the eastern gateway to Puerto Rico's Cordillera Central. The mountains here may not boast the dramatic heights of those found in Jayuya and Utuado, but Cayey has something that attracts islanders far and wide, particularly on the weekends and during holidays. And that is its many *lechoneras,* popular casual eateries that specialize in open-pit roasted pork. Many locals make a day of visiting the area to

dine at all-you-can-eat buffets, dance to the live bands, and shop at roadside vendors, who sell everything from local crafts to homemade cheeses and sweets to gallons of *mavi,* a traditional Taíno beverage made from fermented tree bark of the *mavi* tree.

SIGHTS

Cayey is a 30-minute drive from San Juan or Ponce, and one of the best ways to experience its natural beauty and local culture is to take a short **scenic drive** that loops through the area. From San Juan, take Highway 52 south and exit at Carretera 184. At the end of the exit ramp, turn right and then take an immediate left onto Carretera 184. At the intersection, turn left onto Carretera 763 (a right turn will take you to Reserve Forestal de Carite), then left onto Carretera 765, and right onto Carretera 1. Carretera 1 intersects with Highway 52 at the Caguas Sur Boriken exit. Not only does this drive give you some spectacular views of the mountains, but it will take you by many popular *lechoneras,* some of which have live music. There are many other vendors along the way selling crafts, homemade cheese, candied fruits, and *mavi* champagne.

Reserva Forestal de Carite (Carr. 184, km 27.5, 787/747-4510 or 787/747-4545, Mon.–Fri. 9 A.M.–4:30 P.M., Sat.–Sun. and holidays 8 A.M.–5 P.M., office Mon.–Fri. 7 A.M.–3:30 P.M.) is classified primarily as a subtropical humid forest rich in vegetation, including Honduran mahogany, hibiscuses, eucalyptus, giant ferns, and several varieties of palm. Unfortunately, this forest reserve was severely damaged by Hurricane Georges in 1998, and many of its hiking trails have never been restored. There is one 550-yard trail, though, that ends at Charco Azul, a lovely natural pool. If you don't mind camping in sight of the road, **Area Recreativa Guavate** (Carr. 184, km 27.2) offers nice, shady hillside camping with bathrooms, covered picnic tables, and an outdoor shower. Camping permits must be secured at least 15 days before arrival by calling the forest office or the Department of Natural Resources in San Juan at 787/723-1770.

Museo de Arte Dr. Pio López Martínez (205 Ave. Antonio R. Barceló, 787/738-2161, ext. 2209, Mon.–Fri. 8 A.M.–4:30 P.M., Sat.–Sun. and holidays 11 A.M.–5 P.M.) is an art museum dedicated to local artists with an emphasis on the work of Ramon Frade (1875–1954), who celebrated the island's agricultural community with paintings that dignified the farmer and his contribution to society. Also featured are changing exhibitions of *cartels,*

Puerto Rico's renowned poster art used to publicize festivals, plays, and social concerns.

SHOPPING

Arte Guavate (Carr. 184, km 28.5, 787/263-3588, Mon.–Fri. 9 A.M.–5:30 P.M.) is a small roadside shop selling a wide variety of local crafts and food items. There's a large selection of wooden mortar-and-pestle sets, including one four feet tall, which are instrumental in the preparation of Puerto Rican cuisine. You'll also find hammocks, wood carvings, ceramics, musical instruments, and bottles of homemade Jíbaro Vinaigrette, a flavored vinegar for seasoning meats, vegetables, and salads.

ACCOMMODATIONS

Jajome Terrace (Carr. 15, km 18.6, 787/738-4016, reservations@jajometerrace.com, www .jajometerrace.com, $107 s, $125 d, including taxes) is a small two-story motel-style property with modern rooms, each with a balcony and attractive homey furnishings. Amenities are minimal here. Although there's no pool, there is a banquet room and a terrific upscale open-air restaurant with a gorgeous view of the mountains. Apart from the area around the restaurant, there isn't much in the way of landscaped grounds because the thick tropical forest practically grows right up to your hotel-room door.

FOOD

Cayey is famous for its many *lechoneras.* From Highway 52, exit onto Carretera 184, where you'll find many restaurants serving pit-cooked pork as well as roast chicken stuffed with plantains, *chicharones, pasteles* (mashed plantain or cassava stuffed with meat and steamed in banana leaves), and more. Drive around and check them out until you find one to your liking. Be sure to go hungry and bring a cooler to carry your leftovers home.

◖ Lechonera El Mojito (Carr. 184, km 32.9, 787/263-4675, daily 8 A.M.–8 P.M., $2–20) is the first *lechonera* you encounter after exiting onto Carretera 184 from Highway 52, and you can't miss it thanks to its bright purple exterior. This casual, family-friendly concrete-block restaurant is a gastronomic emporium of fresh roast pork and all the fixings. Take a peek at the whole pigs cooking on a spit over an open fire before taking your place in line to peruse the long steam tables piled high with sliced pork, ribs, pork skins, whole roast chickens, rice and beans, sausages, *tostones, maduras,* yucca, and more. Point out the dishes you want to sample and take a seat at the common tables and wait for a server to deliver your feast. There's a full bar too. Expect a wait if you visit during the weekends or holidays.

(**Jajome Terrace** (Carr. 15, km 18.6, 787/738-4016, lunch and dinner Wed.–Sun., $11.50–24) is one of the rare upscale romantic restaurants to be found in the Cordillera Central. The circular, pavilion-style dining room featuring tile floors and mission-style furniture overlooks a gorgeous view of the mountains and lovely landscaped grounds. The menu features *dorado,* salmon, shrimp, sea bass, chicken, and beef served with your choice of sauces (garlic and béchamel, among others) or stuffings (*madura,* shrimp). The menu also features a selection of *mofongos,* and there's a full bar. This is a great place for a special-occasion meal or a pleasant stopover when traveling between San Juan and Ponce. Reservations are recommended on weekends and holidays.

INFORMATION AND SERVICES

Cayey has two taxi services, **Cayey Metro Taxi** (787/738-8001) and **Cayey Taxi** (787/738-4344). For a car rental, contact **Payless Car Rental** (787/738-7420, www.paylesscayey.com). For your banking needs, go to **Banco Popular** (Centro Comercial Sierra de Cayey, Ave. Antonio R. Barceló, Carr. 14, km 70.6, 787/738-2828). Cayey has two hospitals, **Hospital Menonita de Cayey** (4 Calle Mendoza, 787/263-1001) and **Family Health Center of Cayey** (5 Luis Barreras, 787/738-3011). For pharmacy needs, visit **Walgreens** (Montellano Shopping Center, 787/263-5806).

Aibonito and Barranquitas

Of these two mountain towns, Barranquitas offers the most charming plaza and city center. The recently renovated plaza features a beautiful wrought-iron gazebo in the middle, and the streets around it are lined with bustling shops and museums. But both municipalities have much to offer visitors in search of spectacular natural beauty, history, and annual festivals.

SIGHTS

San Cristóbal Cañon (Carr. 162/Carr. 725, between Aibonito and Barranquitas) is reportedly the biggest canyon in the Caribbean at 4.5 miles long and 500–800 feet deep. It's hard to believe this beautiful deep hole in the earth, now filled with verdant green vegetation, was once a garbage dump. Today it's a popular site for adventure-seeking outdoorsmen and women who want to get away from it all and witness the canyon's natural beauty, including a spectacular river, waterfalls, and shoals. The canyon is not accessible without a trained guide.

Museo Luis Muñoz Rivera (Calle Ubaldino Font, Barranquitas, 787/857-30230, Wed.–Sun. 8 A.M.–noon and 1–4 P.M., $1) is dedicated to one of Puerto Rico's most celebrated native sons, Luis Muñoz Rivera, a poet, journalist, politician, and defender of the island's independence both under Spanish and American rule. Inside this traditional Puerto Rican–style home built in 1857 are many artifacts of Rivera's life, including newspaper clippings, his impressive two-sided walnut desk from 1893, his death mask, and the 1912 Pierce-Arrow that transported his body from his funeral services to his burial site in **Mausoleo Luis Muñoz Rivera** (Calle Padre Berrios, Tues.–Sat. 8 A.M.–4:30 P.M.).

Casa Museo Joaquin de Rojas (Calle Barceló, Barranquitas, 787/857-6293,

Mon.–Fri. 8 A.M.–4:30 P.M., free) is a museum with a mishmash of interesting items that include vintage farm tools, *mundillo* lace, and newspaper clippings about the town's history. Most interesting is a large photograph of Barranquitas taken in 1950. Contemporary artists maintain studios here.

Mirador Piedra Degetau (Carr. 7718, km 0.8, Aibonito, Wed.–Sun. and Mon. holidays 9 A.M.–6 P.M.) is a new, pristinely landscaped park thick with blooming bougainvillea in a riot of colors. There are picnic shelters, bathrooms, a playground, and snack machines, but the focal point of the roadside attraction is the observation tower that offers an amazing view of the mountains and even the sea when visibility is clear.

SPORTS AND RECREATION

San Cristóbal Hiking Tour (P.O. Box 678, Barranquitas, 787/647-3402, walimai@hotmail .com, http://barranquitaspr.org/viajes) offers a variety of weekend excursions in San Cristóbal Cañon from moderate hiking and biking tours to extreme rappelling and mountaineering tours. It also offers tours to Bosque Estatal Toro Negro and other natural sights in the area. Prices range $50–140, depending on the excursion and the number of people in your party.

Acampa (1211 Ave. Piñero, San Juan, 787/706-0695, info@acampapr.com, www .acampapr.com) offers rappelling and rock-climbing tours into San Cristóbal Cañon for experienced adventure travelers. Explore the canyon's waterfalls and river. Acampa also sells and rents camping, hiking, and mountaineering gear at its store in San Juan.

ENTERTAINMENT AND EVENTS

Aibonito is known as the City of Flowers because every year it bursts into a riot of color and floral scents for the **Festival de las Flores** (Carr. 722, km 6.7, 787/735-4070, $3 adults, $2 children), held from the last weekend of June through the first weekend of July. On 25 acres of land, the festival grounds are filled with horticulture and landscaping exhibitions

and more than 50 vendors selling flowers and plants, as well as pottery and garden accessories. There's also live music, and vendors sell food and crafts.

Feria Nacional de Artesanías (23 Calle Muñoz Rivera, Barranquitas, 787/857-6293) held in mid-July features more than 200 artisans from all over the island who flock here to sell local arts and crafts, including wood carvings, musical instruments, ceramics, hammocks, and more.

FOOD

◖ La Piedra Restaurant (Carr. 7718, km 0.8, Aibonito, 787/735-1034, Wed.–Thurs. noon–7 P.M., Fri.–Sat. noon–9 P.M., Sun. noon–6 P.M., $6–18) is a charming little home-style restaurant in a cozy Florida room that contains a full bar, a piano, and tons of potted plants. Puerto Rican cuisine is served, including a wide variety of seafood, steak, and chicken dishes. Be sure to try the desserts made on the premises, including an unusual and refreshing ginger flan.

INFORMATION AND SERVICES

For getting around, taxi service is provided by **Aibonito Taxi** (787/735-7144), and Barranquitas offers **trolley service** (787/857-2500) from the center of town to the business district. Car-rental services are provided by **Barranquitas Car Rental** (Carr. 152, km 1.8, 787/857-7020). Banking services are available at **Banco Popular** branches in Aibonito (Supermercado Aibonito Extra, 96 Calle San José and Carr. 14, km 51.3) and Barranquitas (San Cristobal Shopping Center). Health care is provided by **Mennonite General Hospital Aibonito** (Calle José at Calle Vazquez, 787/735-8001).

OROCOVIS, MOROVIS, AND CIALES

Orocovis and Morovis are small mountain towns with great views and a couple of popular cultural festivals that celebrate the music and foods of the area. Ciales is a charming mountain town where dramatic outcroppings of exposed limestone called *mogotes* tower overhead and the rivers Toro Negro, Yunes, Grande de Manatí, and Cialitos converge both above and below ground, creating an intricate cave system.

Sights

Mirador Orocovis-Villalba (Carr. 143 between Orocovis and Villalba, Wed.–Sun. 9 A.M.–5 P.M.) is a newly constructed park and overlook 2,000 feet above sea level. From here you can see both the island's north and south coasts. There are also a children's playground and picnic tables.

Doña Juana Recreation Center (Carr. 143, km 32.4, 787/724-3724, daily 7:30 A.M.–4 P.M.) is part of Toro Negro Forest. Here you'll find a beautiful large natural pool formed by the waters of the Cordillera Central, perfect for taking a dip. There's also a lookout tower with great views of the mountains.

The biggest draw to Ciales is its underground rivers and caves: **Yuyu Cave, La Virgen Cave, Las Archillas Cave,** and **Las Golondrina Cave,** where you can find sea fossils, stalactites, and columns. For information call 787/871-3500, ext. 266, or contact one of several adventure-tour operators in the area who offer guided expeditions.

In addition to its spectacular caves, Ciales has several modest sights worth seeking out if you're in the area, including the **Museo del Café** (Calle Palmer at Paseo del Aroma, 787/857-6293, Mon.–Fri. 8 A.M.–4:30 P.M.), which celebrates Ciales as the only municipality on the island whose largest agricultural product is still coffee; **Museo Juan Antonio Corretjer** (7 Calle Betances, 787/871-3500, Sat. 8 A.M.–4 P.M.), dedicated to the renowned Puerto Rican poet; and **Puente Mata Plátano José Jiménez** (Carr. 149 at Carr. 132), a historic iron bridge.

Sports and Recreation

Expediciones Palenque (787/823-4354 or 787/306-4382, info@expedicionespalenque .com, www.expedicionespalenque.com) offers daylong spelunking tours to Yuyu Cave for novices, as well as a wall-climbing excursion and base-jumping adventure from Puente Mata Plátano José Jiménez bridge.

Entertainment and Events

Festival de Cuatristas y Trovadores (Plaza de Recreo, Morovis, 787/862-2155) is a celebration of traditional Puerto Rican music and art held in mid-July. Local artisans who make *cuatros,* stringed guitarlike instruments, demonstrate their craft. *Cuatro* musicians and troubadours perform as well.

Festival de Pastel (Orocovis, 787/867-5000, ext. 2295) is a culinary festival held in late November for three days noon–midnight in honor of the *pastel,* a Taíno dish traditionally eaten during the Christmas holidays. Similar to a tamale, it's made of mashed, seasoned plantain filled with fried pork that's wrapped in a banana leaf and steamed. Festivities include live music and artisan vendors.

Food

◖ **Casa Bavaria** (Carr. 15, km 38.3, Morovis, 787/862-7818, casabavaria@prtc.net, www .casabavaria.com, $7.50–36) marks the unlikely intersection of Puerto Rican and German culture and is reason alone to take a day trip to Morovis. In a two-story open-air structure plastered with countless beer signs and banners, Casa Bavaria serves outstanding Puerto Rican and German cuisine. Alongside the usual *mofongo,* shrimp, lobster, and chicken, you can dine on heaping platters of bratwurst, Wiener schnitzel, and sauerkraut. Cocktails are a mere $3.50, and there's an extensive wine list with offerings from Italy, Spain, Chile, and Germany. Dine in the crowded, pleasantly raucous bar, or go around back and take a seat in the quiet dining room overlooking a gorgeous mountain view. There's live music on Saturdays, and Oktoberfest is celebrated the first and second weekends of October with live bands all weekend long. Be forewarned: There's an infectious party atmosphere here that will have you drinking shots of Jägermeister before you know it!

CORDILLERA CENTRAL

Morovis is known for its *pan de la Patita echá,* a delicious braided bread. It's served at any number of the many *panaderías* (bakeries) found here, but the best-known place is **Panadería Patria y Reposteria** (20 Calle Ruiz Belvis and 155 Carretera Desvio, Morovis, 787/862-2867). Believed to be one of the oldest bakeries in Puerto Rico, it was established in 1862. Other options include **Panadería y Reposteria Barahona** (Carr. 155, km 4.1, Morovis, 787/862-2538, daily 8 A.M.–10 P.M.).

Information and Services

Banking services are available at **Banco Popular** branches in Ciales (46A Calle Palmer) and Morovis (49 Ave. Corozal, 787/862-2160). For pharmacy needs, visit **Walgreens** (137 Carr. 200, 787/862-0104).

Jayuya

If you visit only one place in Puerto Rico's Cordillera Central, go to Jayuya. Not only is the municipality rich in Taíno culture and historic sights, but it contains some of the highest peaks on the island. Some mountains are so enormous here that it's possible to see both the north and south coastlines from their crests, and the vegetation is thick with sierra palms, bamboo, banana trees, and brilliantly colorful impatiens. Jayuya also has the best selection of accommodations in the mountain region.

SIGHTS
Cacique Jayuya Monument
Unfortunately it's often closed, but the Cacique Jayuya Monument (Cultural Center, 24 Calle San Felipe, 787/828-1241) honors the great cacique who once ruled the Taíno who lived in the area now named in his memory. In addition to a sculpture of Cacique Jayuya by Tomás Batiste, here you'll see exhibits of archaeological finds from the area and the tomb of a Taíno Indian.

◖ Toro Negro Forest
If you want to see thick, virtually uninhabited tropical jungle as far as the eye can see, so high in the mountains that you can look down on the clouds, Toro Negro Forest (along Ruta Panorámica on Carr. 143 south of Jayuya) is the place to go. From these heights you can see clouds drift between the peaks below you and you're surrounded by tangles of wild bamboo, banana trees, hibiscus, enormous ferns, impatiens, elephant ears, *flamboyan* trees,

and seemingly millions of sierra palms, distinguished by their long straight trunks and pale green foliage towering 30–50 feet high. The roads are steep and twisty, putting a strain on small engines and inducing dizziness—or worse—motion sickness. But it's one of the most exotic sights you'll see on the island and well worth the effort.

Toro Negro contains the highest peak on the island, **Cerro de Punta,** 4,390 feet above

Salto de Doña Juana in Toro Negro Forest

sea level, on the northwestern end of the forest. To reach the summit, park in the lot at Carretera 143, km 17, and hike up about 1.5 miles. **Cerro Maravilla,** along about km 20 on Carretera 143, is 3,800 feet high and is the site of the infamous Cerro Maravilla murders in 1978, in which police officers killed two independenistas who were suspected of planning to sabotage a television transmission tower on the mountain's summit.

In Toro Negro you can also see one of the island's highest waterfalls, **Salto de Doña Juana** (Carr. 149, km 41.5). It can be viewed from the road (it's on the left if you're traveling south) if you look way up high. Although it's not particularly wide, the water propels off the mountaintop with great force, making it a spectacular sight.

The highest peaks of Toro Negro Forest contain dwarf or cloud forest, where the foliage has been stunted from the constant moisture in the atmosphere. The southern part of the forest features many rugged rock cliffs, jagged peaks, and waterfalls. Much of the forest has been subjected to clearing by the logging industry, but long-term reforestation efforts have helped repair some of the damage.

There are 10 trails in the forest, most of which originate from the **information office** (Carr. 143, km 32.4, 787/867-3040, Mon.–Fri. 7:30 A.M.–4 P.M., Sat.–Sun. and holidays 9 A.M.–5 P.M.). One trail is a 10-minute walk to a natural freshwater pool (open Sat.–Sun. and holidays 9 A.M.–5 P.M. Apr.–Sept., $1 adults, children under 10 free). Another popular hike is a 3-km trek to **Torre Observación** lookout tower. A camping area with toilets and showers but no electricity is a 550-yard hike away.

◖ Museo del Cemi

Museo del Cemi (Carr. 144, km 9.3, 787/828-1241 or 787/828-4094, Wed.–Fri. 8 A.M.–4:30 P.M., Sat.–Sun. 10 A.M.–3 P.M., free) makes quite a statement for itself as you drive along Carretera 144. Like a throwback to kitschy mid-century American architecture in which buildings were made to reflect their purpose (e.g., a hot-dog stand shaped like a hot dog), Museo del Cemi is shaped like a huge *cemi*—a triangular artifact with animal characteristics made by the Taíno Indians. Its significance is unknown, but it's believed to have represented a deity and to have contained many powers.

Museo del Cemi

© SUZANNE VAN ATTEN

© SUZANNE VAN ATTEN

La Piedra Escrita

Downstairs is a small collection of Taíno artifacts: necklaces of stone and shells, ritual vomit spatulas, ceremonial maracas, a Dogolito (a phallic symbol of power for caciques), and the mysterious stone collar/belt, the purpose of which is unknown. Upstairs are poster-size photographs of petroglyphs found in Jayuya, Comerio, Utuado, Naguabo, Luquillo, Corozal, and Río Piedras. Next door is **Casa Museo Canales** (787/828-4094, Sat.–Sun. noon–4 P.M., weekdays by appointment, $1 adults, $0.50 children under 12), a historic home typical of 19th-century coffee plantations.

◖ La Piedra Escrita

La Piedra Escrita (Carr. 144, km 7.3, 787/828-1241, free) is one of Puerto Rico's most revered reminders of the island's Taíno culture. The enormous granite boulder measures 32 feet high and 13 feet wide and is located smack-dab in the middle of Río Saliente, creating a natural pool where visitors can go for a swim.

But it's what's on the boulder that is of interest to historians and archaeologists. On the rock's surface are 52 petroglyphs that were carved into the rock by members of indigenous groups sometime between A.D. 600 and 1200. Some of the symbols clearly depict faces of humans and animals while others are geometric or abstract in shape. Because of the quantity of petroglyphs on the rock, some believe La Piedra Escrita was an important ceremonial site, but its significance is ultimately unknown.

Today La Piedra Escrita is a popular tourist sight. A long series of wheelchair-accessible switchback ramps have been built that descend from the stone escarpment overlooking the river down to the water where visitors can get a close-up look at the rock and go for a dip. It's a popular picnic spot on weekends.

ENTERTAINMENT AND EVENTS

Festival Nacional Indígena de Jayuya (Plaza Nemesio R. Canales, calles Nemesio R. Canales and Figuera, 787/828-1241) is an annual three-day celebration of the Taíno culture beginning November 19. Participants don Taíno-style clothing, prepare traditional foods, and perform traditional music and dances. More than 100 artisans sell handmade crafts as well, and many demonstrations and ceremonies are held.

Other festivals include **El Festival del Pueblo del Tomate** held in mid-April to celebrate the municipality's production of tomatoes. Festivities include games, music, and food kiosks. The **Jayuya Patron Saint Festival**

WHEN TAÍNO INDIANS RULED BORIKEN

The Taínos were an indigenous group of people who ruled the island of Puerto Rico (which they called Boriken) when Christopher Columbus and his expedition arrived in 1493. A little more than two decades later, they were virtually wiped out.

But surprising developments have recently revealed that the Taínos may live on in Puerto Rico, and not just in the vestiges of their customs, cuisine, and language that are still prevalent today. Preliminary results from DNA studies recently conducted at the University of Puerto Rico in Mayagüez indicate that nearly half the island's Puerto Rican residents may contain indigenous DNA.

The study of Taíno history and culture is a fairly recent academic undertaking. Previously, what little was known of the peaceful, agrarian society was derived from written accounts by Spanish settlers. But the ongoing study of archaeological sites has uncovered new details about the highly politicized and spiritual society.

The Taínos are thought to have originated in South America before migrating to the Caribbean, where they settled in Puerto Rico, Haiti, the Dominican Republic, and Cuba. Taíno society in Puerto Rico is believed to have developed between A.D. 1100 and 1500. By the time of Columbus's arrival, the island comprised about 20 political chiefdoms, each one ruled by a cacique (chief). Unlike the laboring class, who mostly wore nothing, the cacique wore a resplendent headdress made of parrot feathers, a gold amulet, and a *mao*, a white cotton shawl-like garment that protected the shoulders and chest from the sun.

Second in power to the caciques were the *bohiques* (shamans). Ornamenting their faces with paint and charcoal, they led spiritual rituals and ceremonies, using herbs, chants, maracas, and tobacco to heal the sick. To communicate with the gods and see visions of the future, *bohiques* and caciques inhaled a hallucinogenic powder made from the bright red seeds of the *cohoba* tree. It was ingested in a ceremony that began with a ritual cleansing that involved inducing vomiting with ornately carved spatulas. The powder was then inhaled through tubes created from tubers or bones.

Of special spiritual importance to the Taínos was the enigmatic *cemi*, a three-pointed object carved from stone or wood. Its significance is a mystery, but some believe it was thought to contain the spirit of the god Yocahu. *Cemis* were plentiful, powerful objects, believed to control everything from weather and crops to health and childbirth. Most *cemis*, which were kept in shrine rooms, were representations of animals and men with froglike legs. Some were ornamented with semiprecious stones and gold and are believed to represent the *cohoba*-fueled visions of the caciques and *bohiques*.

The Taínos saw spirituality in every natural thing, even death. Laborers were buried under their houses, called *bohios* – conical huts made from cane, straw, and palm leaves. But chiefs and shamans had special funerary rites. Their bodies were left to decompose in the open, and then their bones and skulls were cleaned and preserved in wooden urns or gourds, which were hung from the rafters. Pity the poor wives of the caciques, who were polygamists. Their favorite wives were buried alive when their husbands died.

Religious ceremonies, called *areytos*, were held in ceremonial plazas or rectangular ball courts, called *bateyes*. Lining its perimeter were monoliths adorned with petroglyphs – carvings of faces, animals, and the sun. This is where feasts, celebrations, sporting events, and ritual dances were held. Music was performed on conch trumpets, bone flutes, wooden drums, maracas, and *güiros*, a washboard-type percussion instrument made from gourds. Sometimes neighboring villagers would join in the festivities, participating in mock fights, footraces, or ball games similar to soccer, played with a heavy bouncing ball made from rubber plants and reeds. As in our modern-day ball games, the consumption of alcoholic beverages – corn beer in Taíno times – was also a highlight of the activities.

When they weren't whooping it up at the *batey*, the Taínos were hard at work growing, gathering, and hunting food. Lucky for them, the island was rich in resources. Peanuts, guavas, pineapples, sea grapes, black-eyed peas, and lima beans grew wild. Fields were cleared for the cultivation of corn, sweet potatoes, yams, squashes, papayas, and yuccas, a staple that was processed into a type of flour used to make cassava bread. Cotton was also grown for the making of hammocks. Iguanas, snakes, birds, and manatees were hunted. The sea provided fish, conchs, oysters, and crabs. Canoes, carved from tree trunks, were used to fish and conduct trade with nearby islands. Some canoes were so huge that they could hold 100 men.

The Taínos were a matrilineal society. Women held a special place in the culture because nobility was passed down through their families. The only commoners to don clothing, married women wore cotton aprons; the longer the *nagua*, the higher the social rank of the wearer. Women spent their time making pottery, weaving hammocks, and processing yucca, a time-consuming and complicated procedure. Babies were carried on their mothers' backs on boards that were tied to the babies' foreheads, a practice that produced the flat heads that Taínos found attractive.

Columbus's arrival marked the beginning of the end for Taíno society. They were already weakened from attacks by the Caribs, an aggressive, possibly cannibalistic indigenous group from South America who captured Taíno women and forced them into slavery. The Spanish followed suit by enslaving many of the remaining Taínos.

It didn't take long for unrest to grow among the Taínos. In 1510, Cacique Urayoan ordered his warriors to capture and drown a Spanish settler to determine if the colonists were mortal. Upon Diego Salcedo's death, the Taínos revolted against the Spanish, but they were quickly overpowered by the Spaniards' firearms. Thousands of Taínos were shot to death, many are believed to have committed mass suicide, and others fled to the mountains.

Several devastating hurricanes hit the island during the next several years, which killed many more Taínos. It has been reported that by 1514, there were fewer than 4,000 Taínos left, and in 1519 a smallpox epidemic is said to have virtually wiped out the rest of the remaining population.

In the last decade, interest in learning more about the Taínos has increased. As pride in the legacy of Taíno society grows, so do efforts to preserve its heritage.

In 2007, what experts are calling the largest and most significant pre-Columbian site in the Caribbean was discovered during the construction of a dam in Jacana near Ponce. The five-acre site contains plazas, bateyes, burial grounds, residences, and a midden mound – a pile of ritual refuse. After a preliminary four-month investigation that included the removal of 75 boxes of skeletons, ceramics, and petroglyphs, the site has been covered back up to preserve it until a full-scale excavation can begin. It is expected to take 15 to 20 years to unearth all the secrets the site contains.

There are two archaeological sites open to the public: **Centro Ceremonial Indígena de Caguana** (Carr. 111, km 12.5, 787/894-7325 or 787/894-7310, www.icp.gobierno.pr) in Utuado and **Centro Ceremonial Indígena de Tibes** (Carr. 503, km 2.5, 787/840-2255, www.nps.gov/nr/travel/prvi/pr15.htm) in Ponce.

And for a taste of Taíno culture, visit Jayuya in November for the Festival Nacional Indígena, featuring traditional music, dance, food, and crafts.

To learn more about Taíno history and culture, visit the websites of the United Federation of Taíno People (www.uctp.org) and the Jatibonicu Taíno Tribal Nation of Boriken (www.taino-tribe.org/jatiboni.html).

honors the Virgen de la Monserrate with religious processions, music, and food kiosks in early September. Christmas is celebrated with a **Magic Forest** featuring large holiday dioramas and storytelling December 1–January 15, and **Three Kings Day** on January 5 features traditional Christmas foods, music, and children's activities. All festivals are held in Complejo Deportivo Filiberto García on Carretera 144 at the entrance to Jayuya. For information call 787/828-1241.

ACCOMMODATIONS

◖ Hacienda Gripiñas (Carr. 527, km 2.5, 787/828-1717 or 787/828-1718, fax 787/828-1719, gripinas@excite.com, www.hacienda gripinas.com, $112 s, $159 d, includes breakfast, dinner, and taxes), built in 1858, was once one of the island's most prosperous coffee plantations. Today, its white wooden structures with green trim and red tin roofs are a unique hotel surrounded by the majestic mountains of the Cordillera Central. The accommodations are rustic but comfortable and include modern bathrooms, excellent beds, air-conditioning, local TV, and amazing mountain views. Some rooms have private balconies, but for those that don't, there is a lovely large common porch with rocking chairs and hammocks overlooking the lush grounds thick with birds and *coqui* tree frogs. The Restaurante Don Pedro serves Puerto Rican cuisine. Amenities have been recently updated with the addition of two swimming pools and a bar.

Hacienda Casa Taína (Carr. 528, km 1.8, 787/828-2270, 787/828-2271, or 787/828-2272, casataina@jayuya.net, www.hacienda casataina.com, $85 one-bedroom, $150 two-bedroom) is a lovely new Spanish Colonial–style hotel with tiled roofs and nicely landscaped grounds with gorgeous views of the mountains. Rooms are brightly painted but sparsely furnished. Amenities include a pool, poolside bar, and restaurant.

Posada Jayuya (49 Guillermo Esteyes, 787/828-7250, fax 787/828-3842, $87 s, $98 d, tax included) is a simple no-frills hotel in the town of Jayuya. The rooms feature modern bathrooms and quality beds, air-conditioning, cable TV, and mini-refrigerators. There's a pool on-site, but no restaurant or bar, although a free continental breakfast is served on weekends and holidays.

Hacienda Gripiñas, a hotel located in a former coffee plantation in Jayuya

FOOD

Restaurante Don Pedro (Hacienda Gripiñas, Carr. 527, km 2.5, 787/828-1717 or 787/828-1718, fax 787/828-1719, gripinas@excite.com, www.haciendagripinas.com, $8–35) serves breakfast and dinner, featuring seafood, steaks, and local cuisine. It's a good option if you stick to simple local dishes, such as the fried meaty ribs, which are tender and tasty. Stay away from more ambitious dishes, such as the onion soup, which comes with a gluey slice of American cheese on top. The attractive dining room in the middle of the hacienda is distinguished by a tree that grows from beneath the floor and spreads its limbs over the tables below.

Kafé de la Tierra Alta (Carr. 144, just west of Jayuya, 787/828-9236, Sun.–Wed. 8 A.M.–9 P.M.) is a clean modern spot serving breakfast and Puerto Rican cuisine, including fried chicken and roast pork.

Panderia Jayuya Cafeteria (Carr. 144, km 1.7, just west of Jayuya, 787/828-3186, daily 6 A.M.–10 P.M.) has a good selection of groceries, produce, baked goods, and a steam table with rice, beans, and other Puerto Rican dishes.

Restaurant La Casona (Carr. 144, km 1.6, just west of Jayuya, 787/828-3347, daily 10 A.M.–10 P.M.) is a great casual rustic restaurant and bar with indoor and patio seating and serving Puerto Rican cuisine. There are two bars, several pool tables, and live music at night.

INFORMATION AND SERVICES

For travel information in Jayuya, visit the **tourism office** (Carr. 144, km 9.3, 787/828-1241, Mon.–Fri. 8 A.M.–4:30 P.M., Sat.–Sun. and holidays 10 A.M.–3 P.M.). Banking services are available at **Banco Popular** (84 Guillermo Estates, 787/828-4120).

Utuado, Adjuntas, and Lares

UTUADO

Utuado is one of the most accessible of Puerto Rico's mountain towns, thanks to Highway 10, which runs south from Arecibo to Utuado. The wide multilane thoroughfare is well-marked and well-maintained, and it offers a spectacular ascent into Puerto Rico's Cordillera Central, where you can see massive mountain peaks towering overhead. The road has been cut right through the mountains in some places, creating dramatic profiles that stand in testament to the engineering feat it took to build the passage. Note, though, that the narrow winding roads that lead off Highway 10 are not for the fainthearted. Proceed on them with caution, especially if it's raining, because mudslides and flooding are not uncommon. Otherwise, don't be deterred from venturing into this region. Its natural beauty is breathtaking, and Utuado is home to the island's most significant Taíno Indian archaeological site.

◖ Centro Ceremonial Indígena de Caguana

Centro Ceremonial Indígena de Caguana (Carr. 111, km 12.5, between Utuado and Lares, 787/894-7325 or 787/894-7310, www.icp.gobierno.pr, daily 8 A.M.–4:30 P.M., $2 adults, $1 children 6–12, children under 6 and seniors free) is one of the island's most significant archaeological sites.

Taíno Indians did not live on the site in Caguana, but dating back to A.D. 1100 they congregated here for religious ceremonies and ball games, leaving behind 12 ceremonial ball fields called *bateyes,* two of which have yet to be excavated. All but one are rectangular fields rimmed with stones and small monoliths, some of which have animal faces and spiral symbols carved into their sides. One is an atypical horseshoe shape. *Bateyes* were central to Taíno culture. This is where men competed with neighboring Taíno groups in a game similar to soccer, played with a ball made from rubber plants and reeds.

A traditional Taíno hut made from tree trunks and palm fronds, called a *bohio,* has been recreated on the site, and there is a small museum of artifacts that unfortunately is closed indefinitely. Many of the artifacts excavated from the site, such as *cemis* (amulets) and stone collars, have been relocated to the Institute of Puerto Rican Culture in San Juan.

Excavation first began on the park in 1915, and it has undergone various stages of excavation and restoration over the years, including a $500,000 overhaul in 2005 that made it more tourist-friendly by planting a promenade of palm trees at the entrance and creating picnic areas and attractive stone walkways through the park.

The best way to get there is to take Highway 10 south from Arecibo to Carretera 111, which is a tight, windy road featuring hairpin curve after hairpin curve. Beware of livestock on this road: Horses and cows can frequently be seen tied up to houses that hug the road, and chickens wander freely.

◖ Bosque Estatal de Río Abajo

Bosque Estatal de Río Abajo (Carr. 621, km 4.4, just west of Hwy. 10, 787/880-6557 or 787/724-3724) is a 5,000-acre mostly subtropical humid forest in the heart of Puerto Rico's karst country, spanning the municipalities of Utuado and Arecibo. Once heavily deforested by industry, the reserve was founded in 1943 and continues to undergo reforestation efforts.

The forest is home to 175 endangered plant species, 47 of which are in danger of extinction, and 34 species of birds. Although it is not open to the public, the forest contains an aviary where the indigenous Puerto Rican parrot is raised in captivity and released in hopes of restoring the endangered species to the island habitat. Recreational facilities include 24 hiking trails, campgrounds, and bare-bones cabins available for rent. Camping permits and guided tours can be arranged by calling 787/724-3724.

Sports and Recreation

Lago Dos Bocas (Carr. 123, north of Utuado, 787/894-3505) is a large artificial mountain lake perfect for kayaking and fishing for sunfish, largemouth bass, catfish, and tilapia. Boats are available from the municipal dock to take visitors to lakefront restaurants on weekends only.

Expediciones Palenque (787-823/4354, 787/306-4382, info@expedicionespalenque .com, www.expedicionespalenque.com) is an adventure-tour operator that takes nature lovers hiking, rappelling, and body-rafting along the Tanamá River. Sights include Cueva del Arco (Arch Cave) and Tunnel Cave. A daylong tour is $90 per person.

Entertainment and Events

The municipality of Utuado commemorates San Miguel Arcángel each year with a **Patron Saint Festival** (787/894-3505) in late September to early October. In addition to the usual religious processions, music, and food kiosks, there are amateur boxing matches, softball games, and domino competitions. It's held in Luis Muñoz Rivera Plaza.

Accommodations

◖ **Casa Grande Mountain Retreat** (Carr. 612, km 0.3, at the intersection of Carr. 140, Barrio Caonillas, 787/894-3939 or 888/343-2272, tarzan@coqui.net, www.hotelcasa grande.com, $92 s, $143 d, includes breakfast and dinner, plus tax) is a truly unique hotel for visitors seeking a retreat from the 21st century deep in the tropical jungle. TVs and radios are prohibited, and the only entertainment at night is listening to the song of the *coqui* tree frog. The 107-acre property features 20 freestanding monastic cabins that contain a bed, a fan, a private bath, a hammock on the porch, and that's it. But what it lacks in luxuries, Casa Grande Mountain Retreat more than makes up for in setting. Deep in the Cordillera Central mountain region, the entire property—formerly a coffee plantation—is completely engulfed by lush, verdant forest. Amenities include a small pool, yoga classes (daily 8 A.M., $10, reservations required), hiking trails, a reading room, and board games. Jungle Jane's Restaurant serves breakfast and dinner daily, and lunch on weekends only.

Villas del Lago (Carr. 140, km 28.1, Barrio Caonillas, 787/894-3481 or 787/894-3464, lcdomartinez@hotmail.com, $75–85) is not to be confused with the Villas del Lago "no-tell motel" at the intersection of Highways 140 and 111. The idyllic, rustic property features a dozen or so wooden cabins perched around Lago Caonillas. The simple cabins feature built-in furniture, small kitchens, balconies, and fans (no air-conditioning). Amenities include a modest restaurant and bar. This quiet, peaceful spot is a great place to get away from it all and chill out with lovely views of the lake.

Food
Some of the tastiest and cheapest food in Puerto Rico can be purchased from street vendors, and the town of Utuado is a great place to experience that. All along Carretera 111 going into and out of town, there are vendors selling grilled *pinchos* (meat kabobs), *pollo al carbon* (barbecue chicken), *grandules* (pigeon peas), and fresh fruit.

Joel Panaderia y Reposteria (Carr. 111, km 4.0, Utuado, 787/814-0715, and 54 Calle Dr. Cueto, Ututado, 787/894-0621, 6 A.M.–10 P.M., $1.75–7) is a casual modern eatery that serves a wide selection of Puerto Rican cuisine, barbecue chicken, burgers and sandwiches. But the real reason to go is fantastic selection of baked goods and pastries, including *mallorcas* (sweet buns), *budin* (bread pudding) and *pastelillo de guayaba* (guava turnover). There are also cakes, doughnuts, and cookies.

Jungle Jane Restaurant (Casa Grande Mountain Retreat, Carr. 612, km 0.3, at the intersection of Carr. 140, Barrio Caonillas, 787/894-3939 or 888/343-2272, tarzan@coqui.net, www .hotelcasagrande.com, daily 8–10:30 A.M. and 6–9 P.M., Sat.–Sun. noon–5 P.M., $12–20) is a pleasant casual restaurant serving an extensive menu of Puerto Rican cuisine and more contemporary dishes. Everything including seafood, steaks, pasta, and vegetarian dishes is available. There's also a full bar.

Restaurante y Pizzeria La Familia (Carr. 111, km 12, Barrio Caguanas, 787/894-7204 or 787/894-7209, Mon. 11 A.M.–4 P.M., Wed.–Thurs. 11 A.M.–9 P.M., Fri.–Sat. 11 A.M.–11 P.M., Sun. 1–10 P.M., $5–15) serves Puerto Rican cuisine and Italian dishes including pizza in a simple salmon-colored building.

Information and Services
Banking services are available at **Banco Popular** (59 Calle Dr. Cueto, 787/894-2700). For pharmacy needs, visit **Walgreens** (Carr. 123, Edificio 940, 787/894-0100).

ADJUNTAS
Situated on La Ruta Panorámico, Adjuntas is known as the "Switzerland of Puerto Rico" because of its cool temperatures. The municipality maintains an average 72 degrees year-round thanks to the high altitude. Adjuntas is also known as the "City of the Sleeping Giant," named after the shape of the mountain range's silhouette. The sleepy little agricultural town is best known for the production of citron and coffee, but in the early 1990s Adjuntas gained notoriety for a rash of reports of UFO sightings in the area. An easy 20-mile drive up Highway 10 from Ponce, Adjuntas is a great centrally located place to explore the Cordillera Central for budget travelers looking for low-cost accommodations.

Sights
Bosque Estatal de Guilarte (intersection of Carr. 518 and Carr. 131, 787/724-3647 or 787/829-5767, Mon.–Fri. 7 A.M.–3:30 P.M., Sat.–Sun. 9 A.M.–5:30 P.M.) is a 3,600-acre subtropical wet forest reserve featuring Monte Guilarte, the third-highest peak on the island at 3,953 feet above sea level. There is one marked trail, which offers a 30-minute hike to the mountain's summit. The forest has 26 bird species and 105 species of trees, including a eucalyptus grove. Unlike other forest reserves, Guilarte has five rustic cabins with bunk beds that rent for $20 a night. A permit is required, and visitors must provide their own bedding.

Casa Pueblo (30 Calle Rodofo Gonzáles, 787/829-4842, www.casapueblo.org, Mon. 8 A.M.–1 P.M., Tues.–Sun. 8 A.M.–3:30 P.M., $2 donation) is a 19th-century structure that has been transformed by a local nonprofit group into a cultural center with exhibition space, a butterfly garden, and a gift shop selling the locally produced Madre Isla coffee. The same group recently established and continues working to restore the nearby **Bosque del Pueblo,** a forest reserve that was once mined for copper. It now contains hiking trails and primitive campgrounds. Permits are required and can be obtained from Casa Pueblo.

Sports and Recreation

Lago Garzas (Carr. 518, south of Adjuntas), a 91-acre artificial lake, is primarily used to generate electricity. But it's also a great little fishing spot for largemouth bass, sunfish, catfish, and shad. A boat launch (787/829-3310) is open Monday–Friday 7 A.M.–7:30 P.M., Saturday–Sunday 9 A.M.–5:30 P.M.

Long-distance runners flock to Adjuntas for **El Gigante Marathon,** a 15-kilometer run held in mid-July. For details, call 787/829-3114.

Accommodations

Monte Río Hotel (18 Calle César González, 787/829-3705, fax 787/829-0766, $45 s, $70 d) is a pink, tri-level hotel with 27 rooms located one block south of the plaza in Adjuntas. The basic rooms are no-frills, but they are air-conditioned and have great views of the town and the mountains. Other amenities include a swimming pool, a restaurant, and a bar.

Villas de Sotomayor (Carr. 123, km 36.7, 787/829-1717 or 787/829-1774, fax 787/829-5105, $110 s/d, $159 t/q) is a small but modern motel-style property with two swimming pools and a recreation center with tennis, volleyball, basketball, and horseshoes. The rooms are tiny but come with TVs and air-conditioning.

LARES

Lares is considered the birthplace of Puerto Rican nationalism because it played a much-revered role in Puerto Rico's independence movement. On September 23, 1868, about 500 Puerto Ricans organized a revolt against Spanish rule in the town of Lares. Local stores and offices owned by Spanish merchants were looted, slaves were declared free, and city hall was stormed. For one day, Lares was free of foreign control for the first time since the arrival of Christopher Columbus.

The revolt was quickly squelched the next day, when rebel forces attempted to take over a neighboring town. The revolutionaries, including leaders Manuel Rojas and Juan Rius Rivera, were taken prisoner, found guilty of treason and sedition, and sentenced to death. But to ease the political tension that was brewing on the island at that time, the revolutionaries were eventually released. Although the revolt, referred to as Grito de Lares, was ultimately unsuccessful, it did result in Spain giving the island more autonomy, and September 23 has become a national holiday.

Today Lares is best known for its production of Alto Grande coffee, a highly prized variety held on par with Jamaica's Blue Mountain and Hawaii's Kona coffees. And on its central plaza is a unique ice-cream shop that folks travel far and wide to visit.

Sights

Centro 23 del Septiembre Plaza (Calle Dr. Pedro Albizu Campos, off Carr. 111) is the central plaza in Lares and it is a testament to the town's brief independence from Spain's rule. In the plaza is a tamarind tree that was planted by beloved independence leader Dr. Pedro Albizu Campos in soil from several independent Spanish-speaking countries. Legend has it that when the tree bears an abundant amount of fruit, Puerto Rico will be free again.

Shopping

Downtown Lares does a thriving retail trade, thanks to dozens of dollar stores, pharmacies, and clothing stores mostly selling inexpensive trendy Latino fashions, from tight bedazzled T-shirts and short denim skirts for girls to graphic T's and cargo shorts for boys. **M&G Accessories** (Centro Calle 23 de Septiembre Plaza beside Heladería de Lares, 787/692-1270 or 787/563-7926, Mon., Wed.–Thurs., Sat. 9 A.M.–5 P.M., Tues., Fri. 9 A.M.–4 P.M., Sun. noon–5 P.M.) is great place to pick up knock-off designer purses and fun pieces of chunky jewelry for dirt cheap.

© SUZANNE VAN ATTEN

Centro 23 del Septiembre Plaza in Lares

CORDILLERA CENTRAL

Food
《 Heladería de Lares (Centro Calle 23 de Septiembre Plaza, Mon.–Thurs. 10 A.M.–5 P.M., Fri.–Sun. 9 A.M.–6 P.M., 787/897-3290 or 787/505-6299, $1.50 per scoop) has nothing like the 31 flavors at Baskin-Robbins. This unusual shop features a wide variety of uniquely flavored ice creams all made on the premises. The confection leans toward a light and fruity formula instead of a heavy butter base, but it's still very creamy and incredibly fresh. Try the sweet, nutty *maiz* (corn) flavor sprinkled with cinnamon. The outstanding pineapple flavor is studded with big chunks of fresh fruit. For something really unusual, try the rice and beans or plantain flavor.

Information and Services
Banking services are available at **Banco Popular** (12 Calle Vilella, 787/897-2670). For health services, go to **Lares Medical Center** (Carr. 111, km 2.9, 787/897-1444).

VIEQUES AND CULEBRA

Vieques and Culebra are two island municipalities a mere 8 and 17 miles, respectively, off the east coast of Puerto Rico, but the lifestyle there is light-years away from that of the main island. Referred to as the Spanish Virgin Islands, Vieques and Culebra are often described as "the way Puerto Rico used to be." The pace of life doesn't just slow down, it comes to a screeching halt. There are no fast-food restaurants or high-rise hotels, no golf courses or casinos, virtually no nightlife, and few tourist sights. And the only way to reach the islands is by plane or ferry. But what they do have are stunning beaches, world-class water sports, and lots of opportunity for R&R.

The small Spanish fort and museum **El Fortín Conde de Mirasol** on Vieques and the **Museo Histórico de Culebra** are the closest things to cultural attraction the islands have to offer. Instead, one of the main reasons to go are the islands' wide sandy beaches, the most popular being **Balneario Sun Bay** in Vieques and **Playa Flamenco** in Culebra. In addition to its beaches, Culebra and Vieques offer fantastic opportunities for diving and snorkeling. If you don't want to go on a group tour, excellent snorkeling from the beach at Playa Carlos Rosario in Culebra is easily accessible. And visitors to Vieques would be remiss not to visit the bioluminescent **Mosquito Bay,** which requires an overnight stay.

PLANNING YOUR TIME

To get to Vieques and Culebra, you can fly from Ceiba or San Juan or take a ferry from

© JIM JOHNSON

HIGHLIGHTS

🌙 **El Fortín Conde de Mirasol:** Tour the last fort built by colonial Spain and see the 4,000-year-old remains of a man exhumed from an archaeological site in Vieques (page 192).

🌙 **Mosquito Bay:** Take a guided kayak or electric pontoon boat to Vieques's bioluminescent bay, where you can get up close and personal with the water that glows an electric blue at night (page 193).

🌙 **Balneario Sun Bay:** Vieques's mile-long, sandy, crescent-shaped beach on crystal-blue waters comes with bathroom, shower, and snack-bar facilities (page 194).

🌙 **Playa Flamenco:** Puerto Rico's most celebrated stretch of white sand and aquamarine water is in Culebra. It's considered one of the most beautiful beaches in the United States (page 206).

🌙 **Diving in Culebra:** Culebra is surrounded by 50 dive sites, and excellent snorkeling can be found right off its beaches. One of the best sites is Playa Carlos Rosario, which features a long coral reef rich with sea life (page 208).

LOOK FOR 🌙 TO FIND RECOMMENDED SIGHTS, ACTIVITIES, DINING, AND LODGING.

Fajardo. If you're visiting for only a day or two, spring for the airfare to save time.

Although it's possible to get to your hotel and some of the islands' beaches using *publicos* (shared vans that carry multiple fares at a time), to fully explore the islands' remote beaches a rental car is recommended. Book early though, because they go fast.

Vieques and Culebra are such small islands that it's possible to spend a day and a night on each one to get a cursory feel for them both. But the reason most people go is to experience the islands' unparalleled natural beauty and soak up plenty of R&R. To do those things properly, it takes a few days to reset your internal clock to "island time" and achieve a blissful state of total relaxation.

HISTORY

Although details are sketchy, Vieques is believed to have been inhabited by a series of indigenous peoples possibly thousands of years before Christopher Columbus "discovered" Puerto Rico in 1493. Based on the discovery of remains found in Vieques, some historians date the earliest inhabitants to the Stone Age era more than 3,500 years ago.

Thanks to a few archaeological digs in Vieques, slightly more is known about the Saladoids, believed to have come from Venezuela around 250 B.C. They were followed by the Ostionoids around 400 B.C. and eventually the Taínos, a highly developed society of agriculturalists who lived on both Vieques and Culebra. The Taínos ruled Puerto Rico from about A.D. 1200 until the Spanish colonists wiped them out in the 1500s.

In the early 1500s, two Taíno brothers in Vieques journeyed to mainland Puerto Rico to help their fellow natives fight the Spanish conquerors. As a result, the governor of Puerto Rico sent troops to Vieques, where all the Taínos were killed or enslaved. For a long time after that, the islands became lawless havens for pirates who sought refuge in the protected harbors and ambushed passing ships.

In 1832 a Frenchman named Le Guillou, known as the founder of Vieques, arrived on the island. Under Spanish authority, he restored order to the island and helped launch a golden era of prosperity. He brought over other Frenchmen from Guadeloupe and Martinique who established sugarcane plantations and processing plants that exported the products to Spain. The operations were manned by hundreds of slaves from Africa and thousands of free workers from surrounding islands. In the early 1800s, the area around Esperanza was a thriving community with an opera house, a movie theater, and a cultural center. But as the town tried to expand to accommodate its growing population, difficulty in clearing the thick vegetation led leaders to relocate the town center to Isabel Segunda in 1844. Vieques continued to enjoy its prosperity until around 1880,

when the sugar industry began to decline because of the development of cheaper sources elsewhere.

It was around this time that Culebra was being settled in fits and starts. The first attempt was in 1875 by a black Englishman named Stevens, who was named governor and given the task of protecting the island's waters from pirates. Later that same year he was assassinated. He was followed in 1880 by a Spaniard, Cayetano Escudero Sanz, who established the first settlement, called San Ildefonso. The island's sole economy was agriculture.

Upon the ratification in 1898 of the Treaty of Paris, which ended the Spanish-American War, Vieques and Culebra came under the rule of the U.S. government. During World War II, the U.S. military became the major landholder on both islands and began to use them for bomb practice and defense-testing sites. Protests begun in Culebra in 1971 led the United States to abandon operations in 1975. But Vieques toughed through 24 more years until a civilian was accidentally killed by a bomb in 1999. Several years of persistent protesting followed, which captured international attention and led to the incarceration of many activists. In 2003 the military abandoned its operations in Vieques. But its legacy lives on, some say, in the island's extraordinarily high rate of cancer.

Vieques

Vieques stands squarely in the nexus of a cultural crossroads. Just 25 miles long and 5 miles wide, it is a rustic, slow-paced island where horses roam freely and going to the beach is just about the only thing to do, at least for now.

In 2003, the Pentagon conceded and the Navy withdrew from Vieques. Its land—15,000 acres on the east side, along with 3,100 acres on the west side that was ceded two years earlier—was handed over to the federal Fish and Wildlife Service, which has classified the property a National Wildlife Refuge. Much of

the land is still off-limits while the Navy continues to clear it of contaminants and unexploded artillery, but so far two natural jewels, Red Beach and Blue Beach, on former Camp Garcia have been opened to visitors.

With the Navy gone, Vieques is on the verge of a tourism explosion. Although efforts are under way to ensure new development doesn't overwhelm the island's natural beauty, it's nearly certain that the sleepy, old-fashioned way of life will be affected.

The east and west ends of the island are still mostly off-limits to civilians, and the island's commercial districts are in the middle of the island. There are two communities, Isabel Segunda on the north coast and Esperanza on the south coast. **Isabel Segunda** is a small, traditional, but fairly charmless Puerto Rican town. Perhaps once the renovation of the plaza is completed, that will change. Many of the island's services lie within its 20 or so blocks, including the only gas stations and ATM. This is also where the ferry docks, and the airport is nearby.

Esperanza is more geared toward tourism. It's largely a residential area with a small strip of guesthouses and restaurants that line the coast overlooking the *malécon,* a picturesque sea walk rimmed by a balustrade. Two of the best reasons to visit Vieques are here: **Sun Bay,** one of the most beautiful public beaches in all of Puerto Rico, and **Mosquito Bay,** one of the world's most spectacular bioluminescent lagoons. Esperanza is also home to quite a few U.S. expatriates, many of whom came for a visit and couldn't bear to leave.

Aside from its gorgeous fine-sand beaches, coral reefs, and mangrove bays, inland Vieques is mostly thick hilly forest and arid, barren stretches of desertlike land. Bats are said to be the only animal native to Vieques, but other wildlife commonly found includes geckos, iguanas, frogs, deer, pelicans, seagulls, egrets, herons, doves, and, of course, horses. Horses are a common mode of transportation in Vieques, and they follow the same traffic laws as automobiles, stopping at four-way stops, and so on. But they also graze and roam freely. The waters around the island are home to several endangered animals, including the manatee and sea turtles.

Accommodations on Vieques tend to be either small luxurious inns or bare-bones guesthouses. Few rooms have TVs or telephones—even the high-end ones. Several interesting restaurants serving international and Caribbean cuisine have opened in recent years. Nearly every business accepts credit cards, unless otherwise noted, and it's a good thing: Vieques is not inexpensive. Because nearly every commodity must be shipped in, prices

© SUZANNE VAN ATTEN

A lovely balustrade lines the *malecón* in Esperanza.

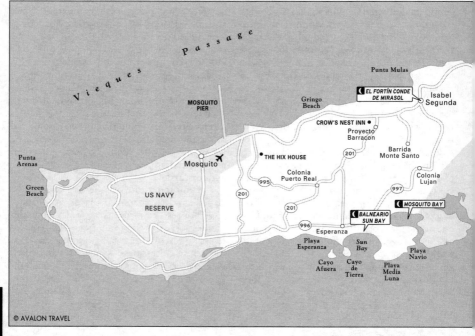

Vieques Passage

Punta Mulas

MOSQUITO PIER

Gringo Beach

EL FORTÍN CONDE DE MIRASOL

Isabel Segunda

CROW'S NEST INN

Proyecto Barracón

THE HIX HOUSE

Barrida Monte Santo

201

Punta Arenas

Mosquito

Colonia Puerto Real

Colonia Luján

Green Beach

995

201

US NAVY RESERVE

201

997

MOSQUITO BAY

BALNEARIO SUN BAY

996   Esperanza

Playa Esperanza

Sun Bay

Playa Navio

Cayo Afuera

Cayo de Tierra

Playa Media Luna

© AVALON TRAVEL

for everything from accommodations to meals rival those in San Juan. Many businesses close on Mondays and during the low-season summer months. Even during the high season, posted business hours may be more of a suggestion than reality. It's always a good idea to call first.

There are occasional water shortages on the island, and plumbing can be a bit of an issue. Signs in public restrooms request that toilet paper be discarded in wastepaper baskets instead of flushed. There are also occasional gasoline shortages, especially on weekends.

Vieques is home to 10,000 inhabitants, and it reportedly has one of the highest unemployment rates in the United States. It's not surprising that petty theft from parked cars is a continuing problem. When in town, visitors are encouraged to keep their cars locked at all times and never to leave anything in them. The greatest threat to car break-ins is at the beach, where culprits use a smash-and-grab tactic.

Drivers are encouraged to leave all the windows rolled down and the sunroof and glove box open to avoid having to pay the cost of replacing a broken window. And always park your car as close to you as possible—preferably away from any bushes and within sight range.

Except for a couple of late-night watering holes, there's little nightlife in Vieques. Since most accommodations don't have TVs and the restaurants typically close by 10 P.M., the best option is just to go to bed so you can hit the beaches early the next day.

With the Navy gone, Vieques is teetering on the cusp of a new era. If you want to see it in its pristine glory, you'd better go soon.

SIGHTS
◖ El Fortín Conde de Mirasol

Built between 1845 and 1855, El Fortín Conde de Mirasol (Fort Count Mirasol, Carr. 989, Isabel Segunda, 787/741-1717, www.enchanted-isle.com/elfortin/index

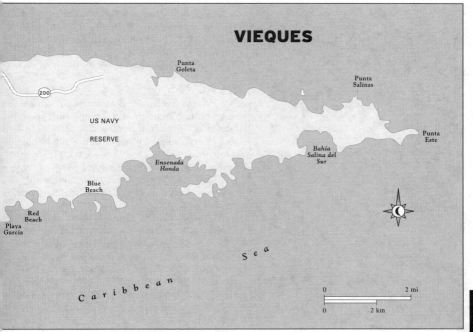

VIEQUES

Punta
Goleta

Punta
Salinas

200

US NAVY

RESERVE

Punta
Este

Ensenada
Honda

Bahía
Salina del
Sur

Blue
Beach

Red
Beach

Playa
García

S e a

C a r i b b e a n

0   2 mi

0   2 km

.htm, Wed.–Sun. 10 A.M.–4 P.M.) was the last fort built by the Spanish in the New World. Never attacked or used in battle, it originally housed Spanish troops and later became a jail and execution site. Among those incarcerated here were fugitive slaves from local sugar plantations and political prisoners who sought Puerto Rico's independence from Spain. Later it was used as a municipal jail until the 1940s, when it was closed and fell into disrepair. In 1989 the Institute of Puerto Rico began restoration of the fort, which still has its original brick floors, exterior walls, and hardwood beams. Today the fort is home to the **Vieques Museum of Art and History,** home of Hombre de Puerto Ferro, the 4,000-year-old remains of a man whose body was discovered in an archaeological site near Esperanza, as well as exhibits dedicated to the island's indigenous people, its historic sugarcane industry, and local artists. It also contains the Vieques Historic Archives.

Often referred to as Vieques Stonehenge, the archaeological site of **Hombre de Puerto Ferro** is on the south side of the island off Carretera 997. About 0.25 mile east of the entrance to Sun Bay, turn inland onto a dirt road that takes you to the fenced-off site. Giant boulders mark the spot where the remains were excavated in 1990. Some believe the boulders were placed around the grave; others say it's a natural phenomenon.

◖ Mosquito Bay

Mosquito Bay (off Carr. 997, near Esperanza, 787/741-0800) is the site of Vieques's celebrated bioluminescent bay, and no trip to the island is complete without a visit. Inside the Balneario Sun Bay complex, Mosquito Bay is a protected wildlife refuge not only because its fragile mangrove ecosystem is vital to the island's environmental health but also because it contains one of the most robust bioluminescent bays in the world. Harmless single-celled dinoflagellates that inhabit the warm water light up

the bay with an electric blue glow when they sense motion.

There are several outfitters in Vieques that provide night excursions on kayaks or an electric pontoon boat for an up-close experience with the phenomenon. For best results, plan your trip during a new moon, when the bay glows brightest.

Other Sights

Built in the late 1800s, **El Faro Punta Mulas** (Calle Plinio Peterson, north of Isabel Segunda, 787/741-0060) looks less like a lighthouse and more like a modest, rectangular government building with a large light on top of it. It's still operational today. Entry is not permitted.

The small **Vieques Conservation and Historic Trust** (138 Calle Flamboyan, Esperanza, 787/741-8850, daily 8 A.M.–4 P.M., gift shop 11 A.M.–4 P.M.) contains modest ecological and archaeological exhibits.

BEACHES

Aside from Mosquito Bay, the main reason to come to Vieques is to enjoy the staggering beauty of its miles of remote, pristine beaches and clear, turquoise waters. Each beach has its own unique characteristics—some are calm and shallow, others have big crashing waves, and still others offer spectacular snorkeling. Several are accessible only from dirt trails, off road or by foot.

Although violent crime is uncommon in Vieques, the island has a petty theft problem, which can be avoided if you use caution. Be vigilant around beaches with bushes where culprits may hide. Never take anything of value to the beach, including digital cameras or personal ID. If someone can't watch your things while you swim, bring a "dry bag," available at dive shops, to contain a car key and a photocopy of your driver's license. Don't leave anything inside your car and be sure to roll all your windows down and open the glove box so it's apparent nothing is inside.

Balneario Sun Bay

The island's best beaches are on the southern coast. The most spectacular is the long white crescent and calm waters of Balneario Sun Bay (Sombé) (Carr. 997, east of Esperanza, 787/741-8198, daily 9 A.M.–5 P.M., $2). It's the only publicly maintained beach in Vieques. Surrounded by a tall cyclone fence, it has plenty of modern, fairly clean facilities, including bathrooms, showers, changing rooms, a snack bar, and guards. Camping is permitted for $10 a day, reservations required (787/741-8198). Adding to the charm of the place is the herd of horses that grazes here.

The Balneario Sun Bay complex also encompasses two smaller, more secluded beaches farther eastward along a sandy road. The first one you'll encounter is **Media Luna**, a

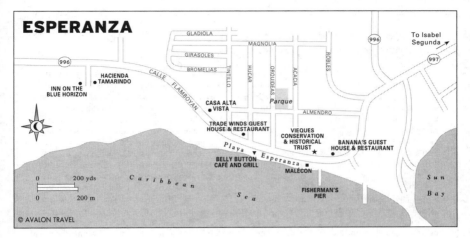

protective cove where the water is shallow. Farther eastward is **Navio Beach,** which sometimes has large waves and is popular with gay beachgoers.

Other Beaches

If you want something remote and untamed, venture onto the former Camp Garcia to get to **Red Beach** and **Blue Beach** (daily 6 A.M.–6 P.M.). Traveling south on Carretera 997, turn left at the sign onto a dirt road about halfway between Isabel Segunda and Esperanza. Follow the signs past the old Navy airstrip and turn right to reach Red Beach, or continue about two more miles and then fork right to arrive at Blue Beach.

On the extreme western end of the island is **Green Beach,** at the end of a dirt road off Carretera 200 (look for the 300-year-old ceiba tree with the massive trunk along the way). It features a narrow strip of sand punctuated by coral outcroppings and a view of the main island. There's good snorkeling to be found here, and lots of starfish to be discovered in the shallow waters along Laguna Kiani, on the north shore as you head eastward from Punta Arenas. But whatever you do, don't stay on Green Beach past about 4 P.M. because that's when the tiny, voracious sand gnats descend.

Esperanza Beach is a fairly unremarkable beach along that community's strip of restaurants and guesthouses. But it's within walking distance if you're staying in town and offers excellent snorkeling, especially around Cayo Afuera, a tiny islet just offshore.

SPORTS AND RECREATION
Mosquito Bay Tours

Any trip to Vieques would be incomplete without a trip to the bioluminescent Mosquito Bay unless, of course, you visit during a full moon, when the ambient light diminishes the visibility of the bioluminescent organisms that light up the water.

Island Adventures (787/741-0720, biobay@biobay.com, www.biobay.com, $25) operates a well-run tour of the bay that lasts about 2.5 hours and starts with a short bilingual lecture. Then guests are bused to Mosquito Bay, where they board an electric pontoon boat that tools around the electric-blue water. Guides are exceedingly friendly and informative. You'll also get a lesson on the constellations. As if that weren't enough, free pickup and drop-off service is provided along Calle Flamboyan in Esperanza.

If you want a more up-close and personal tour of the bay, **Blue Caribe Kayaks** (149 Calle Flamboyan, Esperanza, 787/741-2522) provides kayak tours of Mosquito Bay for $30 per person.

JOURNEY THROUGH THE ELECTRIC-BLUE WATERS OF MOSQUITO BAY

The evening starts at twilight with a bumpy ride through Esperanza in a rattly old school bus. The driver for Island Adventures motors along the seaside strip picking up adventurous patrons of all stripes along the way.

My fellow voyagers include an older couple and their adult daughter, a young family with two inquisitive little boys, a pregnant woman and her husband, and a half dozen rambunctious 20-somethings, whose high spirits suggest they've just left a nearby bar.

We arrive at the Island Adventures headquarters, a converted two-story house with a small office downstairs where we buy our tickets and peruse a small selection of T-shirts and postcards. We're instructed to go upstairs for a brief lecture. There we join others who had forgone the free pickup service and driven themselves.

The room resembles an elementary school science lab. Small tables and chairs fill the back of the room, bookshelves are lined with marine biology texts, and instructional posters fill the walls. Once everyone is assembled, we receive a child-friendly lecture, explaining just why the bioluminescent lagoon in Mosquito Bay glows.

The mangrove bay's rich nutrients and clean warm water create the perfect environment for sustaining the zillions of dinoflagellates that wash into the bay during high tide and remain trapped there when the tide recedes. The microscopic single-celled creature is unique in several ways. For one, it contains properties similar to both plants and animals. But more notably, when it senses motion, it experiences a chemical reaction that creates a burst of light not unlike that of a firefly.

Puerto Rico is said to have as many as seven bays rich in dinoflagellates, although only three are commonly known: Phosphorescent Bay in La Parguera on the southwest coast of Puerto Rico, Laguna Grande in Fajardo on the east coast, and Mosquito Bay in Vieques. Mosquito Bay is touted as one of the most spectacular bioluminescent bays in the world because of its high concentration of dinoflagellates and the absence of pollution and ambient light. Because darkness is required to see the glow, the best nights to tour the bay are when no moon is visible.

After our lecture we pile back into the bus and bounce our way over the rutted roads inside Balneario Sun Bay to reach Mosquito Bay Nature Reserve. Tonight is a new moon, and no matter how hard we peer out the windows, all we see is blackness. The bus pulls all the way up to the water's edge, where several guides and the boat captain await our arrival, and we unload, clutching our cameras and bug spray. A ramp appears from no where, and we walk across it to find our places on the bench seats that run along both sides of the electric pontoon boat.

Silently we motor across the calm waters into the dark lagoon. The sky is filled with constellations, which our guides point out and identify by name. We notice that the lip of the boat's wake looks an eerie pale blue. Then someone stomps loudly several times on the floor of the boat, and we see scores of blue zigzags radiating away from us – the underwater wakes of fish fleeing our path.

As we venture deeper into the lagoon, the night grows darker while the electric-blue glow of the water becomes more vivid.

Before April 2007, when the Department of Natural Resources banned swimming in the island's bioluminescent bays, the climax of the trip came when visitors were permitted to jump in and frolic in the bathtub-warm water, where they could swim, turn flips, and create water angels in the electric-blue drink. Now we must content ourselves with watching the boat's blue wake and spotting electric fish trails through the water. It's still a magical experience, but it's not quite the same.

After we motor back to shore and file onto the bus, we return to town in silence as everyone seems lost in thought. The bus makes intermittent stops in front of the crowded bars, restaurants, and guesthouses that line the strip in Esperanza. One at a time, we disembark and go our separate ways to eat dinner, have a few drinks, and marvel at the wonder of our nighttime journey through the electric-blue waters of Mosquito Bay.

Kayak rentals are also available for $10–15 per hour, $25–35 for four hours, and $45–55 all day. Snorkeling-equipment rentals are also available.

Snorkeling, Diving, and Fishing

The best diving in Vieques can be found along the fringe reefs on the southern side of the island. **Nan-Sea Charters** (787/741-2390, dgephoto1@aol.com, www.nanseacharters.com) offers half-day, two-dive trips starting at $100 from a 28-foot dive boat. One-tank shore dives are $50. Custom coral tours and diving certification courses are also available.

Combine a day of sailing and snorkeling with **Sail Vieques** in Isabel Segunda (787/508-7245, billwillo@yahoo.com). A half-day trip with snorkeling is $50, and a daylong trip to the southern tip of the Bermuda Triangle with snorkeling is $110. Captain Bill also offers a two-hour sunset cruise for $30.

Vieques Adventure Company (69 Calle Orquideas, Esperanza, 787/692-9162, garry@ciequesadventures.com, www.bikevieques.com) offers kayak rentals ($45) and tours, as well as individual kayak fishing tours ($150).

Go inshore fishing for kingfish, amberjack, barracuda, pompano, and tarpon on a 21-foot Ranger bay boat with Captain Franco Gonzalez of **Caribbean Fly Fishing** (61 Calle Orquideas, Esperanza, 787/741-1337 or 787/450-3744, flyfish@coqui.net, www.viequesflyfishing.com).

Mountain Biking

Landlubbers looking to explore inland Vieques can get a guided, off-the-beaten-path mountain-bike tour with **Vieques Adventure Company** (69 Calle Orquideas, Esperanza, 787/692-9162, garry@ciequesadventures.com, www.bikevieques.com). Bikes rent for $35 a day ($25 a day for multiple days) and include a helmet, a lock, and a trail repair kit. Half-day tours are $75. Combination bike-kayak-snorkel tours are also available.

ENTERTAINMENT AND EVENTS
Cockfights

If there is such a thing as politically correct cockfighting, it exists in Vieques, where the birds do not fight until death. Winners are proclaimed by judges before the birds are seriously harmed. Fights are held at **Gallera Puerto Real** (Carr. 200, about three miles west of Isabel Segunda, no telephone), typically on Friday nights and Sunday afternoons, although the schedule changes. Admission is $10; women admitted free. Food and alcohol are served.

Bars

If partying into the wee hours is your idea of the perfect vacation, Vieques may not be the place for you. There are no nightclubs, discos, or casinos on the island, and many of the restaurants close by 10 P.M. There are a couple of watering holes that stay open late, though. Salty sea dogs gravitate to the no-frills **Banana's Beach Bar and Grill** (Calle Flamboyan, Esperanza, 787/741-8700, bananasvieques@gmail.com, www.bananasguesthouse.com, Sun.–Thurs. until 1 A.M., Fri.–Sat. until 2 A.M.). A sign behind the bar proudly proclaims: "This Is A Gin-u-wine Sleazy Waterfront Bar." Ask the bartender what the drink special is, and she's likely to respond: "A beer and a shot." But it also serves a potent rum punch made with three kinds of rum. There are eight small guest rooms on-site if you drink too much and can't drive home.

Apologies to Banana's, but the real "gin-u-wine sleazy waterfront bar" in Vieques is **Al's Mar Azul** (577 Calle Plinio Peterson, Isabel Segunda, 787/741-3400, Sun.–Thurs. 11 A.M.–1 A.M., Fri.–Sat. 11 A.M.–2:30 A.M.). Hanging right over the water, this pleasant dive bar is cluttered with a random collection of junk that looks as if it has been sitting around the place for decades: old lifesaving rings, an inflated blowfish, paper lanterns, the grill off a jeep, a huge plastic turtle, a carved coconut head. It doesn't serve food, but someone will call your order in and pick it up for you at Mamasonga's across the street. It's also home of the annual Spam Cookoff every May. There are some worn pool tables and video poker games if you're compelled to do something besides drink and chat up the locals who hang here. And if you really get bored, there's a dusty bookshelf filled with tattered paperbacks. It's the perfect place to nurse a hangover with a spicy Bloody Mary on Sundays.

Festivals

There are two major festivals in Vieques. The biggest one is **Fiestas Patronales de Nuestra Sra. del Carmen** (787/741-5000), which is held on the plaza of Isabel Segunda Wednesday–Sunday during the third weekend of July. Attractions include parades, religious processions, a small carnival, and lots of live Latin music and dancing. Entertainment usually starts around 9 P.M. and lasts until the wee hours of the morning. Festivities are fueled by *bili,* a traditional beverage made from a local fruit called *quenepa* mixed with white rum, cinnamon, and sugar.

The other big event is the **Cultural Festival** (787/741-1717), sponsored by the Institute of Puerto Rican Culture at El Fortín Conde de Mirasol in Isabel Segunda after Easter. Festivities include folk music and dance performances, a craft fair, and a book fair.

SHOPPING

Shopping outlets are pretty limited in Vieques. For a quality selection of handmade crafts by local and other Caribbean artisans, there's **Kim's Cabin Clothing Boutique and Gifts** (136 Calle Flamboyan, Esperanza, 787/741-3145, daily 9:30 A.M.–5 P.M.). In addition to Haitian metal art and sea-glass earrings, you'll find tropical-print shirts and dresses imported from Indonesia.

Another good source for tropical-print clothing is **Luna Loca** (343 Carr. 200, Isabel Segunda, 787/741-0264, Mon.–Sat. 9 A.M.–5 P.M., Sun. 10 A.M.–4 P.M.). It also has a small selection of jewelry and framed photographs of the island by local artists.

Vibrant original paintings and prints on canvas of tropical flowers, fish, palm trees, and jungle scenes by local artist Siddhia Hutchinson can be found at **Siddhia Hutchinson Fine Art Design Studio and Gallery** (A-15 Calle Mon Repos, Isabel Segunda, 787/741-8780, siddhia@coqui.net, http://siddhiahutchinson .com, daily 9 A.M.–3 P.M.). The artwork has also been tastefully reproduced on ceramics, dinnerware, rugs, and pillows.

ACCOMMODATIONS
$50-100

If you don't mind not being on the beach, the best deal for the budget-minded traveler is **Casa Alta Vista** (297 Calle Flamboyan, Esperanza, 787/741-3296, fax 787/741-3296, casaaltavista@yahoo.com, www.casaaltavista .net, $80 s, $90–95 d, $115–175 for 4 people, plus 9 percent tax). This small, cheerful 10-room guesthouse features newly renovated rooms with modern bathrooms and extra-comfy mattresses. There's no TV, telephone, or pool, but the air-conditioning and mini-refrigerator keep things cool. A rooftop sundeck offers a 360-degree view of the island, three-quarters of it ocean. If it's available, ask for room 12—it has got the best view of the ocean and hillsides. Registration is in the small market on the first floor. This is also where spontaneous jam sessions occasionally occur, thanks to owner and guitar player Mark Biron, who keeps maracas, sticks, cowbells, and *güiros* on hand for anybody who wants to join in. Scooter, bicycle, snorkeling gear, beach chair, umbrella, and cooler rentals are available on-site. There are also a one-bedroom apartment and wheelchair-accessible rooms.

Trade Winds Guest House and Restaurant (Calle Flamboyan, Esperanza, 787/741-8666, fax 787/741-2964, tradewns@coqui.net, www .enchanted-isle.com/tradewinds, $70 s, $80 d, plus 9 percent tax) is a better restaurant than it is a guesthouse, but it's conveniently situated in the middle of Esperanza and across the street from the *malécon* (sea walk). The 10 rooms are small, windowless, and Spartan, but they're clean and have firm mattresses. There's no TV or telephone, but some rooms have air-conditioning. The rooms open onto a scrappy courtyard with plastic patio furniture, and there's a decent restaurant and bar upstairs.

Just want a cheap place to crash? If you

don't plan to spend much time in your room, **Bananas Guesthouse** (Calle Flamboyan, Esperanza, 787/741-8700, atbananas@aol .com, www.bananasguesthouse.com, $55–85 s/d plus 9 percent tax) may meet your needs. In the back of the popular bar and restaurant, Bananas, this bare-bones guesthouse has eight small, rustic, dimly lit rooms with deck flooring. There's no TV or telephone, but some rooms have air-conditioning, screened porches, and mini-refrigerators.

Perched on an inland hillside overlooking the main island is the lovely, lushly landscaped **Crow's Nest Inn** (Carr. 201, km 1.1, Isabel Segunda, 787/741-0033 or 877/276-9763, fax 787/741-1294, thenest@coqui.net, www .crowsnestvieques.com, $90 s, $129 d, $139 one-bedroom suite, $250 two-bedroom suite, plus 9 percent tax; includes continental breakfast). The Spanish hacienda–style inn has 16 well-appointed modern rooms, all with air-conditioning, TV, and a kitchen or kitchenette. There are also a small pool and an excellent restaurant, Island Steakhouse. Snorkeling-gear rental is available.

There's something positively Mediterranean about the exterior appearance of **Casa La Lanchita** (374 N. Shore Rd., Isabel Segunda, 787/741-8449 or 800/774-4712, www .viequeslalanchita.com, $100–175, four-night minimum stay). The bright white four-story structure with archways and balustrades is built right on the sandy beach of a brilliant blue sea and is surrounded by flowering bougainvillea. Despite the posh exterior, the rooms are modestly appointed with budget rattan and metal furnishings, but each room has a private terrace and full-size kitchen.

$150-250

Luxury has many different definitions, and Vieques seems to have a unique hotel to match each one. The ultramodern boutique hotel **Bravo Beach Hotel** (1 N. Shore Rd., Isabel Segunda, 787/741-1128, info@bravobeach hotel.com, www.bravobeachhotel.com, $160–215 s/d, $425 villa, plus 9 percent tax; no children under 18 permitted) is a study in

glamorous minimalism. Nine rooms and a two-bedroom villa are located in a cluster of small bungalows painted pastel shades of green, blue, and yellow. Each room is different, but the spacious interiors all feature stark white walls that create a dramatic contrast to the dark mahogany platform beds and modular furnishings made of wood and glass. Some rooms have ocean-view balconies and floor-to-ceiling windows. One room has 180-degree windows and a king-size canopy bed. Each room has satellite TV, air-conditioning, a mini-refrigerator, wireless Internet, a DVD player, and a PlayStation. The bathroom is stocked with Aveda bath products, and the beds are made with Italian Frette linens. Although it's on the ocean, the hotel doesn't have a swimmable beach. Instead there are two swimming pools, one ocean-side. A poolside bar and lounge serves a limited menu, and the newly opened BBH restaurant serves tapas ranging $8–14 and boasts a large wine selection.

Victorian elegance is the theme at **Hacienda Tamarindo** (Calle Flamboyan, just west of Esperanza, 787/741-0420, fax 787/741-3215, hactam@aol.com, www.hacienda tamarindo.com, $125–230 s, $145–245 d, $175–230 suites, $200–270 two-bedroom suites, plus 9 percent tax and 10 percent service charge). Built around a 200-year-old tamarind tree that's rooted in the lobby and shades the second-floor breakfast room, this beautifully appointed hotel is furnished in a tasteful combination of antique Caribbean and Victorian styles. Folk art, wall murals, and vintage circus posters provide playful touches. There are 13 rooms and three suites. Each one is different, but they all contain basket-weave furnishings, brightly colored bedspreads, and air-conditioning. Rooms have neither TVs nor telephones, but each one comes with folding chairs, oversize towels, and coolers for the beach and pool. The hotel doesn't have a restaurant per se, but it does serve a free breakfast, and a box lunch can be prepared for $8.50 per person if requested the night before. There's also a 24-hour honor bar. No one under age 15 is permitted.

A romantic getaway doesn't get any more lovely or secluded than **Inn on the Blue**

VIEQUES AND CULEBRA

Horizon (Calle Flamboyan, west of Esperanza, 787/741-3318 or 787/741-0527, fax 787/741-0522, innonblue@aol.com, www.innonthebluehorizon.com, $160–370 s, plus 9 percent tax). The small 10-room inn perched on a cliff overlooking the ocean hosts many weddings and is geared primarily toward couples. Rooms are exquisitely furnished with poster beds, antiques, and original artwork. Amenities include a small gym, pool, lighted tennis courts, and an inviting pavilion bar. Rooms have air-conditioning, but no TV or telephone. **Carambola** restaurant serves upscale Caribbean fusion cuisine, and the **Blue Moon Bar and Grill** serves breakfast and lunch in a lovely open-air pavilion-style restaurant overlooking the ocean.

Avant-garde architecture in a thickly wooded setting distinguishes the most unusual hotel in Puerto Rico, **The Hix House** (Carr. 995, km 1.6, 787/741-2302 or 787/741-2797, info@hixislandhouse.com, www.hixislandhouse.com, $195–325 d, plus 9 percent tax and 7 percent service charge). Four unpainted concrete buildings house 13 "lofts," many with open sides, outdoor showers, and ocean views. Designed by architect John Hix to have as little impact on its 13 acres as possible, the property uses solar energy and recycles used water to replenish the vegetation. There's no TV or telephone, but the linens are Frette, the pool is spectacular, and each morning the kitchen is stocked with juices, cereal, breads, and coffee. Yoga classes are conducted in the pavilion, and in-room or garden massages are available.

Over $250

Martineau Bay Resort and Spa (Carr. 200, km 3.4, Isabel Segunda, 787/741-4100, fax 787/741-4171) was closed for a massive remodel project in late 2008. An anomaly on Vieques, it's the first megaresort but most likely not the last. Formerly owned and operated by Wyndham and later bought by W Hotels, the complex has 156 rooms and villas, all either oceanfront or ocean-view. There are also one- to three-bedroom villas. Amenities include a large pool with swim-up bar, full-service spa, fitness room, beach access, tennis courts, and room service. All rooms have air-conditioning, satellite TV, CD players, coffeemakers, hair dryers, and private balconies or terraces. The rooms are large and ultraluxurious, featuring Spanish tile bathrooms, mahogany furniture, and amazing mattresses.

FOOD
Breakfast

There are several terrific breakfast spots in Vieques. In addition to your typical eggs, **Mamasonga** (Calle Plinio Peterson, Isabel Segunda, 787/741-0103, daily 8 A.M.–4 P.M., $3.95–8.95) serves great German apple pancakes and French toast, plus muesli for the health-conscious. Lunch items include black-bean soup, burgers, nachos, Cuban sandwiches, quesadillas, and salads. There's also a full bar.

Another option is **Belly Buttons Café and Grill** (62 Calle Flamboyan, Esperanza, 787/741-3336, daily 7:30 A.M.–2 P.M., $4.50–7.50), serving eggs, French toast, bagels, sandwiches, and salads outside on picnic tables. Call ahead for curb service.

Puerto Rican and Caribbean

Fine dining is a rarity in Vieques, so thank goodness for **(BBH** (Bravo Beach Hotel, 1 N. Shore Rd., Isabel Segunda, 787/741-1128, info@bravobeachhotel.com, www.bravobeachhotel.com, $6–14) with its creative, Caribbean-influenced menu of tapas. The menu is always changing, but plan to dine on the likes of house-cured olives, mussels, seared scallops, duck breast, or New Zealand lamb in the lovely serenity of the minimalist-style setting. Check out the outstanding wine selection in the walk-in wine gallery.

Because many restaurants on Vieques close early, it's good to know where to find a decent restaurant open later in the evening every day. That place is **Richard's Café Restaurant** (Carr. 200, just west of downtown Isabel Segunda, 787/741-5242, daily 11 A.M.–3 P.M. and 5–11 P.M., $6.95–18.95). The dim lighting, fast-food decor, and fake flowers don't create much of an atmosphere inside the pink concrete structure. But it serves good traditional

Puerto Rican cuisine, including *pastelillos, mofongo,* steak, seafood, and lobster. The full bar serves a terrific passion fruit punch, made with Grand Marnier, rum, and pineapple juice.

For a creative take on Caribbean cuisine, there's 【 **Restaurante Bilí** (Amapola Inn, 144 Calle Flamboyan, Esperanza, 787/741-1382, Wed.–Sun. 11 A.M.–4 P.M. and 6–11 P.M., $16.95–29.95). The casual, open-air restaurant's specialties include mini-*empanadillas* stuffed with rabbit and goat cheese, *dorado* in plantain chutney, whole fried snapper, and angel-hair pasta with crab meat stewed in coconut milk. There are also a full bar and a partial view of the ocean.

Also serving Caribbean cuisine is **Trade Winds Restaurant** (Calle Flamboyan, Esperanza, 787/741-8666, fax 787/741-2964, tradewns@coqui.net, www.enchanted-isle .com/tradewinds, daily 8:30 A.M.–2 P.M. and 6–9:30 P.M., $14.50–28). This casual open-air restaurant overlooks the water and serves grilled fish, steak, lobster, pork loin, pasta, *mofongo,* and coconut curry. For dessert, try the piña colada bread pudding with warm rum sauce. There are 10 small guest rooms behind the restaurant.

American and Fusion

Nearby is **Banana's Beach Bar and Grill** (Calle Flamboyan, Esperanza, 787/741-8700, daily 11 A.M.–about 10 P.M., bar stays open later, $5–16.50). This very casual, popular drinking hole serves mostly American pub fare, including burgers, wings, and hotdogs, as well as jerk chicken, ribs, and grilled fish. There are eight small guest rooms in the back.

Although its prices are fairly low by Vieques standards, the gorgeous ambience of 【 **Cafe Media Luna** (351 Antonio G. Mellado/Carr. 200, Isabel Segunda, 787/741-2594, Wed.–Sun. 7–10 P.M., $12–19) makes it feel like a special-occasion restaurant. Dark blue walls, terra-cotta tile floors, and Indian batik wall hangings set a sensual stage for its interesting combination of Asian and Mediterranean dishes, all made from scratch. Specialties include ginger shrimp pancakes with lemon-coconut sauce, avocado

lime cucumber gazpacho, and parmigiana-rosemary–crusted rack of lamb.

Seafood and Steak

If you get your fill of seafood in Vieques, **Island Steakhouse** (Crow's Nest Guesthouse, Carr. 201, km 1.1, Isabel Segunda, 787/741-0033 or 877/276-9763, fax 787/741-1294, thenest@ coqui.net, www.crowsnestvieques.com, Fri.–Tues. 6–10 P.M., $8–27) is ready to serve your carnivorous needs: filet, sirloin, rib eye, porterhouse, *churrasco*—you name it, the place has got it. But non–meat-eaters aren't overlooked: The menu also features whole lobster, fried shrimp, and salmon.

Chez Shack (Carr. 995, km 1.8, 787/741-2175, Mon. and Wed.–Sat. 5:30–10 P.M., $12–30) really is a shack. It's constructed of tacked-up sheets of corrugated metal strung with twinkle lights and surrounded by thick forest, but folks flock here for good food and the steel-drum band. The kitchen has been undergoing some changes in its management and the type of cuisine it serves, and the hours seem to vary from week to week. But everyone swears by the excellent food and convivial mood of this bohemian eatery.

INFORMATION AND SERVICES

All of the services on Vieques are in Isabel Segunda. The **tourism office** (787/741-0800, Mon.–Fri. 9 A.M.–4 P.M.) is on the plaza in Casa Alcaldia (town hall). But for the most comprehensive, up-to-date information, visit www.enchanted-isle.com, www.vieques-island .com, www.viequestravelguide.com, and www .travelandsports.com/vie.htm.

To stay abreast of local news and events, pick up the island's two monthly publications, *Vieques Times* (153 Calle Flamboyan, Esperanza, www.viequestimes.com) and *Vieques Events* (www.viequesevents.net), both printed in English and Spanish.

The island's only bank, with an ATM, is **Banco Popular** (115 Calle Muñoz Rivera, 787/741-2071). Nearby, on the same street, is the **post office** (787/741-3891). You'll find the **police station** (787/741-2020 or 787/741-2121) at Carretera 200, km 0.2, at Carretera 997, and the **fire department** can be reached by calling 787/741-2111. For health services, **Centro de Salud de Familia** (Carr. 997) is open Monday–Friday 7 A.M.–3:30 P.M., and the emergency room is open 24 hours. Serving visitors' pharmacy needs is **Farmacia Antonio** (Calle Benitez Guzman across from Casa Alcaldia, 787/741-8397).

Self-serve laundry **Familia Ríos** (Calle Benítez Castaño, 787/438-1846) is open Sunday–Monday and Wednesday–Friday 6 A.M.–7 P.M., and Saturday 6 A.M.–5 P.M.

GETTING THERE
By Ferry
The **Puerto Rico Port Authority** (in Vieques 787/741-4761, 787/863-0705, or 800/981-2005, daily 8–11 A.M. and 1–3 P.M.) operates a daily ferry service between Vieques and Fajardo.

The **passenger ferry** is primarily a commuter operation, and it can often be crowded—especially on the weekends and holidays when vacationers swell the number of passengers. Reservations are not accepted, but you can buy tickets in advance. Arrive no later than one hour before departure. Sometimes the ferry cannot accommodate everyone who wants to ride. The trip typically takes about an hour to travel between Fajardo and Vieques, and the fare is $4 round-trip per person. Note that ferry schedules can change, but the schedule was as follows:

- **Fajardo to Vieques:** Monday–Friday 9:30 A.M., 1 P.M., 4:30 P.M., 8 P.M.; Saturday–Sunday and Monday holidays 9 A.M., 3 P.M., 6 P.M.

- **Vieques to Fajardo:** Monday–Friday 6:30 A.M., 11 A.M., 3 P.M., 6 P.M.; Saturday–Sunday and Monday holidays 6:30 A.M., 1 P.M., 4:30 P.M.

There is also a weekday **cargo/car ferry,** for which reservations are required. But be aware that most car-rental agencies in Puerto Rico do not permit their automobiles to leave the main island. The best option is to leave your car in Fajardo and rent another car on Vieques. The trip usually takes about two hours, and the cost is $15 for small vehicles and $19 for large vehicles. The schedule is as follows:

- **Fajardo to Vieques:** Monday–Friday 4 A.M., 9:30 A.M., 4:30 P.M.

- **Vieques to Fajardo:** Monday 6 A.M., 1:30 P.M., 6 P.M.

By Air
As almost anyone who's taken the commuter ferry from Fajardo to Vieques will tell you, the best way to get to the island is by air. There are several small airlines that fly to Vieques from the main island, and the flights are fairly inexpensive and speedy.

In San Juan, flights can be arranged from Luis Muñoz Marín International Airport near Isla Verde or from the smaller Isla Grande Airport near Old San Juan. But the shortest, cheapest flight is from the newly opened Jose Aponte de la Torre Airport on the former Roosevelt Roads Naval Base in Ceiba on the east coast. Round-trip flights are about $190 from San Juan and $60 from Ceiba. Flights between Vieques and Culebra are about $70.

Service providers include **Isla Nena Air Service** (787/863-4447, 787/863-4449, or 877/812-5144, islanenapr@centennialpr.net, www.islanena.8m.com); **Vieques Air Link** (787/741-8331 or 888/901-9247, valair@coqui.net, www.viequesairlink.com); **M&N Aviation** (787/791-7008, www.mnaviation.com); and **Air Flamenco** (787/724-1818, airflamenco@hotmail.com, www.airflamenco.net).

GETTING AROUND
Unless you plan to park yourself at one of the island's few full-service hotels and never leave it, you're going to need a rental car to get around. *Publicos* are a great way to get from the ferry or airport to your hotel, but beyond that they're not as reliable as the taxi service mainland Americans may be accustomed to.

If you do rent a car, book it well in advance of your arrival. They get snapped up quickly.

Rental fees start around $50 per day, and penalties can be accrued if you return it with excessive sand inside, damp seats, or less gas in the tank than when you got it. Most vehicles are four-wheel drives because many of the beaches require off-roading to reach. Blowouts are not unusual, so make sure your car has a full-size replacement tire and the tools necessary to change it. If you need assistance changing the tire, the rental-car agency may send someone to help, but again, it will cost you. The seatbelt law is enforced, as are speed limits, which are mostly 35 miles per hour, except in town and on beach roads, where it's 10–15 miles per hour.

There are only three gas stations on the island, one of which appears to be perpetually closed. They're all within a short distance of one another on Carretera 200 in Isabel Segunda, just west of the plaza. Because gas is shipped from San Juan on weekdays only, gas shortages are not unusual, and sometimes gas stations close early on Sundays, since that's the day everyone goes to the beach, including the gas-station operators.

Remember that semiwild horses roam freely on Vieques. Because many roads in Vieques are unlit, it's nearly impossible to see the horses in the dark, so take extra care when driving at night.

Publico

Publicos can typically can be found waiting for fares at the airport or ferry. They can also be called randomly throughout the day for pickup service, although some travelers report that they are not always reliable or timely. Fares are typically $3 in town and $6 to various sites and beaches on the island.

The following is a partial list of *publicos* operating on the island: **Ana Robles or Rafael Perez** (787/313-0599 or 787/486-0267); **Eric** (787/741-0448); **Henry** (787/649-3838); and **Lolo Felix** (787/485-5447).

For travelers seeking transportation from San Juan to Fajardo to catch the ferry to Vieques, **Padin** operates 24-hour *publico* service between Fajardo and the Luis Muñoz Marín International Airport in San Juan. Call Mrs. Rivera at 787/644-3091 or 787/355-6746, or José Padin at 787/644-3091.

Car Rentals

Car rentals start at about $50 per day in Vieques, and most vehicles are jeeps or other four-wheel–drive automobiles. Some agencies will deliver a rental to the airport or your hotel; others require a *publico* ride to the office. Agencies include **Martineau Car Rental** (787/741-0087 or 787/741-3948, www.martineau carrental.com); **Vieques Car and Jeep Rental** (787/741-1037, viequescars@yahoo .com, www.viequescarrental.com); **Island Car Rental** (787/741-1666, iscar@coqui.net, www .enchanted-isle.com/islandcar/); and **Steve's Car Rental** (787/741-8135, stevescarrental@ aol.com, www.enchanted-isle.com/steves). Scooter rentals are available at **Extreme Scooters** (Calle Flamboyan, Esperanza, 787/435-9345).

VIEQUES AND CULEBRA

Culebra

As laid-back as Vieques is, it's practically Las Vegas compared to Culebra. Halfway between mainland Puerto Rico and St. Thomas, the tiny amoeba-shaped archipelago with 23 surrounding cays is just four miles by seven miles. The island is home to 3,000 residents and has one small community—**Dewey** (commonly called "Pueblo" or "Town")—on Ensenada Honda harbor, where the ferry docks.

Culebra has yet to be discovered by the tourism industry, but experienced divers know it as one of the best diving spots in the Caribbean. The clear clean waters are practically untouched by people and their polluting by-products, thanks in part to the arid island's absence of rivers or streams. The result is superb underwater visibility and healthy, intact coral systems that support a wide variety of sea life.

Recognizing the island's vital role as a natural wildlife habitat, President Theodore Roosevelt proclaimed much of the island a National Wildlife Refuge in 1909, which today encompasses 1,568 acres. Nonetheless, in 1939 the U.S. Navy made Culebra its primary gunnery and bomb practice site and continued its operations here until 1975, when it turned its focus to Vieques.

The island is a combination of hilly terrain with dry subtropical forest and a highly irregular coastline punctuated by cliffs, mangrove forests, and spectacular sandy coral beaches. Because it is so sparsely inhabited, Culebra is home to many endangered species and is an important nesting site for birds and sea turtles. Playa Flamenco is celebrated as one of the best beaches in the United States. But there are many other smaller beaches to discover, some completely deserted much of the time.

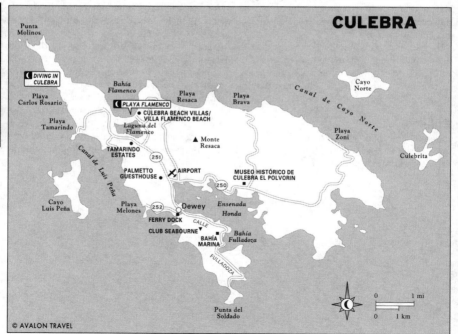

© AVALON TRAVEL

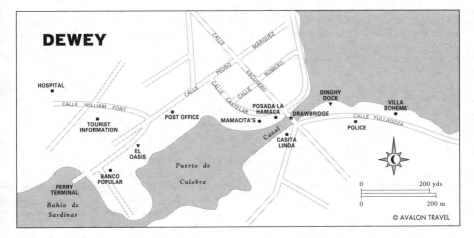

Accommodations in Culebra are mostly small mom-and-pop guesthouses, some little more than spare bedrooms. The operations here are mostly self-serve. In fact, it's not unusual for visitors to have the run of the place when owners decide to head to the beach or bar to while away the day. But there are a handful of small luxury hotels and condo rental units for travelers who want more modern-day amenities or services. There are a dozen or so restaurants, where service typically moves at a snail's pace, and a couple of bars, but little real nightlife.

Because water is shipped from San Juan, shortages are not unusual, and pressure is often low. Some smaller properties have limited hot water or none at all. Plumbing in general can be problematic—the standard practice is to discard toilet paper in the trash instead of flushing it. And alarm clocks are never necessary, because you're sure to be woken by one of the roosters that roam the island. An anomaly in the world, Culebra is virtually crime-free. Instead of petty theft, visitors need only brace themselves against the voracious mosquitoes and sand gnats that tend to invade around dusk.

Culebra is one of the last vestiges of pre-tourism Puerto Rico. Nobody's in a hurry, modern conveniences are few, and all anybody really wants to do is go to the beach. That's the way

people in Culebra like it, and most of them want to keep it that way. Visitors are advised to embrace the island's quirky inconveniences and sleepy pace of life to fully appreciate its many rare charms.

SIGHTS

If you spend any time in Culebra, you're bound to enter the **Culebra National Wildlife Refuge** (787/742-0115, Mon.–Fri. 7:30 A.M.–4 P.M.). It encompasses 1,568 acres, including much of Flamenco Peninsula, where 60,000 sooty terns nest, as well as mangrove forests, wetlands, coastline, surrounding cays (except Cayo Norte), and **Monte Resaca,** the island's highest point at 650 feet, which contains forested canyons, ravines, and a unique habitat known as the boulder forest. The refuge contains excellent beaches, diving, bird-watching, and hiking. Culebrita, Cayo Luis Peña, and Monte Resaca are open daily sunrise–sunset. Other areas are off-limits to visitors. For maps and information, visit the refuge office, east on Carretera 250, just past the cemetery.

Museo Histórico de Culebra El Polvorín (off Carr. 250 toward Playa Brava, 787/405-3768 or 787/742-3832, Thurs.–Sun. 10 A.M.–3 P.M.) is a newly created museum of history on the island that features old maps and photographs of Culebra, Taíno artifacts, traditional canoes made from the zinc plant, and Navy artifacts. It's located at the site of the first settlement in Culebra, in a 1905-era stone building that once stored ammunitions for the Navy.

BEACHES

Once you see Culebra's craggy coastline of hidden coves, private beaches, coral outcroppings, and cays, it's easy to imagine why pirates liked to hide out here. Playa Flamenco is the island's most celebrated beach, and rightly so. But there are many less populated and more remote beaches to be found for those willing to hike in.

◖ Playa Flamenco

Named one of "America's Best Beaches" by the Travel Channel, Playa Flamenco (north on Carr. 251 at dead-end) is one of the main reasons people come to Culebra. It's a wide, mile-long, horseshoe-shaped beach with calm, shallow waters and fine white sand. The island's only publicly maintained beach, it has

bathroom facilities, picnic tables, lounge-chair and umbrella rentals, and a camping area. You can buy sandwiches and alcoholic beverages at Coconuts Beach Grill in front of Culebra Beach Villa, as well as from vendors who set up grills and blenders in the ample parking lot. An abandoned, graffiti-covered tank remains as a reminder of the Navy's presence. It can get crowded on summer weekends and holidays—especially Easter and Christmas.

Other Beaches

If Playa Flamenco is too crowded, take a 20-minute hike over the ridge and bypass the first small beach you encounter to reach the more private **Playa Carlos Rosario,** a pleasant, narrow beach flanked by coral reef and boulders. It offers excellent snorkeling around the long, vibrant stretch of coral reef not too far offshore. Other great snorkeling and diving beaches are **Punta Soldado** (south of Dewey, at the end of Calle Fulladoza), which also has beautiful coral reefs; **Playa Melones,** a rocky beach and subtropical forest within walking

Playa Carlos Rosario has an excellent reef for snorkeling and diving.

© JIM JOHNSON

distance of Dewey; and **Playa Tamarindo,** where you'll find a diversity of soft corals and sea anemones.

Excellent deserted beaches can also be found on two of Culebra's cays—**Cayo Luis Peña** and **Culebrita,** which is distinguished by a lovely but crumbling abandoned lighthouse and several tidal pools. To gain access, it is necessary to either rent a boat or arrange a water taxi. And be sure to bring water, sunscreen, and other provisions; there are no facilities or services on the islands.

At the far eastern side of the island at the end of Carretera 250 is **Playa Zoni,** which features a frequently deserted sandy beach and great views of Culebrita, Cayo Norte, and St. Thomas.

Playa Brava has the biggest surf on the island, but it requires a bit of a hike to get there. To reach the trailhead, travel east on Carretera 250 and turn left after the cemetery, and then hike downhill and fork to the left. Note that Playa Brava is a turtle-nesting site, so it may be off-limits during nesting season from April to June.

Like Playa Brava, **Playa Resaca** is an important nesting site for sea turtles, but it is ill-suited for swimming because of the coral reef along the beach. The hike to Playa Resaca is fairly arduous, but it traverses a fascinating topography through a mangrove and boulder forest. To get there, turn on the road just east of the airport off Carretera 250, drive to the end, and hike the rest of the way in.

Turtle Watch

Culebra is one of three nesting grounds for hawksbill and leatherback turtles, the latter of which is the largest species of turtle in the world, weighing between 500 and 1,600 pounds. From April to early June, the sea turtles spend the evenings trudging up the beach at Playa Resaca and Playa Brava to dig holes and lay eggs before returning to the sea in grand displays of sand-tossing to cover their tracks. The Puerto Rico Department of Natural and

VIEQUES AND CULEBRA

© JIM JOHNSON

Visitors must take precautions not to disturb the sea turtles during nesting season, from April to June.

Environmental Resources (787/556-6234 or 877/77-CORAL—877/772-6725, fax 530/618-4605, info@coralations.org, www.coralations.org/turtles) accepts volunteers to catalog the turtles when they nest.

SPORTS AND RECREATION
C Diving

Culebra more than makes up for its dearth of entertainment options with its wealth of diving opportunities. There are reportedly 50 dive sites surrounding the island. They're mostly along the island's fringe reefs and around the cays. In addition to huge diverse coral formations, divers commonly spot sea turtles, stingrays, puffer fish, angel fish, nurse sharks, and more.

Among the most popular dive sites are **Carlos Rosario (Impact),** which features a long, healthy coral reef teeming with sea life, including huge sea fans, and **Shipwreck,** the site of *The Wit Power,* a tugboat sunk in 1984. Here you can play out your *Titanic* fantasies and witness how the sea has claimed the boat for its habitat.

Many of the best dive sites are around Culebra's many cays. **Cayo Agua Rock** is a single 45-foot-tall rock surrounded by sand and has been known to attract barracudas, nurse sharks, and sea turtles. **Cayo Ballena** provides a 120-foot wall dive with spectacular coral. **Cayo Raton** is said to attract an inordinate number and variety of fish. And **Cayo Yerba** features an underwater arch covered in yellow cup coral, best seen at night when they "bloom," and a good chance to see stingrays.

The island's sole diving and snorkeling source, **Culebra Divers** (across from the ferry terminal in Dewey, 787/742-0803, info@culebradivers.com, www.culebradivers.com), offers daily snorkeling trips for $45. One-tank dives are $60, and two-tank dives are $85, including tanks and weights. Snorkeling and dive gear is available for rent. It's also a good place to go for advice on snorkeling from the beach.

Other Water Sports

For water-sport equipment rentals, **Culebra**

Water Toys (next to El Batey in Dewey, 787/742-1122, cell 787/246-1718 or 787/406-2224, www.islaculebra.com/culebra-water-toys/english.html, daily 8 A.M.–5 P.M.) offers snorkel gear for $10, kayaks and pedal boats for $40, rowboats for $50, sailboard gear for $60, and fishing skiffs for $125. It also offers water-taxi service to Culebrita, Cayo Luis Peña, Carlos Rosario, Vieques, and St. Thomas.

Mountain Biking

Culebra Bike Shop (Calle Fulladoza, 787/742-2209 or 787/209-2543, daily 9 A.M.–6 P.M.) rents 21- and 24-speed mountain bikes, as well as boogie boards and snorkeling equipment.

ENTERTAINMENT

Nightlife is limited on Culebra, but sometimes even nature lovers and beachcombers need to cut loose. **El Batey** (Carr. 250, km 1.1, 787/742-3828, Fri.–Sat. 10 P.M.–2 A.M., also serves lunch) provides that opportunity. Dancing is the primary attraction at this large no-frills establishment, where DJs spin salsa, merengue, and disco on Friday and Saturday nights. It also serves deli sandwiches and burgers ($3–5) during the day.

Everybody who goes to Culebra ends up at **Mamacita's** (64 Calle Castelar, 787/742-0090, www.mamacitaspr.com, Sun.–Thurs. 4–10 P.M., Fri.–Sat. 4–11 P.M.) at some point. The popular open-air watering hole right on the canal in Dewey attracts both locals and visitors alike. Two side-by-side tin-roofed pavilions provide shade for the cozy oasis appointed with brightly painted tables and chairs surrounded by potted palms. The blue tiled bar is tricked out with colorful folk art touches painted in shades of turquoise, lime green, and lavender. Behind the bar you can buy cigarettes and condoms, and you can get a spritz of bug spray free of charge when the sand gnats attack. Happy hour is 3–6 P.M. daily. Try the house special cocktail, the bushwhacker, a frozen concoction of Kahlúa, Bailey's Irish Cream, coconut cream, rum, and amaretto. Check the chalkboard for excellent daily dinner specials.

SHOPPING

Shopping is limited to mostly shops selling tourist trinkets, but **Butiki** (74 Calle Romero, Dewey, daily 9 A.M.–6 P.M., 708/935-2542, www.butikiculebra.com) stands out for offering a great selection of batik fabrics, purses, jewelry by local artisans, and seascape oil paintings by owner Evan Schwarze.

ACCOMMODATIONS

Some properties require a minimum stay, although exceptions may be made for a surcharge. It's worth asking if you don't mind the extra cost.

Under $50

Playa Flamenco Campground (Playa Flamenco, 787/742-7000, $20, cash only) is not necessarily the place to go if you want a quiet spot to commune with nature. It's more like party central on weekends, holidays, and in summer, when the grounds can get crowded. Facilities include toilets, outdoor showers, and picnic tables. Reservations are required. If you can't get through by phone, write Autoridad de Conservactión y Dessarrollo de Culebra, Attn.: Playa Flamenco, Apartado 217, Culebra, PR 00775.

$50-100

The majority of Culebra's properties are small, modest self-serve operations that are more true to the rustic spirit of the island. Staying at **Villa Arynar B&B** (Calle Fulladoza on Ensenada Honda bay, 787/742-3145, berniefrancette@cs.com, www.culebra-island.com, Oct.–May, $90 s/d, $595 week) is like visiting friends. The two-story private home is right on the bay and surrounded by vegetation. Accommodations are limited to two spare bedrooms with a shared bathroom, but guests are free to enjoy the large decks, fishing pier, and common room with couches and a refrigerator. Owners and visitors alike eat breakfast together on the deck. Adults only.

For those who want to stay in the town of Dewey, just walking distance from the ferry dock, there are several options. **Mamacita's**

Guesthouse (64 Calle Castelar, 787/742-0090, $102. s, $115 d, including tax) is a pastel-colored hodgepodge of balconies and archways squeezed between Calle Castelar and the canal. The hostel-like accommodations are strictly functional and feature air-conditioning and satellite TV in the bedrooms. It's best suited for those just looking for a place to crash and a hopping bar and excellent restaurant on-site. Laundry facilities and boat dockage are available for guests. Internet access is available for a fee.

Visitors get more bang for the buck next door at ◖ **Posada La Hamaca** (68 Calle Castelar, 787/742-3516, info@posada.com, www.posada.com, $85 s, $97 d, $108 studio, $160 one-bedroom that sleeps 8, plus 9 percent tax). The Spanish-style guesthouse is under new management and has updated itself with new furnishings and fresh paint inside and out. The 10 rooms are light, airy and tidy, and they come with satellite TV, air-conditioning, mini-refrigerators, free Internet, and hot water. There's a large shady deck overlooking the canal out back with two gas grills. Beach towels, coolers, and free ice are provided for trips to the beach.

Palmetto Guesthouse (128 Manuel Vasquez, two blocks behind Carlos Jeep, 787/742-0257 or 787/235-6736, palmettoculebra@yahoo.com, www.palmettoculebra.com, $96 s, $115 d) is a modest six-unit property in the residential part of Dewey, within walking distance of the airport. One of the few properties that doesn't boast a view of the water, it makes up for its location with the "we aim to please" attitude of its owners, former Peace Corps volunteers Mark and Terrie Hayward. The small, tidy rooms are appointed with modern furnishings, air-conditioning, and mini-refrigerators. Common areas include two kitchens, a computer with Internet access, and a TV with a DVD/VCR player (but no cable or satellite access). Beach chairs, umbrellas, boogie boards, and coolers are provided free of charge for a small deposit. The shady backyard has a deck and gas grill. Co-owner Mark Hayward also operates an informational website on Culebra at http://culebrablog.com.

$100-150

Despite its weathered exterior, **Casita Linda** (by canal bridge in Dewey, 787/435-0430 or 787/742-0360, casitalindabeach@cs.com, $119–225) offers three simple, cheerful, modern one- and two-bedroom apartments on the canal. Amenities include kitchens or kitchenettes, air-conditioning in the bedrooms, and porches, patios, or terraces. Some units sleep up to six people.

《 Villa Boheme (368 Calle Fulladoza, 787/742-3508, http://villaboheme.com, $95–125 s, $130–135 d, plus 9 percent tax) has a lovely Spanish hacienda–style exterior and landscaped grounds right on Fulladoza Bay. Inside are 11 cheerfully appointed rooms with air-conditioning and hot water. Some rooms have private balconies and small kitchens; others share a communal kitchen in the patio area, which also contains satellite TV. A large terrace spans the length of the rambling property and overlooks the bay. Guests may use the dock, equipped with water and electricity, for $2 per foot per night. Moorings are also available for rent.

In town on Ensenada Honda is **Casa Ensenada** (142 Calle Escudero, 787/742-3559 or 866/210-00709, www.casaensenada.com, $125–175 for two, plus 9 percent tax). Despite its small size and modest aesthetics, this three-room guesthouse has everything you could need. Rooms are outfitted with air-conditioning, satellite TV, VCRs, hot showers, and kitchenettes, and there are a telephone, high-speed Internet, fax, and copier on-site. For trips to the beach, towels, chairs, coolers, umbrellas, and ice are available.

Nearby is **《 Vista Bella Apartments** (on Ensenada Honda, 787/644-6300 or 787/742-0549, visabellaculebra@yahoo.com, www.culebra-island.com, $120 studio, $163 one-bedroom that sleeps four, $218 two-bedroom that sleeps six). Four new, modern, and spacious apartments come with kitchens, air-conditioning, large covered balconies, and a spectacular view of Ensenada Honda.

$150-250

There are two hotels right on Playa Flamenco, which is the main reason to recommend either one. Just be sure to bring your insect repellent—it gets buggy. **Culebra Beach Villas** (Playa Flamenco, 787/767-7575, 787/754-6236, or 877/767-7575, cbrental@prtc.net, www.culebrabeachrental.com, $125 studio, $175–185 one-bedroom, $225 two-bedroom, plus 9 percent tax) offers 33 individually owned cottages and rooms with air-conditioning and kitchens, some with TVs but no Internet or telephones. The rooms are fairly Spartan, but the cottages have decks and covered porches. The service is minimal, although linens and towels are provided. Request a newer unit in the back of the complex if available. Basic pub fare can be had at the open-air waterside Coconuts Beach Grill.

The other option is **Villa Flamenco Beach** (Playa Flamenco, 787/742-0023, Nov.–Aug., $140 efficiency, $120–135 studio, plus 9 percent tax). A party-hardy vibe emanates from the two-story pink-and-green concrete structure, which contains six units. There are four studio apartments with kitchenettes, air-conditioning, and hot water, which sleep two, and two efficiency apartments with full kitchens, hot water in the shower only, and no air-conditioning, which sleep four. A couple of rooms have beachfront balconies. The place is low-key and self-serve.

The most luxurious option in this price range is **《 Club Seabourne** (Carr. 252, Calle Fulladoza on Ensenada Honda, 787/742-3169 or 800/981-4435, fax 787/742-0210, www.clubseabourne.com, $189 pool cabana room, $219 one-bedroom villa, $329 two-bedroom, including tax), which qualifies as Culebra's first foray into the world of modern boutique hotels. The quiet, remote, 14-unit hotel features a cluster of old-fashioned yellow-clapboard free-standing villas with pitched tin roofs that overlook Fulladoza Bay on Ensenada Honda. Rooms have air conditioning, but no TV or telephones. A lovely landscaped pool surrounded by umbrella tables overlooks the bay, as does the poolside bar, Sea Shells Bar and Grill. Fine dining can be had at White Sands Restaurant, serving Caribbean cuisine on a screened porch. Rates include continental breakfast, courtesy cocktails, one hour of free kayak rental, and transportation to and from the airport and ferry. Kayaks, snorkeling equipment, bikes, beach chairs, and umbrellas are available for rental, and picnic lunches are available by request.

Even more modern amenities can also be found at **Bahía Marina** (Punta Soldado Rd., km 2.4, 787/742-0535, 866/CULEBRA—866/285-3272, fax 787/742-0536, info@bahia-marina.net, www.bahiamarina.net, $151–179 one-bedroom apartment, $295 two-bedroom, plus tax). This hilltop row of 16 corporate-looking apartments with sleeper sofas in the sitting rooms comes with kitchenettes, air-conditioning, cable TV, and ocean-view balconies. There's also a large pool and an open-air bar and restaurant.

For total seclusion, you can't do much better than **Tamarindo Estates** (off Carr. 251 just south of Playa Flamenco, 787/742-3343, jose2@tamarindoestates.com, www.tamarindo estates.com, $190 plus $20 per pair of children, plus 9 percent tax). The property is on the wildlife refuge and features 12 simply furnished, hillside cottages on 60 acres overlooking the water and Cayo Luis Peña. Units are three or six to a building, and they look like they were furnished by a flea market, which gives them a quaint homespun vibe. Each one contains a TV, a VCR, air-conditioning in the bedroom, a fully equipped kitchen, a screened porch, and a rooftop veranda. Internet access is available in the common computer room. The rocky beach directly in front of the property offers great snorkeling, and a short hike north is a sandy beach for swimming. There's also a small pool on-site, but no restaurant or bar.

FOOD

Culebra is not particularly renowned for its restaurants, although there are a couple of establishments that are changing that. The concept of service is very different here from what stateside dwellers may be accustomed to. Things move at a slow, casual pace, so it's best to be patient and prepared to linger for awhile. Also,

note that operating hours can change unexpectedly, and some restaurants close up shop completely for weeks at a time.

Puerto Rican

Most of the restaurants in Culebra serve fairly modest fare. One popular spot is **Dinghy Dock** (Calle Fulladoza, south of the drawbridge, on Ensenada Honda, 787/742-0024, 787/742-0233, or 787/742-0518, info@dinghydock.com, www.dinghydock.com, daily 8 A.M.–2:30 P.M., 6:30–9 P.M., dinner $9–30). The name of this funky little eatery and bar is self-explanatory: Boats literally dock beside your table at this casual waterfront spot. Plastic patio chairs line a narrow dock under a hanging roof. The cuisine is by and large Puerto Rican, featuring Angus steaks and seafood, including tuna and lobster at night, waffles and French toast for breakfast. Check out the huge tarpon that swim below waiting for a handout. There is a full bar.

Seafood and Steak

The sensual delights of **◖ Juanita Bananas** (1 Barrio Melones, 787/742-3171 or 787/402-5852, www.juanitabananas.com, Fri.–Mon. 5:30–10 P.M., $22–32, cash only) start before you even enter this romantic yet casual fine-dining restaurant. The Eden-like grounds are filled with flowers, fruit trees, fresh herbs, and a vegetable garden, which provide many of the ingredients in chef Jennifer Daubon's sublime contemporary Caribbean cuisine. Specialties include *panko*-crusted snapper, citrus-marinated salmon, and conch fritters. Sundays feature sushi specials. Reservations suggested, and BYOB.

Another romantic fine-dining option is Club Seabourne resort's **White Sands Restaurant** (Calle Fulladoza on Ensenada Honda, 787/742-3169, fax 787/742-0210, www.clubseabourne .com, Wed.–Sun. 6–9:30 P.M., $18–22). A cozy screened porch overlooking Fulladoza Bay is the setting for a menu with an emphasis on seafood, including lobster, scallops, salmon, and halibut.

Dining doesn't get much more casual than

at ◖ **Barbara Rosa** (189 Calle Escudero, 787/397-1923, Tues.–Sun. 11:30 A.M.–9 P.M., $6–16, cash only) where you literally dine in the front yard of the cook's house. Diners peruse a handwritten menu and place their orders at the counter for excellent, inexpensive seafood dishes, including fish and chips, crab cakes, and *dorado*.

◖ **Mamacita's** (64 Calle Castelar, by the canal south of the drawbridge, 787/742-0322, restaurant daily 8 A.M.–3 P.M. and 6–9 P.M., bar Sun.–Thurs. 10 A.M.–10 P.M., Fri. 10 A.M.–11 P.M., $14–20, plus 15 percent gratuity) is a colorful open-air restaurant and bar serving excellent Caribbean-American–style dishes featuring *dorado, churrasco,* pork, and pasta, as well as a few pub-style appetizers. The dinner menu changes nightly and recently included a terrific dish of grilled *dorado* in cilantro lime aioli. Mamacita's doubles as a popular watering hole at night and rents rooms too.

Shipwreck Bar and Grill (at Bahía Marina, Calle Punta Soldado, km 2.4, 787/742-0535, www.bahiamarina.net, daily 4–10 P.M., $10–24) is a casual open-air eatery in the corporate environs of the Bahía Marina hotel, high up on a hill overlooking the water. The menu serves everything from burgers and conch fritters to whole snapper, *mofongo,* and New York strips.

Italian

◖ **El Eden & Neptune Bar** (on an unnamed gravel road across the canal from Mamacita's, Dewey, 787/742-0509, Thurs.–Sat. 9 A.M.–9 P.M., Sun. 9 A.M.–2 P.M., Mon. 9 A.M.–6 P.M., $17–24) is a quirky little place owned by Richard Cantwell and Luz Rivera, who have put a lot of love and care into this eclectic combination deli, fine dining restaurant, tiki bar, wine shop, and grocery. All breads and desserts are made on-site using minimal processed foods and as many local products as possible. Lunch features deli sandwiches and daily specials, and the dinner menu changes weekly, but the risottos are their specialty. Other options may include gnocchi in pesto, veal marsala, and *churrasco.* For dessert,

try the passion fruit or Kahlúa mousse. There's a great tiki bar with shell-encrusted mirrors and bamboo if you just want to drink.

Lunch and Light Fare

Pandeli Bakery (17 Calle Pedro Marquez at the corner of Calle Escudero, Carr. 250, 787/742-0296, Mon.–Sat. 5:30 A.M.–5 P.M., Sun. 6:30 A.M.–5 P.M., $2.25–5.95) is a cool, modern, cozy bakery serving breakfast, sandwiches, burgers, empanadas, and pastries. There's also a small selection of dry goods and wines.

Hot pizza and ice-cold beer are the reasons to visit **El Oasis** (Calle Pedro Marquez, Dewey, 787/742-3175, Thurs.–Mon. 6–10 P.M., $7–20, cash only). The menu includes a few pasta dishes and salads, and the bar is a popular gathering spot for the drinking crowd.

Visitors to Playa Flamenco can find sustenance at **Coconuts Beach Grill** (in front of Culebra Beach Villas, $3–6, cash only). Its hours are irregular, but usually on the weekends this casual open-air eatery serves a limited selection of sandwiches and cocktails.

INFORMATION AND SERVICES

The **Culebra Tourism Department** (787/742-3521 or 787/742-3116, ext. 441 or 442, Mon.–Fri. 8 A.M.–4:30 P.M.) is in the yellow concrete building on Calle William Font in Dewey. For the most up-to-date information on the island, visit www.culebra-island.com, www.islaculebra.com, and www.culebra.org.

Because many businesses accept only cash, it's important to know where the island's ATM is. **Banco Popular** (787/742-3572, Mon.–Fri. 8:30 A.M.–3:30 P.M.) is across from the ferry terminal on Calle Pedro Marquez. You'll find the **post office** (787/742-3862, Mon.–Fri. 8 A.M.–4:30 P.M.) at 26 Calle Pedro Marquez, and **laundry facilities** can be found at Mamacita's Guesthouse (64 Calle Castelar, 787/742-0090).

The **police department** (787/742-3501) is on Calle Fulladoza just past Dinghy Dock. For medical services, **Hospital de Culebra** (Calle

William Font, 787/742-3511 or 787/742-0001, ambulance 787/742-0208) operates a clinic Monday–Friday 7 A.M.–4:30 P.M., as well as 24-hour emergency service and the island's only pharmacy.

GETTING THERE
By Ferry
The **Puerto Rico Port Authority** (in Culebra 787/742-3161, 787/741-4761, 787/863-0705, or 800/981-2005) operates a daily ferry service between Culebra and Fajardo from the town of Dewey.

The **passenger ferry** is primarily a commuter operation, and it can often be crowded—especially on the weekends and holidays. Reservations are not accepted, but you can buy tickets in advance. Be aware that on weekends and holidays, the ferry can sell out, leaving disappointed travelers behind. The trip typically takes about 1.5 hours to travel between Fajardo and Culebra. The fare is $4.50 round-trip per person, with an additional charge of $2 for beach or camping equipment. Note that ferry schedules can change, but the schedule was as follows:

- **Fajardo to Culebra:** Daily 9 A.M., 3 P.M., 7 P.M.

- **Culebra to Fajardo:** Daily 6:30 A.M., 1 P.M., 5 P.M.

There is also a weekday **cargo/car ferry** between Culebra and Fajardo, for which reservations are required. But be aware that most car-rental agencies in Puerto Rico do not permit their automobiles to leave the main island. The best option is to leave your car in Fajardo and rent another car on Culebra. The trip usually takes about 2.5 hours, and the cost is $15 for small vehicles and $19 for large vehicles. The schedule is as follows:

- **Fajardo to Culebra:** Monday, Tuesday, and Thursday 4 A.M. and 4:30 P.M.; Wednesday and Friday 4 A.M., 9:30 A.M., 4:30 P.M.

- **Culebra to Fajardo:** Monday, Tuesday, and Thursday 7 A.M. and 6 P.M.; Wednesday and Friday 7 A.M., 1 P.M., 6 P.M.

By Air
There are several small airlines that fly to Culebra from the main island, and the flights are fairly inexpensive and speedy. The only catch is that it's not for the faint of heart. Landing on the tiny island requires a steep descent over a mountaintop that takes your breath away.

In San Juan, flights can be arranged from Isla Grande Airport for about $190 round-trip, or from the new Jose Aponte de la Torre Airport in Ceiba, on the east coast of the big island, for about $66 round-trip. Service providers include **Isla Nena Air Service** (787/863-4447, 787/863-4449, or 877/812-5144, islanenapr@centennialpr .net, www.islanena.8m.com); **Vieques Air Link** (787/741-8331 or 888/901-9247, va-lair@coqui.net, www.viequesairlink.com); **M&N Aviation** (787/791-7008, www.mn aviation.com); and **Air Flamenco** (787/724-1818, airflamenco@hotmail.com, www.air flamenco.net).

Isla Nena Air Service also provides service between Culebra and Vieques for about $70.

GETTING AROUND
Between the *publicos* and water taxis, it is possible to get around Culebra without renting a vehicle, but it is not necessarily advisable. If you want to explore the island, jeeps and scooters are available for rent. Just be sure to book early—two to three months in advance is recommended.

There are few roads on Culebra, but they can be narrow, steep, and riddled with potholes. Parking and seatbelt laws are strictly enforced, and for some odd reason, driving bare-chested can get you a ticket.

Note that many places don't have traditional addresses with street names and numbers. If you ask people for an address, they're more likely to describe its physical location in relation to something else, as in "beside El Batey," or "across from the ferry." Also, nobody who lives in Culebra calls Dewey by its name. It's usually just referred to as "Pueblo" or "Town."

VIEQUES AND CULEBRA

Water Taxi

There are several water-taxi operators who will take you to Culebrita for about $40 and to Cayo Luis Peña for $25. They include **Culebra Dive Shop** (787/742-0566); **Willy's Water Taxi** (787/742-3537); and **Culebra Water Toys** (787/742-1122, cell 787/246-1718 or 787/406-2224), which also provides service to Carlos Rosario, Vieques, and St. Thomas.

Cayo Norte Water Taxi (787/742-0169 or 646/924-6362) provides service to Cayo Norte.

Publico

If you arrive at the airport and there aren't any *publicos* there, strike out walking a short distance to Willys. From the airport turn left and go one block past the stop sign; he's on the right. Otherwise, you can give one a call to take you from point A to point B, although night service can be spotty. Operators include **Willys** (787/742-3537), **Kiko** (787/514-0453), **Samuel** (787/649-9641), and **Seguramente** (787/590-1375). It costs $2 to go from the airport to "downtown" Dewey or from Dewey to Flamenco Bay.

Car Rentals

Several agencies provide jeep rentals for about $60 per day, although some travelers report success at negotiating a better rate. Bring a copy of your insurance policy to avoid steep insurance charges. The following operators provide delivery service at the airport, ferry, or hotel of choice: **Jerry's Jeeps** (across from the Culebra airport entrance, 787/742-0587 or 787/742-0526); **Carlos Jeep Rental** (787/742-3514 or 787/613-7049, cjrental@coqui.net); and **Dick and Cathie's Jeep Rental** (787/742-0062, cash only).

Another option is to rent a scooter from **Culebra Scooter Rental** (at the Culebra airport, 787/742-0195, www.culebrascooter rental.com, 8:30 A.M.–6 P.M., $40 per day).

BACKGROUND

The Land

GEOGRAPHY

Puerto Rico is a rectangular island, situated roughly in the middle of the **Antilles,** a chain of islands that stretches from Florida to Venezuela and forms the dividing line between the Atlantic Ocean and the Caribbean Sea. The Antilles are divided into two regions—Greater Antilles and Lesser Antilles. Puerto Rico is the smallest and easternmost island of the Greater Antilles, which include Cuba, Hispañola (Dominican Republic and Haiti), and Jamaica.

In addition to the main island, which is 111 miles east to west and 36 miles north to south, Puerto Rico comprises several tiny islands or *cayos,* including Mona and Desecheo off the west coast and Vieques, Culebra, Palomino, Icacos, and others off the east coast. The northern and eastern shores of Puerto Rico are on the Atlantic Ocean, and the southern shores are on the Caribbean Sea. To the west is Mona Passage, an important shipping lane that is 75 miles wide and 3,300 feet deep.

The island was believed to have been formed between 135 million and 185 million years ago when a massive shift of tectonic plates crumpled the earth's surface, pushing parts of it down into deep recesses below the ocean floor and pushing parts of it up to create the island. This tectonic activity resulted in volcanic eruptions, both underwater and above it.

© SUZANNE VAN ATTEN

Two significant things happened as a result of all this geologic activity. The **Puerto Rico Trench** was formed off the island's north coast. At its greatest depth, it is 28,000 feet below sea level, making it the deepest point known in the Atlantic Ocean. Secondly, it formed the mountainous core of Puerto Rico that spans nearly the entire island from east to west and reaches heights of 4,390 feet above sea level. Volcanic activity is believed to have been dormant in Puerto Rico for 45 million years, but the earth is always changing. The Caribbean plate is shifting eastward against the westward-shifting North American plate, which has resulted in occasional earth tremors through the years. Although this activity is suspected to have led to the volcanic activity in Montserrat in recent years, its danger to Puerto Rico is its potential to cause earthquake—not volcanic—activity.

Puerto Rico has three main geographic regions: mountains, coastal lowlands, and karst country. More than 60 percent of the island is mountainous. The island's mountains, which dominate the island's interior, comprise four ranges: **Cordillera Central, Sierra de Cayey, Sierra de Luquillo,** and **Sierra Bermeja.** The largest and highest range is Cordillera Central, which spans from Caguas in the east to Lares in the west. Its highest point is Cerro Punta (4,390 feet above sea level), in the Toro Negro Forest near Jayuya. Sierra de Luquillo is in the northeast and contains the Caribbean National Forest, home to El Yunque rain forest. These two mountain ranges feature dramatic pointed peaks and lush tropical vegetation. Sierra de Cayey, in the southeast between Cayey and Humacao, and Sierra de Bermeja, in the southwest between Guánica and the island's southwestern tip, are smaller in area and height, drier, and less forested.

The **coastal lowlands** span more than 300 miles around the rim of the island, 8–12 miles inland in the north and 2–8 miles inland in the south. Formed through time by erosion of the mountains, the coastal lowlands are important agricultural areas that benefit from the rich soil and water that wash down from the mountains. Much of the area is defined by sandy or rocky beaches and mangrove swamps, although the mangrove forests are being whittled away by development.

The island's third region is unique. The **karst region** spans the island's northern interior, from San Juan in the east to Aguadilla in the west, and the southern interior, from Ponce in the east to San Germán in the west. It can also be found in isolated pockets throughout the island, as well as on Mona Island off the west coast. The karst region is distinguished by a fascinating landscape of sinkholes, cliffs, caves, and conical, haystack-shaped hills called *mogotes*. More than 27 percent of Puerto Rico's surface is made up of limestone, and its erosion from rain helped create the beguiling patchwork of hills and holes. One of limestone's unique properties is that it reprecipitates and forms case rock that is impervious to chemical and climatic change, which has basically frozen the odd formations in time. In addition, water produced by reprecipitation bubbles up to hydrate the earth's surface, and drips down, creating subterranean rivers and caves.

As a result of its karst region, Puerto Rico has some of the most significant cave systems in the Western Hemisphere and the third-largest underground river, Río Camuy. The public can tour part of the massive cave system at **Las Cavernas del Río Camuy** in the municipality of Camuy.

In addition to Río Camuy, Puerto Rico's other major rivers include the north-running **Grande de Arecibo,** the island's longest; **La Plata, Cibuco, Loíza,** and **Bayamón,** which run north; and **Grande de Añasco,** which runs west. There are no natural lakes in Puerto Rico, although 15 reservoirs have been created by damming rivers. But there are several natural lagoons, including **Condado** and **San José** in San Juan, **Piñones** and **Torrecillas** in Loíza, **Joyuda** in Cabo Rojo, **Tortuguero** in Vega Baja, and **Grande** in Fajardo.

CLIMATE

Puerto Rico's climate is classified as **tropical marine,** which means it's typically sunny, hot, and humid year-round. The temperature fluctuates between 76°F and 88°F in the coastal plains and 73–78°F in the mountains. Humidity is a steady 80 percent, but a northeasterly wind keeps things pretty breezy, particularly on the northeast side of the island.

Nobody wants rain during a tropical vacation, but precipitation is very much a part of life in Puerto Rico. Although there are periods when the deluge is so heavy that you might think it's time to build an ark, rains are generally brief and occur in the afternoons. The average annual rainfall is 62 inches. Although it rains throughout the year, the heaviest precipitation is from May to October, which is also hurricane season. The driest period is January to April, which coincides with the tourism industry's high season. Keep in mind that the north coast receives twice as much rain as the south coast, so if the outlook is rainy in San Juan, head south.

Hurricanes are a very real threat to Puerto Rico. It is estimated that the island will be hit by a major hurricane every 30 years. The most devastating storm in recent history was Hurricane Hugo in September 1989, which rendered billions of dollars of damage and left some areas without electricity and water for several weeks. Hurricane Georges in September 1998 was no picnic either.

For the latest information on weather conditions in Puerto Rico, visit the National Weather Service at www.srh.noaa.gov/sju.

ENVIRONMENTAL ISSUES

Because Puerto Rico is part of the United States, local industry is subject to the same federal environmental regulations and restrictions as in the United States.

Puerto Rico's greatest environmental threats concern its vanishing natural habitat and the resulting impact on soil erosion and wildlife. Reforestation efforts are under way in many of the island's national parks and forest reserves, and organized efforts are under way to protect and rebuild endangered wildlife populations, especially the Puerto Rican parrot, the manatee, and the leatherback sea turtle.

Many of the island's environmental protection efforts are overseen by the Conservation Trust of Puerto Rico, whose headquarters is based in **Casa de Ramón Power y Girault** (155 Calle Tetuán, San Juan, 787/722-5834, www .fideicomiso.org, Tues.–Sat. 10 A.M.–4 P.M.), where visitors can peruse exhibits and pick up printed information on its projects.

In Vieques, the biggest environmental concern surrounds the ongoing cleanup of the grounds once occupied by the U.S. Navy, which stored munitions and performed bombing practice on the island. After years of protest by local residents, the Navy withdrew in 2003, but much of its land (18,000 acres) is still off-limits to the public while efforts to clear it of contaminants and the live artillery that still litters the ocean floor are under way. The cancer rate in Vieques is 27 percent higher than that of the main island, and many blame it on the presence of unexploded artillery leaking chemicals into the water and the release of chemicals into the air when the artillery is detonated, which is the Navy's way of disposing of it.

Flora

For such a small island, Puerto Rico has a wide diversity of biological environments.

For instance, Bosque Estatal de Guánica in the southwestern corner of the island is classified as a subtropical dry forest, where cacti, grasses, and evergreen trees hosting Spanish moss and mistletoe compete for water and nutrients from sun-bleached rocky soil. On the opposite end of the island is the Caribbean National Forest, which contains subtropical moist forest, also called rain forest. Palm trees, a multitude of ferns, *tabonuco* trees, orchids, and bromeliads grow here. And along the coast are mangrove forests, where the mighty land-building trees flourish in the salty water and provide vital habitat to marine life.

The first extensive study of Puerto Rico's diverse flora was undertaken in the early 1900s, thanks to American botanists Nathaniel and Elizabeth Britton, founders of the New York Botanical Gardens. Their annual trips to the Caribbean, beginning in 1906, led to the publication in 1933 of *The Scientific Survey of Puerto Rico and the Virgin Islands,* the first systematic natural history survey in the Caribbean region.

TREES

The official tree of Puerto Rico is the **ceiba,** also called silk-cotton tree or kapok tree. Often the tallest tree in the forest, the ceiba attains heights of 150 feet and has a ridged columnar trunk and a massive umbrella-shaped canopy. Its far-reaching limbs often host aerial plants, such as moss and bromeliads.

The ceiba was important to the island's indigenous Taínos because its thick trunks were perfect for carving into canoes. Its flowers are small and inconspicuous, but it produces a large ellipsoid fruit that, when split open, reveals an abundance of fluffy fibers, called kapok.

Arguably Puerto Rico's most beautiful tree, though, is the **flamboyan,** also known as royal poinciana. If you visit the island between June and August, you're sure to notice the abundance of reddish-orange blooms that cover the flamboyan's umbrella-shaped canopy. It is a gorgeous sight to behold. The tree is also distinguished by fernlike leaves and the long brown seedpods it produces.

Probably the most plentiful and easily identifiable tree in Puerto Rico is the mighty palm, which grows throughout the island. There are actually many varieties of palm in Puerto Rico. Among them are the **coconut palm,** which has a smooth gray bark marked by ring scars from fallen fronds and which bears the beloved coconut in abundance; the **royal palm,** distinguished by its tall, thin straight trunk that grows to 25 feet and sports a crown of leaves that are silver on the underside; the **Puerto Rican hat palm,** featuring a fat tubular trunk and fan-shaped frond; and the **sierra palm,** which has a thin straight trunk and thick thatch.

El Yunque Caribbean National Forest is home to more than 1,000 plant species, 23 of which are endemic to the area.

Puerto Rico's **mangrove** forests are found in swampy coastal areas throughout the island. Much of the island's coast was once covered in mangrove, but a lot of it has been destroyed to make way for commercial development. Fortunately efforts are under way to preserve many of the island's last remaining mangrove forests in parks in Piñones, Boquerón, Fajardo, Vieques, and elsewhere.

The mangrove tree is a unique plant. For one thing, it is able to grow along the ocean's shallow edges, absorbing, processing, and secreting salt from the water. But what's truly amazing about the mangrove, and what makes it so vital to marine life, is its adaptive root system. Because the trees grow in thick, oxygen-deprived mud, they sprout aerial roots to absorb oxygen from the air and nutrients from the surface of the water. The aerial roots take many different forms, including thousands of tiny pencil-shaped roots sticking up from shallow waters; big knee-shaped roots that emerge from the ground and loop back down; and roots that sprout from branches.

Between its complex tangle of roots and its low-lying compact canopy, the mangrove forest plays several important roles in the environment, primarily by providing habitat to local wildlife. Its branches are a haven to nesting birds, and its underwater root systems protect crabs, snails, crustaceans, and small fish from predators. Mangrove forests also help protect the coastal plains from violent storms, reduce erosion, and filter the ocean waters. And finally, mangrove forests actually build land by providing nooks and crannies within their root systems that capture soil, aerate it, and create conditions where other plants can grow.

Puerto Rico is rich in plants that have edible, medicinal, or other practical uses. For the Taíno Indians, the island's forests served as their pharmacy and grocery store.

The **mamey** is prized not only for the delicious fruit it bears but also for its fragrant flowers and lovely appearance. Resembling a Southern magnolia, the mamey grows to 60 feet high and features a short stout trunk and dense foliage with long, glossy, leathery dark-green leaves. The flowers feature 4–6 white petals and have a lovely fragrance. The fruit is brown and leathery on the outside, and inside can be sweet and tender or crisp and sour, depending on the variety. Another popular tree that bears edible fruit is the **mango.** The ubiquitous leafy tree grows in forests, backyards, and alongside roadways, and in the summer each tree bears what appears to be hundreds of mangoes. When ripe, the fruit is covered with a thick yellow and brown skin, but inside is a soft succulent fruit similar to a peach. You'll often see locals on the side of the road selling bags of them out of their trucks.

The curious **calabash tree** served an entirely different purpose in Taíno culture. Its greatest value was in the large, round, gourd-like fruit that sprouts directly from the tree's trunk. After the fruit was cleansed of its pulp, the remaining shell was dried and used as a bowl for food preparation and storage. Sometimes the bowls were decorated with elaborate carvings etched into the sides before the shell dried. Carved calabash bowls are popular souvenir items today.

FLOWERING PLANTS

Like any good tropical island, Puerto Rico has a bounty of flowering plants. Probably the one most commonly encountered, particularly in gardens but also in the wild, is the beautiful sun-loving **bougainvillea.** The plant produces great clusters of blossoms with thin papery petals, which come in an assortment of colors, including pink, magenta, purple, red, orange, white, and yellow. The plant is actually a vine, but in Puerto Rico bougainvillea often grows freestanding, with its long thin branches hanging heavy with blooms.

The mountains are home to many varieties of flowering plants, including one that home gardeners in the States may recognize—the shade-loving **impatiens,** a lovely ground-covering plant with white blooms. They can be seen blooming in great drifts along mountain banks. Other mountain flowering plants include more than 50 varieties of **orchids,** but don't look for corsage-sized blossoms—Puerto Rico's orchids tend to be small, some the size of a fingernail. Where you find orchids, you can usually find **bromeliads,** which, like the orchid, grows on other plants that serve as hosts. Bromeliads are typically distinguished by overlapping spirals of leaves with a tubular punch of color in the center, but the family includes some atypical variations, including **Spanish moss** and the **pineapple,** both of which grow on the island.

Other plants found commonly in Puerto Rico are a large variety of ferns, large and small, in the mountains. Along the beaches, the sea grape, a low-lying compact shrub that grows in clusters, creates a cave-like reprieve from the sun. Several varieties of cactus grow in the subtropical dry forest along the southwestern coast and on the islands of Vieques and Culebra.

Fauna

MAMMALS

The only mammal native to Puerto Rico is the bat. Eleven species live on the island, including the **red fig-eating bat,** which roosts in the forest canopy in the Caribbean National Forest, and the **Greater Antillean long-tongued bat,** which lives in caves and feeds on fruits and nectar from flowers.

Thanks to colonial trade ships, **rats** were introduced to the island in the late 1400s. They thrived here in great abundance, causing havoc on sugar plantations. Then someone had the brilliant idea of introducing **mongooses** from India to keep the rat population down. Unfortunately, mongooses are active during the day, and rats are active at night, so the effort failed, and now there's a mongoose problem. They have no natural predators on the island, and they live up to 40 years. Mongooses are to be avoided at all costs as they are major carriers of rabies.

Paso Fino horses are a common form of transportation in rural areas of Puerto Rico, especially in Vieques and Culebra, where they roam the island freely.

Some parts of Puerto Rico also have a **feral dog** problem. It's not uncommon to see roving packs of mangy, skeletal canines rummaging for scraps in small towns and rural areas.

BIRDS AND INSECTS

Puerto Rico is a bird-watcher's paradise, but the one endemic bird you probably won't see is the **Puerto Rican parrot.** Although once

prolific throughout the island, the endangered bird's population is a mere 35 or so that live in the wild today because of the loss of habitat to development. They are found in the Caribbean National Forest.

In 1987 the U.S. Fish and Wildlife Service initiated a program to raise Puerto Rican parrots in captivity and release them into the Caribbean National Forest in hopes of building up the population. Unfortunately, success has been stymied by hurricanes and predators, primarily the red-tailed hawk. But the efforts continue, and today there are about 150 living in captivity in aviaries in Luquillo and Bosque Estatal Río Abajo.

It's highly unlikely a visitor to El Yunque will see a Puerto Rican parrot, but just in case, keep your eyes peeled for a foot-long, bright green Amazon parrot with blue wingtips, white eye rings, and a red band above its beak. When in flight, it emits a repetitive call that sounds like a bugle.

Other species of birds found in more plentiful numbers in Puerto Rico include sharp-skinned hawks, broad-wing hawks, bananaquits, Puerto Rican todies, red-legged thrushes, stripe-headed tanagers, brown pelicans, lizard cuckoos, elfin woods warblers, hummingbirds, and nightjars, which nest silently on the ground by day and fly in search of prey at night.

At dusk, many of Puerto Rico's wilderness beaches come under attack by **sand fleas,** also called no-see-ums: vicious, minuscule buggers

The Mona iguana, found only on Mona Island off Puerto Rico's west coast, grows up to four feet in length and lives up to 50 years of age.

that have a fierce bite. If they attack, your best defense is to pack up as quickly as possible and call it a day.

REPTILES AND AMPHIBIANS

Of all the creatures that call Puerto Rico home, none are as beloved as the tiny **coqui** tree frog, the island's national symbol. A mere 1–1.5 inches long fully grown, the *coqui* is difficult to spot, but you can definitely hear the male's distinctive "co-QUI" call at dusk or after a rain. Despite the ubiquity of their cheerful chirp, of the 16 varieties that live in Puerto Rico, only two make the eponymous sound, which serves to attract a mate and repel reproductive competitors.

Unlike many frogs, the *coqui* does not have webbed appendages and does not require water to live or reproduce. In fact, *coquis* are never tadpoles. The female *coqui* lays its eggs on leaves, and tiny little froglets emerge fully formed from the eggs. Although they're born with tails, they lose them posthaste.

It is considered good luck to spot a *coqui*,

and there are many other legends surrounding them. One is that a little boy was transformed into a frog because he misbehaved, and now he comes out and sings at sunset. Another involves a bird that was stripped of its wings but was later turned into a frog so it could climb back into the trees where it once lived.

The one creature visitors to Puerto Rico are sure to spot is a **lizard.** The island is literally crawling with them, varying in species from the ubiquitous four-inch **emerald *anoli,*** which is sure to slip inside the house if a window is left open, to the **Puerto Rican giant green lizard,** an imposing reptile that can grow up to 16 inches long and lives mostly in the limestone hills.

But Puerto Rico's mack-daddy lizard is the prehistoric-looking **Mona iguana,** which grows up to four feet long. Mona Island off the west coast of Puerto Rico is the only natural habitat for the Mona iguana, but there is a tiny mangrove *cayo* in the bay at La Parguera where a small population is kept for research purposes and which can be seen by boat. Although an herbivore, the Mona iguana has an intimidating appearance because of its horned snout and the jagged bony crest down its back. The Mona iguana lives up to 50 years.

Snakes are few in Puerto Rico, but they do exist. Fortunately, they are all nonpoisonous. The **Puerto Rican boa** is an endangered species. The longest snake on the island, it grows up to six feet and is quite elusive.

MARINE LIFE

Unlike many islands in the Caribbean, Puerto Rico's underwater coral reef systems are still mostly healthy and intact. And where there's a healthy reef system, there is an abundance of marine life.

Among Puerto Rico's endangered marine creatures is the **manatee**, a 1,000-pound submarine-shaped mammal with a tail, two small flippers, and a wrinkled, whiskered face. The slow-moving herbivore lives in shallow, still waters, such as lagoons and bays. Their only natural predator is man, and because they often float near the water's surface, they are particularly susceptible to collision with watercraft. The U.S. Fish and Wildlife Service operates a recovery program for the manatee, and if you spot one, you're likely to see its tracking device, which looks like a walkie-talkie attached to its back.

Also endangered are the **hawksbill** and **leatherback sea turtles,** the latter of which is the world's largest species of sea turtle, weighing between 500 and 1,600 pounds. There are several important turtle nesting sites in Puerto Rico, along the north shore and on the islands of Mona and Culebra. The turtles nest between April and June by climbing up on the beach at night and burying their eggs in the sand before returning to the sea. Unfortunately, turtle nests are vulnerable to animals and poachers, who prize the eggs. Several government agencies are involved in protected the nesting sites. If visitors want to help out, they should contact the Puerto Rico Department of Natural and Environmental Resources (787/556-6234 or 877/77-CORAL—877/772-6725, fax 530/618-4605, info@coralations.org, www.coralations .org/turtles), which accepts volunteers to catalog the turtles during nesting season.

Besides its endangered species, Puerto Rico has countless other varieties of thriving marine life from **rays** and **nurse sharks** to **puffer fish** and **parrot fish.** The reefs themselves are sights to behold, with their **brain coral, sea fans,** and **yellow cup coral,** which blooms at night.

And although typically associated with colder waters, migrating **humpback whales** can be spotted along the island's west coast between January and March.

History

INDIGENOUS CULTURES

The earliest known inhabitants of Puerto Rico were the **Archaic** or **Pre-Ceramic** cultures, which are believed to have lived on the island from 3000 B.C. until A.D. 150. They were loosely organized in small nomadic groups of about 30 who occupied encampments for brief periods. What little is known about this culture has been deduced from a couple of burial sites and a few excavated stone and shell artifacts, such as flint chips, scrapers, and pestles. They are believed to have been primarily hunters and gatherers who did not cultivate crops

or make pottery. There are two main theories about the origins of the Archaic culture. It is believed they either originated in South America and migrated to Puerto Rico by way of the Lesser Antilles or they originated in the Yucatán Peninsula and crossed from Cuba and Hispañola.

The Archaic were followed by the **Arawak,** who migrated from Venezuela. The earliest Arawak were classified as **Igneri** or **Saladoid,** and they lived in Puerto Rico from 300 B.C. to A.D. 600. The Igneri were superb potters, whose ceramics were distinguished by white paint on a red background. They also produced small *cemis,* three-side amulets believed to have religious significance. Their society was organized in villages of extended-family houses situated around a central plaza, under which the dead were buried. In addition to hunting and gathering, the Igneri cultivated crops.

Around A.D. 600, the Igneri culture evolved into two separate cultures that are grouped together under the name **Pre-Taíno.** The **Elenoid** lived on the eastern two-thirds of the island while the **Ostionoid** lived on the western third of the island. The Elenoid culture is distinguished by a coarse, thick style of unpainted ceramics. The Ostionoid produced pottery similar to the Igneri's, except that it was painted in shades of pink and lilac. Little is known about Pre-Taíno culture. Both cultures continued to hunt, fish, gather, and farm. Although they had centralized villages, there is evidence that many Pre-Taíno split into nuclear families and lived in houses separate from one another scattered throughout the island. It is during this time that many Taíno customs began to appear. The Pre-Taíno were the first to construct *bateyes,* rectangular ball courts, and central plazas, which were square or round. They produced larger *cemi* amulets than found in Igneri culture, and they began carving petroglyphs—typically human or animal faces—into stones.

The most significant Igneri and Pre-Taíno archaeological site in Puerto Rico is **Centro Ceremonial Indígena de Tibes** near Ponce. In addition to seven *bateyes* and two plazas, a cemetery containing the remains of 187 people was discovered here.

Around A.D. 1200, the Pre-Taíno evolved into the **Taíno** culture. Of all the indigenous groups that lived in Puerto Rico, the most is known about the Taíno perhaps because they were the ones to greet Christopher Columbus when he arrived in 1493, and several Spanish settlers wrote historical accounts about their culture.

The Taíno society was highly organized and hierarchal. They lived in self-governing villages called *yucayeques.* Commoners lived in conical wood-and-thatch huts called *bohios* while the chief, or cacique, lived in a rectangular hut called a *caney.* They were a highly spiritual culture and would gather on sacred grounds, distinguished by plazas and *bateyes* (ball courts), to perform their religious ceremonies and compete in ball games.

The Taínos produced highly complex ceramics, as well as wood and stone implements, such as axes, daggers, *dujos* (ceremonial stools), and stone collars, the purpose of which is unknown. In addition to hunting, fishing, and gathering, they were highly developed farmers. The Taínos were also highly spiritual, and they created many *cemi* amulets, which were much more complex than those of past cultures, and stone carvings.

The Taínos were a peaceful culture, a fact that was severely challenged by the arrival of the Spanish conquistadors as well as the marauding Caribs, a highly aggressive, warrior culture that originated in Venezuela and roamed the Antilles plundering goods and capturing women. A hotly debated topic in scholarly discussions about the Caribs is whether or not they practiced cannibalism. The Taíno culture vanished around 1500 after the arrival of the Spanish conquistadors. Those not killed and enslaved by the Spanish died from a smallpox epidemic.

The public can visit a significant Taíno archaeological site called **Centro Ceremonial Indígena de Caguana** in Utuado, in the Cordillera Central mountain region.

COLONIZATION

Christopher Columbus was on his second voyage in his quest to "discover" the New World when he arrived in Puerto Rico in 1493. There is debate as to where exactly Columbus, called Colón by the Spanish, first disembarked on the island. That momentous occasion is claimed by Aguada, on the northwest coast of the Atlantic, and Guánica, on the southwest coast of the Caribbean. Either way, he didn't stick around long enough to do much more than christen the island San Juan Bautista, after John the Baptist.

It wasn't until 1508 that Juan Ponce de León, who had been on the voyage with Columbus, returned to the island to establish a settlement. The Taíno provided no resistance to his arrival. In fact, Taíno cacique Agueybana allowed Ponce de León to pick any spot he wanted for a settlement so long as the Spanish would help defend the Taíno against the Caribs. His choice of Caparra, a marshy mosquito-ridden spot just west of what is now San Juan, was a poor one.

Around 1521 the settlement was relocated to what is now Old San Juan, and in 1523 Casa Blanca was built to house Ponce de León and his family, although by that time the explorer had left for Florida, where he met his demise. Originally the new settlement was called Puerto Rico for its "rich port." It's not clear why—possibly a cartographer's mistake—but soon after it was founded, the name of the settlement was switched with the name of the island.

San Juan quickly became a vital port to the Spanish Empire. An important stopover for ships transporting goods from the New World to Europe, it soon became a target for foreign powers. To protect its interests, Spain began a centuries-long effort to construct a formidable series of fortresses to defend the harbor and the city.

Construction of the island's first Spanish fort, La Fortaleza, began in 1533. The small structure, which to this day serves as home to the island's governor, was built to store gold and protect it from Carib attacks. The port quickly grew in importance, and Spain's enemies—England, Holland, and France—began to threaten it with attacks. More elaborate defense systems were needed. To protect the city's all-important harbor, construction of El Morro castle began in 1539, forming the nucleus of the city's fortifications. Through the years it was expanded to four levels and five acres before completion in 1787.

To protect the city from attack by land, San Cristóbal castle was begun in 1634. By the time it was completed in 1783, it was the city's largest fort, spanning 27 acres. That same year began the 200-year construction of La Muralla,

the massive stone wall that once encircled the city and much of which still stands. It contained five gates which were closed at night and guarded at all times.

The English were the first to significantly damage the city. In 1595, Sir Francis Drake led 26 vessels in an attack that partially burned the city but was successfully repelled. The next English attack proved more fruitful. Led by George Clifford, the earl of Cumberland, troops landed in Santurce in 1598 and occupied the city for several months before illness and exhaustion forced them to abandon their stronghold.

The most devastating attack to date came when 17 Dutch ships led by Boudoin Hendricks attacked in 1625. And in 1797 the British, led by Sir Ralph Abercrombie, attacked again.

Meanwhile, other settlements were being established throughout the island. The area now known as Aguada was established as Villa de Sotomayor in 1508, but it was destroyed by Indians in 1511. In 1516, Franciscan friars built a monastery nearby, which was destroyed by Indians 12 years later. A new monastery was built in 1590, followed by a chapel in 1639. Also an important stopover for ships on their way to Spain from South America, it suffered attacks by the English, French, and Dutch. San Germán was founded in 1573 and was attacked by pirates, the English, and the Dutch. Arecibo followed in 1606.

Attack by foreign powers waned in the 1800s, and the island's sugarcane and coffee plantations flourished because of the slave labor that was brought in from Africa. But by the 1860s, a new challenge to Spanish rule arose in the form of an independence rebellion that was brewing among the island's rural class.

On September 23, 1868, about 500 Puerto Ricans organized a revolt, proclaiming the mountain town of Lares free of Spanish rule. Local stores and offices owned by Spanish merchants were looted, slaves were declared free, and city hall was stormed. The revolt was quickly squelched the next day, when rebel forces attempted to take over a neighboring town. The revolutionaries, including leaders

Manuel Rojas and Juan Rius Rivera, were taken prisoner, found guilty of treason and sedition, and sentenced to death. But to ease the political tension that was brewing on the island at that time, the revolutionaries were eventually released. Although the revolt, referred to as **Grito de Lares,** was unsuccessful, it did result in Spain's giving the island more autonomy.

Colonial reforms were made, national political parties were established, and slavery was abolished. But at the same time, restrictions were imposed on human rights, such as freedom of the press and the right to gather. Meanwhile, the Spanish Empire was beginning to crumble. It eventually lost all its Caribbean colonies except Cuba and Puerto Rico, and increased tariffs and taxes were imposed on imports and exports to help fund Spain's efforts to regain control of the nearby Dominican Republic. Living conditions in Puerto Rico deteriorated as the economy declined. Illiteracy was high; malnutrition and poverty were rampant. Violent clashes broke out between desperate residents and Spanish merchants, who monopolized trade on the island.

SPANISH-AMERICAN WAR

As the 19th century drew to a close, tensions had grown between Spain's declining empire and the rising world power of the United States, which had set its sights on the Caribbean islands to protect its growing sea trade. Under pressure from the United States, Spain granted Puerto Rico constitutional autonomy and the island was preparing to hold its first self-governing elections when the Spanish-American War was declared in April 1898.

The war was fought mostly in the waters around Cuba and the Philippines, but in May San Juan was pounded with artillery for three hours from warships led by U.S. Admiral William T. Sampson. The attack was a misguided effort to flush out a Spanish squadron commander who was not in San Juan at the time. Both of San Juan's major forts sustained damage. The top of El Morro's lighthouse was destroyed, and several residences and government buildings were damaged.

In July, 18,000 U.S. troops were sent to secure Puerto Rico. Landing in Guánica, ground troops began working their way northwest to San Juan, but before they could arrive, Spain agreed to relinquish sovereignty over the West Indies. With the signing of the Treaty of Paris in December 1898, Puerto Rico was ceded to the United States.

U.S. RULE AND THE FIGHT FOR INDEPENDENCE

For two years after the Spanish-American War, the United States operated a military government in Puerto Rico until 1900, when the first civilian government was established. The governor, his cabinet, and the senate-like Higher House of Delegates was appointed by the U.S. president. A 35-member Local House of Delegates and a resident commissioner, who represented Puerto Rico in the U.S. House of Representatives but had no vote, were elected by popular vote. In 1917, Puerto Ricans were granted U.S. citizenship by President Woodrow Wilson.

Living conditions in Puerto Rico advanced very little in the first 30 years under U.S. rule. A couple of hurricanes between 1928 and 1932 left the economy—dependent solely on agriculture—in ruins. Homelessness and poverty were rife. The unhappy state of affairs fueled the organization of another independence movement led by the Harvard-educated nationalist leader Pedro Albizu Campos. The doctor chafed against U.S. rule and asserted it had no claims to the island because it had been given its independence from Spain before the Spanish-American War broke out.

A gifted orator, Campos traveled throughout Latin America garnering support for Puerto Rico's independence and was named president of the island's Nationalist Party, which had formed in 1922. In 1935, four Nationalists were killed by local police under the command of a Colonel E. Francis Riggs in an event referred to today as the Río Piedras Massacre. The next near, Riggs was killed in retaliation by two Nationalists, who were arrested and executed without a trial. Campos was arrested for his suspected role in the death. The first jury trial found him innocent, but a second trial found him guilty and he was sentenced to prison.

On Palm Sunday in 1937, a Nationalist Party demonstration was organized in Ponce, Campos's hometown, to protest the independence leader's incarceration. Just as the march was getting under way, police fired on the crowd, killing 19 people and injuring 200 in what went down in history as the Ponce Massacre. It was a huge blow to the independence movement, and with Campos imprisoned, it seemed as though the fight for freedom had been quelled. Instead, the incident merely drove the movement underground and possibly fueled its embrace of violent tactics.

To quell the brewing unrest, protect its interests, and benefit from the island's resources, the United States took several momentous steps beginning in the 1940s that had far-reaching effects on Puerto Rico's culture. During World War II, several large military bases were established on the island—Fort Buchanan Army Base in Guaynabo, Ramey Air Force Base in Aguadilla, Roosevelt Roads Naval Station in Ceiba, and Vieques Navy Base—which significantly boosted the economy. In 1940 a major hydroelectric-power expansion program was undertaken, providing electric power throughout the island and attracting U.S. industry. In 1947, President Harry S. Truman agreed to give Puerto Rico more control of its local government, and the next year the island chose its first self-elected governor, Luis Muñoz Marín, a member of the Popular Democratic Party.

But by this time, Campos had finished serving his time and returned to Puerto Rico, where he reinvigorated efforts to achieve independence—this time, at any cost.

On November 1, 1950, two Puerto Rican nationalists—Oscar Collazo and Griselio Torresola—attempted to assassinate President Truman at the Blair House, where the president and his family were living while the White House was being renovated. Approaching the house from opposite sides, they attempted but failed to shoot their way in. After the gunfire ended, Torresola and one police officer were dead, and two police officers were wounded. Collazo was sentenced to death, but Truman commuted the sentence to life. Campos was again arrested and found guilty of his role in planning the assassination attempt. He spent the remainder of his life in and out prison until his death in 1965.

In 1952, Puerto Rico adopted a new constitution, and Commonwealth status was established. The island had more self-governing powers than ever before. This was the beginning of the long debate that still rages today over Puerto Rico's political status. While roughly half the population is content with Commonwealth status, an equal number of residents have worked steadily toward trying to achieve statehood.

Puerto Rico's first self-elected governor, Luis Muñoz Marín, was a New Deal–style reformist with progressive ideas who served four terms as governor of Puerto Rico. In partnership with the United States, he initiated many programs that advanced economic and cultural development throughout the island and significantly improved the infrastructure. Under his leadership, an economic development program called Operation Bootstrap was successfully launched to entice global industry to the island with federal and local tax exemptions. *The Economist* described it as "one century of economic development…achieved in a decade." The standard of living leapt to new heights, and the tourist trade soon exploded. The next three decades, from the 1950s through the 1970s, was a huge period of growth and development for the island. But some believed Operation Bootstrap was a throwback to colonial ideals in which the island's resources were exploited without fair compensation, rendering the island increasingly more dependent on the United States.

The island suffered several setbacks in the 1980s. The energy crisis and U.S. recession sent the tourist trade into decline, and many of San Juan's glamorous high-rise hotels fell into disrepair, some shuttering altogether. Hurricane Hugo in 1989 dealt a devastating blow, and Operation Bootstrap was discontinued, which sent many manufacturers packing.

Meanwhile, the independence movement was quietly gaining momentum, and peaceful protest was not part of the agenda. Two pro-independence organizations formed in the 1970s. The Popular Boricua Army, commonly known as Los Macheteros, primarily operated in Puerto Rico. The Armed Forces of Puerto Rican National Liberation (FALN) operated in the United States. The two organizations communicated their desire for independence with terrorist attacks.

One of FALN's most notorious attacks was setting off a briefcase bomb in 1975 in New York City's Fraunces Tavern, a historic landmark where George Washington delivered his farewell speech to colonial troops during the Revolutionary War. Four patrons were killed. Other bombs were detonated in a Harlem tenement, Penn Station, and JFK Airport. All told, FALN set off 72 bombs in New York City and Chicago, killing five people and injuring 83.

In 1981, Los Macheteros infiltrated the Puerto Rican Air National Guard base and blew up 11 military planes, causing $45 million in damage. In 1983 members of Los Macheteros raided a Wells Fargo depot in Hartford, Connecticut, wounding a policeman and making off with $7.2 million, ostensibly to fund the organization's efforts.

Sixteen instigators from both organizations were eventually captured and sentenced to federal prison, bringing the terrorist acts to a halt. In 1999, President Clinton granted them clemency.

TODAY

The dawn of a new century found Puerto Rico in a heated contest with the U.S. military over its Navy base in Vieques. For years the military had been using the island for bombing practice and ammunitions storage. But in 1999, civilian David Sanes was accidentally killed by a bomb in Vieques, which set off an organized protest effort that raged for several years and grew stronger in numbers through time. The military finally relented, pulling out of Vieques in 2003. Without the base in Vieques, the U.S. Navy decided it didn't need the Roosevelt Roads Naval Station in Ceiba, and it was closed in 2004, taking with it its estimated $250 million-a-year infusion into the local economy. With Ramey Air Force Base having closed in the mid-1970s, Fort Buchanan is the last remaining U.S. military base on the island.

The independence movement in Puerto Rico has long since abandoned its violent ways, and in truth, only 5 percent of the population wants independence. But every once in a while, something occurs that reminds islanders of the movement's presence and its bloody history. As recently as 2005, the FBI killed—some say ambushed—Los Macheteros organizer Filiberto Ojeda Ríos in a shoot-out at his home in Hormigueros. The 72-year-old man was the ringleader in the 1983 Wells Fargo attack and had evaded authorities ever since. To some, the fact that Ojeda was killed on September 23—a holiday honoring the independence movement's 1868 uprising against Spain—seemed to send a clear reminder to *independenistas* that their past activities had not been forgotten.

The single most defining characteristic of Puerto Rico's political climate today is the decades-old debate over whether it should remain a territory of the United States, become a state, or achieve independence. Which way the tides would turn were residents given the opportunity to decide their fate is anyone's guess, since popular opinion is equally divided between pro-Commonwealth and pro-statehood stances.

Economy and Government

ECONOMY

Puerto Rico has one of the best economies in the Caribbean, but it's still well below U.S. standards. Approximately 44 percent of the population lives below the poverty level. In 2008 the unemployment rate was 12 percent, and annual per capita income was $12,000. The island is heavily dependent on U.S. aid, and the government is the largest employer.

From colonial times until the 1940s, the island's largest industry was sugar production. But that industry went into decline when sugar prices plummeted as other sources became available.

In 1948 the federal and local governments came together to introduce an economic development program called Operation Bootstrap. In addition to bringing land reforms, roads, and schools to neglected parts of the island, it stimulated industrial growth by giving federal and local tax exemptions to U.S. corporations that established operations in Puerto Rico. Many major manufacturing firms set up shop, and before long the production of pharmaceuticals and electronics far eclipsed agriculture on the island. The period from the 1950s through the 1970s was a huge period of growth and development. The standard of living achieved new heights very quickly, and the tourism industry began to blossom.

© AVALON TRAVEL

But in the latter part of the 20th century, Puerto Rico's economy suffered a series of setbacks. First the energy crisis and U.S. recession put a damper on the tourist trade in the 1980s. Then in the 1990s, Operation Bootstrap's tax incentives were discontinued and the North American Free Trade Agreement (NAFTA) was enacted, which sent industries packing to Mexico, where labor was cheaper. Adding insult to injury, in 2004 the United States closed the Roosevelt Roads Naval Station, which contributed $250 million a year to the local economy.

But there is a new vigor fueling the economy of Puerto Rico today, and it's apparent in the many cranes and construction projects under way throughout the island. Economic development has turned its attention aggressively toward tourism during a time, especially after 9/11,

when U.S. travelers are seeking destinations closer to home. Port Authority improvements to San Juan's 12 ship docks and seven piers have made it the largest port in the Caribbean. The brand-new 113-acre Puerto Rico Convention Center beside the Isla Grande Airport near Old San Juan was completed in late 2005, making it the largest convention center in the Caribbean. New road construction projects are under way, and seemingly every town is renovating its central plaza. An estimated five million tourists visit the island each year.

GOVERNMENT ORGANIZATION

Puerto Rico is a self-governing commonwealth of the United States. Its residents are U.S. citizens, but they can't vote for members of Congress or the president. A resident

PUERTO RICO MUNICIPALITIES

commissioner represents the island's interests in Washington but cannot vote on legislative matters. Businesses pay federal taxes, but individuals do not, although they do contribute to federal programs such as Social Security and Medicare. Individuals also pay about 32 percent of their income in local taxes.

Ever since Puerto Rico became a commonwealth in the early 1950s, its residents have debated the best course for the island's political future. A small but fervent number want independence, but the rest of the island is evenly divided between pro-statehood and pro-commonwealth factions. Statehood would mean more federal funding and a voice in national decisions. Those opposed to statehood fear losing their Spanish language and heritage in the rush toward Americanization. For the first time since the United States claimed the island as a territory in 1898, Puerto Rico may be in the position of deciding its own fate. A U.S. task force has recommended the island hold a public vote to determine its future status no later than Dec. 31, 2009.

In some ways, Puerto Rico is already like a state. The United States oversees all federal affairs, including interstate trade, foreign relations, customs, immigration, currency, military service, judicial procedures, transportation, communications, agriculture, mining, and the postal service. The local Puerto Rican government oversees internal affairs. The head of government is an elected governor, and there are two legislative chambers—the House and the Senate. The island's capital is based in San Juan. The island is divided into 78 municipalities, and each one is governed by a popularly elected mayor and municipal assembly.

POLITICAL PARTIES

Puerto Ricans are passionate about politics. Political rallies are frequent, and during election years, political alliances are proclaimed by flag-waving caravans that drive through towns honking their horns and broadcasting speeches from loudspeakers. Puerto Rico has one of the highest percentages of voter turnout in the United States, with 81.7 percent in 2004.

There are three political parties in Puerto Rico. The **Popular Democratic Party** is pro-commonwealth, the **New Progressive Party** is pro-statehood, and the **Puerto Rican Independence Party** is pro-independence. Those who embrace independence represent only 5 percent of the population. The rest of the island is fairly evenly divided between pro-statehood and pro-commonwealth factions.

How Puerto Ricans might vote should they be given the option of statehood is hard to say. Four straw votes have been held since 1967—the most recent in 1998 when 50.3 percent of the voters wanted "none of the above." So clearly, anything can happen. It will be interesting to see what path Puerto Rico chooses should the United States give it the power to decide.

JUDICIAL SYSTEM

The judicial system in Puerto Rico is structured the same as in the United States. The highest local court is the Supreme Court, consisting of a chief justice and six associate justices appointed by the governor. There is a Court of Appeals, Superior Court, a civil and criminal District Court, and Municipal Court. The U.S. Federal Court, based in San Juan, has final authority.

People and Culture

NATIONAL IDENTITY

There is a saying on the island that Puerto Ricans are like porpoises: They can barely keep their heads above water, but they're always smiling. It's an apt description. In 2005, Puerto Ricans were proclaimed the happiest people on earth, according to a highly reported study by the Stockholm-based organization World Values Survey. Despite high poverty and unemployment rates, it seems nothing can put a damper on the lively, fun-loving Puerto Rican spirit. Most Puerto Ricans like to celebrate big and often. In fact, there are reportedly more than 500 festivals a year on the island, and everything is a family affair involving multiple generations of relatives. Music is usually at the heart of most gatherings, and Puerto Ricans are passionate about their opinions and love few things more than to debate politics or sports for hours.

The culture of Puerto Rican life has been significantly shaped by its history. It was originally inhabited by a society of peaceful, agriculturally based indigenous people who migrated to the island from South America. But beginning in 1508, the island became a Spanish colony, and for the next four centuries European influence reigned. Towns were developed according to Spanish custom around central plazas and churches. The Church spread Catholicism, and Spanish became the official language.

Because the majority of colonists were men, the Spanish Crown officially supported marriage between Spanish men and Taíno women, leading to a population of mixed offspring. The Spanish also brought in slaves from Africa to work the island's many coffee and sugar plantations, and they too produced offspring with the Taíno and Spanish colonists, producing what for years was called a population of mulattoes.

Perhaps because of this historic mixing of races, racial tensions are relatively minimal in Puerto Rico. There are some levels of society that proudly claim to be of pure European blood, and darker-skinned populations are sometimes discriminated against. But in general, Puerto Rico is a true melting pot of races in which skin comes in all shades of white and brown, and the general population is fairly accepting of everyone else.

When the United States took control of Puerto Rico in 1898, the island underwent another enormous cultural transformation. Suddenly U.S. customs and practices were imposed. English became a common second language, and has at times been proclaimed the official language. The U.S. dollar became the legal tender. American corporations set up shop, bringing with them an influx of American expatriates whose ways of dress, cuisine, and art were integrated into the existing culture. Much of this influence came in the form of the military, due to the many military bases that were established on the island. Some people credit that influence on the relative stability and orderliness of public life, particularly as compared to other Caribbean islands. The island's governmental and judicial systems are organized similarly to the United States, and many U.S. social services are offered on the island.

Inroads of contemporary American culture have been made into much of island life, but Puerto Ricans are fiercely proud of their Spanish heritage. Since becoming a U.S. territory a little more than 100 years ago, Puerto Rico has undergone a seismic shift in its national identity that has divided the island politically. Puerto Ricans are U.S. citizens, and they enjoy many—but not all—the privileges that entails. The issue of Puerto Rico's future political status has been an ongoing debate for more than 50 years, and it is as much a part of the island's national identity as its Spanish language and customs. Roughly half the island's population wants to remain a U.S. commonwealth, in large part because they believe that status ensures the preservation of their Spanish

FIESTAS PATRONALES SCHEDULE

The most elaborate and renowned Fiestas Patronales take place in San Juan and Loíza, but all of the municipalities' celebrations honoring their patron saints offer visitors a unique opportunity to get a concentrated dose of local culture. The following is a list of some of the island's Fiestas Patronales.

FEBRUARY

- **Manatí:** La Virgen de La Candelaria, February 2
- **Mayagüez:** La Virgen de La Candelaria, February 2
- **Coamo:** La Virgen de La Candelaria and San Blas, February 3

MARCH

- **Loíza:** San Patricio, March 17
- **Lares:** San José, March 19
- **Luquillo:** San José, March 19

MAY

- **Arecibo:** Apóstol San Felipe, May 1
- **Maunabo:** San Isidro, May 15
- **Toa Alta:** San Fernando, May 30

JUNE

- **Barranquitas:** San Antonio de Padua, June 13
- **Dorado:** San Antonio de Padua, June 13
- **Isabela:** San Antonio de Padua, June 13
- **San Juan:** San Juan Bautista, June 23
- **Orocovis:** San Juan Bautista, June 24
- **Toa Baja:** San Pedro Apóstol, June 30

JULY

- **Culebra:** Virgen del Carmen, July 16
- **Hatillo:** Virgen del Carmen, July 16
- **Morovis:** Virgen del Carmen, July 16
- **Aibonito:** Santiago Apóstol, July 25
- **Fajardo:** Santiago Apóstol, July 25
- **Guánica:** Santiago Apóstol, July 25
- **Loíza:** Santiago Apóstol, July 25
- **San Germán:** San Germán, July 31

AUGUST

- **Cayey:** Nuestra Señora de la Asunción, August 15
- **Adjuntas:** San Joaquín and Santa Ana, August 21
- **Rincón:** Santa Rosa de Lima, August 30

SEPTEMBER

- **Jayuya:** Nuestra Señora de la Monserrate, September 8
- **Moca:** Nuestra Señora de la Monserrate, September 8
- **Salinas:** Nuestra Señora de la Monserrate, September 8
- **Cabo Rojo:** San Miguel Arcangel, September 29
- **Utuado:** San Miguel Arcangel, September 29

OCTOBER

- **Yabucoa:** Los Angeles Custodios, October 2
- **Naguabo:** Nuestra Señora del Rosario, October 7
- **Vega Baja:** Nuestra Señora del Rosario, October 7
- **Quebradillas:** San Rafael Arcangel, October 24

NOVEMBER

- **Aguadilla:** San Carlos Borromeo, November 4

DECEMBER

- **Vega Alta:** La Inmaculada Concepción de María, December 8
- **Vieques:** La Inmaculada Concepción de María, December 8
- **Ponce:** Nuestra Señora de la Guadalupe, December 12

culture. The other half wants to become a U.S. state so they can have full privileges of citizenship, including the ability to vote for the U.S. president and have full representation in Congress.

Recently, Congress has taken actions that could put the future of Puerto Rico's political status to a popular vote on the island. Until a vote is held, the future of Puerto Rico's 3.9 million citizens hangs in the balance between two cultures.

GENDER ROLES

When it comes to gender roles, Puerto Ricans are fairly traditional. However, like the rest of the industrial world, women have made inroads into the formerly male world of business and sports, particularly in urban areas. At one time it was common practice among the island's most traditional families for young women to be accompanied by chaperones in the form of an aunt or older sister when they began dating, but that practice is quickly vanishing.

Vestiges of machismo still exist among male populations. Attractive young women may attract unwanted catcalls, usually expressed with a "s-s-s" sound, or calls of *"Mira, mami!"* But in general, Puerto Rican men can be quite chivalrous in ways American women may be unaccustomed to. Having a bus seat relinquished for their comfort and the holding of doors are courtesies commonly encountered.

RELIGION

Before the arrival of Christopher Columbus in 1493, Puerto Rico's indigenous population was comprised of highly spiritual individuals who worshipped multiple gods believed to reside in nature. It was a common belief that these gods controlled everything from the success or failure of crops to one's choice of a spouse.

All that began to change when Ponce de León arrived in 1508, bringing with him several Roman Catholic priests who ministered to the new colony and set about converting the Taíno Indians to the faith, beginning with baptisms. In 1511, Pope Julius II created a diocese in Caparra, the island's first settlement.

Today, depending on the source, Puerto Rico's population is between 75 and 85 percent Roman Catholic. Although weekly church attendance is far below that figure, the Catholic Church has great influence on Puerto Rican life. Each town has a Catholic church at its center and celebrates its patron saint with an annual festival. Although many patron-saint festivals have become much more secular over time, they typically include a religious procession and special Mass to mark the day. Images of saints are common items in traditional households, and you can't enter a church without seeing clusters of women lighting candles, praying, or kissing the hem of the dress worn by a statue of Mary.

Some Puerto Ricans practice a hybrid form of religion called *espiritismo,* which combines elements of the Catholic religion and Indian beliefs in nature-dwelling spirits that can be called on to effect change in one's life. Similarly, some Puerto Ricans of African descent practice Santería, introduced to the island by Yoruba slaves from West Africa. It also observes multiple gods and combines elements of Catholicism. Practitioners of both religions patronize the island's *botanicas,* stores that sell roots, herbs, candles, soaps, and amulets that are employed to sway the spirits to help individuals achieve success, whether it be in business, love, or starting a family.

Once the United States arrived in Puerto Rico in 1898, Protestantism began to grow on the island, and all major sects are represented. Pentecostal fundamentalism has developed in recent decades, and there is a small Jewish community on the island as well.

HOLIDAYS AND FESTIVALS

No matter when you visit Puerto Rico, there's a good chance there's a holiday or festival going on somewhere on the island. Among the biggest festivals are Ponce's **Carnaval** in February; Hatillo's **Festival de Máscaras** and **Dia de Los Inocentes** in December; and **Festival Nacional Indígena** in Jayuya in November. For more information on those festivals, see their respective chapters.

Being a U.S. commonwealth, Puerto Rico has adopted an American-style celebration of Christmas, but it also celebrates the more traditional **Los Reyes Magos,** also known as **Three Kings Day,** on January 6. On January 5, children fill shoeboxes with grass to feed the Wise Men's camels and place them under their beds. In the morning, the grass is gone and in its place is a present.

But most notably, all 78 municipalities in Puerto Rico honor their patron saints with annual festivals called **Fiestas Patronales.** Although special Masses and religious processions may be a part of the celebrations, secular festivities such as musical performances, dancing, traditional foods, artisan booths, and games often take precedence. The festivals typically take place in the main plaza.

LANGUAGE

Puerto Rico has two official languages: Spanish and English. Many Puerto Ricans living in metropolitan areas are bilingual, but by far the majority of the population uses primarily Spanish. Spanish is spoken in the public school system, and English is taught as a foreign language.

In recent years, the designation of Puerto Rico's official language has been caught in a political volley between the pro-statehood and pro-commonwealth factions. In 1991, Governor Rafael Hernández Colón, a proponent of commonwealth status, declared Spanish as the sole official language. He was preceded by Governor Pedro Rosselló, a proponent of statehood, who changed the official language to English. But for now, both languages enjoy official status.

EDUCATION

Puerto Rico has a 94 percent literacy rate, and its educational system is structured the same as in the United States—kindergarten through 12th grade. In addition to the public school system, the Catholic Church operates a private school system. Both systems teach in Spanish. There are also several English-language private schools on the island.

There are several institutions of higher learning in Puerto Rico, the largest one being the Universidad de Puerto Rico, with campuses in Mayagüez, San Juan, Río Piedras, and Humacao. Other schools include Universidad Polytechnica de Puerto Rico, Universidad Intermericana de Puerto Rico, Universidad Carlos Albizu, and Universidad del Sagrado Corazón. There are also two arts schools— Escuela de Artes Plásticas de Puerto Rico and Conservatorio de Música de Puerto Rico.

The Arts

Puerto Rico is a melting pot of indigenous, Spanish, and African influences, and nowhere is that more apparent than in the island's rich cultural life. Food, music, art, dance—they all reflect different aspects of the cultures that came together over time to create *la vida criolla.*

MUSIC

Music is a huge part of Puerto Rican life. Sometimes it seems as though the whole island reverberates to a syncopated beat, thanks to the strains of music that waft from outdoor concerts, open windows, barrooms, passing cars, and boom boxes. Nearly every weekend there is a holiday or festival in Puerto Rico, and at the core of its celebration is always music. During a recent stay in Old San Juan, each morning began with the sound of a lone elderly man walking up the deserted street singing a heartbreaking lament that echoed off the 18th-century buildings.

The island has made many significant contributions to the world of music at large, starting with the birth of a couple of uniquely Puerto Rican instruments. The national instrument of Puerto Rico is the *cuatro,* an adaptation of the

Spanish guitar that features 10 strings arranged in five pairs and typically carved from solid blocks of laurel. Several classic Puerto Rican instruments date to the indigenous people, including the popular *güiro.* Similar in principle to the washboard, the *güiro* is a hollowed gourd with ridges cut into its surface, which is scraped rhythmically with a comblike object. Other prevalent local instruments that reflect African influence are the *barril,* a large drum originally made by stretching animal skin over the top of a barrel; the *tambour,* a handheld drum similar to a tambourine but without the cymbals; and the maraca, made from gourds and seeds.

Some of Puerto Rico's earliest known musical styles are *bomba* and *plena,* which have roots in the African slave culture. They're both heavy on percussion and lightning-fast rhythms. *Bomba* features call-and-response vocals and is accompanied by frenzied dancing in which the dancers match their steps to every beat of the drum. In *plena,* the emphasis is on the vocals, which are more European in origin and retell current events or local scandals. Local *bomba* masters include Los Hermanos Ayala, traditionalists from Loíza, and the more contemporary Cepedas, based in Santurce, San Juan. Reviving interest in *plena* is the band Plena Libre.

Akin in philosophy to the origins of American country music, *música jíbaro* is the folk sound of Puerto Rico's rural mountain dwellers, called *jíbaros.* Performed by small ensembles on *cuatro, güiro,* bongos, and occasionally clarinets and trumpets, *música jíbaro* is more Spanish in origin than *bomba* or *plena,* although the Caribbean influence is unmistakable. Vocals, which play an important part in *música jíbaro,* are usually about the virtues of a simpler way of life. There are two types of *música jíbaro*—*seis* and *aguinalda. Seis* is typically named after a particular town, and the lyrics are often improvised and sung in 10-syllable couplets. *Aguinaldos* are performed around Christmas by roaming carolers. Ramito (1915–1990) is considered Puerto Rico's quintessential *jíbaro* artist.

While Puerto Rican slaves grooved to *bomba* and the farmers played their folk tunes, Puerto Rico's moneyed Europeans turned their attentions to classical music, eventually giving birth around 1900 to *danza,* a romantic classical style of music often described as Afro-Caribbean waltz. Originating in Ponce, *danza* was performed on piano, cello, violin, and *bombardino* (similar to a trombone) for dancers who performed structured, ballroom-style steps. The form is celebrated in Ponce with the annual Semana de la Danza in May. *Danza's* most famous composers were Manuel Gregorio Tavarez (1843–1883) and his pupil, Juan Morel Campos (1857–1896).

In 1956, renowned Catalan cellist and composer Pablo Casals moved to Puerto Rico, and a year later Festival Casals was born. The international celebration of classical music continues today in concert halls in San Juan, Ponce, and Mayagüez every June and July. In Old San Juan there is a museum dedicated to Casals, featuring his music manuscripts, instruments, and recordings.

Of course, salsa is the music most associated with Puerto Rico today. A lively, highly danceable fusion of jazz, African polyrhythms, and Caribbean flair, salsa is performed by large ensembles on drums, keyboards, and horns. When people refer to Latin music, they usually mean salsa. It is the predominant form of music heard on the island, so just stop in almost any bar or restaurant advertising live music and you're likely to hear it. Watching expert salsa dancers move to the music is as entertaining as listening to the music. Born in New York City but Puerto Rican by heritage, percussionist and composer Tito Puente (1923–2000) was a major influence on salsa music. Other masters include Celia Cruz (1924–2003) and Willie Colón, but there are scores of popular Puerto Rican salsa artists who perform today.

The biggest thing happening in Puerto Rican music now, though, is reggaetón. An exciting blend of American hip-hop, *bomba, plena,* and Jamaican dancehall, the musical form is Puerto Rican–born and bred, and it's starting to gain notice worldwide. A big part of its explosive growth is due to the popularity of Daddy Yankee, who grew up in the public housing projects of San Juan and who's managed to cross over into the American market. Reggaetón festivals have become a popular pastime in Puerto Rico, but you can also hear it in nightclubs and blasting from car windows. And once again, Puerto Rico's culture comes back to its Afro-Caribbean roots. Other popular reggaetón artists include Don Omar, Tego Calderón, Ivy Queen, and Calle 13.

VISUAL ARTS

The visual arts have been a thriving art form in Puerto Rico for centuries, and its artists' output runs the gamut from baroque European-influenced paintings to contemporary conceptual pieces that challenge the definition of art.

Puerto Rico's best-known early artists were José Campeche (1751–1809) and Francisco Oller (1833–1917). Campeche was of mixed race, born in San Juan to a freed slave, Tomás Campeche, and a native of the Canary Islands, María Jordán Marqué. He was primarily a self-taught artist, first learning the skill from his father, but he studied for a time with Luis Paret, an exiled Spanish painter who lived in Puerto Rico for awhile. As was common at the time, Campeche primarily painted portraits of wealthy landowners and religious scenes in heavily ornamented detail, which was in keeping with the rococo style of the day. He painted more than 400 paintings during his lifetime, the majority of them commissions. Campeche's *The Virgen de la Soledad de la Victoria* was the first acquisition of the Museo de Arte de Puerto Rico, where you can see many other examples of his work.

Oller was born in Bayamón and studied art at the Academia de Bellas Artes in Madrid from 1851 to 1853. He also studied in Paris from 1858 to 1863, where he was a contemporary of Pissarro, Cézanne, and Guillaumins and exhibited at several Paris salons. Influenced by realist and impressionist styles, his work encompassed portraits, landscapes, and still lifes. But once he returned for good to Puerto Rico in 1884, his work became primarily realist in nature, typically rendered in somber colors. His subjects tended to focus on traditional Puerto Rican ways of life. One of his most famous paintings is *El Velorio (The Wake)*, which depicts a rural family gathered in a home for an infant's wake and which can be seen in a gallery at the University of Puerto Rico in Río Piedras. Oller's work has been acquired by many important museums, including the Musée d'Orsay in Paris.

Two other important early artists were Miguel Pou (1880–1968) and Ramón Frade (1875–1954), whose paintings celebrated the dignity of *jíbaro* (peasant) life.

Another internationally recognized artist was island transplant Jack Delano (1914–1997), a significant photographer who chronicled the Puerto Rican people and way of life from 1941 until his death. Born in Kiev, Ukraine, he first came to Puerto Rico in 1941 on assignment for the U.S. Farm Security Administration in conjunction with President Franklin D. Roosevelt's New Deal programs. The program sent many famous photographers throughout the United States to document rural life. In addition to Delano, they included Walker Evans, Dorothea Lange, Marjory Collins, and Gordon Parks, among others. After the war, Delano returned to Puerto Rico in 1946, settled there permanently, and continued to photograph the island's changing culture. His work is journalistic in nature but is deeply imbued with a respect for the human condition. In addition to his photography, Delano was a musical composer of sonatas.

Beginning in the 1940s, a radical new art form exploded in Puerto Rico that reflected growing concern among artists and writers that the island's native culture was being subsumed by American influence. That sentiment was expressed in visually striking representations of graphic poster art, called *cartels*. Originally funded by the local government, artists produced colorful illustrations of important books, plays, songs, and poems, as well as political slogans and quotations. Eventually the art form evolved away from its boosterish origins. Some artists used the form to criticize the government and social issues, while others celebrated the island's natural and architectural beauty. Today it's most commonly seen advertising festivals. Among its most celebrated artists are Lorenzo Homar (1913–2004), who was a recipient of the National Medal of Honor and cofounder of the Centro de Arte de Puertorriqueño, which played an important role in advancing the graphic art form. The Museo de Arte de Puerto Rico has a gallery devoted to an excellent collection of *cartels*.

Another significant artist was Rafael Tufiño (1922–2008), whose somber paintings captured the island's people and customs, as well as its pockets of squalor. Tufiño was also a cofounder of the Centro de Arte de Puertorriqueña and a faculty member for the Puerto Rico Institute of Culture's art school, Escuela de Artes Plásticas.

Puerto Rico's arts scene continues to evolve. Recognizing the positive impact art can have on the economy, then-governor Sila M. Calderón initiated in 2001 a $25 million program to fund the **Puerto Rico Public Art Project,** which has put in place scores of contemporary site-specific public art installations throughout the island. Many works are meant to be functional, in the form of bus stops, park benches, and vendor kiosks, or to enliven the roadways of major thoroughfares and stops along the new commuter rail service (Tren Urbano). Pieces vary from murals to conceptual multimedia installations to earthworks, and 20 percent of the works are created by Puerto Rican artists. Among the local and international artists participating are Ana Rosa Rivera, Víctor Vázquez, Ramón Berríos, Lourdes Correa Carlo, Charles Juhasz, and Liliana Porter.

For details on the project, including maps and descriptions of the pieces, visit www.artepublicopr.com, in English and Spanish.

CRAFTS

Puerto Rican artisans produce a variety of crafts unique to the island's culture. The most distinctive craft is the **Vejigante mask,** a brilliantly colored object made from coconut shells or papier-mâché featuring large protruding horns.

The masks represent the Moors in annual festivals revolving around street pageants that reenact Spain's defeat of the Moors in the 13th century. Although there are several artists who create the masks, the Ayala family in Loíza are considered the masters of the form. Prices range about $30–250. *Vejigante* figurines made from a variety of materials, including ceramic, glass, and metal, are also popular collectible items made by local artisans and come in all price ranges.

Puerto Rico's oldest and most traditional craft form is the **santo,** primitive-looking woodcarvings of Catholic saints. *Santos* originated with low-income families who wanted representations of their favorite saints to display in their homes, but who couldn't afford the expensive plaster ones available for purchase. Today, *santos* are highly collectible, and many museums, including Museo de las Americas in Old San Juan, exhibit priceless collections of vintage *santos*. New *santos* can be found in the island's finer crafts and gift shops and cost $80–500.

Mundillo is a delicate, handmade lace created by tying fine threads using bobbins,

© SUZANNE VAN ATTEN

a *mundillo* in progress

which facilitate weaving the threads into an intricate pattern. The lace is used to embellish tablecloths, handkerchiefs, and christening gowns, among other things. The art form has roots in Spain, but the *mundillo* pattern is specific to Puerto Rico. It's primarily produced in and around the tiny town of Moca near Aguadilla on the west coast, where several artisans live. *Mundillo* can be purchased at finer gift shops around the island and at some festivals. Because it is so labor-intensive, *mundillo* is somewhat pricey. A handkerchief rimmed with a small amount of *mundillo* starts around $30, but a handkerchief made entirely of *mundillo* can cost more than $100.

The crafting of woven cotton **hammocks** is an art form that continues a tradition started by the Taíno Indians, who used them not only to sleep on but also for food storage and other utilitarian purposes. The town of San Sebastián in the western fringe of the Cordillera Central is the best known source of the hammock, but they're available at most crafts and gift shops throughout the island starting at about $30.

Other popular low-priced craft items include **seed jewelry,** colorful earrings, bracelets, and necklaces made from the seeds of trees and plants on the island; **güiros,** percussion instruments made from gourds; and landscape paintings on pieces of rough-hewn wood.

LITERATURE

Literature in Puerto Rico has historically revolved around national identity and the tension of being U.S. citizens in a Latino culture. Its literary heritage began to emerge in the mid-1800s, and among its earliest notable works was *El Gíbaro* (1849) by Manuel Alonso y Pacheco. Part prose, part poetry, *El Gíbaro* celebrated the simple life of Puerto Rico's farmers, called *jíbaros.*

But the first writer to receive literary prominence was Alejandro Tapia y Rivera (1826–1882) of San Juan, a playwright and abolitionist who wrote many works, including biographical pieces on important Puerto Ricans such as Spanish admiral Ramón Power y Giralt, artist José Campeche, and the pirate Roberto Cofresí.

One of Puerto Rico's early writers who was revered throughout the Caribbean and South America was Eugenio María de Hostos (1839–1903), a writer and educator who led civic-reform movements throughout Latin America. His seminal work is *Peregrinación de Bayoán* (1863), a work of fiction that illustrated injustices under the Spanish regime and called for independence from Spain.

After Puerto Rico came under control of the United States, a new crop of writers, called the Generation of '98, began to flourish. Fueled primarily by politics, several writers of this era combined the art of poetry with the craft of journalism. José de Diego (1867–1918) of Aguadilla and Luís Muñoz Rivera (1859–1916) of Barranquitas were significant poets and journalists who fueled the island's independence movement with their words. Diego, considered a precursor of the modernist movement in Puerto Rico, produced several books of poetry, including *Pomarrosas, Jovillos, Cantos de Rebeldía,* and *Cantos del Pitirre.* Rivera's most significant work was a book of poems called *Tropicales.*

One of the most important writers of this era was Antonio S. Pedriera (1899–1939), whose work *Insularismo* examined how U.S. political control had affected Puerto Rican culture in the first 35 years.

In the 1940s, there was a mass migration of Puerto Ricans to the United States—primarily New York City—and the island's literature took a significant shift reflecting that phenomenon. Suddenly there was an output of work by Puerto Rican immigrants who found themselves grappling with issues of dual identity. In 1951, Playwright René Marqués (1919–1974) of Arecibo wrote his most critically acclaimed play, *The Oxcart,* which chronicled the mass exodus of Puerto Ricans to New York City. Also noteworthy is *A Puerto Rican in New York* (1961) by Jesús Colón (1918–1974), who was born in Cayey but grew up in the United States.

The 1960s and 1970s saw the birth of a literary movement called Nuyorican literature. Nuyorican is the name given to New Yorkers of Puerto Rican heritage. Some of the most notable writers of this movement were Piri Thomas, author of *Down These Mean Streets* (1967), and Nicholasa Mohr, who wrote *Nilda* (1973), both of which dealt with life in the urban barrios of New York City. By the 1980s, the Nuyorican movement exploded on the spoken-word scene with work that had a strong political message. New York's Nuyorican Poets Café was and still is the epicenter of this movement, providing a forum for such celebrated poets as Ponce-born Pedro Pietri (1944–2004), for whom a street in New York City was recently named, and New York–born Felipe Luciano, founder of the Young Lords activist group. Also once a regular at Nuyorican Poets Café was Gurabo-born Miguel Piñero (1946–1988), who was a playwright and actor. His play *Short Eyes,* about life in prison, won the New York Drama Critics Award for Best American Play in 1974. His life was depicted in a film starring Benjamin Bratt called *Piñero.*

Puerto Rican literature continues to flourish today thanks to many contemporary writers living on the island and in the United States, including poet Victor Hernández Cruz and novelists Esmeralda Santiago, who wrote *When I Was Puerto Rican* (1993) and *El Amante Turco* (2005), and Ernesto Quiñonez, author of *Bodega Dreams* (2000) and *Chango's Fire* (2004), among others.

For an excellent survey of Puerto Rican literature, read *Boricuas: The Influential Puerto Rican Writings, an Anthology* (Ballantine, 1995), featuring excerpts of works by some of the writers mentioned here, as well as many others.

DANCE

Dance plays an important role in Puerto Rican culture because it goes hand in hand with the island's rich musical heritage. But for the most part, dance is about moving to the groove of live music or DJs, whether it's at a nightclub, an outdoor concert in the town plaza, or at one of the island's countless festivals. Dance is integral to *bomba, plena,* salsa, and reggaetón music, and the thing all those forms of movement have in common is this: It's all in the hips! The exception is the ballroom style of *danza.*

When it comes to dance performance, the island leader is Guateque, the folkloric ballet of Puerto Rico. For more than 20 years this 40-member dance company and school based on Corozal has been preserving and performing the island's traditional dances, as well as adapting them into new productions. Past productions include *Los Taínos de Borkén* and *Los Dioses (The Gods),* which depict daily life and spirituality of the island's indigenous Indians.

ESSENTIALS

Getting There

BY AIR

Puerto Rico has two international airports, Luis Muñoz Marín International Airport (SJU) in Isla Verde, San Juan; and Rafael Hernández International Airport (BQN) in Aguadilla on the west coast. The only other airport to service flights from the United States is Mercedita International Airport (PSE) in Ponce on the South coast.

Regional airports serving commercial travel are Isla Grande Airport (SIG) near Old San Juan; Jose Aponte de la Torre Airport (RVR) in Ceiba; Eugenio María de Hostos Airport (MAZ) in Mayagüez; Vieques Airport (VQS) in Isabel Segunda; and Culebra Airport (CPX) in Culebra. Airports in Fajardo and Humacao have been closed to commercial service.

Air fares to Puerto Rico fluctuate in price throughout the year, but the cheapest rates can typically be secured during the off-season, May–October, which is also hurricane season.

From North America

Direct flights to San Juan are available from Atlanta, Boston, Chicago, Dallas/Fort Worth, Fort Lauderdale, Miami, New York City, Newark, Orlando, Philadelphia, and Washington, D.C.

© OMAR VEGA

The following airlines offer flights to San Juan from the United States:

- **AirTran** (800/247-8726, www.airtran.com)

- **American Airlines** (800/433-7300, www.aa.com)

- **Continental Airlines** (800/231-0856 or 800/523-3273, www.continental.com)

- **Delta Air Lines** (800/221-1212 or 800/325-1999, www.delta.com)

- **JetBlue Airways** (800/538-2583, www.jetblue.com)

- **Spirit Airlines** (800/772-7117, www.spiritairlines.com)

- **United Airlines** (800/864-8331, www.ual.com)

- **U.S. Airways** (800/428-4322, www.usairways.com)

Direct flights to Aguadilla are operated by Jet Blue (from Orlando and from JFK in New York City); Spirit Airlines (from Fort Lauderdale); Delta (from Newark); and Continental (from Newark). Direct flights to Ponce are operated by Jet Blue (from JFK in New York City and from Orlando).

In Canada, direct flights to San Juan are operated by Air Canada (888/247-2262, www.aircanada.com) from Montréal and Toronto.

From Europe

British Airways (www.britishairways.com) offers connecting flights from the United Kingdom to San Juan via New York City or Miami. **Iberia** (www.iberia.com) offers direct flights to San Juan from Madrid.

From Australia

Connecting flights from Australia are operated by **United** (through Los Angeles and Chicago) and **American Airlines** (through New York City).

From the Caribbean

Several small airlines offer flights to San Juan from throughout the Caribbean. They include **Air Sunshine** (888/879-8900, www.airsunshine.com) from St. Croix, St. Thomas, Tortola, Virgin Gorda, and Vieques; **Cape Air** (800/352-0714, www.flycapeair.com) from St. Croix, St. Thomas, and Tortola; and **Liat Airline** (888/844-5428, www.liatairline.com) from 22 destinations in the eastern Caribbean.

BY CRUISE SHIP

San Juan is the largest port in the Caribbean, and it is a port of call or point of origin for nearly two dozen cruise-ship lines. The cruise ship docks lie along Calle La Marina in Old San Juan.

A few of the most popular cruise-ship lines serving San Juan include:

- **Carnival Cruise Lines** (866/299-5698, www.carnival.com)

- **Celebrity Cruises** (800/647-2251, www.celebritycruises.com)

- **Holland America Line** (877/724-5425, www.hollandamerica.com)

- **Norwegian Cruise Line** (800/327-7030, www.ncl.com)

- **Princess Cruises** (800/PRINCESS— 800/774-6237, www.princess.com)

- **Radisson Seven Seas Cruises** (877/505-5370, www.rssc.com)

BY FERRY

Ferries del Caribe (787/832-4800, www.ferriesdelcaribe.com), which provides transportation between Mayagüez and Santo Domingo, Dominican Republic, on a 12-hour overnight voyage, is primarily a car ferry but sometimes it's like a cruise ship. On select dates, you can book a cabin and make it a mini-vacation by enjoying the restaurant, lounge, game room, and disco. Catch it from the Mayagüez ferry terminal (787/831-3368, fax 787/831-3345, Mon.–Fri. 8 A.M.–9 P.M.) at 31 Avenida Gonzalez Clemente.

Getting Around

Puerto Rico's easy accessibility from the States and the compact lay of the land make it a great place to go for a long weekend. Many visitors simply fly into San Juan and stay there. There are plenty of great restaurants, nightclubs, shops, beaches, and historical sights within walking or taxi distance. A reliable bus transit system and a new rail line called Tren Urbano provide inexpensive transportation throughout the city. It's understandable why some visitors are hesitant to leave behind the capital city's charms.

But escaping the bustle of the city and experiencing the island's unique natural beauty is highly recommended and easily achieved. Car-rental agencies are plentiful, and the roads are well marked and maintained. Because the island is so small, it's possible to make a day trip to any sight on the island. Just keep in mind that Puerto Rico has a high volume of traffic, which can slow your progress. Travel through the central mountain region especially can take longer than might be expected because of the narrow winding roads. Always figure in extra travel time when planning a road trip.

CAR

Visitors who plan to venture outside of San Juan should plan to rent a car. This is by far the best way to explore the island. Most of the major American car-rental agencies have locations throughout the island, and there are several local agencies as well. For the most part, roads are well maintained and well marked. Gasoline is sold by the liter, speed limits are measured in miles per hour, and distance is measured in kilometers. And all road signs are in Spanish. International driving licenses are required for drivers from countries other than the United States.

Driving around San Juan can be bit nerve-racking for those not accustomed to inner-city driving. The sheer number of cars on the island guarantees congested roadways, so be sure to schedule extra time for road trips. Drivers tend to speed and don't leave much space between cars. They also can be creative when it comes to navigating traffic—rolling through stops and driving on the shoulder of the highway is not uncommon. Ponce has, hands-down, the

DRIVING VOCABULARY

vaya – go
derecha – right
izquierda – left
derecho – straight ahead
doble – turn
cuadras – blocks
esquina – corner
cruzar – to cross
cruce – crossroads
luz – traffic light
luces – traffic lights
lejos – far
al centro – downtown
estacionamiento – parking
calle – street
Carr. or *carretera* – highway
autopista – limited access toll roads

ROAD SIGNS
alto – stop
hacia – to
salida – exit
norte – north
sur – south
este – east
oeste – west
Int. – approaching intersection, or interior route
ramal – business route
despacio – slow
cuidado – be careful
calle sin salida – dead-end street
desvio – detour

PUERTO RICO'S HIGHWAYS AND DRIVING DISTANCES

The island's major highways are:

- **PR 26:** East-west, San Juan airport to Condado; also known as Baldorioty de Castro Avenue

- **PR 18:** North-south, connecting PR 22 and PR 52, San Juan

- **PR 66:** Northwest-southeast, Canovanas to San Juan

- **PR 22:** East-west, San Juan to Arecibo (toll); also known as Jose de Diego Expressway

- **PR 52:** North-southwest, San Juan to Ponce (partially toll); also known as Luis a Ferre Expressway

- **PR 30:** Northwest-southeast, Caguas to Humacao

- **PR 53:** North-south, Fajardo to Yabucoa

Driving distances from San Juan to:

- **Aguadilla:** 81 miles (130 kilometers)

- **Arecibo:** 48 miles (77 kilometers)

- **Barranquitas:** 34 miles (55 kilometers)

- **Cabo Rojo:** 111 miles (179 kilometers)

- **Cayey:** 30 miles (48 kilometers)

- **Dorado:** 17 miles (27 kilometers)

- **Fajardo:** 32 miles (52 kilometers)

- **Guánica:** 94 miles (151 kilometers)

- **Humacao:** 34 miles (55 kilometers)

- **Jayuya:** 58 miles (93 kilometers)

- **La Parguera:** 107 miles (172 kilometers)

- **Luquillo:** 28 miles (45 kilometers)

- **Mayagüez:** 98 miles (158 kilometers)

- **Ponce:** 70 miles (113 kilometers)

- **Rincón:** 93 miles (150 kilometers)

- **Salinas:** 46 miles (74 kilometers)

- **Utuado:** 65 miles (105 kilometers)

worst drivers. It's practically a free-for-all, and they blow their car horns constantly.

Take extra precautions when driving in the mountains. Fortunately the traffic is light, but the roads are narrow and winding. Drivers who travel these roads every day tend to proceed at a perilously fast clip. If the driver behind you appears impatient or tailgates, pull over and let him pass. On roads with a lot of blind curves, it is common practice to blow the car horn to alert oncoming traffic you're approaching. If it's raining, beware of small mudslides and overflowing riverbanks, which sometimes close roads. And whatever you do, don't look down! But really, it's not as bad as it sounds. Driving through Puerto Rico's majestic mountains is well worth a few shattered nerves.

There is an excellent, major, limited-access highway system—called **Autopista**—that dissects and nearly encircles the island, some of which are toll roads ($0.25–1.25 per toll). The speed limits range 50–65 miles per hour.

The rest of the island's numbered roads are called *carreteras*, typically written as the abbreviation "carr.," followed by a number, such as Carr. 193. Major *carreteras* often have spur routes that either go into a town's center or along its beachfront. A road number followed by the letter "R" or the word "Ramal" indicates a spur route that goes through a town's commercial district. Beachfront routes are often indicated by the abbreviation "Int." or an addition of the numeral "3" after a road number.

Addresses are typically identified by road and kilometer numbers, for instance: Carr. 193, km 2. Look for the white numbered kilometer posts alongside the road to identify your location. In towns, streets are called *avenida* (abbreviated as Ave.) and *calle.*

TAXI

Most towns in Puerto Rico are served by at least one taxi service. San Juan has several reliable tourist-taxi services that serve the areas where visitors congregate. It's possible to flag one down day or night in Isla Verde and Condado, and in Old San Juan, there are two taxi stands—on Plaza de Colón and Plaza de Armas. You can also call one. Operators include **Metro Taxi** (787/725-2870), **Major Taxi** (787/723-2460), **Rochdale Radio Taxi** (787/721-1900), and **Capetillo Taxi** (787/758-7000).

Fares between the airport and the piers in Old San Juan are fixed rates. From the airport, the rates are $10 to Isla Verde, $14 to Condado, and $19 to Old San Juan. From the piers, the rates are $12 to Condado, $19 to Isla Verde. Metered fares are $3 minimum, $1.75 initial charge, and $0.10 every 19th of a mile. The first three pieces of luggage are $0.50; additional luggage is $1 per piece. Customers pay all road tolls.

PUBLICO

Publicos, also known as *guaguas* or *carros publicos,* are privately owned transport services that operate communal van routes throughout specific regions of the island. In addition, most towns are served by local *publicos. Publico* stops are usually found on a town's main plaza. This is a very inexpensive but slow way to travel because as riders get off at their appointed stops, the van will wait indefinitely until it fills up with new riders before heading to the next stop.

Publico transportation from San Juan to outlying areas is provided by **Blue Line** (787/765-7733) to Río Piedras, Aguadilla, Aguada, Moca, Isabela, and other areas; **Choferes Unidos de Ponce** (787/764-0540) to Ponce and other areas; **Lina Boricua** (787/765-1908) to Lares, Ponce, Jayuya, Utuado, San Sebastían, and other areas; **Linea Caborrojeña** (787/723-

9155) to Cabo Rojo, San Germán, and other areas; **Linea Sultana** (787/765-9377) to Mayagüez and other areas; and **Terminal de Transportación Publica** (787/250-0717) to Fajardo and other areas.

BUS

Autoridad Metropolitana de Autobuses (787/250-6064 or 787/294-0500, ext. 514, www.dtop.gov.pr/ama/mapaindex.htm) is an excellent public bus system that serves the entire metropolitan San Juan area until about 9 P.M. It's serviced by large, air-conditioned vehicles with wheelchair access, and the cost is typically a low $0.75 per fare (exact change required). Bus stops are clearly marked along the routes with green signs that say "Parada," except in Old San Juan, where you have to catch the bus at **Covadonga Bus and Trolley Terminal,** the large terminal near the cruise-ship piers at the corner of Calle la Marina and Calle J. A. Corretjer. When waiting for a bus at a Parada, it is necessary to wave at the driver to get him to stop.

RAIL

In 2005, San Juan launched **Tren Urbano,** its first long-awaited commuter train service. The system runs mostly aboveground and has 15 stations, many of which house a terrific collection of specially commissioned public art. The train connects the communities of Bayamón, the University of Puerto Rico in Río Piedras, Hato Rey, and Santurce at Sagrado Corazón University. The train runs daily 5:30 A.M.–11:30 P.M. Fares are $1.50. For information call 866/900-1284 or visit www.ati.gobierno.pr.

AIR

Local air service within Puerto Rico, including Vieques and Culebra, is provided by several airlines, including **Isla Nena Air Service** (787/863-4447, 787/863-4449, or 877/812-5144, islanenapr@centennialpr.net, www.islanena.8m.com); **Vieques Air Link** (787/741-8331 or 888/901-9247, valair@coqui.net, www.viequesairlink.com); **M&N Aviation**

(787/791-7008, www.mnaviation.com); and **Air Flamenco** (787/724-1818, airflamenco@hotmail.com, www.airflamenco.net).

FERRY

Agua Expreso (787/729-8714) provides ferry service from Pier 2 in Old San Juan to Cataño across the San Juan Bay 6 A.M.–10 P.M. The 10-minute ride costs $0.50 one way. You can also take a commuter car ferry down the Marin Pena Channel south of Santurce, which connects with the Nuevo Centro station of the Tren Urbano.

The **Puerto Rico Port Authority** (in Vieques 787/741-4761, 787/863-0705, or 800/981-2005; in Culebra 787/742-3161, 787/741-4761, 787/863-0705, or 800/981-2005; in Fajardo 787/863-0705 or

787/863-4560) operates daily passenger ferry service and weekday cargo and car ferry service between Fajardo on the east coast to the islands of Vieques and Culebra. Reservations are not accepted, but you can buy tickets in advance. Arrive no later than one hour before departure. Sometimes the ferry cannot accommodate everyone who wants to ride. The passenger ferry takes about one hour to get from Fajardo to Vieques and 1.5 hours from Fajardo to Culebra. The fare is $4.50 round-trip per person. The cargo/car ferry trip takes about two hours to get from Fajardo to Vieques and about 2.5 hours from Fajardo to Culebra. The cost is $15 for small vehicles and $19 for large vehicles. Note that car-rental agencies in Puerto Rico prohibit taking rental cars off the main island.

Sports and Recreation

Puerto Ricans are rabid sports enthusiasts and their three biggest passions can be described as the three B's: boxing, baseball, and basketball.

BOXING

Puerto Rico has produced many world-class boxers, starting with the island's first NBA world champion in the bantamweight class, Barceloneta native Sixto Escobar, who first won the title in 1934. In 1948, bantamweight boxer Juan Evangelista Venegas became the first Puerto Rican to win an Olympic medal. To date, Puerto Rico has won six Olympic medals in boxing. Isabela native Juan Ruíz made history by becoming the first Latino WBA heavyweight champion by beating Evander Holyfield in 2001.

Félix "Tito" Trinidad is considered by many to be Puerto Rico's best all-time boxer. A champion in both welterweight and middleweight divisions, Trinidad announced his retirement in 2002 with a record of 42 wins, 35 by knockout, and only two losses. Since then he has come out of retirement twice to compete

three more times, losing his last match in 2008 to Roy Jones. Trinidad's most celebrated win was the defeat of welterweight champion Oscar de La Hoya in an event called The Fight of the Millennium held at Mandalay Bay in Las Vegas in 1999. His victorious return to the island was marked by a jubilant turnout of thousands of fans who greeted him at the Luis Muñoz Marín International Airport in San Juan.

BASEBALL

With origins dating back to the late 19th century, baseball was the first team sport to emerge in Puerto Rico's modern times. Currently the island is home to a winter league featuring six regional teams from Bayamón, Caguas, Carolina, Mayagüez, Ponce, and Santurce. Each year the winning team competes in the Caribbean Series in February, playing against winning teams from Dominican Republic, Mexico, and Venezuela.

For the first time in history, opening day for Major League baseball was held in San Juan in 2001 with a game between the Toronto Blue Jays and the Texas Rangers. The game was appropriately held in San Juan's Hiram Bithorn Stadium, named after the Chicago Cubs pitcher and the first Puerto Rican to play in the Major Leagues.

Today more than 100 Major League players are from Puerto Rico, but the island's most famous player is undoubtedly Hall of Famer Roberto Clemente, who played 18 seasons with the Pittsburgh Pirates. Clemente died in an airplane crash off the coast of San Juan on New Year's Eve in 1972 on his way to deliver aid to earthquake victims in Nicaragua.

BASKETBALL

Although once extremely popular, basketball has seen a decline in interest in recent years, which has put the future of the National Superior Basketball League in jeopardy. Established in 1932, it currently consists of 12 regional teams. The island is also home to the Puerto Rican National Basketball Team, which competes in international events. The team made history in the 2004 when it defeated the U.S. Dream Team in the Olympics in Greece.

Puerto Rican athletes who have gone on to play for the NBA include Carlos Arroyo (Orlando Magic) and Jose Barea (Dallas Mavericks).

GOLF

Because of its verdant natural beauty, Puerto Rico has become something of a golf mecca for travelers. There are more than 20 courses on the island, most of them resort courses that tend to be upgraded and improved on a regular basis. The majority of courses are located on the eastern side of the island from Dorado in the north to Humacao on the southeast coast.

Puerto Rico hosted its first PGA tour, the Puerto Rico Open, in 2008 at the Trump International Golf Club in Rio Grande. The island's best known professional golfer is Juan "Chi Chi" Rodriguez. The story has it that the PGA Hall of Famer was first introduced to the game when he was a child working as a water carrier on a sugar plantation and discovered golf caddies were better paid.

HORSE RACING AND RIDING

The development of the Paso Fino breed of horse is closely intertwined with the history of Puerto Rico, starting with the arrival of Juan Ponce de León in 1508. Among the explorer's cargo were 50 horses from which the birth of the breed can be traced.

Horse races were once held in the streets of Old San Juan as far back as 1610. Today gamblers can bet on winners at the big modern Hipódromo Camarero in Canóvanas, about 10 miles east of San Juan. Races are held Wednesdays through Mondays.

Horses are still used as a mode of transportation in rural parts of the main island and throughout Vieques and Culebra. There are several stables that offer trail rides, including **Pintos R Us** (Carr. 413 Int., Barrio Puntas, Rincón, 787/361-3639, www.pintosrus.com), **Hacienda Carabalí** (Carr. 992, km 3, Luquillo, 787/889-5820 or 787/889-4954, www.hacienda carabalipuertorico.com), and **Tropical Trail Rides** (Carr. 4466, km 1.8, Isabela, 787/872-9256, info@tropicaltrailrides.com, www.tropical trailrides.com).

COCKFIGHTING

Pitting spur-wearing gamecocks against each other in a battle for the finish is a legal and a popular sport with gamblers—so much so that it's televised. Although birds do sometimes fight to the death, efforts have been made to make the sport more humane. Spurs have been shortened from 2.5 inches to 1.5 inches in length, and injured cocks may be removed from a fight.

There are more than 100 licensed cockfighting arenas in Puerto Rico. Arenas are typically found in barnlike structures in rural areas of the island, but San Juan has a modern facility in Isla Verde, Club Gallistico de Puerto Rico, which caters to a more urban crowd with food and beverage service.

WATER SPORTS

As noted throughout this book, water sports are a huge draw in Puerto Rico. Visitors come from all over the world to surf its western shores, where regional and national competitions are held. Diving and snorkeling are popular on the southwest coast and around the smaller islands off the east coast. Sailing, big game fishing, and kite-boarding are other popular sports.

TOUR OPERATORS

Puerto Rico has a slew of tour operators offering a variety of adventures that span the spectrum from guided city walks to deep-sea dives to mountain-climbing hikes. All tour companies require reservations.

Historical Walking Tours

Legends of Puerto Rico (Old San Juan, 787/605-9060, fax 787/764-2354, info@legendsofpr.com, www.legendsofpr.com) offers a variety of daytime and nighttime walking tours of Old San Juan that revolve around a variety of topics from history, pirate legends, and crafts. It also offers a Modern San Juan tour and hiking tours of the karst region, El Yunque, and mangrove forests.

Adventure Nature Tours

Acampa (1211 Ave. Piñero, San Juan, 787/706-0695, info@acampapr.com, www.acampapr.com) offers a large selection of hiking, rappelling, and rock-climbing adventure tours throughout the island. Sights include San Cristóbal Cañon, Río Tanamá, El Yunque, Toro Negro Forest, Mona Island, and Caja de Muerto Island. Acampa also sells and rents camping, hiking, and mountaineering gear at its store in San Juan.

AdvenTours (787/889-0251 or 787/831-6447, www.adventourspr.com) is an ecotourism operator offering hiking, kayaking, and biking tours out of Mayagüez, Rincón, Luquillo, and Vieques. Sights include a coffee plantation, El Yunque, archaeological sites, and more.

Aquatica Dive and Surf (Carr. 110, km 10, Gate 5, Ramey, Aguadilla, 787/890-6071, Mon.–Sat. 10 A.M.–5:30 P.M., Sun. 9 A.M.–3 P.M., aquatica@caribe.net, http://premium .caribe.net/~aquatica) has mountain-bike tours of the west coast as well as dive and snorkel trips and surf instruction.

Expediciones Palenque (787/823-4354 or 787/306-4382, info@expedicionespalenque .com, www.expedicionespalenque.com) offers a variety of daylong spelunking, rappelling, body-rafting, and base-jumping tours in the Cordillera Central. This is strictly for adventure travelers in good physical condition. Sights include Río Tanamá, Yuyú Cave, Tunnel Cave, and Arch Cave.

San Cristóbal Hiking Tour (P.O. Box 678, Barranquitas, PR 00794, 787/857-2094 or 787/647-3402, walimai@hotmail.com, http://barranquitaspr.net/viajes/english.htm) offers a variety of weekend excursions in San Cristóbal Cañon from moderate hiking and biking tours to extreme rappelling and mountaineering tours. It also offers tours to Bosque Estatal Toro Negro and other natural sights in the area.

Dive, Snorkeling, and Boating Tours

Adventure Tourmarine (Carr. 102, Joyuda, 787/375-2625 or 787/255-2525, tourmarinepr@yahoo.com, www.tourmarinepr.com) offers snorkeling, dive, and fishing tours along the west coast, as well as two-day camping trips to Mona Island.

Aventuras Tierra Adentro (787/766-0470, www.aventuraspr.com) offers daylong adventure expeditions into the wild. Saturdays are devoted to rock climbing, rappelling, and body-rafting in a canyon. Sundays are reserved for hiking, rappelling, and swimming in the Río Camuy cave system. This adventure is for the physically fit and adventurous.

East Island Excursions (Puerto Del Rey Marina, Fajardo, 877/937-4386 or 787/860-3434, fax 787/860-1656, www.eastwindcats .com) offers sailing and snorkel trips aboard a 62-foot sailing catamaran with a glass bottom and a slide, a 65-foot power catamaran, or a 45-foot catamaran. Excursions are available to Vieques, Culebra, Culebrita, and St. Thomas.

Encantos Ecotours Suroeste (Placita La Parguera, 787/808-0005 or 787/272-0005, fax 787/789-1730) offers nighttime kayak tours of Bahía Fosforescente in La Parguera, as well as

© JOHN W. THOMPSON

diving off the coast of Rincón

snorkeling, bike, and hiking tours in Bosque Estatal de Guánica.

Island Adventures (787/741-0720, Esperanza, Vieques, biobay@biobay.com, www.biobay.com) offers nighttime tours of the bioluminescent Mosquito Bay aboard an electric pontoon boat.

Las Tortugas Adventures (4 Calle La Puntilla, San Juan, 787/725-5169, info@kayak-pr .com, www.kayak-pr.com) offers a variety of half- and full-day snorkel and kayak tours on the east coast, launching from Bahía Las Croabas in Fajardo. Tours include Las Cabezas de San Juan in Fajardo, the bioluminescent lagoon, mangrove forest in Piñones, and excursions to Cayo Icacos, Cayo Diablo, and Monkey Island.

Mona Aquatics (Calle José de Diego, next to Club Naútico, Boquerón, 787/851-2185, fax 787/254-0604, www.monaaquatics.com) offers dive tours, sunset cruises, and nighttime tours of Bahía Fosforescente. It also provides overnight camping and diving trips to Mona Island.

Sea Ventures Dive Center (www.dive puertorico.com; Carr. 3, km 51.2, Fajardo, 787/863-3483 or 800/739-3483, www.dive fajardo.com; Copamarina Beach Resort, Carr. 333, km 6.5, Guánica, 877/348-3267 or 800/468-4553, www.divecopamarina.com; and 110 Harbour Dr., Palmas del Mar, Humacao, 787/781-8086 or 787/739-3483, www.dive palmasdelmar.com) has three locations from which it offers a variety of diving and snorkeling tours along the east and southwestern coasts. Destinations include Vieques, Culebra, and Cayo Santiago (Monkey Island) in Naguabo.

Taíno Divers (Black Eagle Marina, Carr. 413, 787/823-6429, www.tainodivers.com, daily 9 A.M.–6 P.M.) offers daily snorkeling, dive, and whale-watching tours along the west coast. Fishing charters are also available.

Fishing Tours
Caribbean Fly Fishing (61 Calle Orquideas, Esperanza, Vieques, 787/741-1337 or 787/450-3744, flyfish@coqui.net, www.caribbean flyfishingco.com) offers inshore kingfish,

amberjack, barracuda, pompano, and tarpon fishing trips on a 21-foot Ranger bay boat.

Light Tackle Adventure (Boquerón pier, Cabo Rojo, 787/849-1430 or 787/547-7380, www.lighttackleadventure.8k.com) specializes in light-tackle and fly-fishing excursions. It also provides kayak tours of the Cabo Rojo salt flats, Boquerón Bay, Joyuda, and La Parguera. Bird-watching tours on the Cabo Rojo salt flats are also available.

Tropical Fishing Charters (Sea Lovers Marina, Fajardo, 787/379-4461, www.tropical fishingcharters.com) offers year-round big-game fishing, specializing in blue marlin, from May to October.

Surfing Schools

Aquatica Dive and Surf (Carr. 110, km 10, Gate 5, Ramey, Aguadilla, 787/890-6071, Mon.–Sat. 10 A.M.–5:30 P.M., Sun. 9 A.M.–3 P.M., aquatica@caribe.net, http://premium.caribe.net/~aquatica) offers surfing instruction as well as mountain-bike tours and dive and snorkeling trips. They are accredited by the National Surf Schools and Instructors Association.

WOW Surfing School (San Juan, 787/955-6059, info@gosurfpr.com, www.gosurfpr.com) was founded by international surf champion William "Chino" Sue-A-Quan. Accredited by the National Surf Schools and Instructors Association, it offers instruction at two locations: Isla Verde just east of the Ritz Carlton, and Playa Escambron by Hotel Normandie in Puerta de Tierra between Condado and Old San Juan.

Rincón Surf School (787/823-0610, info@rinconsurfschool.com, www.rinconsurfschool.com) conducts a surf school for beginners and experienced surfers looking to up their game. You can get a 2.5-hour private lesson, or between one and five full days of class instruction. It also offers a Surf & Yoga Retreat for women.

Surf 787 Summer Camp (Carr. 115, Rincón, 787/448-0968 or 949/547-6340, www.surf787.com) offers accommodations and surf instruction for adults only from December through April. From June through September, children ages 11–17 can attend the kid's day and overnight surf camp featuring a full day of surf instruction, three meals a day, and evening activities.

Accommodations and Food

Accommodations in Puerto Rico run the gamut from world-class luxury resorts to rustic self-serve guesthouses, which offer little more than a bed to crash on and a help-yourself attitude when it comes to getting clean linens, ice, and other items you might need. In between are a variety of American hotel chains in all price ranges and a number of small, independent hotels and inns. There are also some unique hotels of historic significance, such as **El Convento** in San Juan, a former Carmelite convent built in 1651, and **Hacienda Gripiñas,** a former coffee plantation in Jayuya located high up in the Cordillera Central mountains.

Outside San Juan there are accommodations designated by the Puerto Rico Tourism Co. as *paradores* (www.gotoparadores.com),

independently owned and operated country inns. There are 18 properties in all, with the largest concentration located on the western half of the island. Note, though, the designation of *parador* is not a recommendation, and the quality of the properties are wildly divergent between the superior and the inferior. For details, see www.gotoparadores.com.

ACCOMMODATION RATES

Overnight stays in Puerto Rico can range from $39 at Hotel Colonial in Mayagüez to $1,070 for a Cliffside suite at the **Horned Dorset Primavera** in Rincón. Generally, however, room rates fall between $100 and $250. There are no traditional all-inclusive resorts in Puerto Rico, where meals are included with the price of the room, although Copamarina Resort in Guaníca and the Horned Dorset Primavera in Rincón offer all-inclusive packages.

A tax is applied to all accommodations, but many properties include the tax in the rate, so ask to be sure. Typically the tax is 9 percent of the rate, but hotels with casinos charge 13 percent tax. Resorts usually add on a resort service fee, which is typically an additional 9 percent.

Many accommodations offer two rates—the most expensive is during high season (typically January–April), the least expensive is during low season (May–December). If you're traveling during high season, be sure to book your room early or you may find your options limited. Note that the high season for destinations and accommodations catering to Puerto Rican travelers may be during the summer months. Some accommodations have a third rate charged during the Christmas holiday season, which may be even more pricey than the high-season rates. Most accommodations may be booked online.

PUERTO RICAN CUISINE

Puerto Rican cuisine is a hearty fare called *cocina criolla,* which means creole cooking. A typical *criolla* dish contains fried or stewed meat, chicken, or seafood, combined with or accompanied by rice and beans. Stewed dishes usually begin with a seasoning mix called *sofrito,* which includes salt pork, ham, lard, onions, green peppers, chili peppers, cilantro, and garlic. *Adobo,* a seasoning mix comprising peppercorn, oregano, garlic, salt, olive oil, and vinegar or fresh lime juice, is rubbed into meats and poultry before frying or grilling. Tomato sauce, capers, pimento-stuffed olives, and raisins are also common ingredients in Puerto Rican cuisine. Two items are integral to the preparation of *cocina criolla*—a *caldero,* a cast-iron or cast-aluminum cauldron with a round base, straight sides, and a lid; and a mortar and pestle, which is used to grind herbs and seeds.

The plantain is a major staple of the Puerto Rican diet. Similar to a banana but larger, firmer, and less sweet, it is prepared in a variety

of ways. *Tostones* is a popular plantain dish. The fruit is sliced into rounds, fried until soft, mashed flat, and fried again until crisp. They're typically eaten like bread, as a starchy accompaniment to a meal. It's sometimes served with a tomato-garlic dipping sauce or something akin to Thousand Island dressing.

But probably the most popular way plantain is served is in *mofongo,* a mashed mound of fried, unripe plantain, garlic, olive oil, and *chicharrón* (pork crackling). *Mofongo relleno* is *mofongo* stuffed with meat, poultry, or seafood, and *piononos* are appetizer-size stuffed *mofongo. Amarillos,* which translates as "yellows," is the same thing as the Cuban *maduras* and is made from overripe plantains that have been sliced lengthwise and fried in oil until soft and sweetly caramelized. Bananas are also popular in *cocina criolla,* especially *guineitos en escabeche,* a green-banana salad marinated with pimento-stuffed olives in vinegar and lime juice.

Rice also figures prominently in Puerto Rican food. Most restaurants serving *comida criolla* will list several *arroz* (rice) dishes such as *arroz con habichuelas* (beans), *arroz con pollo* (chicken), *arroz con juyeyes* (crab), *arroz con camarones* (shrimp), and *arroz con gandules* (pigeon peas). Typically in this dish the ingredients have been stewed until damp and sticky in a mixture of tomatoes and *sofrito.* A similar dish is paella, a Spanish import featuring an assortment of seafood. *Asopao,* a thick stew, is another popular rice dish, and *arroz con leche* (milk) is a favorite dessert similar to rice pudding.

Pork is very popular in Puerto Rico, and it has a variety of names: *lechon, pernil, cerdo.* But chicken and beef are common, and occasionally you'll come across *cabro* (goat) and guinea hen. Popular meat dishes include *carne guisada* (beef stew), *chuletas fritas* (fried pork chops), *carne empanado* (breaded and fried steak), *carne encebollado* (fried steak smothered in cooked onions), and *churrasco,* an Argentine-style grilled skirt steak. Restaurants along the coast usually specialize in a wide range of seafood, including *camarones* (shrimp), *langosta* (lobster), *pulpo* (octopus), and *carrucho* (conch). Fish—typically fried whole—can be found on nearly every menu, the choices usually being *chillo* (red snapper), *dorado* (mahimahi), or occasionally *bacalao* (dried salted cod).

Interestingly, you'll usually find the exact same dessert options at most restaurants. They will include flan (a baked caramel custard), *helados* (ice cream), and *dulce de guayaba* (guava in syrup) or *dulce de lechosa* (papaya in syrup) served with *queso del pais,* a soft white cheese. Occasionally restaurants will offer *tembleque,* a coconut custard, particularly around the Christmas holidays.

An American-style breakfast is fairly commonly found, although Puerto Ricans often eat their eggs and ham in toasted sandwiches called *bocadillos.* American coffee can sometimes be found, but the traditional *café con leche,* a strong brew with steamed milk, is highly recommended. *Bocadillos* are often eaten for lunch, particularly the *Cubano,* a toasted sandwich with ham, roasted pork, and cheese. The *media noche* is similar to the Cubano, but it's served on a softer, sweeter bread.

Although American fast-food restaurant chains can be found in Puerto Rico, the island has its own traditional style of fast-food fare often sold from roadside kiosks. Offerings usually include fried savory pies and fritters made from various combinations of plantain, meat, chicken, cheese, crab, potato, and fish.

Puerto Rican Cocktails

The legal drinking age in Puerto Rico is 18. Although all types of alcoholic beverages are available, rum is the number 1 seller. There are three types of rum: white or silver, which are dry, pale, and light-bodied; gold, which is amber-colored and aged in charred oak casks; and black, a strong, 151-proof variety often used in flambés. Favorite rum drinks are Cuba Libre, a simple mix of rum and Coke with a wedge of lime; piña colada, a frozen blended combination of rum, cream of coco, and pineapple juice; and mojito, a Cuban import made from rum, simple syrup, club soda, fresh lime juice, and tons of fresh muddled mint.

When it comes to beer, Puerto Ricans prefer a light pilsner, and you can't go wrong with Medalla. It's brewed in Mayagüez and won the bronze in its class at the World Beer Cup 1999. Presidente beer, made in the Dominican Republic, is also popular.

Conduct and Customs

ETIQUETTE

A certain formality permeates life in Puerto Rico. It's customary to acknowledge one another, including shop owners, with a greeting: *buenas dias* for good day, *buenas tardes* for good afternoon, and *buenas noches* for good evening. If you approach someone to ask the time or for directions, preface your question with *perdóneme* (excuse me). When a waiter delivers your meal, he or she will say *buen provecho,* and it's customary to say the same to diners already eating when you enter a restaurant.

Traditionally Puerto Ricans are exceedingly cordial. Even in San Juan, rudeness is rarely encountered. If you're lost or need help, they will cheerfully point you in the right direction. But Puerto Ricans don't typically display much interest in fraternizing with tourists. Americans who venture into bars catering primarily to the local dating scene may get a chilly reception if they're perceived as romantic rivals. The exception is bars that depend on the tourist dollar or that are in towns with a large U.S. expatriate population, such as Rincón or Vieques, where you're likely to know everybody's name by the time you leave.

Dress appropriately for the occasion. Although most upscale restaurants don't necessarily require a coat and tie, some do, so inquire. Otherwise, a well-groomed, nicely attired appearance is expected. And never wear beach attire, skimpy halter tops, or short shorts anywhere but the beach or pool. Although young fashionable Puerto Rican women may sometimes dress provocatively, visiting American women are advised to use some modesty or risk attracting unwanted male attention.

To the relief of nonsmokers, smoking has been banned in all restaurants, lounges, clubs, and bars in Puerto Rico, with the exception of establishments with outdoor seating. Public drinking has also been banned.

MACHISMO

Machismo appears to be becoming somewhat a thing of the past, particularly in San Juan, where mainland American influence is heaviest. The days of men verbally harassing or flashing young women is no longer a common occurrence, although vestiges of it remain around some wilderness beaches where perpetrators are far from the *policía*'s eyes. Nevertheless, it is interesting that *cabron* is a favored, mock-aggressive greeting among many men in Puerto Rico. Technically it means "goat," but its idiomatic translation is a man who's cuckolded by a cheating wife. There was a time when calling a man a *cabron* was a sure way to get a black eye, and used in the heat of an argument, it still is. But today it's more commonly used as a term of affection between male friends.

Meanwhile, the flip side of machismo—Old World chivalry—is still very much alive and well in Puerto Rico, especially among older men who appear to take pride in their gestures of kindness toward women.

CONCEPTS OF TIME

San Juan operates much like any big American city. The pace of life is fast, service is expedient, and everybody's in a hurry. But the farther you get away from San Juan, and most markedly in Culebra and Vieques, things tend to operate on "island time"—that is, at an extremely leisurely pace. You may be the only person in the restaurant, but it may still take 30 minutes or longer to receive your meal. Posted hours of operation are more suggestion than reality. Visitors are best advised to chill out and accept that this is just the way things are in Puerto Rico. If fawning service is required to have a good time, then stick with the resorts.

Tips for Travelers

VISAS AND OFFICIALDOM

No passports or visas are required for U.S. citizens entering Puerto Rico. Those visiting the island from other countries must have the same documentation required to enter the United States. Visitors from the United Kingdom are required to have a British passport but do not need a visa unless their passports are endorsed with British Subject, British Dependent Territories Citizen, British Protected Person, British Overseas Citizen, or British National (Overseas) Citizen. A return ticket or proof of onward travel is necessary. Australian visitors must have a passport and can stay up to 90 days without a visa.

CUSTOMS

Travelers must pass through customs at the airport in Puerto Rico before leaving the island to make sure no prohibited plants or fruits are taken off the island. Permitted items include avocados, coconuts, papayas, and plantains. Mangoes, passion fruits, and plants potted in soil are not permitted. Pre-Columbian items or items from Afghanistan, Cuba, Iran, Iraq, Libya, Serbia, Montenegro, and Sudan may not be brought into the United States. There are no customs duties on items brought into the United States from Puerto Rico.

EMBASSIES

Because Puerto Rico is a commonwealth, there are no U.S. embassies or consulates here. Several countries are represented locally by consulates, though, including the United Kingdom (Torre Chardon, Suite 1236, 350 Ave. Chardon, San Juan, PR 00918, 787/758-9828, fax 787/758-9809, btopr1@coqui.net) and Canada (33 Calle Bolivia, 7th Floor, Hato Rey, San Juan, PR 00917-2010, 787/759-6629, fax 787/294-1205).

GAY AND LESBIAN TRAVELERS

Most likely due to the predominant influence of the Catholic church in Puerto Rican society, homosexuality is illegal on the island; however, the law is rarely, if ever, enforced. Despite Puerto Rico's strong patriarchal society in which a traditional sense of manhood is highly prized, homosexuality is generally accepted across the board, even in rural areas. In fact, San Juan is something of a mecca for the LGBT traveler. There are many hotels and nightclubs that cater specifically to a gay and lesbian clientele, and certain beaches are known to attract a gay crowd. San Juan is also a popular port of call for gay cruises.

WOMEN TRAVELING ALONE

Puerto Rico is perfectly safe for women traveling alone or in groups. But precautions should be taken. Dressing provocatively can attract catcalls and other forms of unwanted attention, and bathing suits should never be worn anywhere but at the beach or pool. Women traveling solo should avoid remote wilderness beaches and late-night bars that cater primarily to locals. Safety in numbers is a good rule to follow when going out at night.

STUDY AND VOLUNTEER OPPORTUNITIES

Spanish Abroad (5112 N. 40th St., Suite 203, Phoenix, AZ 85018, 888/722-7623 or 602/778-6791, www.spanishabroad.com) offers Spanish-language immersion classes with homestays in

Hato Rey, San Juan. The **Vieques Humane Society** (787/741-0209, viequeshumane society@hotmail.com, www.viequeshs.org) offers a private room, shared bath and kitchen (and limited transportation) in exchange for volunteering to work with animals and/or a clinic for 20 hours a week.

WHAT TO TAKE

The activities you plan to pursue in Puerto Rico will dictate what you will need to pack. If you plan to sunbathe by day and hit the discos by night, pack your swimsuit and trendiest club wear. If a shopping marathon is on the agenda, pack comfortable walking shoes and an empty duffel bag for carrying back your loot. If you want to go hiking in the mountains, long lightweight pants and hiking boots are in order. If you stay in the mountains overnight, bring a light jacket.

No matter what you do, bring sunscreen, bug spray, a wide-brimmed hat, an umbrella, and some bottled water. You'll need protection from the sun and the occasional sand-flea attack while you're on the beach. And if you're traveling during the rainy season, expect a brief shower every day. You'll be grateful for some light raingear such as a poncho and waterproof shoes or sandals.

Light cotton fabrics are always recommended. Puerto Rico's temperatures fluctuate between 76–88°F on the coastal plains and 73–78°F in the mountain region. The humidity hovers around a steady 80 percent. Note that wearing bathing suits or short shorts is inappropriate anyplace other than the pool or beach, and a few restaurants require a jacket and tie.

If you plan to navigate the island by car, bring a Spanish-English dictionary and a current, detailed road map. Just about every business on the island accepts credit cards and debit cards, and virtually every town has at least one ATM. The only time you'll need cash is if you plan to shop or buy food from roadside vendors, which you definitely should do.

HEALTH AND SAFETY

The quality of health care in Puerto Rico is comparable to that in the United States, and all major towns have one or more hospital and pharmacy, including Walgreens. Unlike in Mexico, the water is as safe to drink as it is in the United States, and fruits and vegetables are fine to eat.

There are no major health issues facing the island, save the occasional outbreak of dengue fever, a viral infection spread by mosquitoes. Symptoms include fever, headache, body aches, and a rash, and it lasts about seven days. In rare cases it can be fatal—usually when the victim has been previously infected with the disease. Visitors are at low risk for contracting dengue fever unless there's an active outbreak, but using mosquito repellent is a good preventative measure.

A visitor's biggest physical threat is most likely sunstroke. Summer can be brutally hot, especially in urban areas. It's important to drink lots of water, especially if you're doing a lot of walking or other physical activity. A hat and sunscreen are recommended. Or you could do as some of the local women do and use umbrellas to keep the beating rays at bay.

Crime

Most of the crime in Puerto Rico revolves around the drug trade. The island is on a drug-transportation route that begins in Venezuela and passes through the Dominican Republic and into Puerto Rico on the way to the U.S. mainland. Add to that a poverty level of 44 percent, and you have a certain level of desperation. Ponce and Loíza have experienced high rates of murder, but most crimes are of the petty street variety—especially theft from automobiles or snatched purses. The street drug trade in San Juan operates out of La Perla, a former squatter's village outside the city wall beside Old San Juan.

Prostitution is illegal in Puerto Rico, although there's at least one strip club in San Juan that's reputed to be a bordello. Prostitutes do sometimes work the streets—even in quiet towns such as Mayagüez—and they're often more likely to be transgendered men than women.

The most common threat to visitors is having their possessions stolen from a rental car. Never leave anything of value visible in your car and always keep it locked. There are also occasional reports of carjackings and stolen vehicles. The police patrol San Juan regularly, and they keep their blue lights flashing all night long to announce their presence. For any emergency—crime, fire, wreck, injury—dial 911 for help.

Information and Services

MAPS AND TOURIST INFORMATION

Before you go, contact the **Puerto Rico Tourism Company** (800/866-7827) to request that it send you free of charge its extensive tourist-information packet, which includes brochures, maps, pictures, and details on hotels, tours, and attractions. It's a great planning tool. You can also visit its website at www.gotopuertorico.com for more information. Another great site is www.travelandsports.com.

Once you've arrived on the island, visit the Puerto Rico Tourism Company's information center, in Old San Juan near the cruise-ship piers in a small yellow colonial structure called **La Casita** (Plaza de Dársenes, Old San Juan, 787/722-5208 or 787/724-6829, fax 787/722-5208, www.gotopuertorico .com, Sat.–Wed. 9 A.M.–8 P.M., Thurs.–Fri. 9 A.M.–6:30 P.M.). It's not only a great source for maps and promotional brochures on various tourist sites, hotels, and tours, but you can also sip on a free rum cocktail. Call 800/866-7827 to order travel information.

For information specifically on the capital city, visit the **Tourism Office of San Juan**

(250 Calle Teután at Calle San Justo, Old San Juan, 787/721-6363, Mon.–Sat. 8 A.M.–4 P.M.). It offers self-guided audio tours of Old San Juan in English and Spanish for $9.99 per person. There's also a small selection of promotional materials for local tourist sites, hotels, and tours.

Many of the island's towns have their own tourist offices, usually on or near the plaza and often in the *alcadia* (city hall) building. Unfortunately, many of them tend to be open sporadically, despite posted hours of operation.

There are also free maps and travel publications, such as *Places to Go, Bienvenidos,* and *Qué Pasa!* magazines, available at many stores, restaurants, and hotels.

For a detailed road map of the island, International Travel Maps of Canada (www .itmb.com) is your best option, but you'll have to order online before you go. The same goes for National Geographic's excellent illustrated map of the Caribbean National Forest, available from its website, www.nationalgeographic .com/maps.

MONEY

Puerto Rico's form of currency is the U.S. dollar, which is sometimes referred to as *peso*. Full-service banks with ATMs are plentiful, the most common one being Banco Popular. Banking hours are Monday–Friday 9 A.M.–3:30 P.M. Credit cards and debit cards are accepted virtually everywhere. The only time cash is required is when buying items from roadside vendors and occasionally even they will accept plastic.

A sales tax, between 5.5 percent and 6.7 percent depending on the municipality, has recently been instituted in Puerto Rico, and hotel taxes can vary depending on the type of property. Hotels with casinos charge 11 percent tax, and hotels without casinos charge 9 percent tax. There may also be resort fees, energy surcharge fees, and other charges. When determining the price of a hotel room, ask whether or not the tax is included in the stated price.

Tipping practices are the same as in the United States—15–20 percent of the bill, unless a gratuity has already been added.

COMMUNICATIONS AND MEDIA
Postal Service
Mail service is provided by the U.S. Postal Service. Although mailing letters and postcards to and from the island costs the same as in the United States, international rates apply when shipping items to the island. United Parcel Service and overnight shipping companies such as Federal Express also operate on the island.

Telephone
Puerto Rico has one area code—787—and it must always be dialed when placing a call. Nevertheless, all calls are not local, so long-distance rates may apply. U.S. cell phones with nationwide service should function fine in Puerto Rico.

Newspapers and Magazines
Daily newspapers include **El Nuevo Dia** and **Primera Hora,** both in Spanish. Ponce has a newsweekly, **La Perla del Sur. The New York Times** and **The Miami Herald** can be commonly found in hotels and newsstands in San Juan.

Television
Broadcasting is regulated by the U.S. Federal Communications Commission. There are three commercial channels: **Telemundo** (channel 2), **Televicentro** (channel 4), and **Univision** (channel 11), and one public channel—**TUTV** (channel 6). Local programming features sitcoms, talk shows, news, and soap operas, all in Spanish. Multichannel cable and satellite TV is also available.

Radio
- **WRTU:** 89.7 FM; University of Puerto Rico music, news, culture.
- **Cadena Salsoul:** 98.5 FM (San Juan), 101.1 FM (south), 100.3 FM (west); salsa.

- **WOSO:** 1030 AM; news, information, entertainment sports in English.
- **Alfa Rock:** 105.7 FM (northeast), 106.1 FM (southwest); rock music.
- **La Mega Station:** 106.9 FM (San Juan); pop music.

WEIGHTS AND MEASURES

Puerto Rico uses the metric system. Gasoline is bought in liters (1 gallon = 3.7 liters), and distance is measured in kilometers (1 mile = 1.61 kilometers). The exception is speed, which is measured in miles per hour.

Time Zone

Puerto Rico observes Atlantic standard time and does not practice daylight saving time. Therefore, time in Puerto Rico is one hour later than Eastern standard time November–March and the same as Eastern daylight time from the second Sunday in March until the first Sunday in November.

RESOURCES

Glossary

ajillo garlic
al centro downtown
alto stop
amarillos fried ripe plantains
appertivos appetizers
arroz rice
asado roasted
asopoa rice stew
autopista divided limited-access highway
avenida avenue
azucar sugar
bacalao dry salted codfish
bahía bay
balneario publicly maintained beach
barbacoa meat grilled over a fire or charcoal; also the name of the grill
barrio neighborhood
batata white yam
batey ceremonial ball field used by Taíno Indians
bebida beverage
bocadillo sandwich, typically toasted
bohique Taíno spiritual leader
Borinquen Taíno name for Puerto Rico
bosque estatal public forest
botánica shop that sells herbs, scents, and candles used by practitioners of *espiritismo* or *santería*
cabro goat
cacique Taíno chief
café coffee
calle street
camarones shrimp
capilla chapel
carne beef

carretera road
carrucho conch
cayos cays, islets
cebollado onion
cemi Taíno amulet
cerdo pig
chillo red snapper
chorizo spicy pork sausage
chuletas chops, typically pork
churrasco grilled, marinated skirt steak
cocina criolla Puerto Rican cuisine
coco coconut
coqui tiny tree frog that emits an eponymous chirp
criolla creole; means "Puerto Rican-style"
cruce crossroads
cruzar to cross
cuadras blocks
cubano toasted sandwich with pork, ham, cheese, and pickles
derecha right
derecho straight
doble turn
dorado mahimahi
empanado breaded and fried meat
ensalada salad
espiritismo Taíno-based religion that believes deities reside in nature
esquina corner
estacionamiento parking
este east
faro lighthouse
fiestas patronales festivals that celebrate the patron saints of towns
frito fried

gandules pigeon peas
guayaba guava
habichuelas beans
helado ice cream
hielo ice
horno baked
izquierda left
jámon ham
jíbaro rural mountain resident, hillbilly
juevos eggs
juyeyes crab
laguna lagoon
langosta lobster
leche milk
lechon pork
lechonera restaurant serving pit-roasted pork and other local delicacies
lechosa papaya
lejos far
luces traffic lights
luz traffic light
malécon sea-wall promenade
mantequilla butter
mariscos seafood
máscaras masks
media noche sandwich similar to a *cubano*, but on a softer, sweeter bread
mercardo market
mofongo cooked unripe plantain mashed with garlic and olive oil
mogote conical, haystack-shaped hill
mondongo beef tripe stew
mundillo handmade lace that's created with bobbins
muralla wall
ñame yam
norte north
Nuyorican a Puerto Rican person who migrated to New York
oeste west
pan bread
panadería bakery
panapen breadfruit
papas potatoes
parador privately owned inn in a rural area

parque park
pechuga de pollo chicken breast
pernil pork
pescado fish
picadillo seasoned ground beef used to stuff *empanadillas*
pimiento pepper
piña pineapple
playa beach
postre dessert
publicos public transportation in vans that pick up multiple riders along an established route
pueblo town center
pulpo octopus
queso cheese
queso del pais soft white cow cheese
relleno stuffed food item, as in *mofongo relleno*
reserva forestal forest reserve
sal salt
salida exit
santería Afro-Caribbean–based religion that observes multiple gods
santos small wood carvings of Catholic saints
setas mushrooms
sopa soup
sorullos or sorullitos fried cheese and corn-meal sticks
sur south
Taíno people who were indigenous to Puerto Rico when it became a Spanish colony
tocino bacon
tostones twice-fried, flattened pieces of plantain
vaya go
vejigante horned mask worn in festivals
yautia taro root, similar to a potato
yuca cassava, a root vegetable

Abbreviations

Ave. Avenida
Bo. Barrio
Carr. Carretera
Int. approaching intersection, or interior route

Spanish Phrasebook

Your Puerto Rico adventure will be more fun if you use a little Spanish. Puerto Ricans, although they may smile at your funny accent, will appreciate your halting efforts to break the ice and transform yourself from a foreigner to a potential friend.

Spanish commonly uses 30 letters – the familiar English 26, plus four straightforward additions: *ch*, *ll*, *ñ*, and *rr*, which are explained in *Consonants* below.

PRONUNCIATION

Once you learn them, Spanish pronunciation rules – in contrast to English – don't change. Spanish vowels generally sound softer than in English. (Note: The capitalized syllables below receive stronger accent.)

Vowels

a like ah, as in "hah": *agua* "AH-gooah" (water), *pan* "PAHN" (bread), and *casa* "CAH-sah" (house)

e like ay, as in "may": *mesa* "MAY-sah" (table), *tela* "TAY-lah" (cloth), and *de* "DAY" (of, from)

i like ee, as in "need": *diez* "dee-AYZ" (ten), *comida* "ko-MEE-dah" (meal), and *fin* "FEEN" (end)

o like oh, as in "go": *peso* "PAY-soh" (weight), *ocho* "OH-choh" (eight), and *poco* "POH-koh" (a bit)

u like oo, as in "cool": *uno* "OO-noh" (one), *cuarto* "KOOAHR-toh" (room), and *usted* "oos-TAYD" (you); when it follows a *q* the **u** is silent; when it follows an *h* or has an umlaut, it's pronounced like "w"

Consonants

b, d, f, k, l, m, n, p, q, s, t, v, w, x, y, z, and ch
pronounced almost as in English; **h** occurs, but is silent – not pronounced at all

c like k as in "keep": *cuarto* "KOOAR-toh" (room), Tepic "tay-PEEK" (capital of Nayarit state); when it precedes *e* or *i*, pronounce *c* like s as in "sit": *cerveza* "sayr-VAY-sah" (beer), *encima* "ayn-SEE-mah" (atop)

g like g as in "gift" when it precedes *a, o, u,* or a consonant: *gato* "GAH-toh" (cat), *hago* "AH-goh" (I do, make); otherwise, pronounce *g* like h as in "hat": *giro* "HEE-roh" (money order), *gente* "HAYN-tay" (people)

j like h, as in "has": *Jueves* "HOOAY-vays" (Thursday), *mejor* "may-HOR" (better)

ll like y, as in "yes": *toalla* "toh-AH-yah" (towel), *ellos* "AY-yohs" (they, them)

ñ like ny, as in "canyon": *año* "AH-nyo" (year), *señor* "SAY-nyor" (Mr., sir)

r lightly trilled, with tongue at the roof of your mouth like a very light English *d*, as in "ready": *pero* "PAY-doh" (but), *tres* "TDAYS" (three), *cuatro* "KOOAH-tdoh" (four).

rr like a Spanish *r*, but with much more emphasis and trill. Let your tongue flap. Practice with *burro* (donkey), *carretera* (highway), and *Carrillo* (proper name), then really let go with *ferrocarril* (railroad).

Note: The single small but common exception to all of the above is the pronunciation of Spanish **y** when it's being used as the Spanish word for "and," as in "Ron y Kathy." In this case, pronounce it like the English ee, as in "keep": Ron "ee" Kathy (Ron and Kathy).

Accent

The rule for accent, the relative stress given to syllables within a given word, is straightforward. If a word ends in a vowel, an *n*, or an *s*, accent the next-to-last syllable; if not, accent the last syllable.

Pronounce *gracias* "GRAH-seeahs" (thank you), *orden* "OHR-dayn" (order), and *carretera* "kah-ray-TAY-rah" (highway) with stress on the next-to-last syllable.

Otherwise, accent the last syllable: *venir* "vay-NEER" (to come), *ferrocarril* "fay-roh-cah-REEL" (railroad), and *edad* "ay-DAHD" (age).

Exceptions to the accent rule are always marked with an accent sign: á, é, í, ó, or ú, such as *teléfono* "tay-LAY-foh-noh" (telephone), *jabón* "hah-BON" (soap), and *rápido* "RAH-pee-doh" (rapid).

BASIC AND COURTEOUS EXPRESSIONS

Most Spanish-speaking people consider formalities important. Whenever approaching anyone for information or some other reason, do not forget the appropriate salutation – good morning, good evening, etc. Standing alone, the greeting *hola* (hello) can sound brusque.

Hello. *Hola.*
Good morning. *Buenos días.*
Good afternoon. *Buenas tardes.*
Good evening. *Buenas noches.*
How are you? *¿Cómo está usted?*
Very well, thank you. *Muy bien, gracias.*
OK; good. *Bien.*
Not OK; bad. *Mal; feo.*
So-so. *Más o menos.*
And you? *¿Y usted?*
Thank you. *Gracias.*
Thank you very much. *Muchas gracias.*
You're very kind. *Muy amable.*
You're welcome. *De nada.*
Good-bye. *Adios.*
See you later. *Hasta luego.*
please *por favor*
yes *sí*
no *no*
I don't know. *No sé.*
Just a moment, please. *Momentito, por favor.*
Excuse me. *Disculpe* or *Con permiso.*
I'm sorry. *Lo siento.*
Pleased to meet you. *Mucho gusto.*
How do you say...in Spanish? *¿Cómo se dice...en español?*
What is your name? *¿Cómo se llama usted?*
Do you speak English? *¿Habla usted inglés?*
Is English spoken here? (Does anyone here speak English?) *¿Se habla inglés?*
I don't speak Spanish well. *No hablo bien el español.*
I don't understand. *No entiendo.*
My name is ... *Me llamo ...*
Would you like ... *¿Quisiera usted ...*
Let's go to ... *Vamos a ...*

TERMS OF ADDRESS

When in doubt, use the formal *usted* (you) as a form of address.

I *yo*
you (formal) *usted*
you (familiar) *tú*
he/him *él*
she/her *ella*
we/us *nosotros*
you (plural) *ustedes*
they/them *ellos* (all males or mixed gender); *ellas* (all females)
Mr., sir *señor*
Mrs., madam *señora*
miss, young lady *señorita*
wife *esposa*
husband *esposo*
friend *amigo* (male); *amiga* (female)
sweetheart *novio* (male); *novia* (female)
son; daughter *hijo; hija*
brother; sister *hermano; hermana*
father; mother *padre; madre*
grandfather; grandmother *abuelo; abuela*

TRANSPORTATION

Where is ... ? *¿Dónde está ... ?*
How far is it to ... ? *¿A cuánto está ... ?*
from...to ... *de...a ...*
How many blocks? *¿Cuántas cuadras?*
Where (Which) is the way to ... ? *¿Dónde está el camino a ... ?*
the bus station *la terminal de autobuses*
the bus stop *la parada de autobuses*
Where is this bus going? *¿Adónde va este autobús?*
the taxi stand *la parada de taxis*
the train station *la estación de ferrocarril*
the boat *el barco*
the airport *el aeropuerto*
I'd like a ticket to ... *Quisiera un boleto a ...*
first (second) class *primera (segunda) clase*
roundtrip *ida y vuelta*
reservation *reservación*
baggage *equipaje*
Stop here, please. *Pare aquí, por favor.*
the entrance *la entrada*
the exit *la salida*

the **ticket office** *la oficina de boletos*
(very) near; far *(muy) cerca; lejos*
to; toward *a*
by; through *por*
from *de*
the right *la derecha*
the left *la izquierda*
straight ahead *derecho; directo*
in front *en frente*
beside *al lado*
behind *atrás*
the corner *la esquina*
the stoplight *la semáforo*
a turn *una vuelta*
right here *aquí*
somewhere around here *por acá*
right there *allí*
somewhere around there *por allá*
street; boulevard *calle; bulevar*
highway *carretera*
bridge; toll *puente; cuota*
address *dirección*
north; south *norte; sur*
east; west *oriente (este); poniente (oeste)*

ACCOMMODATIONS
hotel *hotel*
Is there a room? *¿Hay cuarto?*
May I (may we) see it? *¿Puedo (podemos) verlo?*
What is the rate? *¿Cuál es el precio?*
Is that your best rate? *¿Es su mejor precio?*
Is there something cheaper? *¿Hay algo más económico?*
a single room *un cuarto sencillo*
a double room *un cuarto doble*
double bed *cama matrimonial*
twin beds *camas gemelas*
with private bath *con baño privado*
hot water *agua caliente*
shower *ducha*
towels *toallas*
soap *jabón*
toilet paper *papel higiénico*
blanket *frazada; manta*
sheets *sábanas*
air-conditioned *aire acondicionado*
fan *abanico; ventilador*

key *llave*
manager *gerente*

FOOD
I'm hungry. *Tengo hambre.*
I'm thirsty. *Tengo sed.*
menu *lista; menú*
order *orden*
glass *vaso*
fork *tenedor*
knife *cuchillo*
spoon *cuchara*
napkin *servilleta*
soft drink *refresco*
coffee *café*
tea *té*
drinking water *agua pura; agua potable*
bottled carbonated water *agua mineral*
bottled uncarbonated water *agua sin gas*
beer *cerveza*
wine *vino*
milk *leche*
juice *jugo*
cream *crema*
sugar *azúcar*
cheese *queso*
snack *antojo; botana*
breakfast *desayuno*
lunch *almuerzo*
daily lunch special *comida corrida* (or *el menú del día* depending on region)
dinner *comida* (often eaten in late afternoon); *cena* (a late-night snack)
the check *la cuenta*
eggs *huevos*
bread *pan*
salad *ensalada*
fruit *fruta*
mango *mango*
watermelon *sandía*
papaya *papaya*
banana *plátano*
apple *manzana*
orange *naranja*
lime *limón*
fish *pescado*
shellfish *mariscos*
shrimp *camarones*

(without) meat (sin) carne
chicken pollo
pork puerco
beef; steak res; bistec
bacon; ham tocino; jamón
fried frito
roasted asada
barbecue; barbecued barbacoa; al carbón

SHOPPING

money dinero
money-exchange bureau casa de cambio
**I would like to exchange traveler's
  checks.** Quisiera cambiar cheques de
  viajero.
What is the exchange rate? ¿Cuál es el tipo
  de cambio?
How much is the commission? ¿Cuánto es
  la comisión?
Do you accept credit cards? ¿Aceptan
  tarjetas de crédito?
money order giro
How much does it cost? ¿Cuánto cuesta?
What is your final price? ¿Cuál es su último
  precio?
expensive caro
cheap barato; económico
more más
less menos
a little un poco
too much demasiado

HEALTH

Help me please. Ayúdeme por favor.
I am ill. Estoy enfermo.
Call a doctor. Llame un doctor.
Take me to . . . Lléveme a . . .
hospital hospital; sanatorio
drugstore farmacia
pain dolor
fever fiebre
headache dolor de cabeza
stomach ache dolor de estómago
burn quemadura
cramp calambre
nausea náusea
vomiting vomitar

medicine medicina
antibiotic antibiótico
pill; tablet pastilla
aspirin aspirina
ointment; cream pomada; crema
bandage venda
cotton algodón
sanitary napkins use brand name, e.g. Kotex
birth control pills pastillas anticonceptivas
contraceptive foam espuma anticonceptiva
condoms preservativos; condones
toothbrush cepilla dental
dental floss hilo dental
toothpaste crema dental
dentist dentista
toothache dolor de muelas

POST OFFICE AND COMMUNICATIONS

long-distance telephone teléfono larga
  distancia
I would like to call . . . Quisiera llamar a . . .
collect por cobrar
station to station a quien contesta
person to person persona a persona
credit card tarjeta de crédito
post office correo
general delivery lista de correo
letter carta
stamp estampilla, timbre
postcard tarjeta
aerogram aerograma
air mail correo aereo
registered registrado
money order giro
package; box paquete; caja
string; tape cuerda; cinta

CUSTOMS

border frontera
customs aduana
immigration migración
tourist card tarjeta de turista
inspection inspección; revisión
passport pasaporte
profession profesión
marital status estado civil

single *soltero*
married; divorced *casado; divorciado*
widowed *viudado*
insurance *seguros*
title *título*
driver's license *licencia de manejar*

AT THE GAS STATION

gas station *gasolinera*
gasoline *gasolina*
unleaded *sin plomo*
full, please *lleno, por favor*
tire *llanta*
tire repair shop *vulcanizadora*
air *aire*
water *agua*
oil (change) *aceite (cambio)*
grease *grasa*
My...doesn't work. *Mi...no sirve.*
battery *batería*
radiator *radiador*
alternator *alternador*
generator *generador*
tow truck *grúa*
repair shop *taller mecánico*
tune-up *afinación*
auto parts store *refaccionería*

VERBS

Verbs are the key to getting along in Spanish. They employ mostly predictable forms and come in three classes, which end in *ar*, *er*, and *ir*, respectively:

to buy *comprar*
I buy, you (he, she, it) buys *compro, compra*
we buy, you (they) buy *compramos, compran*

to eat *comer*
I eat, you (he, she, it) eats *como, come*
we eat, you (they) eat *comemos, comen*

to climb *subir*
I climb, you (he, she, it) climbs *subo, sube*
we climb, you (they) climb *subimos, suben*

Here are more (with irregularities marked in **bold**):

to do or make *hacer*
I do or make, you (he she, it) does or makes *hago, hace*
we do or make, you (they) do or make *hacemos, hacen*

to go *ir*
I go, you (he, she, it) goes *voy, va*
we go, you (they) go *vamos, van*

to go (walk) *andar*
to love *amar*
to work *trabajar*
to want *desear, querer*
to need *necesitar*
to read *leer*
to write *escribir*
to repair *reparar*
to stop *parar*
to get off (the bus) *bajar*
to arrive *llegar*
to stay (remain) *quedar*
to stay (lodge) *hospedar*
to leave *salir* (regular except for *salgo*, I leave)
to look at *mirar*
to look for *buscar*
to give *dar* (regular except for *doy*, I give)
to carry *llevar*
to have *tener* (irregular but important: *tengo, tiene, tenemos, tienen*)
to come *venir* (similarly irregular: *vengo, viene, venimos, vienen*)

Spanish has two forms of "to be." Use *estar* when speaking of location or a temporary state of being: "I am at home." "*Estoy en casa.*" "I'm sick." "*Estoy enfermo.*" Use *ser* for a permanent state of being: "I am a doctor." "*Soy doctora.*"

Estar is regular except for *estoy*, I am. *Ser* is very irregular:

to be *ser*
I am, you (he, she, it) is *soy, es*
we are, you (they) are *somos, son*

NUMBERS

zero *cero*
one *uno*
two *dos*
three *tres*
four *cuatro*
five *cinco*
six *seis*
seven *siete*
eight *ocho*
nine *nueve*
10 *diez*
11 *once*
12 *doce*
13 *trece*
14 *catorce*
15 *quince*
16 *dieciseis*
17 *diecisiete*
18 *dieciocho*
19 *diecinueve*
20 *veinte*
21 *veinte y uno or veintiuno*
30 *treinta*
40 *cuarenta*
50 *cincuenta*
60 *sesenta*
70 *setenta*
80 *ochenta*
90 *noventa*
100 *ciento*
101 *ciento y uno or cientiuno*
200 *doscientos*
500 *quinientos*
1,000 *mil*
10,000 *diez mil*
100,000 *cien mil*
1,000,000 *millón*
one-half *medio*
one-third *un tercio*
one-fourth *un cuarto*

TIME

What time is it? *¿Qué hora es?*
It's one o'clock. *Es la una.*
It's three in the afternoon. *Son las tres de la tarde.*
It's 4 A.M. *Son las cuatro de la mañana.*
six-thirty *seis y media*
a quarter till eleven *un cuarto para las once*
a quarter past five *las cinco y cuarto*
an hour *una hora*

DAYS AND MONTHS

Monday *lunes*
Tuesday *martes*
Wednesday *miércoles*
Thursday *jueves*
Friday *viernes*
Saturday *sábado*
Sunday *domingo*
today *hoy*
tomorrow *mañana*
yesterday *ayer*
January *enero*
February *febrero*
March *marzo*
April *abril*
May *mayo*
June *junio*
July *julio*
August *agosto*
September *septiembre*
October *octubre*
November *noviembre*
December *diciembre*
a week *una semana*
a month *un mes*
after *después*
before *antes*

(Courtesy of Bruce Whipperman, author of *Moon Pacific Mexico*.)

Suggested Reading

HISTORY AND POLITICS

Carrión, Arturo Morales. *Puerto Rico: A Political and Cultural History.* W.W. Norton & Co., 1984. An examination of Puerto Rico's Commonwealth status and how it got there.

Monge, José Trias. *Puerto Rico: The Trials of the Oldest Colony in the World.* Yale University Press, 1999. (Paperback). An examination of Puerto Rico's political status through history and an outlook on its future.

Odishelidze, Alexander, and Arthur Laffer. *Pay to the Order of Puerto Rico: The Cost of Dependence.* Allegiance Press, 2004. A look at Puerto Rico's political status from an outsider—a Russian native. Although Puerto Rico's options for future political status are well documented, the author openly favors statehood.

Rouse, Irving. *The Taínos: Rise and Decline of the People Who Greeted Columbus.* Yale University Press, reissue 1993. A history of the Taíno culture based on intensive study of archaeological sites.

ARTS AND CULTURE

Delano, Jack. *Puerto Rico Mio: Four Decades of Change.* Smithsonian Books, 1990. Includes 175 duotones of former Farm Security Administration photographer Jack Delano's visual chronicle of the island and its people. Includes essays in Spanish and English by educator Arturo Morales Carrión, historian Alan Fern, and anthropologist Sidney W. Mintz.

Muckley, Robert L., and Adela Martinez-Santiago. *Stories from Puerto Rico.* McGraw-Hill, 1999. A collection of legends, ghost stories, and beloved true accounts that reflect the island's folklore. In English and Spanish.

Santiago, Roberto, ed. *Boricuas: Influential Puerto Rican Writings—An Anthology.* One World/Ballantine, 1995. A fantastic collection of poems, speeches, stories, and excerpts by Puerto Rico's greatest writers, past and present, including Jesús Colón, Pablo Guzman, Julia de Burgos, and many more.

NATURE AND WILDLIFE

Lee, Alfonso Silva. *Natural Puerto Rico/Puerto Rico Natural.* Pangaea, 1998. An examination of the fauna of Puerto Rico by Cuban biologist Alfonso Silva Lee. In Spanish and English.

Oberle, Mark W. *Puerto Rico's Birds in Photographs.* Humanitas, 2000. More than 300 color photographs document 181 species of birds found in Puerto Rico. Comes with a CD-ROM including audio clips and more photographs.

Raffaele, Herbert. *A Guide to the Birds of Puerto Rico and the Virgin Islands.* Princeton University Press, 1989. Contains information on 284 documented species as well as 273 illustrations.

Simonsen, Steve. *Diving and Snorkeling Guide to Puerto Rico.* Pisces Books, 1996. A guide to the best diving and snorkeling sites around the island.

CHILDREN'S BOOKS

Bernier-Grand, Carmen T. (author), and Ernesto Ramos Nieves (illustrator). *Juan Bobo: Four Folktales from Puerto Rico.* HarperTrophy, 1995. Four humorous folktales about the trials and tribulations of the lovable, misguided little boy Juan Bobo.

Ramirez, Michael Rose (author), and Margaret Sanfilippo (illustrator). *The Legend of the Hummingbird: A Tale from Puerto Rico.* Mondo, 1998. Learn about Puerto Rico's history, climate, and traditions in this beguiling tale of transformation.

Internet Resources

TRAVEL INFORMATION

Puerto Rico Tourism Co.
www.gotopuertorico.com

Produced by the Puerto Rico Tourism Co., this is an excellent source of well-researched information on history, culture, events, and sights with a promotional slant. Download or request a copy of the current Master Guide, an extensive source of current listings produced by Travel and Sports Inc.

Travel and Sports Inc.
http://travelandsports.com

An enormous database of current travel information, including hotels, restaurants, sights, transportation, water sports, and more. It has a great interactive map and publishes a quarterly Master Guide distributed by the Puerto Rico Tourism Co., available in English, Spanish, French, German, and Portuguese.

Let's Go to Ponce
www.letsgotoponce.com

General tourist information on Ponce and the south Coast.

Tourism Association of Rincón
www.rincon.org

In addition to a plethora of general tourist information on Rincón, this site provides info services of interest to residents, including locations for churches, hair salons, and cleaners. Plus, there's some great photography.

Enchanted Isle
www.enchanted-isle.com

Enchanted Isle is a top-notch site for all things concerning Vieques and Culebra. This is your source for hotels, restaurants, sights, sports, weather, transportation, and more. Also a great source for private vacation rentals and real estate.

Vieques Travel Guide
www.viequestravelguide.com

A reliable source of vacation rentals, tourist sights, shops, transportation, and more on Vieques.

Isla Culebra
www.islaculebra.com

A terrific source for vacation rentals on Culebra. The best feature is its very active, informative travel forum. Post a question and someone will know the answer.

HISTORY, POLITICS, AND CULTURE

Historic Places in Puerto Rico
www.nps.gov/history/nr/travel/prvi

The National Park Service site provides details on all the historic sites that fall under its purview.

Music of Puerto Rico
www.musicofpuertorico.com

Excellent source for information on Puerto Rican music from folk and *danza* to *bomba* and salsa to reggaetón. Also contains audio clips, biographies of native musicians, lyrics, and musical history.

Public Art
www.artepublicopr.com/english

Official source for Puerto Rico's $25 million public art project, including project proposals, artists' biographies, and maps to the sites.

Puerto Rico and the Dream
www.prdream.com

An intelligent and discriminating site about the history, culture, and politics of Puerto Rico that includes audio files of oral histories, galleries of select art exhibitions, historical timelines, archival photos, and discussion forums. The site really has its finger on the pulse of all matters important to Puerto Ricans.

Puerto Rican Painter
www.puertoricanpainter.com

An all-inclusive look at local artists currently working in Puerto Rico, the site includes a list of galleries, artist biographies, and galleries of artwork.

Taíno Cyber Culture Center
www.indio.net/taino

A clearinghouse for links to articles on Taíno history, news, research, and culture.

NATURE AND WILDLIFE

U.S. Fish and Wildlife Service
www.fws.gov/caribbean

The U.S. Fish and Wildlife Service operates this site featuring information on the island's wildlife refuges, geographic regions, and efforts to restore the population of Puerto Rican parrots.

U.S. Forest Service
www.fs.fed.us/r8/caribbean/index.shtml

The authority on the El Yunque Caribbean National Forest by the U.S. Forest Service. Contains interactive and downloadable maps, and information on recreation areas.

WATER SPORTS

Scuba Diver Magazine
http://dive.scubadiving.com

Plug "Puerto Rico" into the website's search engine and you'll find a link to lots of articles with details on dive sites around the island. Includes information on conditions, visibility, and types of marine life to be found.

Wannasurf
www.wannasurf.com/spot/Central_America/Puerto_Rico

An excellent source for surfing Puerto Rico's beaches, containing maps, reports, recommendations, and tips.

Index

List of Maps

Acknowledgments

Above all I want to thank my parents, Ted and Jo Teagle, who instilled in me a passion for travel. Had they not been adventurous enough to move our family to Puerto Rico in the early 1970s, this book would never have happened. I also want to thank my sons, Derrick and Drew, who bring so much joy to my life and inspire me to be my best every day.

I want to thank my lifelong friend Caryl Altman Howard for introducing me to this beguiling island and for playing a major role in some of my fondest memories of life in Puerto Rico.

Fellow author Craig Seymour was an invaluable source of advice, encouragement, and support throughout the research and writing process. I can't imagine having taken this journey without his wisdom and humor, and I will always be indebted to him. And special thanks go to Amy Tinaglia, Scottie Williams, Shelly Williams, and Frederick Noble, who accompanied me on portions of my research trips. They not only made the experience that much more fun, but their unique insights helped inform the content.

Jennifer Bhagia-Lewis was an enormous help in fact-checking and researching many of the minute but vital details contained herein. Thanks to her, all the phone numbers, websites, and rates were correct as of publication. I'm also grateful to photographer Omar Vega for sharing his artistic vision in the better photographs that grace this book.

And in Puerto Rico, I owe much gratitude to impromptu tour guides Stan Kolb, Cheche, Justino del Valle, and John "Rocky" Thompson for their generous hospitality, kindness, and insight into island life.

And finally, I'd like to acknowledge those I hold dear who not only endure my constant yammering about Puerto Rico but who just generally make my world go round: Sun Rim Brank, Rick Cheney, Bonnie Cornelius, Chris Edmonds, Janet Guy, Lea Holland, Anne Murray Mozingo, Lynn Peisner, Jerry Portwood, and Kelly Robinson.

www.moon.com

DESTINATIONS | ACTIVITIES | BLOGS | MAPS | BOOKS

MOON.COM is all new, and ready to help plan your next trip! Filled with fresh trip ideas and strategies, author interviews, informative blogs, a detailed map library, and descriptions of all the Moon guidebooks, Moon.com is all you need to get out and explore the world—or even places in your own backyard. As always, when you travel with Moon, expect an experience that is uncommon and truly unique.

MAP SYMBOLS

▭▭▭ Expressway	◖ Highlight	✗ Airfield	⚓ Golf Course
▭▭▭ Primary Road	○ City/Town	✕ Airport	Ⓟ Parking Area
▭▭▭ Secondary Road	◉ State Capital	▲ Mountain	⛰ Archaeological Site
‑‑‑‑‑ Unpaved Road	⊛ National Capital	✚ Unique Natural Feature	♟ Church
‑‑‑‑‑ Trail	★ Point of Interest		⛽ Gas Station
············ Ferry	• Accommodation	⥤ Waterfall	Glacier
‑·‑·‑ Railroad	▾ Restaurant/Bar	♠ Park	Mangrove
▭▭▭ Pedestrian Walkway	▪ Other Location	⬛ Trailhead	Reef
▥▥▥ Stairs	△ Campground	⛷ Skiing Area	Swamp

CONVERSION TABLES

$$°C = (°F - 32) / 1.8$$
$$°F = (°C × 1.8) + 32$$

1 inch = 2.54 centimeters (cm)
1 foot = 0.304 meters (m)
1 yard = 0.914 meters
1 mile = 1.6093 kilometers (km)
1 km = 0.6214 miles
1 fathom = 1.8288 m
1 chain = 20.1168 m
1 furlong = 201.168 m
1 acre = 0.4047 hectares
1 sq km = 100 hectares
1 sq mile = 2.59 square km
1 ounce = 28.35 grams
1 pound = 0.4536 kilograms
1 short ton = 0.90718 metric ton
1 short ton = 2,000 pounds
1 long ton = 1.016 metric tons
1 long ton = 2,240 pounds
1 metric ton = 1,000 kilograms
1 quart = 0.94635 liters
1 US gallon = 3.7854 liters
1 Imperial gallon = 4.5459 liters
1 nautical mile = 1.852 km

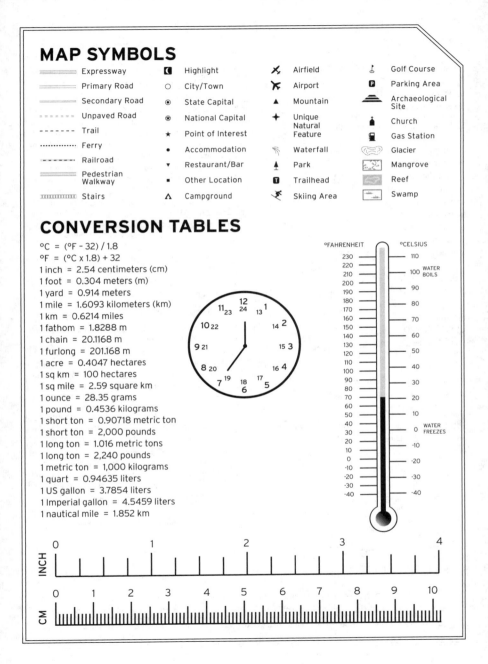

MOON PUERTO RICO

Avalon Travel
a member of the Perseus Books Group
1700 Fourth Street
Berkeley, CA 94710, USA
www.moon.com

Editor and Series Manager: Kathryn Ettinger
Copy Editor: Christopher Church
Graphics Coordinators: Sean Bellows,
   Kathryn Osgood
Production Coordinators: Sean Bellows,
   Domini Dragoone, Elizabeth Jang
Cover Designer: Sean Bellows
Map Editor: Brice Ticen
Cartographer: Kat Bennett
Proofreader: Julie Littman
Indexer: Valerie Sellers Blanton

ISBN-13: 978-1-59880-182-8
ISSN: 1932-0957

Printing History
1st Edition – 2006
2nd Edition – September 2009
5 4 3 2 1

Front cover photo: palm trees on shoreline along
Piñones © Thomas R. Fletcher/Alamy

Title page photo: pastel-colored houses in Old San
Juan © Suzanne Van Atten

Interior color photos: page 4 Condado Beach
© Omar Vega; page 5 (left) Capilla del Cristo © Omar
Vega; (center) balconies in Old San Juan © Suzanne
Van Atten; (right) hot springs of Baños de Coamo
© Suzanne Van Atten; page 6 (thumbnail) Faro
de Punta Tuna © Suzanne Van Atten; (bottom) La
Muralla © Omar Vega; page 7 (top left) windsurfing in
Condado © Omar Vega; (top right) graffiti reflecting a
sense of national pride © Suzanne Van Atten; (bottom
left) Monumento al Indio © Omar Vega; (bottom right)
Carnaval in Ponce © Lagustin/Dreamstime.com;
page 8 © Omar Vega; pages 9–13 all © Suzanne Van
Atten; page 14 (top) courtesy of National Astronomy
& Ionosphere Center; (bottom) © Omar Vega; page 15
© Suzanne Van Atten; page 16 © Peter Bowden;
page 17 © Fotoamateur49/Dreamstime.com; page 18
© Alexphoto01/Dreamstime.com; page 19 © Ervphotos/
Dreamstime.com; page 20 © Dave Clausen

Printed in Canada by Friesens

KEEPING CURRENT

If you have a favorite gem you'd like to see included in the next edition, or see anything
that needs updating, clarification, or correction, please drop us a line. Send your
comments via email to feedback@moon.com, or use the address above.